PRAISE FOR

THE GROUND TRUTH

"Assail[s] the government's official depiction of 9/11 as so much public relations flimflam . . . [and] superbly renders the knuckle-biting tension and confusion engendered by the hijackings . . . Farmer's accomplishment is to throw 9/11 into fresh relief. A precise and reliable accounting of what happened has been absent until now. This is it."

—Jacob Heilbrunn,
The New York Times Book Review

"*The Ground Truth* is an important reexamination of the events before, during, and after the September 11 attack on the World Trade Center. As you read it, you may not know whether to laugh or cry. Laughter comes because Farmer paints a picture of government officials who seem like Monty Python running their Ministries of Silly Walks. The tears come when you discover the dozens of missed opportunities to stop this tragedy well before the hijackers boarded a jet. Farmer is particularly well equipped to write this book . . . and all of it is presented in a compelling, well-written style that is almost thrillerlike in its narrative."

—*Minneapolis Star-Tribune*

"Farmer deftly hones in on the nation's bureaucratic morass leading up to September 11 and the government's failure to respond on the day of the attacks, distinguishing his book from other accounts. He highlights the ineptitude of American bureaucracy and the inherent flaws of its national security, and he shows that the horrific attacks could easily occur again unless there is a drastic federal overhaul." —*The American Prospect*

THE GROUND TRUTH

THE UNTOLD STORY OF AMERICA UNDER ATTACK ON 9/11

JOHN FARMER

RIVERHEAD BOOKS

New York

RIVERHEAD BOOKS
Published by the Penguin Group
Penguin Group (USA) Inc.
375 Hudson Street, New York, New York 10014, USA
Penguin Group (Canada), 90 Eglinton Avenue East, Suite 700, Toronto, Ontario M4P 2Y3,
Canada (a division of Pearson Penguin Canada Inc.)
Penguin Books Ltd., 80 Strand, London WC2R 0RL, England
Penguin Group Ireland, 25 St. Stephen's Green, Dublin 2, Ireland
(a division of Penguin Books Ltd.)
Penguin Group (Australia), 250 Camberwell Road, Camberwell, Victoria 3124, Australia
(a division of Pearson Australia Group Pty. Ltd.)
Penguin Books India Pvt. Ltd., 11 Community Centre, Panchsheel Park, New Delhi—110 017,
India
Penguin Group (NZ), 67 Apollo Drive, Rosedale, North Shore 0632, New Zealand
(a division of Pearson New Zealand Ltd.)
Penguin Books (South Africa) (Pty.) Ltd., 24 Sturdee Avenue, Rosebank, Johannesburg 2196,
South Africa

Penguin Books Ltd., Registered Offices: 80 Strand, London WC2R 0RL, England

While the author has made every effort to provide accurate telephone numbers and Internet
addresses at the time of publication, neither the publisher nor the author assumes any
responsibility for errors, or for changes that occur after publication. Further, the publisher does
not have any control over and does not assume any responsibility for author or third-party
websites or their content.

The author will donate a portion of his earnings from sales of this book to Rutgers University
School of Law, Newark, to further faculty research, and to the New Jersey Institute for Social
Justice.

Chart on pages 356–374 prepared with the assistance of Laurel DuMont
The transcript on pages 256–261 appears courtesy of ABC News.

First Riverhead hardcover edition: September 2009
First Riverhead trade paperback edition: September 2010
Riverhead trade paperback ISBN: 978-1-59448-478-0

The Library of Congress has catalogued the Riverhead hardcover edition as follows:

Farmer, John J.
    The ground truth : the untold story of America under attack on 9/11 / John Farmer.
        p.   cm.
    Includes bibliographical references and index.
    ISBN 978-1-59448-894-8
    1. September 11 Terrorist Attacks, 2001.   2. Terrorism—United States.   I. Title.
    HV6432.7.F37   2009   2009023297
    973.931—dc22

History has many cunning passages, contrived corridors
And issues, deceives with whispering ambitions,
Guides us by vanities. . . .
Neither fear nor courage saves us. Unnatural vices
Are fathered by our heroism.

—T. S. ELIOT, "Gerontion"

Facts are stubborn things.

—JOHN ADAMS, "Argument in Defense of the
Soldiers in the Boston Massacre Trials," 1770

*This book is dedicated to
9/11 Commission Team 8—the "Whiskey Tango Foxtrot" team—
to my parents, and to Beth, with love.*

*It honors the memory of my cousin Joseph F. Errichiello, Jr. (1979–2004),
and mother-in-law, Dorothy Hollis Jackson (1922–2004), who died in the
spring of 2004, as the 9/11 Commission was completing its work.*

CONTENTS

THE GROUND TRUTH

INTRODUCTION

THE VIEW FROM THE GROUND

The story of the al Qaeda terrorist plot that culminated in the 9/11 attacks, and of the American government's response to it, has been told well, from differing perspectives, on several occasions. The Report of the Congressional Joint Inquiry is a fascinating—and often scathing—reconstruction of FBI and CIA activity before 9/11. *The 9/11 Commission Report*, which I assisted in writing, recounts accurately the events as we were able to reconstruct them; it is the collaborative work of a remarkably diverse and talented group of staffers and commissioners. Steve Coll's *Ghost Wars* and Lawrence Wright's *The Looming Tower* focus on developments in Afghanistan and the evolving al Qaeda organization, respectively, and are both outstanding. With respect to NORAD's immediate response to the attacks, Michael Bronner, with whom I consulted during his work on the Universal Pictures production of *United 93*, gets it right in an excellent piece in the August 2006 edition of *Vanity Fair*. The work of the 9/11 Commission itself has been documented by Commission chairman Tom Kean and vice chairman Lee Hamilton in their book *Without Precedent*.

Why, then, another book about 9/11? Put simply, before now the story could not be told as it is told here. In particular, three developments since *The 9/11 Commission Report* was issued have made possible, and necessary, this reexamination of our nation's response: the declassification of many of the primary-source records of the day, which makes it possible to portray the events as they were lived; the release of investigative reports by the Inspectors General of the Departments of Defense and Transportation, which, I shall argue, ignore critical evidence in concluding that government officials did not knowingly mislead the public about the events of 9/11; and the occurrence of Hurricane Katrina, which sheds essential, if tragic, light on the government's failure to recognize and learn from the "ground truth" of 9/11.

The account of the nation's response to the 9/11 attacks set forth in *The 9/11 Commission Report* is accurate, and true, but the vast majority of the tape recordings, transcripts, and contemporaneous records from September 11, 2001, were treated as classified throughout the investigation, ostensibly because of their possible use as evidence in the prosecution of Zacarias Moussaoui. Although we on the Commission sought to declassify the relevant records, we were working against a stringent deadline. An "audio monograph" of the day's events that we prepared—an account that allowed the voices of the day to tell the story—did not survive the vetting process, and a supplemental monograph that we prepared, which was finally released in January 2005, was drastically condensed and had significant sections blacked out. Only now that most of the relevant tapes and transcripts have been declassified is it possible to tell the story in all of its drama.

That more complete primary-source record sheds light on an important but little-noticed aspect of the 9/11 story. In the course of our investigation into the national response to the attacks, the 9/11 Commission staff discovered that the official version of what had occurred that morning—that is, what government and military officials had told Congress, the Commission, the media, and the public about who knew what when—was almost entirely, and inexplicably, untrue. Pressed for time and committed to the central purpose of finding the facts, however, the Commission had referred the issue of whether any of these officials had knowingly lied to or misled the public about the facts of that day to the

Inspectors General of the Department of Defense and the Department of Transportation.

Months passed, then a year, then two years, a period longer than the life of the Commission itself. Finally, on September 1, 2006, the Friday afternoon before Labor Day, the Department of Transportation Inspector General released its report. This was followed, on September 12, 2006—the day after the anniversary of the attacks, when the attendant media scrutiny had subsided—by the release of the Department of Defense Inspector General's report. The releases of both reports were timed, in short, to attract as little notice as possible, despite—or perhaps because of—both reports' conclusion that there was no proof of deliberate falsification. The Department of Transportation Inspector General's report ascribed the false information Federal Aviation Administration officials had provided to "a lack of attention to the details," and although it found FAA officials' explanations "unreasonable," it did not find evidence for an alternative explanation. The Department of Defense Inspector General's report ascribed the inaccuracies of Pentagon officials to their being focused at that point not on what had occurred but on the struggle to protect the homeland; it also claimed that efforts to piece together what had occurred were compromised by the military's inadequate record-keeping procedures on 9/11.

This book challenges these conclusions. It does so by setting forth in detail, and as the events were lived, what happened on 9/11 and in the days that followed—including how the government's explanation of events evolved. Not only did the Department of Defense maintain adequate records—principally tapes at the National Military Command Center and at operational positions in the Northeast Air Defense Sector (NEADS) and contemporaneous logs maintained up and down the chain of command—but the events of the day as entered in the records were both unmistakable and unmistakably different from what officials had claimed. Furthermore, as 9/11 Commissioners Gorelick, Ben-Veniste, and Gorton have pointed out, those records were consulted as early as the first few days after the attacks, as the bureaucracy pieced together what had occurred. At some level of the government, at some point in time, this book concludes, there was a decision not to tell the truth about what happened.

The Ground Truth retells the 9/11 story in a new and, I hope, compelling and illuminating way: not primarily in terms of the evolution of doctrines or the interplay of departments or personalities, but in units of time. My purpose is to discuss our government's growing awareness of and reaction to the al Qaeda terrorist threat as it was lived, when the government had first years, then months, then weeks, then days, then hours, then minutes, and finally seconds to redefine its mission and respond.

This way of organizing the narrative makes for an exciting, true-to-life read. As the units of time are compressed, and the number of national security agencies and actors capable of interdicting the plot narrows to two relatively obscure units, the FAA and NORAD (the North American Aerospace Defense Command), the story of 9/11 acquires a narrative momentum that is no less compelling for our knowledge of how the story ends. Equally important, telling the story in shrinking units of time is the best way to appreciate both the uniqueness of what happened that morning and its remarkable similarity to all that had led up to this encounter with a new form of warfare.

Of all the misleading accounts told by a government to its people, our government's account to its people about what happened on 9/11 is certainly not the most egregious. It didn't escalate a war, as did the Johnson administration's fabrication of the Gulf of Tonkin incident in 1965. It didn't provide a pretext for aggression, as did the government's manipulation of intelligence regarding the existence of weapons of mass destruction in Iraq. Nor did it precipitate a constitutional crisis, as did the Nixon administration's lies about Watergate or President Clinton's lies about his relationship with Monica Lewinsky.

In the grand scheme of things, then, the government's deception about how we were defended on 9/11 may seem minor. This book in no way seeks to overstate its significance. In its own way, however, the government's failure to tell the truth about what happened on 9/11 has had far-reaching effects.

Because the government's story didn't make sense, it raised as many questions as it answered, thus fueling conspiracy theories that persist regarding 9/11. One purpose of *The Ground Truth* is to lay at least some of these theories to rest by identifying and establishing the deception that actually did occur. The perpetuation of the untrue official version remains a betrayal of every citizen who demanded a truthful answer to the simple question: What happened?

More important, because the government's version of what occurred on 9/11 overstated the efficiency and effectiveness of our national defense response, it obscured that day's essential reality, and its causes: a radical disconnect between those who were putatively in charge of conducting our nation's defense and those who were on the ground, making operational decisions. Because the government didn't tell the truth, in other words, we lost the "ground truths" of 9/11; (1) there was no connection or collaboration between Washington and the ground-level commanders, as a result of which (2) our national decision-makers in Washington—or, in the case of President Bush, in the air—were irrelevant to how we were defended during that critical time period.

Leadership was irrelevant on 9/11, moreover, not because of how quickly the critical events happened—essentially, within a two-hour period—but because there had been a persistent and pervasive estrangement throughout the 1990s between leadership of the national security departments and the ground-level bureaucratic personnel, as the government attempted to adapt to the world's changing post–Cold War realities.

The government's failure to acknowledge the radical disconnect made it easy to respond to the 9/11 attacks by the predictable method of creating a new bureaucracy, the Department of Homeland Security, while responding to the immediate conditions of the last attack, patching the holes in the air defense system by ensuring connectivity between the FAA and NORAD, modernizing radar coverage, increasing the number of fighter jets on alert, and revising the applicable rules of engagement to enable a quicker response the next time planes are hijacked for use as weapons. But the next attack is unlikely to duplicate the last, and the deficiencies in the response to 9/11, once they are appreciated, point to a more fundamental problem. They were a direct consequence of the way that government bureaucracies function: as top-heavy silos of isolated and narrowly defined missions, jealous of the information to which they are privy and structured not to solve problems but to deflect responsibility. In this sense, as we shall see, the problems that plagued FAA and NORAD on 9/11 itself were no different from those faced by the FBI, the CIA, the DoD, INS, or the other agencies of the federal bureaucracy in the years, months, weeks, and days leading to 9/11. The compressed time frame within which the FAA and NORAD had to act simply made those problems more glaringly apparent and, perhaps, more painful to admit.

By obscuring the truth of what happened on 9/11, the government was able to avoid confronting the consequences of that ground truth: that the fault for failing to detect or to interdict the attacks lay in the nature of modern government itself, and that until we address the way that bureaucracies function, until we truly "reinvent government," the passage of new statutes or the creation of new procedures or entirely new departments, like the Department of Homeland Security, will be unavailing. Thus, Congress responded to the principal recommendation of the 9/11 Commission by creating a new office, the Director of National Intelligence, but ignored completely the Commission's insistence that that office have budgetary authority over the intelligence community in order to be effective. Instead, it left 80 percent of the intelligence budget under the authority of the Department of Defense. As 9/11 Commissioner John Lehman pointed out, such an approach was "the exact opposite of what we had recommended," because it left the "sprawling mess" of our national intelligence bureaucracy "untouched . . . to create another bureaucracy of more than 1,000 people in the Office of the Director of National Intelligence."

Unless we change government, we will fail to protect ourselves, with horrifying consequences, as was made painfully clear in 2005, during Hurricane Katrina. As I will show, the problems the government encountered in responding to Katrina mirrored, and in many cases replicated, the problems experienced on 9/11. These similarities are the more significant because, unlike 9/11, Katrina was not a surprise, but an event that had been forecast and planned for years ahead of time. That government failed in identical ways in preparing for and responding to such disparate events makes clear that the problems were not incidental to unique events but central to the American way of government.

The aftermaths of both 9/11 and Katrina were a bacchanalia of blame. If the failures had occurred in a single agency of government, with respect to a single crisis, the assessment of individual blame would be appropriate. But when the failure occurs in multiple departments across the government, in differing crises, and is of virtually the same nature regardless of who is leading the department, such individual scapegoating misses the point. What failed in the history of 9/11 and in the Katrina crisis was not an individual department head or two, but government itself. If we are to address the systemic failures that undermined our nation's responses to the 9/11 attacks and Katrina, we must change fundamentally the way government functions.

This conclusion stems not just from having studied 9/11 as senior counsel to the 9/11 Commission, but also from having experienced it and attempted to manage it (and other crises) as the head of a large governmental agency. From June 1999 until January 2002, I served as New Jersey's attorney general, leading a department of nearly 10,000 people, including nearly 700 lawyers and nearly 3,000 officers of the New Jersey State Police, with a budget of nearly $1 billion. I have experienced firsthand just how difficult it is to reorient a government bureaucracy in the face of new realities. I brought to my work on the

9/11 Commission and to my study of Hurricane Katrina the perspective gained by managing crises such as 9/11, the anthrax attacks of 2001, and Tropical Storm Floyd, and addressing troubling social issues such as racial profiling and sexual predators; my work on the Commission and in learning about Katrina, in turn, have reinforced my belief that there are some basic truths about the ways in which government agencies function that must be addressed if we are to prepare for and respond effectively to future crises.

In joining the discussion of how to change government, *The Ground Truth* demonstrates precisely how government failed in dealing with the 9/11 conspiracy. It portrays the national defense story of 9/11 as the events were actually experienced that morning; it shows that those events were the trailing consequence of policy decisions taken years, even decades, before. Only by experiencing the attacks as they occurred can one appreciate the dislocation to which the military's air defenders and the FAA's civilian air traffic controllers were subjected, and the crucible of their having to think and react "outside the box." Equally important, only by learning about the human drama of that effort can one evaluate in its proper context the rhetoric throughout the 1990s about "reinventing government" and defending America in the post–Cold War world.

The response on the ground on 9/11 was the trailing consequence of those post–Cold War policy debates, the dysfunctional choices they produced, and the government-wide failure to interdict the 9/11 plot. It is the most powerful challenge to the claims of the departing Clinton administration that it had successfully "reinvented government" to meet post–Cold War challenges and that terrorism had been its highest national security priority, and of the Bush administration that it had mobilized to counter the threat. Given the state of national preparedness that I shall describe, and the way that the national defense was conducted, those claims simply cannot be true. The failure to anticipate the attacks of 9/11 was, indeed, as the Commission concluded, a "failure of imagination," but it was more than that; it was a collapse of competence, and an exposure of the continuing need for fundamental change in the ways in which departments of government are permitted to function.

It is impossible, in other words, to separate the way the defense of America against the 9/11 attacks was conducted from the way the systems designed to prevent a surprise attack on America were configured. As we shall see, because of the essential estrangement between policy leaders and the personnel of the departments they led, despite all the debates and discussion, our national defense apparatus—both domestic and foreign—had been left largely unchanged.

This is the essential truth of our national response on 9/11: for all of the rhetoric and all of the billions of dollars of government spending to "reinvent government" to adapt to the challenges of a New World Order, the Cold War did not end in 1991; for all practical purposes, it did not end until 9:03 a.m. on September 11, 2001, when United Airlines Flight 175, the second hijacked plane, crashed into the second tower of the World Trade Center. Only then did it become apparent that America was under attack. Later that morning, as Air National Guard personnel searched their antiquated radarscopes for phantom hijacked aircraft, a staff sergeant on the floor at the Northeast Air Defense Sector in Rome, New York, stated what so many across the government were thinking: "This is a new kind of war." Tragically, it was.

This is its story.

PART ONE

YEARS

The evolution of the "planes conspiracy," and of the U.S. government's attempts to counter al Qaeda, has received comprehensive book-length treatment in *The 9/11 Commission Report*, in Steve Coll's *Ghost Wars*, and in Lawrence Wright's *The Looming Tower*. The following sections do not attempt to replicate that history, but draw from it to set the context for the government's response on September 11 by highlighting the ways in which the evolving conspiracy touched upon various components of America's vast and far-flung early-warning system. As the conspiracy grew from its origins in Afghanistan to include more participants in more parts of the world, accessing more types of travel and communication technologies, it became susceptible to detection by one or more of the multitude of American national security and law enforcement agencies. Each agency's alert system, from the Central Intelligence Agency's human intelligence to the National Security Agency's electronic eavesdropping to the Federal Bureau of Investigation's network of field offices, would register what amounted to seismic indications of what became the 9/11 conspiracy. But the greater fault lines lay within and among the agencies themselves. These fault lines estranged the top officials within departments, who set policy, from the career professionals who carry it out, and ensured that the seismic readings taken in one department were not shared with other departments. As a consequence, even though the seismic disturbances grew stronger and stronger as 9/11 approached, every effort to get a clear reading was frustrated.

Also frustrated, it should be noted at the outset, was the 9/11 Commission staff's effort to question certain critical al Qaeda detainees who have direct knowledge of the 9/11 conspiracy. As *The 9/11 Commission Report* makes clear, the staff's access to detainees was "limited to the review of intelligence reports . . . We submitted questions for use in the interrogations, but had no control over whether, when, or how questions of particular interest would be asked. Nor were we allowed to talk to the interrogators so that we could better judge the credibility of the detainees and clarify ambiguities in the reporting. We were told that our requests might disrupt the sensitive interrogation process." Because of this, the detainees' answers were scrutinized closely for reasonableness and corroboration. Undisclosed to the Commission, we now know, were the facts that many of the interrogations were conducted using waterboarding and other "enhanced" interrogation techniques, and that many of the sessions had been videotaped. The existence of those tapes was withheld from the Commission, and the tapes themselves were later destroyed. Their destruction is the subject of an ongoing criminal investigation, and is an apt premise to the "tale of tales" of 9/11 recounted in Part Four of this book.

TWO MEN IN A CAVE: 1996–1997

Like many watershed historical events, the terrorist attacks of September 11, 2001, have acquired, in the perspective of eight years, a patina of inevitability. For al Qaeda members, it has become Holy Tuesday, its consequences bearing a divine signature. But to two men meeting in a cave in Tora Bora, Afghanistan, in mid-1996 to discuss potential attacks against the United States, the success of the "planes operation" they would mastermind nearly five years later seemed anything but inevitable.

The two men were Osama bin Laden and Khalid Sheikh Mohammed. Although their paths had crossed briefly during the jihad against the Soviet occupation of Afghanistan in the 1980s, they had pursued independent and largely parallel paths since.

Bin Laden had come to his willingness to attack the United States gradually. He was a man of ascetic temperament who, unlike many of his siblings in a billionaire family, had been educated not in the West but in Saudi Arabia and had seen little of the non-Muslim world; his worldview was initially parochial, even as his ambition was global. Like many in the Islamic fundamentalist world of the late 1980s, bin Laden believed that, as one commentator summarized it, "the secular Arab governments must be overthrown before the greater enemy, the West, can be tackled." Once the Communist threat had been removed from Afghanistan, the consensus among jihadists was that the next phase of jihad should "concentrate upon its own state context, whose regime is the 'nearest enemy' in Muslim legal lingo. 'Further away enemies,' such as the state of Israel or the United States, are to be tackled later, after the seizure of power." Lawrence Wright puts it this way: "What did bin Laden want? . . . The tragedy of Palestine was a constant theme in his speeches, yet he was reluctant to participate in the intifada against Israel. . . . Bin Laden hated Yasser Arafat because he was a secularist. Nor did he relish the prospect of war against Arab governments. At the time, he envisioned moving the struggle to Kashmir, the Philippines, and particularly the Central Asian republics where he could continue the jihad against the Soviet Union. Notably, the United States was not yet on anyone's list."

Over time, however, as it became clear that jihad in oppressive states like Egypt or Saudi Arabia would be exceedingly difficult to carry out, and as his base of operations moved from Afghanistan to Sudan to Saudi Arabia and back to Afghanistan, bin Laden came to see the United States as "the head of the snake," the source of support for both Israel and the corrupt Middle Eastern governments against which he struggled, and, beyond this, the source of evil and corruption in the world. "America continues to claim that it is upholding the banner of freedom and humanity," bin Laden would tell an interviewer in November 1996, "while these deeds that they did [the dropping of the atomic bombs on Hiroshima and Nagasaki and the imposition of sanctions on Iraq], you would not find that the most ravenous of animals would descend to." Stung by the refusal of the Saudi government to allow him to raise an army of mujahideen to drive the Iraqis from Kuwait, and its reliance instead on the United States military, bin Laden turned on the Saudi government that had enriched his family and called for jihad to end the sacrilege of a non-Muslim presence in Arabia. From his new base in Sudan, bin Laden denounced both his home Saudi government and the United States, and al Qaeda leaders issued a fatwa calling for jihad against the Western occupation of Muslim lands.

Bin Laden used Sudan as his base from 1992 to 1996. During this time, al Qaeda became increasingly confrontational with the United States. Al Qaeda operatives bombed two hotels in Aden where United States military personnel typically stayed en route to Somalia, and played a role in supporting the Somali warlords who shot down two U.S. Black Hawk helicopters in 1993; al Qaeda claims the United States withdrawal from Somalia in 1994 as a major victory. In November 1995, a car bomb was detonated outside a joint United States–Saudi National Guard training facility in Riyadh; credit was later claimed by al Qaeda associates. Ultimately, international pressure brought upon the Sudanese government, particularly from the United States, led that government to expel bin Laden in 1996. He returned to Afghanistan, determined to strike the United States as his primary enemy. As Michael Scheuer, the former head analyst of the CIA's bin Laden unit, put it, bin Laden "labored in public and private" to reverse the favored sequence in which Arab governments, and then the United States, are attacked and overthrown, and claimed, to the contrary, that "'if the United States is beheaded, the Arab Kingdoms will wither away.'" It was with this mind-set that bin Laden sat down in mid-1996 with Khalid Sheikh Mohammed.

Khalid Sheikh Mohammed, or "KSM," as he has become known, differed from bin Laden in almost every respect. Where bin Laden is tall and exceptionally thin, KSM is shorter and portly. Where bin Laden is ascetic, KSM is worldly; Lawrence Wright describes him as "pious but poorly trained in religion; an actor and a cutup; a drinker and a womanizer. Whereas bin Laden was provincial and hated travel, especially in the West, Mohammed was a globe-trotter fluent in several languages, including English, which he perfected while studying mechanical engineering at North Carolina Agricultural and Technical State University, a mostly black school in Greensboro." Perhaps because he had seen more of the world and had lived and studied in the United States, KSM's animus toward the United States was more narrowly drawn and less theological than bin Laden's. According to the 9/11 Commission, KSM's animus toward the United States "stemmed not from his experiences there as a student, but rather from his violent disagreement with U.S. foreign policy favoring Israel."

By all accounts, including KSM's own, the two men had not seen each other since the Afghanistan jihad of the late 1980s, when KSM had worked as an administrative assistant to bin Laden's mentor (and, later, rival), Abdullah Azzam. Like bin Laden, however, in the intervening years KSM had come to see the United States as his principal enemy, and had acted upon his animus, although not as a formal member of al Qaeda.

He had played an extremely minor role in his nephew Ramzi Youssef's plot to topple the World Trade Center in 1993, having wired $660 to the account of one of Youssef's co-conspirators, Mohammed Salameh, on November 3, 1992, some three months before the attack. According to KSM, he had learned of the plot from his nephew while both were in Afghanistan in 1991 or 1992, and had discussed his nephew's progress in the course of several phone calls in succeeding months. After the February 26 bombing, KSM and Youssef, who had escaped back to Pakistan, conspired to carry out the so-called Bojinka Plot, which involved blowing up twelve commercial airliners over the Pacific Ocean over a two-day period. They had acquired materials for explosives, and had successfully tested a bomb aboard a Philippine airliner en route to Tokyo, killing the passenger under whose seat Youssef had planted the bomb, before authorities in Manila foiled the plot by discovering the bomb-making laboratory when it accidentally exploded.

KSM remained at large throughout 1994 and 1995. Even as his nephew was betrayed and captured in Islamabad on February 7, 1995, KSM was traveling around the world, to Sudan, Yemen, Malaysia, and Brazil. In early 1996, aware that U.S. authorities were pursuing him, he fled to Afghanistan, where he sat down with Osama bin Laden in the remote caves of Tora Bora to discuss their common interests. Each had been effectively pushed beyond the margin of the civilized world. Thanks in part to pressure exerted by the United States, bin Laden had lost his Saudi citizenship and his sanctuary in Sudan; KSM may or may not have been aware that he was the subject of a sealed indictment in the Southern District of New York—there are reports that he was warned by a government official in Qatar—but he was very much aware that he was a fugitive from American justice.

Accounts of the meeting conflict as to both date and substance. Some accounts place the meeting in 1997; others, including KSM's, place it in 1996. KSM claims he bore no particular allegiance to either bin Laden or al Qaeda when the two met, and would have accepted the support of another mujahideen organization to carry out his schemes. Indeed, from his perspective, "bin Laden was in the process of consolidating his new position in Afghanistan while hearing out others' ideas, and had not yet settled on an agenda for future anti-U.S. operations." Even at this late date, according to KSM, bin Laden did not seem enthusiastic about attacking the U.S. homeland directly. KSM briefed bin Laden on his activities in the several years since they had last seen each other, and then presented a menu of schemes for potential strikes against the United States. Among these was a plan to train pilots to crash airplanes into buildings. Bin Laden was noncommittal at best, deflecting any discussion of specific plans but inviting KSM to join al Qaeda and to live in Afghanistan as part of the movement. KSM declined the request.

Bin Laden's initial reserve is easy to understand. By 1996, he was a man without a country, meeting in a cave complex left over from the war against the Soviet Union in one of the remotest corners of the earth. Tora Bora is the northern slope of a range of mountains that straddle the then ungoverned Tribal Areas of northwest Pakistan and Afghanistan. Composed largely of quartz and feldspar, the Tora Bora, or "Black Dust," is shot through with caves that are nearly impenetrable by means of conventional explosives. During the 1980s jihad against the Soviet Union, bin Laden had financed the expansion of existing caverns and the construction of new ones; it had become the base for bin Laden and the Arab mujahideen in the 1980s, and it would become the base to which he retreated and from which he would make his escape from the Americans in February 2002. It may have been the only place in the world where bin Laden felt truly safe.

Any plan as elaborate as the plan KSM described to bin Laden in their initial meeting would require the recruitment and training of multiple personnel, the expenditure of a great deal of money, and nearly worldwide logistical support. It would, in other words, require that al Qaeda develop a level of sophistication in planning and execution that it had yet to manifest in its other operations.

More important, and more daunting, were the defenses of the enemy. By 1996, the United States was the unquestioned dominant economic, cultural, and military force in the world. The collapse of the former Soviet Union in 1991 had left only one global superpower, and that superpower possessed the most extensive arsenal, the greatest number of military bases around the world, the most sophisticated signals intelligence system, and perhaps the greatest system of law enforcement detection the world had yet seen. Any proposed attack using commercial airplanes as weapons would have to circumvent a system of intelligence, national defense, and law enforcement whose explicit primary purpose was to prevent a surprise attack upon the United States. The operation would be imperiled from its inception, subject to exposure by various U.S. government agencies at various stages of the plot, depending on whether the conspirators were operating abroad or domestically.

As long as the focus of the planning and training took place outside the United States, in the safe-haven training camps in Afghanistan, and in meetings in foreign countries, the planners' communications would be vulnerable to discovery by the National Security Agency, which could capture virtually any form of electronic communication; the NSA operates "a dozen or more listening posts around the world, each one of which intercepts two million faxes, e mails, telephone calls and other signals every *hour*." In addition, activity in their training camps could be detected via imagery satellites operated by the Department of Defense's National Reconnaissance Office.

Assuming that the al Qaeda plotters somehow evaded electronic detection, their foreign operations were vulnerable to detection through the human intelligence provided by the Central Intelligence Agency. The CIA was entwined with the fundamentalist jihadi movement from early on, and was for much of the 1980s one of its greatest benefactors, pouring billions of dollars' worth of weapons and other supplies into Afghanistan as the mujahideen fought the Soviets. This experience acquainted the Agency with many of the critical players in the jihadist movement. The bombing of the World Trade Center in February 1993 by Ramzi Youssef, followed by the foiled plot by followers of Omar Abdel Rahman (sometimes called the "Blind Sheikh") to blow up New York City's bridges, tunnels, and prominent buildings later that year, elevated Islamist terrorism to the top of the post–Cold War national security priority list. A 1995 National Intelligence Estimate concluded that loosely organized, transnational terrorist groups, obtaining weapons, financing, and other forms of support from various governments, factions, and individual benefactors like bin Laden, posed the greatest emerging threat to national security.

Furthermore, by the time KSM and bin Laden had their meeting in

1996, the CIA was aware of the threat posed by those individual bene-factors and by the al Qaeda organization; the Agency was actively col-lecting intelligence on bin Laden by 1996. CIA Director John Deutch that year established in the Agency's Counterterrorist Center a special "station," of about a dozen officers, that came to focus on learning about the background, intentions, movements, and capabilities of Osama bin Laden. It was the first time in its history that an Agency station's mission had targeted a person rather than a country, and the first time it created a "station" that was not country-based; the "bin Laden station" was lo-cated in Langley, Virginia, a short distance from CIA headquarters. By 1997, the Agency, through the station, had "learned that al Qaeda had a military committee that was planning operations against U.S. interests worldwide and was actively trying to obtain nuclear material." In late 1996, a former bin Laden aide, Jamal al-Fadl, became a protected govern-ment witness and told the Agency that, while in Sudan, bin Laden had sought actively to purchase nuclear material.

Although the Agency had largely abandoned Afghanistan after the Soviet withdrawal, agents soon reestablished contacts within the country; by 1997 "these contacts contributed to intelligence about bin Laden's local movements, business activities, and security and living arrange-ments, and helped provide evidence that he was spending large amounts of money to help the Taliban." The Agency became confident, as a con-sequence of these renewed contacts, that it was, according to the chief of the Counterterrorist Center, "near to providing real-time information about bin Laden's activities and travels in Afghanistan."

That "real-time" intelligence about Osama bin Laden's whereabouts could be passed easily to law enforcement, to military intelligence, and to the covert operations agents of the CIA, and the most powerful nation in human history could then be engaged to destroy bin Laden, his orga-nization, and the plot against America. There was precedent to support the belief that this could occur. In May 1997, assisted by a clan of Afghan tribal fighters, by Pakistani intelligence, and by a Baluchi tribal leader, a team of "black ops" operatives from the FBI and the CIA flew into Pakistan and apprehended Mir Amal Kasi, the Baluchi sniper who had opened fire on the entrance to CIA headquarters in 1993, as he left his hotel room for morning prayers. A triumphant George Tenet announced to CIA employees assembled in Langley, "No terrorist should sleep soundly as long as this agency exists." The same clan of Afghan fighters that assisted in capturing Amal Kasi was then enlisted, in late 1997, to provide intelligence about bin Laden and to work with the CIA and the military to formulate a plan to capture him.

In short, the CIA, the NSA, and the other intelligence arms of the Department of Defense, the State Department, and other agencies of the United States government comprised, by design, a vast early-warning system. It was, as Steve Coll points out, "a vast, pulsing, self-perpetuating, highly sensitive network on continuous alert. Its listening posts were attuned to even the most isolated and dubious evidence of pending attacks. Its analysts were continually encouraged to share information as widely as possible among those with appropriate security clearances. . . . From George Tenet to the lowest-paid linguist in the Counterterrorist Center, the system was biased toward sounding the alarm." The "planes operation" would have to evade detection by this system in order to succeed.

Bin Laden was also faced with the real possibility of interdiction and destruction by the United States military, which had emerged from the Cold War as the most powerful military in world history. Formed after World War II, along with the CIA, with the express mission of preventing "another Pearl Harbor" the Department of Defense had become, by the mid-1990s, the most powerful department of the federal government, controlling, in addition to other programs, 80 percent of the intelligence budget, and housing the NSA, the National Reconnaissance Office (NRO), the Defense Intelligence Agency (DIA), and tactical intelligence units assigned to each of the armed services. The strategy it had adopted to prevent a surprise attack had become known as "force projection" and involved establishing a U.S. military presence throughout much of the world. By the end of the twentieth century, the Department of

Defense would confirm the existence of 725 bases in thirty-eight countries around the world, with an aggregate replacement value estimated at $118 billion. An important function of these bases—in some cases their overriding function—was surveillance of potential threats against the United States, including terrorism.

The military had also developed and deployed several different types of forces to combat terrorism. Inspired by Israeli commandos' successful hostage rescue at Entebbe in 1976, and by West German special forces' successful attack on terrorists in 1977, the military created the Delta Force, a highly trained rapid-response team it could deploy virtually anywhere in the world. In addition, the military had responded to the Libyan-sponsored bombing of a Berlin disco in 1986 with air strikes against Libya, and with Tomahawk missiles against Iraq in 1993, upon learning of Iraqi plans to assassinate President George H. W. Bush. Thus, the full array of American military might could be recruited to the service of bin Laden's and al Qaeda's destruction, once the United States decided to strike and had acquired a target.

There was thus reason for concern that an operation as complex as the proposed planes operation, with so many actors and moving parts, and with so great a level of sophistication required, would be detected before the plan even left Afghanistan.

Assuming that the plan did proceed beyond the training phase in Afghanistan and the terrorists, having evaded the NSA's intercepts, the NRO's satellite surveillance, the surveillance of the hundreds of military bases projected around the world, and the CIA's intelligence agents and analysts, moved beyond Afghan and other international borders to attempt to enter the United States, other levels of security would come into play. Entry into the United States could be restricted by the State Department through the visa process, and by placing suspected terrorists on the terrorist watchlist. After it was discovered in 1993 that Omar Abdel Rahman, the "Blind Sheikh," had traveled freely despite having conspired to assassinate Egyptian president Anwar Sadat, the State Department moved aggressively to improve the terrorist watchlist system. By the late 1990s, "State had created a worldwide, real-time electronic database of visa, law enforcement, and watchlist information." As part of this system, State maintained a "TIPOFF" list of known and suspected terrorists that, by 2001, contained 60,000 names. State was also empowered, by legislation passed in 1994, to designate certain organizations as terrorist organizations, without giving notice to those organizations or affording them a right to challenge the designation; providing material support to those organizations became a federal felony, regardless of whether the person aiding the organization was aware that it had been so designated by the State Department.

The State Department was assisted in its efforts by the Immigration and Naturalization Service, which had automated the terrorist watchlist in response to the World Trade Center bombing in 1993. In addition, INS created a new "lookout" unit and assigned one person from that unit to assist the State Department in watchlisting suspected terrorists, and in working with the FBI and CIA to determine what to do with such individuals when they appeared at points of entry into the United States. According to the 9/11 Commission, by 1998, ninety-seven suspected terrorists had been denied entry to the United States because of their presence on the terrorist watchlist. There was a good chance, then, that the al Qaeda operatives might be turned away at the airports and ports and border crossings of America, and never get their opportunity to strike.

Assuming that the terrorists surmounted the final obstacle of State Department watchlisting and immigration status and managed to make their way into the United States, they would pass into the jurisdiction of domestic law enforcement, primarily that of the Federal Bureau of Investigation. If they did so, they would be met with an agency that, through its fifty-six field offices across the country, its thousands of special agents, and its legions of informants and cooperating witnesses, had eyes and ears in virtually every American community. Thirty-four of those offices, moreover, housed a Joint Terrorism Task Force, in which

Bureau agents worked with state and local law enforcement officers to share information and to coordinate investigations.

The Bureau recognized early the dangers posed by terrorist attacks and had mobilized aggressively against them. Authorized by Congress to investigate terrorist attacks against Americans that occur outside the United States, and to arrest perpetrators abroad without gaining consent from host governments, the Bureau had investigated the bombing of Pan Am Flight 103, the plane that blew up over Lockerbie, Scotland, in December 1988. The Bureau's investigation went where the evidence led it, not to Syria or Iran, as many had suspected, but to Libya, which later acknowledged responsibility for the attack. Within days of the 1993 bombing of the World Trade Center, Bureau agents had identified a truck remnant as part of a Ryder rental truck that had been reported stolen in Jersey City the day before the bombing. Mohammed Salameh, the recipient of KSM's wire transfer a few months prior, had reported the van stolen and kept calling the rental agency to ask for his $400 deposit back. Within weeks, the Bureau had Salameh and two of his cohorts in custody, had begun the two-year manhunt for Ramzi Youssef, and had traced the activity of all of the conspirators to the Farouq Mosque in Brooklyn, where the Blind Sheikh was prominent. An informant at the mosque learned of a plot later that year to blow up New York's bridges, tunnels, and prominent buildings; as a consequence of this investigation, the plot was disrupted, and the Blind Sheikh and several co-conspirators were prosecuted successfully by the Justice Department.

After these events, the discovery in 1995 of the Bojinka Plot, KSM and Youssef's plan to "blow up twelve American airplanes in Asia, assassinate the pope, bomb the U.S. and Israeli embassies in Manila, and crash an airplane into CIA headquarters," caused heightened concern in the Bureau about the domestic consequences of overseas events. It responded by increasing the number of overseas FBI offices from twenty-three in 1996 to forty-four by the end of the century. Many of the new offices were located in cities like Cairo, Islamabad, Tel Aviv, and Riyadh, in order that the threat from radical Islam abroad could be more effectively monitored.

When in the spring of 1995 a Japanese terrorist organization called Aum Shinrikyo released a weapon of mass destruction—sarin nerve gas—into the Tokyo subway, killing twelve people and injuring five thousand, and Timothy McVeigh bombed the Murrah Federal Building in Oklahoma City, killing 168 Americans, the Bureau responded by changing its organizational structure to meet the threat. Director Louis Freeh created a headquarters Counterterrorism Center, and exchanged senior counterterrorism officials with the CIA. The Bureau mirrored the CIA's creation of a "bin Laden station" by creating a special unit within the Counterterrorism Center devoted exclusively to bin Laden; federal law enforcement in Manhattan launched a secret grand jury investigation into bin Laden's financial support of terrorist operations. The following year, the Bureau underwent a radical reform in its mission, elevating terrorism, espionage, and other national security threats to the top of its priority list for the first time in its history. This change in priorities signaled a sea change in the Bureau's organizational culture, from a law enforcement agency focused primarily on solving crimes that have already occurred to one devoted to preempting attacks before they could be carried out. "Meeting the strategic goals," the Bureau's blueprint for reform noted, "requires that the FBI supplement its reactive capability with bold and innovative proactive efforts designed to deter and prevent—to the maximum extent feasible—criminal activities that threaten vital American interests."

If the al Qaeda terrorists were successful in running the long gauntlet leading from possible NSA detection abroad, to CIA detection, to military interdiction, to State Department watchlisting and immigration barriers, to detection and interdiction by the FBI or other domestic law enforcement, they would still have to be able to board the airplanes, hijack them, and fly them accurately enough to crash them into the chosen targets. To accomplish this final task, the al Qaeda operatives would have to contend with the Federal Aviation Administration's multilayered security system. The FAA system was designed so that "the failure of any one layer of security would not be fatal, because additional layers would provide backup security." Those layers were, respectively, intelligence, passenger prescreening, checkpoint screening, and onboard security.

The FAA had a forty-person intelligence unit, which received large volumes of intelligence data from the FBI, CIA, and other intelligence agencies. This unit would sift the intelligence to identify both specific plots and general threats. If a given terrorist or plot escaped detection at this level, passenger prescreening was employed to deny access to potential terrorists. Passenger prescreening consisted of two elements. First, the FAA published a "no-fly" list of people deemed a direct threat to civil aviation; anyone on that list would be denied access. Second, all airlines used "an FAA-approved computerized algorithm [the Computer Assisted Passenger Prescreening System, or CAPPS] designed to identify passengers" whose profile suggested that they might pose a risk to aircraft.

Assuming that the terrorists went undetected by the FAA intelligence section, and also passed the passenger prescreening tests, they would still have to go through the standard checkpoint screening to which all passengers were subjected: metal detectors and X-ray machines designed to interdict weapons and other prohibited items. Since the 1988 bombing of Pan Am Flight 103, moreover, the FAA's security systems had been tested by "red teams," undercover agents who would travel with weapons and other prohibited items and attempt to defeat the airport security systems.

The al Qaeda operatives would then have to hijack the planes successfully, and fly them accurately enough to hit their targets. Waiting for them at the end of the gauntlet would be the North American Aerospace Defense command, known as NORAD. A joint United States–Canadian command, NORAD was established in 1958, at the height of the Cold War. Its mission, "air sovereignty," was control of the airspace above the domestic United States, as well as surveillance and control of the airspace of Canada and the United States. It was empowered to enforce "air sovereignty" through the use of fighter jets kept on constant alert around the perimeter of the continent. Even if the terrorists were successful in every prior phase and in hijacking and flying the planes, NORAD presented the possibility that they would never reach their targets.

As he sat in exile in his cave at the edge of the world, it is easy to see why bin Laden would be cautious about attempting something as complex as the planes operation, regardless of how determined he was to strike at "the head of the snake." He was facing a multibillion-dollar edifice of national defense and security every bit as imposing—intimidating, even—as the Twin Towers of the World Trade Center, and his own organization had never attempted an operation involving as many people, communications, and training, and with as great a likelihood of failure or betrayal.

Over the next three years, bin Laden and al Qaeda would test the structure of American security and improve the sophistication of their own organization. Al Qaeda would find that, like the Twin Towers themselves, the strength of the American security apparatus was more apparent than real, and that—again, like the Towers—as imposing as it appeared from the outside, it was fragile at its core. Like the Towers, and, of necessity, before them, it would collapse.

Virtually every executive-branch department involved in the national defense against bin Laden and al Qaeda was, as UCLA political science professor Amy Zegart has characterized American intelligence agencies, "flawed by design," beset by internal obstacles to sharing information, by external boundaries that inhibited interaction between departments, and, most important, by a pervasive estrangement of the departments' leadership from their career agents and employees. These dysfunctional features culminated in the most radical estrangement: namely, that of the president of the United States, regardless of party affiliation, from the career government service. These fault lines would become increasingly apparent—and their effects increasingly tragic—as the time and opportunities to stop Bin Laden, KSM, and al Qaeda were compressed from years, to months, to weeks, to days, to hours, to minutes, and, finally, to seconds.

1998

By 1998, bin Laden was becoming more comfortable in his Afghanistan surroundings, and bolder in his public pronouncements. On February 23, 1998, bin Laden held a press conference to present the world with a manifesto from the newly formed International Islamic Front for Jihad Against Jews and Crusaders. Signed by Islamist extremist leaders from Egypt, Pakistan, Bangladesh, Afghanistan, and Kashmir, the document accused the United States of "occupying the most sacred lands of Islam: the Arabian Peninsula. It has been stealing its resources, dictating to its leaders, humiliating its people, and frightening its neighbors. It is using its rule in the Peninsula as a weapon to fight the neighboring peoples of Islam." The manifesto concluded by giving "all Muslims the following judgment: The judgment to kill and fight Americans and their allies, whether civilians or military, is an obligation for every Muslim who is able to do so in any country."

This pronouncement did not go unnoticed at the CIA's Counterterrorist Center, which issued an alert memo immediately. Shared with *The Washington Post* by a member of Congress the day it was issued, the memo noted that this fatwa was "the first from these groups that explicitly justify attacks on American civilians anywhere in the world." The Counterterrorist Center, relying on its Afghan sources from the 1980s who could provide "real-time" intelligence on bin Laden's whereabouts, formulated an elaborate plan to kidnap him while he slept at Tarnak Farms, his complex on the outskirts of Kandahar. The eighty-building complex had been mapped by satellite imagery, and intelligence had identified the specific building in which bin Laden slept. The Afghanis would storm the compound, grab bin Laden, then hold him until the CIA flew him out of the country.

On May 20, 1998, the kidnap plan underwent a full-scale, four-day dry run. The plan was reviewed by the commander of Delta Force, and although there were concerns that such an intricate operation was beyond the grasp of the CIA, and left too much discretion in the hands of the tribal leaders, the Pentagon identified "no showstoppers." The Counterterrorist Center evaluated the likelihood of success at well under 50 percent, but nevertheless warned of the risk of not acting: "Sooner or later, Bin Laden will attack U.S. interests, perhaps using WMD." Ultimately, however, caution prevailed. CIA director Tenet canceled the operation because of the low probability of success and the high probability of collateral casualties or other disastrous consequences. The date by which bin Laden was to have been transported out of Afghanistan in CIA custody, July 23, 1998, came and went.

Two weeks later, on August 7, 1998, American embassies in Kenya and Tanzania were bombed minutes apart in al Qaeda's and bin Laden's most sophisticated attack to date. Hundreds were killed, thousands injured. There had been no warning. Bin Laden's February press conference had resulted in a series of general alerts by the State Department, but no information specific enough to act upon. Repeated expressions of concern by the U.S. ambassador to Kenya that the embassy building was too close to a major street and vulnerable to a car or truck bomb were never acted upon.

One of the conspirators, Wadih el Hage, had been tracked by the CIA's Counterterrorist Center and the FBI from Afghanistan to Nairobi in 1996 and 1997. The FBI removed el Hage from a flight in New York in late 1997 and had him testify before a federal grand jury. He denied any association with bin Laden, was released, and moved to Texas; authorities believed that they had disrupted his East African cell. They hadn't.

Every component of the national security apparatus was energized by these attacks. On August 8, CIA director Tenet informed the White House that he had reliable intelligence that there would be a meeting of high-level Islamist terrorists near Khost, Afghanistan, on August 20, and that bin Laden would likely attend. The White House reviewed and rejected a Pentagon plan for a Special Forces raid into Afghanistan. The size of the force required was deemed too great, the timing too slow, and the choice of targets ill-defined. Instead, the president and his aides decided to launch cruise missiles at the site of the reported meeting, and at another site in Sudan, a chemical plant believed to manufacture the precursor chemicals for VX nerve gas.

On August 17, 1998, President Clinton testified under oath and gave a national address about his illicit relationship with Monica Lewinsky, acknowledging the affair after months of denials. On August 20, seventy-five Tomahawk cruise missiles struck the reported site of the Afghanistan meeting. More than twenty jihadist trainees were killed, and scores wounded. Bin Laden and the hundred or so expected Islamist leaders, however, were not there. The chemical plant in Sudan was also struck, with thirteen cruise missiles, killing a night watchman. It turned out to be an ordinary chemical plant. The soil sample on which the intelligence had been based to support the attack might have indicated a VX precursor, or "it might as well have been weed killer," as Tim Weiner notes in *Legacy of Ashes*.

In the immediate aftermath of the failed cruise missile attacks, Taliban leaders, including Mullah Omar, indicated a willingness to discuss bin Laden's status in their country, and perhaps to expel him. By September, however, Taliban leaders had decided not to agree to expulsion. As a consequence of this refusal, Saudi Arabia broke off diplomatic relations with the Taliban government.

The White House issued secret orders to the U.S. Navy to deploy forces, including two submarines bearing cruise missiles, in the Arabian Sea, just off the coast of Pakistan. Within six weeks of the embassy bombings, intelligence reports indicated that bin Laden was once again staying at the Tarnak Farms complex. Concerns about the possible destruction of a hospital on the grounds, and a lack of confidence that bin Laden would in fact be staying at the complex—the intelligence was based on a single, uncorroborated source—led the president to decide against ordering the missiles to be fired. He had been willing to risk the loss of civilian lives in the August 20 attack, he claimed, because the chances of success had been greater.

President Clinton signed a written authorization, known as a Memorandum of Notification (MON), for the CIA to work with tribal assets in Afghanistan to use force to capture bin Laden and other al Qaeda leaders. The original capture plan was renewed, but the language authorizing government agents to "apprehend with lethal force as authorized" was ambiguous. As Steve Coll explains, "Some CIA officers and supervisors . . . worried that if an operation in Afghanistan went bad, they would be accused of having acted outside the memo's scope. . . . Under American law . . . Clinton might have signed MONs that made no reference to seeking bin Laden's arrest, capture, or rendition for trial. He might have legally authorized the agency to carry out covert action for the sole purpose of killing bin Laden, al-Zawahiri, and other al Qaeda leaders. But Clinton did not choose this path." Instead, in an attempt to reach consensus with the Justice Department, the authorizing language was "convoluted and 'Talmudic.'"

As a consequence, the American response reflected ambivalence at the highest levels of government about exactly what course to pursue: "On the one hand, they ordered cruise missile–equipped submarines to patrol secretly under the Arabian Sea. They hoped to use the submarines to kill bin Laden if they could find him sitting still long enough to strike. On the other hand, they authorized the CIA to carry out operations designed at least on paper to take bin Laden alive." This ambivalence was, if anything, reinforced by the criticism President Clinton received for the perceived "wag the dog" political timing of the August 20 strike. The 9/11 Commission concluded that "the failure of the strikes, the 'wag the dog' slur, the intense partisanship of the period, and the nature of the al Shifa evidence [namely, that the United States had bombed a mere pharmaceutical plant] likely had a cumulative effect on future decisions about the use of force against bin Laden." Political damage and operational uncertainty led ineluctably to inaction.

The president also signed an executive order authorizing the freezing of any assets that could be linked to Osama bin Laden. In addition, the Pentagon began to draw up elaborate plans for ground operations involving the injection of special forces to kill or capture bin Laden.

On a parallel legal track, the Justice Department announced on November 4, 1998, that a grand jury in the Southern District of New York had indicted Osama bin Laden, among others, for the embassy bombings. The government offered a $5 million reward for information leading to the arrest of bin Laden or one of his lieutenants, Mohammed Atef.

Bin Laden responded to the missile attacks and indictment in two ways. First, for his protection, he increased the numbers of his personal bodyguards and took to moving around frequently, sleeping in a different location each night. Second, he escalated his jihad against the United States. He responded to the news of the reward for his capture by offering a higher reward—$9 million—for the assassination of the secretary of state, the secretary of defense, the FBI director, or the CIA director. In late 1998 or early 1999, he met again with KSM and authorized him to go ahead with the planes operation.

According to KSM, the embassy bombings represented a "watershed" in the story of the 9/11 conspiracy. They convinced him that bin Laden was serious about attacking American interests directly. They demonstrated the increasing military sophistication of al Qaeda that was being developed in the training camps of Afghanistan. In addition, the aggressive American response—missile attacks, diplomatic pressure on the Taliban to expel him, the indictment—had made clear that the stakes involved in bin Laden's struggle against the United States were by 1999, for bin Laden, life and death.

On December 4, 1998, CIA director Tenet, in a memo to his senior deputies, stated: "We must now enter a new phase in our efforts against bin Laden. Our work to date has been remarkable and in some instances heroic; yet each day we all acknowledge that retaliation is inevitable and that its scope may be far larger than we have previously experienced. . . . We are at war. I want no resources or people spared in this effort." The same day, President Clinton's Presidential Daily Briefing was headlined "Bin Laden Preparing to Hijack U.S. Aircraft and Other Attacks." Two weeks later, the CIA received intelligence that bin Laden would be spending the night of December 20 at the governor's residence in Kandahar;

from the field, the CIA's station chief advised, "Hit him tonight—we may not get another chance." The national security team decided against recommending that cruise missiles be launched, because of the potential for collateral damage and because of doubts about the intelligence. Former CIA director Tenet explains, "We could never get over the critical hurdle of being able to corroborate Bin Laden's whereabouts, beyond the single thread of data provided by Afghan tribal sources. . . . As much as we all wanted Bin Laden dead, the use of force by a superpower requires information, discipline, and time. We rarely had the information in sufficient quantities or the time to evaluate and act on it."

1999

The U.S. government's intense focus on bin Laden seemed to pay off early in 1999, when intelligence yielded another opportunity to strike bin Laden. The CIA's Afghan tribal allies provided intelligence that bin Laden was staying at a hunting camp in western Afghanistan. The CIA and the National Imagery Mapping Agency (NIMA) located the site and mapped it thoroughly. A CIA tracking team reported that they had located bin Laden at the camp, where he appeared to be a guest of sheikhs from the United Arab Emirates (UAE). Furthermore, the camp was located far from any urban concentrations, and it appeared that bin Laden would be staying there for some time. The CIA's team on the ground concluded that this was a viable target, and the sentiment in the Counterterrorist Center was that cruise missiles should be launched: "Let's just blow the thing up. And if we kill bin Laden, and five sheikhs are killed, I'm sorry. What are they doing with bin Laden? He's a terrorist. You lie down with the dog, you get up with fleas." On February 8, 1999, the military began to prepare to launch cruise missiles.

President Clinton was facing impeachment at the time of his briefing on the opportunity to strike bin Laden while he was staying at the hunting camp. In addition, the intelligence on bin Laden's presence in the camp was not absolutely certain, and the Emirates were important strategically for the United States in the region. CIA director Tenet and National Security Advisor Sandy Berger recommended against the strike; President Clinton decided not to pursue it. This decision angered and embittered CIA ground-level operatives: "We knew he was there. We had assets in place. There was little risk to life and limb to anybody—not our Afghan colleagues, nobody on the American side. And it would have been, we thought, definitive. We could take him out." Their anger intensified when, after White House Counterterrorism coordinator Richard Clarke called a UAE official to voice concerns over Emirate officials' relations with bin Laden, the hunting camp was hurriedly dismantled, thus removing an attractive future target.

Little more than one month later, in March or April 1999, KSM was summoned to Kandahar and instructed by bin Laden to begin planning for the planes operation. KSM, who had formally joined al Qaeda in late 1998 or early 1999, had advanced several other proposals by this time, involving attacks in Israel, Thailand, Singapore, Indonesia, and the Maldives, but now he was told by bin Laden and others to focus on the planes operation. He was also told, apparently, to scale back his original conception. According to KSM's testimony submitted to the 9/11 Commission, the original plan called for the following: "a total of ten aircraft to be hijacked, nine of which would crash into targets on both coasts—they included those eventually hit on September 11 plus CIA and FBI headquarters, nuclear power plants, and the tallest buildings in California and the state of Washington. KSM himself was to land the tenth plane at a U.S. airport and, after killing all adult male passengers on board and alerting the media, deliver a speech excoriating U.S. support for Israel, the Philippines, and repressive governments in the Arab world."

This grandiose proposal was not approved by bin Laden, who thought that it was impractical and vulnerable to compromise. The plan was refined and scaled back during a series of meetings in the spring of 1999 at a complex called al Matar, near Kandahar. The initial meetings focused on target selection, with bin Laden wanting to destroy the White House, the Pentagon, and the Capitol, KSM the World Trade Center and the Capitol. The planes operation was one of several in the planning stages by 1999; mujahideen were rotating in and out of training camps in Afghanistan, learning the rudiments of international travel, martial arts, explosives, and countersurveillance tactics.

Even as KSM and bin Laden were meeting in the spring of 1999 in Kandahar to plan the planes operation, the CIA's assets in Afghanistan were offering their most detailed and accurate reporting to date of his whereabouts. In May 1999, over a five-day period, several sources reported details on bin Laden's comings and goings in and around Kandahar. This was, by consensus, the most reliable intelligence possible. The military was ready with its cruise missiles. There were three opportunities to fire on bin Laden in thirty-six hours. "This was in our strike zone," a senior military officer would tell the 9/11 Commission. "It was a fat pitch, a home run." As the Commission's report elaborated, "He expected the missiles to fly. When the decision came back that they should stand down, not shoot, the officer said, 'We all just slumped.'" He told the Commission that "he knew of no one at the Pentagon or the CIA who thought it was a bad gamble. Bin Laden 'should have been a dead man' that night."

Oddly, neither George Tenet nor Sandy Berger had a clear memory of this episode when speaking with the 9/11 Commission; days before, however, faulty intelligence had resulted in calamity elsewhere in the world. As part of NATO's bombing campaign to force Serbia to remove its troops from Kosovo, the CIA had selected as a target the Yugoslav Federal Directorate of Supply and Procurement. Using tourist maps to help them locate the Directorate, the CIA delivered coordinates to the Pentagon, which loaded them into the bombs' guidance system. The bombs were delivered on target. Unfortunately, the target turned out to be the Chinese embassy. The resulting humiliation undermined the confidence of national security leadership, from the president down, in the competence of the CIA. The thirty-six-hour window in Kandahar closed.

Kandahar in May 1999 was the last serious opportunity that the government had to kill bin Laden with cruise missiles before 9/11, and it was close to the last moment when decapitating al Qaeda would in itself have ended the planes operation. In the course of their spring meetings in Kandahar, bin Laden and KSM had identified several of the future suicide hijackers; the plan was rapidly expanding beyond the small circle of leaders.

During his spring 1999 Kandahar meetings with KSM, bin Laden selected four mujahideen to serve as martyrs to jihad in the planes operation: Khalid al Mihdhar, Nawaf al Hazmi, Abu Bara al Yemeni, and Khallad (Tawfiq bin Attash). Hazmi and Mihdhar, Saudi nationals who already possessed United States visas, had fought as mujahideen in Bosnia and had visited the al Qaeda training camps in Afghanistan on numerous occasions. Bin Laden designated them for pilot training.

As the plot broadened to include multiple participants and to contemplate international travel, KSM realized that for certain proposed hijackers, gaining entry into the United States would likely prove impossible. Khallad, for instance, a Yemeni with known terrorist ties, was denied a visa. As the plan broadened in scope, in other words, other aspects of the American national security system were implicated, and their security measures had to be negotiated. It became apparent, as the 9/11 Commission concluded, that "because individuals with Saudi passports could travel much more easily than Yemeni, particularly to the United States, there were fewer martyrdom opportunities for Yemenis." Accordingly, al Qaeda would ultimately select for martyrdom only those individuals who were most likely to be able to travel internationally and to enter the United States without raising concern. There was a bias favoring Saudis and Egyptians because of their nations' favorable status with the U.S. State Department, and favoring individuals with little or no prior involvement with jihad.

Throughout the fall of 1999, the chosen mujahideen, with the exception of Mihdhar, received intensive training at a select al Qaeda camp near Kabul, and then, in December 1999, by KSM himself in Karachi, Pakistan. They were trained in rudimentary English, exposed to Western culture, and taught how to function in America. In early 2000, they traveled to Kuala Lumpur.

While the planes operation began to take shape, officials in Washington struggled to come up with a revised strategy to deal with bin Laden and al Qaeda. In July, President Clinton authorized the CIA to work with foreign governments to apprehend bin Laden. The president also extended the authorizations to cover not just bin Laden, but senior al Qaeda leadership as well. At the CIA, new leadership at the Counterterrorist Center formulated "the Plan," a multifaceted approach to combating al Qaeda that included working with Pakistani intelligence, training and arming the Uzbeks, assisting Afghan tribal leader Ahmed Shah Massoud and the Northern Alliance in the fight against the Taliban and bin Laden, and deploying a joint force consisting of CIA and Special Forces personnel. The last option was never deemed feasible; each of the first three was considered to have a likelihood of success of less than 15 percent.

By the fall of 1999, however, the emphasis of the national security apparatus went from proactive efforts to capture or kill bin Laden to defensive activation of every layer of the national security establishment. As Steve Coll puts it, "It had been a rough autumn for the threat-reporting managers at the CIA's Counterterrorist Center. Beginning in September they picked up multiple signs that Bin Laden had set in motion major terrorist attacks timed to the turn of the year." CIA director Tenet forecast between five and fifteen attacks centering on the millennium. "Because the U.S. is bin Laden's ultimate goal," he counseled, "we must assume that several of these targets will be in the U.S." Although this message was greeted with some skepticism at the White House, where staffers believed that fear of the consequences of failing to report a genuine threat was leading the CIA to overreport threats, the national security establishment was galvanized into action when Jordanian intelligence disrupted a plot to bomb a Radisson Hotel on New Year's Eve, and when a random customs check at the Canadian border yielded the arrest of an operative loosely affiliated with al Qaeda who had intended to bomb Los Angeles International Airport.

By mid-December 1999, the United States was on full alert. A record number of Foreign Intelligence Surveillance Act wiretaps were issued. An associate of the LAX bomber was arrested in Brooklyn, New York. Foreign embassies and CIA operatives were placed on high alert. Director Tenet contacted twenty intelligence chiefs in foreign countries and requested that they arrest anyone associated with bin Laden. State and local law enforcement were briefed on the threat; in New Jersey, emergency plans were developed in the event of an attack on Manhattan. Everyone was told essentially the same thing; as Director Tenet put it in a memo to CIA officers abroad: "The threat could not be more real."

No attacks materialized. It is unclear, in retrospect, whether the efforts of law enforcement and national security personnel were decisive in deterring attacks, whether the publicity surrounding the arrest of the LAX bomber and the Jordanian plotters caused al Qaeda to stand down, or whether al Qaeda was simply not prepared as of the millennium to launch a major attack, and was relying on outliers such as the LAX bomber. Two critical misses, however, suggest that the American national security warning system had been more lucky than good. Despite the heightened state of alert by NSA, NIMA, DIA, CIA, and foreign intelligence services throughout the world, no one picked up a failed attack in Yemen, where a team of al Qaeda terrorists had intended to bomb a U.S. Navy ship but had sunk their own small boat when they overloaded it with explosives. Perhaps more important, no one—not even German intelligence—reported the curious travel, on the eve of Ramadan in late November, of a group of four students in Hamburg to Pakistan and then to Afghanistan. Led by Mohammed Atta, the Hamburg group, which included Ramzi bin al Shib, Ziad Jarrah, and Marwan al Shehhi, would complement Mihdhar and Hazmi and form the core of the 9/11 attackers.

Another indication that the government's success in thwarting potential millennium attacks had been fortuitous came in an after-action report, the *Millennium After-Action Review*, prepared by the National Security Council staff under the supervision of Richard Clarke. Preparing to testify before the 9/11 Commission in 2003, former National Security Advisor Sandy Berger paid several visits to the National Archives to review Clinton-era documents. While purportedly looking over the documents before their delivery to the 9/11 Commission, Berger took several bathroom breaks. Archives staff suspicions were aroused on September 2, when he appeared to have stuffed documents in his socks; he later admitted having removed a copy of the *Millennium After-Action Review* on that date, but denied having stuffed it in his socks. The Archives staff began numbering the documents provided to Berger. When he returned, a month later, on October 2, he found, to his surprise, more copies of the *Millennium After-Action Review*. He waited until he was alone, then stuffed several documents in his pockets and left the building. According to the record of Berger's interview with the National Archives Inspector General, "It was dark. He did not want to run the risk of bringing the documents back into the building. He headed towards a construction site area on Ninth Street. Mr. Berger looked up and down the street, up into the windows of the Archives and DoJ [Department of Justice], and did not see anyone. He removed the documents from his pockets, folded the notes in a 'V' shape, and . . . walked inside a construction fence and slid the documents under a trailer." Berger returned to the Archives building, and after seven p.m., "left the building, retrieved the documents and notes from the construction site, and drove back to his office." On October 4, an Archives official called Berger and told him that documents were missing. Berger "lied" to the official, "telling [him] he did not take the documents. Mr. Berger drove to his office late that afternoon. On the night of October 2, he had destroyed, cut up into small pieces, three of the four documents. These were put into the trash." Berger pleaded guilty to a misdemeanor, and admitted to shredding three copies of the *Review;* it is not clear whether the copies contained hand-written notes, or whether he removed other documents. The 9/11 Commission was not informed that he had destroyed documents, or that he had had access to original documents. It is a fair inference that the destroyed documents would not have reflected positively on the Clinton administration's performance.

Testifying before the 9/11 Commission, then Attorney General John Ashcroft described the report as recommending "disrupting the Al Qaeda and terrorist presence here using immigration violations, minor criminal infractions and tougher visa and border controls." The *Review*, according to Ashcroft, warned of a substantial Al Qaeda presence within the United States, "capable of supporting additional terrorist attacks here."

The fact that America was not attacked during the millennium, in other words, was a result not of impregnable defenses but of the fortuity of alert customs inspectors in Port Angeles, Washington, and the lack of a fully mature plan. Furthermore, the actions of former National Security Advisor Berger in smuggling sensitive documents out of the National Archives, taken together with the CIA's destruction of interrogation tapes, are indications of the lengths to which government officials of the highest bipartisan ranks proved willing to go to frustrate the 9/11 Commission's search for the truth.

2000

The potential value of the Hamburg group to the planes operation was recognized immediately by al Qaeda's leadership. They were, as Lawrence Wright describes them, "educated, technical men, with English skills ranging from rudimentary to fluent. They did not need to be told how to live in the West. Visas would be no problem. All they needed was to learn how to fly and to be willing to die."

Originally intending to go to Chechnya for jihad against the Russians, the Hamburg contingent of Islamists traveled instead to Afghanistan because they were informed that travelers to Chechnya were being detained in Georgia. Once in Afghanistan, they were singled out immediately by Mohammed Atef and introduced to bin Laden, to whom they swore loyalty. They were then informed that they had been selected for a secret, as yet undisclosed, mission. At a Ramadan feast hosted by bin Laden himself, they were informed that they had been selected to be martyrs. They were instructed to return to Hamburg, and to enroll in flight schools. They returned in early January 2000. Their trip had been concealed from German authorities by their friends, including Mounir el Motassadeq, who terminated Shehhi's lease and used a power of attorney to pay bills from Shehhi's bank account, and also assisted Ziad Jarrah. As a result, no intelligence regarding the travel of the four future hijackers was gathered or passed. With the free travel of Atta and his comrades from Hamburg to Afghanistan and back, the enormous warning apparatus of U.S. national security had been bypassed successfully. Penetration of the United States itself was one step away.

The other hijacking team, which had been selected earlier, was not as fortunate. In their case, the early-warning system worked precisely according to design. During the course of the FBI's investigation of the embassy bombings, investigators had come across a phone number in Yemen that appeared to be used as a routing clearinghouse for al Qaeda phone messages. That number, to which Khalid al Mihdhar's father-in-law subscribed, was monitored thereafter by the NSA. The NSA monitoring picked up a conversation about a meeting that would take place in early January 2000 in Kuala Lumpur, Malaysia; attending, according to the conversation, would be Khalid al Mihdhar and two others, named Nawaf and Salem. The NSA reported that "something nefarious might be afoot."

CIA agents tracked Mihdhar to Dubai, where he was staying, en route to Malaysia. They broke into his hotel room and photographed his passport, which reflected that Mihdhar had a multi-entry U.S. visa that would not expire until April 2000. They faxed the passport to the Counterterrorist Center, which notified intelligence services around the world and advised them that "we need to continue the effort to identify these travelers and their activities . . . to determine if there is any true threat posed." The Counterterrorist Center had also briefed the CIA leadership, Sandy Berger, and the National Security Council staff. According to the 9/11 Commission, FBI director Freeh and others at the Bureau were also made aware of the meeting in Kuala Lumpur, "though the FBI noted that the CIA had the lead and would let the FBI know if a domestic angle arose."

The CIA requested that Malaysian intelligence provide surveillance of the meeting, which was held on January 5, 2000, at a condominium resort overlooking a golf course designed by Jack Nicklaus. The meeting, which involved several known or suspected al Qaeda members, was not wiretapped. Cofer Black, who oversaw the intelligence operation as the head of the Counterterrorist Center, explained: "We surveil them. We surveil the guy they're there to meet. Not close enough to hear what they're actually saying, but we're covering, taking pictures, watching their behavior. They're acting kind of spooky. They're not using the phone in the apartment. They're going around, walking in circles, just like junior spies. Going up to phone booths, making a lot of calls. It's like, 'Who are these dudes?'"

In the Counterterrorist Center, the FBI liaison learned of Mihdhar's American visa and wrote a memo requesting permission to share the information about the meeting in Kuala Lumpur and the possibility that one or more of the participants would be traveling to the United States. The FBI agent was told, "This is not a matter for the FBI." The Bureau agent appealed to his counterpart, the CIA agent who was stationed at FBI's headquarters in order to facilitate information sharing; he forwarded the memo he had written and asked if it was "a no-go, or should I remake it in some way?" According to Lawrence Wright, he never received a response and the issue was forgotten. On January 8, Mihdhar, Hazmi, and a third man flew from Kuala Lumpur to Bangkok, where they were lost to surveillance. One week later, Hazmi (who, it turned out, also had a valid entry visa) and Mihdhar flew to Los Angeles unde-tected by the American early-warning system. No one had thought to add Mihdhar's name to the TIPOFF watchlist, despite his now known association with al Qaeda and his multi-entry U.S. visa.

When, in March of 2000, the CIA's Bangkok station reported that Nawaf al Hazmi had flown to Los Angeles on January 15 on a United Airlines flight, no one outside the CIA's Counterterrorist Center was informed. Neither Hazmi nor Mihdhar was placed on the TIPOFF watch-list even then, and, as the 9/11 Commission concluded, "None of this information—about Mihdhar's U.S. visa or Hazmi's travel to the United States—went to the FBI, and nothing more was done to track [them] until January 2001, when the investigation of another bombing, that of the U.S.S. *Cole*, reignited interest in Khallad," who had also attended the meeting in Kuala Lumpur and had been photographed with Mihdhar. As Lawrence Wright observes, the failure to wiretap the meeting in Kuala Lumpur meant that "the opportunity to discover the plots that culmi-nated in the bombing of the USS *Cole* and the 9/11 attack was lost."

If Mihdhar and Hazmi narrowly evaded detection as they made their way into the United States, the Hamburg cell managed to penetrate the United States without raising a single red flag. Upon their return from Afghanistan, the four changed their conduct and appearances to make themselves inconspicuous. They avoided associating with radicals, whom they knew would be watched, shaved their beards, and wore Western-style clothing. With the exception of Ziad Jarrah, their families and friends noticed that they seemed to be acting like their old selves again. They also researched flight schools in Europe and the United States, ultimately deciding that it would be preferable to train in the United States. Atta, Shehhi, and Jarrah obtained new passports before seeking U.S. visas, claiming that their old passports had been lost. Bin al Shib, who did not obtain a new passport, was unable to obtain a visa and had to remain behind in Germany. Bin al Shib was excluded not because of concerns about his membership in al Qaeda, which was unknown, but rather because of "the generalized suspicion that visa applicants from Yemen . . . might join the ranks of undocumented aliens seeking work in the United States." Marwan al Shehhi arrived in Newark on May 29. Mohammed Atta arrived in Newark on June 3. Ziad Jarrah arrived in Newark on June 27. By the end of June, three of the four 9/11 pilots were in the United States, ready to be trained to fly by Americans.

All three settled on aviation schools in Florida, and were in training by the fall of 2000. They paid for their training and living expenses with $114,500 wired to them by KSM's nephew. None of them raised any suspicions among American authorities.

Hazmi and Mihdhar settled in San Diego during the winter and spring of 2000, intending to learn English and take flying lessons. They were befriended by a group of Muslim men who attended the same mosque, and who shared many of their Islamist views and their hostility toward America. The pair proved to be poor students of both English and flying; by the end of May, they had given up learning to fly. On June 10, Mihdhar exposed the planes operation to potential compromise when he flew home, unannounced, to visit his family in Yemen. KSM was outraged by this undisciplined act, and sought to drop Mihdhar from the planes operation, but bin Laden intervened on his behalf.

Hazmi sat tight in San Diego and awaited the arrival of a fourth pilot, Hani Hanjour, who had lived in the United States at various times throughout the 1990s and already had a pilot's license when he arrived in Afghanistan for training in jihad. When senior al Qaeda leadership discovered that they had a trained pilot in their midst who had also lived in America, Hanjour was recruited immediately to the planes operation. He arrived in San Diego and met Hazmi on December 8, 2000.

While the 9/11 pilots were undergoing training in the United States through the fall of 2000, the attention of U.S. national security officials was diverted by an attack halfway around the world. On October 12, 2000, al Qaeda members loaded a small boat with explosives, sped alongside a U.S. Navy destroyer, the USS *Cole*, and detonated their boat, blasting a $250 million hole in the ship's side, killing seventeen members of the *Cole*'s crew and wounding at least forty. Investigators from the FBI, the Naval Criminal Investigative Service, and the CIA were dispatched immediately to assist in investigating the attack.

By the second half of November 2000, despite significant conflicts both between U.S. and Yemeni law enforcement officials and among the U.S. contingent, al Qaeda's responsibility for the *Cole* attack had been established. In particular, the al Qaeda operative Khallad had been identified by captured *Cole* conspirators as having been the intermediary in the plot between al Qaeda's leadership—presumably bin Laden—and the suicide bombers. But the CIA and other intelligence agencies could not prove that bin Laden was responsible; a November 25 memo from Richard Clarke and Sandy Berger to President Clinton stated that while the available evidence strongly suggested that "the attack had been carried out by a large cell whose senior members belonged to al Qaeda," al Qaeda responsibility was still an "unproven assumption."

This investigation and analysis coincided with the U.S. presidential election of 2000, which was still very much undecided as of late November. Investigators continued to work the case into December, and on December 21 presented the latest findings to senior national security staff. The presentation concluded that the CIA had "no definitive answer on [the] crucial question of outside direction of the attack—how and by whom." The report noted that the Yemeni government claimed that Khallad had directed the attacks from Afghanistan, perhaps as bin Laden's intermediary, but added that the intelligence supporting the Yemeni government's claim had not been shared with the CIA. The CIA did conclude, however, that it could establish that Khallad was an al Qaeda operative through both signals and human intelligence.

This was not sufficient proof, in the estimation of President Clinton and National Security Advisor Berger, to warrant the use of military force against the Taliban or bin Laden. President Clinton told the 9/11 Commission, "The election and change of power was not the issue. . . . If the agencies had given him a definitive answer, he said, he would have sought a U.N. Security Council ultimatum and given the Taliban one, two, or three days before taking further action against both al Qaeda and the Taliban. But he did not think it would be responsible for a president to launch an invasion of another country just based on a 'preliminary judgment.'" The analysts in the CIA's Counterterrorist Center were frustrated: "They found connections between the bombers and an al Qaeda operative who had recently spent time at a Kandahar guesthouse. But they could not prove bin Laden's personal responsibility for the attack—at least, the evidence would not meet the standards of a criminal indictment. Nor could they provide specific proof of bin Laden's role that Clinton could cite if he wished to publicly justify retaliation. Yet the CIA's officers told colleagues that they were dead certain of bin Laden's involvement."

In response to the *Cole* bombing, the Pentagon outlined thirteen options for the use of military force against the Taliban or bin Laden; it was described as a primer on the "extraordinary complexity" of proceeding with a "boots on the ground" approach. The "overwhelming message," Richard Clarke concluded, "was, 'We don't want to do this.'" The remaining alternative, an alliance with Ahmed Shah Massoud and the Northern Alliance, was rejected by the senior national security staff at the White House. Nothing was done.

The Clinton administration's account of its failure to respond to the *Cole* bombing is difficult to accept, particularly if one is to believe that it had been seeking actively since 1998 to capture or kill bin Laden. If it is true, as claimed, that the White House believed it had authorized the killing of bin Laden in 1998 and never rescinded that authorization, and if it is true, as claimed, that the president would have authorized his assassination at any time thereafter if the government had acquired actionable intelligence, then why the insistence, after the *Cole* bombing, that the White House be provided with "specific proof" capable of supporting an indictment before retaliating against bin Laden? There was certainly substantial proof of al Qaeda involvement, and the head of al Qaeda was preaching incessantly the destruction of America. If the Clinton administration had truly authorized action against bin Laden already—and for the prior two years—and if it truly was "at war" with al

Qaeda and bin Laden, it should not have needed "definitive proof" after the *Cole* bombing to have taken action.

The year 2000 ended, then, with no response to the *Cole* bombing from the American government. The year that had begun in exultation that the millennium had come and gone without a major attack ended in the dispiriting reality that the largest attack since the embassy bombings had come and gone with no response. That would be left to the incoming Bush administration. In Afghanistan, al Qaeda recruits flooded the training camps, and money poured in from sympathetic Muslims around the world. In America, three al Qaeda members progressed with their pilot training in Florida, while Hazmi and the fourth pilot, Hanjour, left San Diego and headed east.

PART TWO

2001

MONTHS

The future hijackers encountered the national security apparatus several times in early 2001, mostly as a consequence of international travel. The travel of the hijackers and their points of contact with U.S. and other government security in the course of that travel is set forth at length in *The 9/11 Commission Report*; see also the chart on pages 337–356.

Khalid al Mihdhar was not the only member of the planes operation to feel estranged by life in the United States and decide to go home for a visit. Ziad Jarrah traveled twice in January, to visit his girlfriend in Germany and his ailing father in Beirut. He traveled again to see his girlfriend in mid-March. Shehhi, whose family had become concerned and reported him missing to the United Arab Emirates government, traveled to Morocco in January, and to Egypt in late April, in part to visit Atta's father. He called his family in January and told them he was still living and studying in Hamburg. That news ended a search for him that had been under way by the Hamburg police.

Mohammed Atta traveled to Hamburg in January on business. He met with Ramzi bin al Shib, and told him that the three pilots in America had completed their training and were awaiting orders. He added that they had been joined by a fourth, Hani Hanjour. Upon his return to Florida on January 10, 2001, he wired money to bin al Shib in Hamburg so that bin al Shib could travel to Afghanistan and meet with al Qaeda leadership.

Both Shehhi and Atta were stopped and questioned by INS officials when they attempted to reenter the country. Although neither was able to present a student visa, both persuaded the officials that they needed to return to the United States so that they could complete their flight-school training.

Atta also encountered law enforcement on April 26, when he was stopped in Florida in a routine traffic stop. He presented his international driver's license, but apparently resolved to get a U.S. license; on May 2, he and Jarrah visited the Florida Division of Motor Vehicles office in Lauderdale Lakes to get Florida driver's licenses.

During the spring and early summer, the future hijackers settled in two locations. Atta and Jarrah settled in Florida in April, and were joined on May 2 by Shehhi. Hazmi and Hanjour settled in Paterson, New Jersey, renting an apartment in May. They were joined eventually in their apartment by four other future hijackers: Hazmi's brother Salem, Majed Moqed, Ahmed al Ghamdi, and Abdul Aziz al Omari. Mihdhar would join them in early July.

The remaining hijackers, the so-called muscle—twelve of whom (out of a total of thirteen) were Saudi nationals—began arriving in the United States in late April 2001, and were in place with the arrival of Mihdhar on July 4. They had secured their U.S. tourist visas before leaving home for training in Afghanistan at the training camps that were known to but not attacked by American national security, even after the attack on the *Cole* had been linked to al Qaeda.

That training included hijacking techniques, martial arts, explosives, bodybuilding, and rudimentary English. They trained in the use of knives by butchering a sheep and a camel. According to KSM, they "learned to focus on storming the cockpit at the earliest opportunity when the doors first opened, and to worry about seizing control over the rest of the plane later. The operatives were taught about other types of attack as well, such as truck bombing, so that they would not be able to disclose the exact nature of their operation if they were caught. According to KSM, the muscle did not learn the full details—including the plan to hijack planes and fly them into buildings—before reaching the United States."

Thus, the training of the "muscle" hijackers reflected the reality recognized by bin Laden in the plot's earliest stages: as the number of people involved increased from two or three to seven or eight, to a dozen, to the nineteen hijackers and everyone in al Qaeda who was needed to assist them, so did the likelihood that the plot would be identified at some level of U.S. security and thwarted by the Americans before the hijackers ever had a chance to board the flights. By the spring and early summer of 2001, as the nineteen hijackers began to travel and to congregate, with the assistance of al Qaeda operatives throughout the Middle East, Europe, and the United States, the plot was closer to both fruition and detection.

It came closest to detection in May and June, when a CIA representative to the FBI's International Terrorism Center began to look into the possible relationship between Khalid al Mihdhar, who had not yet returned to the United States, and Khallad, the mastermind of the *Cole* bombing who had also been involved in the embassy bombings. At one point, the CIA had believed that Khallad and Mihdhar were the same person, but the FBI had determined conclusively that they were not. Tom Wilshire, the CIA representative, underscored the importance of Khallad in an e-mail to his supervisors: "OK. This is important. This is a major-league killer, who orchestrated the Cole Attack and possibly the Africa bombings."

An FBI agent assigned to the CIA's Counterterrorist Center had been assisting the FBI in New York in investigating the *Cole* attack. She was trying to trace the movements of Fahd al Quso, who had traveled to Bangkok in January 2000 to give money to Khallad. Because this occurred just after the meeting in Kuala Lumpur, the CIA decided to share with the FBI some of the surveillance photographs taken of that meeting, to see whether the Bureau's agents could identify any of the participants.

On June 11, representatives of the CIA met with the FBI in New York.

They were briefed on the progress of the Bureau's *Cole* investigation. Then they showed the Bureau three surveillance photographs from the Kuala Lumpur meeting. One of the CIA agents had reviewed NSA intercepts regarding the Kuala Lumpur meeting before meeting with the FBI; accordingly, she knew that members of an "operational cadre" of al Qaeda were planning to travel to Kuala Lumpur, and that among these were "Nawaf, Salem, and Khalid." She further learned that before the meeting, the CIA had identified "Khalid" as Khalid al Mihdhar, and that it had tracked his travel from Yemen until his arrival in Kuala Lumpur on January 5, 2000. Because the databases she searched contained the caveat that "their contents could not be shared with criminal investigators without the permission of the Justice Department's Office of Intelligence Policy and Review," she determined that she could share none of the intelligence regarding Mihdhar with the Bureau at the June 11 meeting. Another CIA representative at the meeting knew the additional facts that Mihdhar possessed a United States visa, that his visa indicated that he intended to travel to New York, that Hazmi had traveled to Los Angeles, and that intelligence had placed Mihdhar in Khallad's company. He made a similar decision that the information could not be shared with the FBI's criminal investigators.

The CIA representatives, after some heated exchanges about why they were not more forthcoming, did share with the Bureau the name Khalid al Mihdhar, but that was all. They promised to try to get permission to pass further information along. The CIA declined to share Mihdhar's passport number or date of birth, which would have allowed the FBI to place him on the TIPOFF list and bar his entry into the country; nor did the CIA itself forward Mihdhar's name to the State Department for inclusion on the list. On June 13, two days after the June 11 meeting, Khalid al Mihdhar received a U.S. visa. He flew to Newark on July 4.

In the spring of 2001, as the nineteen hijackers began traveling, different components of the American national security apparatus began to pick up signals that a major operation might be imminent. As the 9/11 Commission notes, "The level of reporting on terrorist threats and planned attacks increased dramatically to its highest level since the millennium alert." This increased intensity was reflected in national security briefings throughout the spring and early summer, bearing titles such as "Bin Laden Public Profile May Presage Attack," "Bin Laden Network's Plan Advancing," and "UBL: Operation Planned in U.S." (May); "Bin Laden Attacks May Be Imminent," "Bin Laden and Associates Making Near-Term Threats," and "Bin Laden Planning High-Profile Attacks" (June). Reports "similar to these" were made available to President Bush, Vice President Cheney, and National Security Advisor Condoleezza Rice in morning meetings with Tenet.

What was the nature of the intelligence? In early May, a walk-in to the FBI claimed that there was a plan to launch attacks on London, Boston, and New York. On May 16, a phone call to a foreign embassy was reported warning that al Qaeda was planning an attack on the U.S. using "high explosives." In late May, the system picked up rumors that there was an al Qaeda plot to hijack an airplane or storm an embassy in an effort to free the Blind Sheikh, Omar Rahman. The FAA issued an information circular to the airlines advising of the possibility of "an airline hijacking to free terrorists incarcerated in the United States." On May 24, the Counterterrorism Center received reports concerning plots in Yemen, Italy, and Canada. Counterterrorism Chief Cofer Black rated the threat level as just slightly less than during the millennium crisis.

Toward the end of June, Richard Clarke advised Rice that the threat reporting had reached "a crescendo." Six separate intelligence reports, according to Clarke, indicated that al Qaeda personnel were talking about a pending attack. The intelligence reporting "consistently described the upcoming attacks as occurring on a calamitous level, indicating that they would cause the world to be in turmoil and that they would consist of possible multiple—but not necessarily simultaneous—attacks."

The government acted upon the perceived threat in early July. On July 2, the FBI Counterterrorism Center sent a message to federal agencies and to state and local law enforcement agencies summarizing threat information regarding bin Laden. The memo advised that there was an increased volume of threat reporting related to groups "aligned with or sympathetic to Usama Bin Laden." The memo emphasized, however, the potential for attacks abroad, and further stated that "the FBI has no information indicating a credible threat of terrorist attack in the United States."

The federal agencies were convened by Richard Clarke. On July 5, he met with representatives of the INS, the FAA, the Coast Guard, the Secret Service, Customs, the CIA, and the FBI to discuss the federal response to the threat. Attendees of the meeting later reported to the 9/11 Commission that "they were told not to disseminate the threat information they received at the meeting. They interpreted this direction to mean that although they could brief their superiors, they could not send out advisories to the field."

On July 10, 2001, Special Agent Ken Williams of the FBI's Phoenix field office sent a memo to the bin Laden and Radical Fundamentalist units at FBI headquarters, and to two agents in the New York field office, warning that there were "an inordinate number of individuals of investigative interest" taking flying lessons at Arizona flight schools. He named ten people he had investigated with possible terrorist ties, one of whom was an associate of Hani Hanjour, and warned of a possible "effort by Usama Bin Laden to send students to the United States to attend civil aviation schools." The memo was marked "routine"; however, it was not shown to the acting FBI director or distributed to other field offices, and Williams later indicated that "the Phoenix memo was not an alert about suicide pilots."

That same day, director Tenet and his deputies met with National Security Advisor Condoleezza Rice and her deputy to describe for them the nature of the threat reporting that the intelligence community had been receiving. According to Tenet, his deputy began the briefing by predicting that "there will be a significant terrorist attack in the coming weeks or months!" Tenet's staff reported that bin Laden and other al Qaeda leaders had been discussing a near-term attack, and that Islamic extremists were traveling in large numbers to Afghanistan and leaving countries such as Yemen. "Attack preparations have been made. Multiple and simultaneous attacks are possible, and they will occur with little or no warning. Al-Qa'ida is waiting us out and looking for vulnerability."

On July 18, the State Department advised the public of an increased risk of terrorist attacks in the Arabian Peninsula. On July 19, on a periodic conference call with the FBI's field offices, Acting Director Thomas Pickard mentioned that, in light of the increased threat reporting, the Bureau needed to have "evidence response teams ready" in case of an attack. "He did not ask field offices to try to determine whether any plots were being considered within the United States."

On July 31, an FAA circular alerted the aviation community to "reports of possible near-term terrorist operations . . . particularly on the Arabian Peninsula and/or Israel." The circular stated that the FAA had "no credible evidence of specific plans to attack civil aviation," but noted that some active terrorist groups did "plan and train for hijackings."

By late May, bin Laden was obviously aware that news of an impending attack was spreading through al Qaeda's ranks, and that this increased the likelihood of detection. As Richard Clarke and the CIA Counterterrorist Center were advising that attacks might be imminent, bin Laden was meeting bin al Shib in early May and instructing him to convey to Atta that the teams should "focus on their security and that of their operation"; at several points that spring and summer bin Laden pressed to advance the date of the attacks, fearing detection.

The hijacking teams, in place in New Jersey and Florida, focused on preparing for their mission. The muscle hijackers opened local bank accounts, acquired postal addresses, and joined local gyms, presumably to stay in physical shape for their role. Several obtained photo identification, first in New Jersey and then at the Virginia Department of Motor Vehicles. The pilots took cross-country surveillance flights, studying the types of planes they would be flying. In late May, Shehhi flew from New York to Las Vegas via San Francisco. In early June, Jarrah flew from Baltimore to Las Vegas via Los Angeles. At the end of June, Atta flew from Boston to Las Vegas via San Francisco. Each flew first class, aboard United Airlines. In addition, Jarrah and Hanjour rented small planes in Pennsylvania and New Jersey, and flew the "Hudson corridor," a low-altitude "hallway" along the Hudson River that paralleled the New York skyline, including the World Trade Center. Hanjour rented small aircraft on several occasions from the Caldwell Flight Academy in New Jersey; on July 20, he and Hazmi flew from Fairfield, New Jersey, to Gaithersburg, Maryland, a route that took them close to Washington, D.C.

Once all of the hijackers were in place, Atta flew to Spain on July 8 to meet for the last time with bin al Shib. The two men stayed in Cambrils, a town near Barcelona. Bin al Shib returned to Germany on July 16; Atta flew back to Florida on July 19. According to bin al Shib, he told Atta that bin Laden was extremely worried about the security of the mission, given the number of operatives in the United States. He pressed Atta to select a date for the attack. Atta replied that he had been preoccupied with "organizing the arriving hijackers and still needed to coordinate the timing of the flights so that the attacks would occur simultaneously." Atta said he would need five to six weeks to prepare. Bin al Shib advised Atta that bin Laden had instructed that the other hijackers not be informed of the date until the last minute for security reasons. Bin al Shib, however, wanted advance notice of at least a week so that he could travel to Afghanistan and inform bin Laden.

Atta told bin al Shib that he understood that bin Laden wanted to hit the White House but that he thought the target was too difficult. He stated, further, that he had asked Hanjour and Hazmi to rent small aircraft and evaluate the target for feasibility; Hanjour and Hazmi had already, according to Atta, flown reconnaissance flights near the Pentagon. Hanjour was assigned to the Pentagon, Jarrah the Capitol, and Atta and Shehhi the World Trade Center. Atta also told bin al Shib that he, Jarrah, and Shehhi had had no trouble carrying box-cutters aboard their cross-country reconnaissance flights, and that the time to storm the cockpits would be when the cockpit doors were first opened, usually ten to fifteen minutes into the flight. He also told bin al Shib that he wanted to hijack planes departing on long flights because they would be full of fuel, and that he preferred Boeing aircraft since they were easier to fly than Airbus.

Atta shared bin Laden's concern about detection. He complained to bin al Shib that several of the hijackers wanted to contact their families to say good-bye, which he had forbidden. He also advised bin al Shib to obtain new phone lines when he returned to Germany in order to preserve security. Bin al Shib gave Atta eight necklaces and bracelets that Atta had had him buy, so that the hijackers, clean-shaven and well-dressed, could pass for wealthy Saudis.

Upon his return to Germany, bin al Shib obtained two new phones. With one, he communicated with Atta. With the other, he communicated with KSM and others, notably Zacarias Moussaoui. Bin al Shib called KSM in Afghanistan and briefed him on Atta's progress. Bin al Shib informed KSM that the most serious potential glitch in the operation was that Atta was having trouble with one of the proposed pilots, Ziad Jarrah. Bin al Shib believed that this resulted from Jarrah's repeated desire to visit his family, specifically his German girlfriend, Aysel Senguen. On July 20, Senguen purchased a one-way ticket for Jarrah to fly to Germany from Miami. On his previous four trips, Jarrah had always flown with a round-trip ticket. Atta drove him to the airport on July 25; bin al Shib picked him up in Düsseldorf. Jarrah insisted on seeing Senguen immediately, so he and bin al Shib arranged to meet a few days later. When they did, they had "an emotional conversation" in which bin al Shib urged Jarrah to live up to his commitment.

KSM, concerned that Jarrah might be backing out of the operation, instructed bin al Shib to wire money to Zacarias Moussaoui. Moussaoui had been taking flying lessons in Norman, Oklahoma, beginning in February, but had stopped in May. Bin al Shib wired money to him in late July, and he reserved training time for mid-August on a 747 flight simulator in Eagan, Minnesota. Given the timing of the wire transfers to Moussaoui, the 9/11 Commission speculates that "KSM may have instructed Binalshibh [sic] to send money to Moussaoui in order to help prepare Moussaoui as a potential substitute pilot for Jarrah." If he did, however, he never put Moussaoui in contact with Atta, and by the time Moussaoui began training, Jarrah had returned to Florida from his final trip to Germany.

As the hijackers' international travels dwindled to a few flights at the end of July, the intelligence about the impending attack decreased correspondingly. On July 27, Richard Clarke informed Rice that the spike in intelligence about a near-term al Qaeda attack had ceased. He advised, however, that the alert level should remain high, because some of the reporting indicated that bin Laden's plans had been delayed, not canceled.

WEEKS

Notwithstanding the fall-off in threat reporting at the end of July, President Bush was alerted to the possibility of a domestic terrorist attack in his daily briefing of August 6, 2001, headlined "Bin Laden Determined to Strike in US." The report cited FBI information since the embassy bombings in 1998 that indicated "a pattern of suspicious activity in this country consistent with preparations for hijackings or other types of attacks, including recent surveillance of federal buildings in New York," and concluded that the FBI had "approximately 70 full field investigations throughout the US that it considers Bin Laden–related." President Bush was briefed three more times by Tenet before 9/11. None of those briefings touched on the threat of a domestic attack.

During the first three weeks of August, the hijackers finalized their plans. On August 4, Atta drove to the Orlando airport to pick up a final hijacker, Mohamed al Khatani. Khatani was detained by INS officials, however, because he spoke no English, was traveling with a one-way ticket and little money, and could not explain what he planned to do while in the United States. He was sent back to Dubai.

On August 7, Atta flew to Newark, probably to meet with Hazmi and coordinate the operation; two days later, two of the "muscle" hijackers who had been staying in Paterson with Hazmi, Hanjour, and Mihdhar flew to Miami. While in New Jersey, Atta, Hanjour, and Hazmi purchased first-class tickets on transcontinental flights routed to Las Vegas. Atta, Hazmi, and Hanjour met and stayed in Las Vegas on August 13–14.

The third week of August, the hijackers bought small knives; on August 22, Jarrah purchased a GPS unit and three aeronautical charts in Miami. The next day, Atta flew again to Newark. On August 25, Hazmi and Mihdhar traveled from Paterson to William Paterson University in Wayne, New Jersey. Using the university library's Internet terminals, they purchased airline tickets for September 11. Atta had told bin al Shib that he wanted to wait until after the first week in September, when Congress would be back in session.

Even as they were buying their tickets, just ten miles away, in Lower Manhattan, the Manhattan FBI office had just been tasked with searching for Hazmi and Mihdhar. Maggie Gillespie, an FBI agent detailed to the CIA's Counterterrorist Center, had been following up on the details of the Kuala Lumpur meeting since late July. She had found that Hazmi had traveled to Los Angeles in 2000, that Mihdhar had also been in the country, and that he had returned on July 4. On August 23, she notified INS, the State Department, Customs, and the FBI of this information, and asked them to put Hazmi and Mihdhar on their watchlists. She did not notify the FAA. A colleague intelligence analyst at Bureau headquarters sent a message to the head of New York's antiterrorism squad, reporting the information and ordering the unit to determine whether Mihdhar was still in the United States. His possible involvement with the bombers of the *Cole*, she wrote, made him "a risk to the national security." She added, however, that no criminal agents could be involved in the search; this counsel was repeated the next day by a CIA supervisor. This application of "the wall" infuriated the New York bureau's experienced antiterrorism investigators. "Show me where this is written that we can't have the intelligence," Special Agent Steve Bongardt demanded on a number of occasions. "If this guy is in the country, it's not because he's going to fucking Disneyland!" On August 25, when the New York FBI's criminal investigators' appeals to allow them to open a criminal investigation of Mihdhar were turned down, Bongardt wrote to intelligence analyst Dina Corsi: "Whatever happened to this—someday somebody will die—and wall or not—the public will not understand why we are not more effective and throwing every resource we had at certain 'problems.' Let's hope the National Security Law Unit will stand behind their decisions then, especially since the biggest threat to us now, UBL [bin Laden], is getting the most 'protection.'" That same day, just across the Hudson River, Hazmi and Mihdhar visited the library at William Paterson University, went online, and purchased their airline tickets for the morning of September 11.

The plot was still, however, in danger of detection. KSM's activation of Zacarias Moussaoui as an operative, whatever its motivation, came close to compromising the planes operation. His flight instructor in Minnesota became suspicious when he did not present any of the normal qualifications of people training on the Boeing 747 simulator, and when he also indicated that he did not intend to become a commercial pilot, but wanted to use the simulator as "an ego-boosting thing." He also asked questions about whether the cockpit doors would be locked or unlocked during flight. The flight instructor contacted the FBI in Minnesota, which referred the matter to the Minnesota Joint Terrorism Task Force. Its investigation began on August 15.

Investigators learned quickly that Moussaoui was a French national who had expressed Islamist sympathies, had traveled to Pakistan and perhaps to Afghanistan, and had overstayed his student visa. Moussaoui had $32,000 in a bank account and no plausible explanation for his possession of that amount. He had made plans to receive martial arts training and to purchase a global positioning device. He was arrested by the INS and a deportation order was signed on August 17.

On August 18, the FBI case agent requested a special warrant under the Foreign Intelligence Surveillance Act (FISA) to search Moussaoui's computer. The FISA warrant was sought because the FBI's legal analysts and federal prosecutors believed that the Bureau lacked probable cause to connect the contents of the laptop to criminal activity. Under FISA at that time, however, the Bureau needed to be able to demonstrate probable cause that Moussaoui was an "agent of a foreign power." On August 22 and 27, the French provided information linking Moussaoui to an Islamist rebel leader in Chechnya. The Minneapolis office of the Bureau believed that this information should be sufficient to support a FISA warrant; FBI headquarters disagreed, and its National Security Law Unit declined to submit the FISA application. On August 24, the case agent contacted the CIA's Counterterrorist Center and requested assistance with the investigation. That day, the CIA sent a cable to London and Paris, describing Moussaoui as a potential "suicide hijacker."

While the FBI continued to debate what to do about Moussaoui, and investigators continued to seek evidence sufficient to support a FISA warrant, and the FBI's intelligence agent searched databases for Hazmi and Mihdhar, the hijackers in the United States were finalizing their plans. Atta and bin al Shib continued to debate the merits of the White House versus the Capitol as a target; bin al Shib reminded Atta repeatedly that bin Laden preferred the White House, and Atta replied, repeatedly, that it would prove a much more difficult target to hit. Atta ultimately agreed to keep the White House as a target, but insisted that the Capitol remain as an alternative should the White House prove too difficult. Atta passed the word to bin al Shib that the chosen date would be September 11; bin al Shib in turn passed the word to al Qaeda operatives in Hamburg and the United Arab Emirates that if they were planning to return to Pakistan, they had better do so in the near future. One al Qaeda contact in the UAE received a return transfer of $46,000 in unused funds from the hijackers in late August. All had returned to Pakistan by the first week of September. Bin al Shib, likewise, planned his return for early September. There is evidence that Hazmi telephoned friends in San Diego during the third week of August and informed them that something was about to happen; according to witnesses, his friends accelerated wedding plans and began behaving strangely in the days leading up to 9/11.

As August gave way to September, the government remained ensnared in its own rules proscribing information-sharing between intelligence and law enforcement and between foreign and domestic agencies. The FBI intelligence agent assigned to find Hazmi and Mihdhar continued to search databases of New York–area hotels, but not with alacrity; the lead was assigned to him as "routine," meaning that he had thirty days to open an intelligence case and begin to search for Mihdhar.

The designation of the lead as "routine" seems bizarre, given the hair-trigger sensitivity of the Bureau to the intense threat-reporting of the summer. Indeed, the special agent who requested the search indicated that he wanted "to get this going as soon as possible." But like most Bureau agents at that time, she believed that criminal investigations took priority, and she later told Justice Department officials that she did not consider the Mihdhar investigation to be "bigger" than other pending matters. As Amy Zegart concludes, "Good instincts led the analyst to take unusual steps to expedite the search, but old attitudes prevailed: when pressed to prioritize the manhunt relative to the bureau's traditional law enforcement work, she put down 'routine.'"

As the debate raged in the lower echelons of the FBI over whether to seek a Foreign Intelligence Surveillance Act warrant for Zacarias Moussaoui's laptop, no one briefed either Acting FBI Director Thomas Pickard or Assistant Director for Counterterrorism Dale Watson about the case. On August 27, the acting special agent in charge of the Min-neapolis field office called the International Terrorism Operations Sec-tion to complain about the handling of the case; when chided that he was just trying to get everyone "spun up," he replied that, to the contrary, he was "trying to keep someone from taking a plane and crashing into the World Trade Center." He declined, however, to take the matter fur-ther up the chain of command.

On August 23, Director of Central Intelligence Tenet was informed about the Moussaoui case in a briefing titled "Islamic Extremist Learns to Fly." He was told some of the particulars of the case, and that the CIA was working on the matter with the FBI. Tenet has indicated that, not-withstanding his alarm about the intensity of threat reporting, no connection to al Qaeda was apparent to him. Furthermore, he did not share this briefing with the FBI, the White House staff, or the president; because the arrest was made domestically, he viewed it as an FBI matter, not within his portfolio.

As August ended, the plot had fully ripened. No one within the United States national security early-warning system knew the plot existed, or how close—how agonizingly close—investigators were to discovering and disrupting it.

DAYS

The Bush administration's National Security Council Principals Committee met on September 4. It was their first formal meeting to be devoted primarily to the question of what to do about Afghanistan, al Qaeda, and bin Laden. The members were presented with a draft National Security Decision Directive outlining a revised U.S. policy toward al Qaeda and Afghanistan. The stated goal of the directive was the elimination of bin Laden and his organization. The measures it proposed to undertake to achieve this goal included increased support, over a three-year period, for Ahmed Shah Massoud and the Northern Alliance, the principal Afghani opponents of the Taliban.

Another potential proposal involved empowering the CIA to deploy an armed pilotless aircraft, the Predator, to Afghanistan, and authorizing the CIA to use it to assassinate bin Laden. There was ambivalence within the CIA about whether it was desirable to have this power; this ambivalence may have been reflected in Tenet's presentation of the option at the meeting. The committee approved support for the Northern Alliance, while expressing reservations about the funding source, but deferred on the issue of the Predator. The Air Force itself had no interest in deploying the Predator, viewing it as an untested robot.

Hazmi, Mihdhar, and the other future hijackers of American Airlines

Flight 77 moved during the first week of September from New Jersey to Laurel, Maryland, where they checked into a motel and worked out at a local gym. They met with Atta on September 7, when he arrived on a flight from Miami to Baltimore. Two days later, Atta flew from Baltimore to Boston, where he met Shehhi, who would pilot United Flight 175, at his hotel. Atta called his father that night, presumably to say goodbye. Ziad Jarrah received a speeding ticket early that morning in Maryland as he drove north to meet the United 93 team in Newark; he wrote an emotional farewell letter to his German girlfriend.

The Bush administration's plan to support the Northern Alliance was dealt a severe blow on September 9. Its leader Ahmed Shah Massoud sat down for an interview with two reporters who claimed to work for an Arab television news organization. In reality, they were al Qaeda operatives; their television camera concealed a bomb, which detonated as the interview began, killing Massoud and thus decapitating the Northern Alliance.

On September 10, Atta picked up one of his crew for American Flight 11 and the two drove from Boston to Portland, Maine. They checked into a hotel, had pizza, and shopped at a convenience store. The rest of their team stayed at a hotel in Newton, Massachusetts. The team assigned to United Flight 175 stayed at a hotel in Boston. The team assigned to United 93 stayed at a Newark Airport Days Inn. The team assigned to American 77 moved from its hotel in Laurel, Maryland, to a hotel in Herndon, Virginia.

As the hijackers gathered in their hotels, the national security deputies convened again on September 10. They finalized the three-year plan to support the Northern Alliance, notwithstanding the death of Massoud. In addition, the CIA was instructed to prepare a separate section of the Decision Directive to supersede the existing Clinton administration authority in order to authorize "a broad range of other covert activities, including authority to capture or to use lethal force" against al Qaeda and bin Laden. The White House wanted the authority to be broad enough to "cover any additional UBL-related covert actions contemplated."

But the time for stopping a domestic attack by taking out bin Laden, or anyone in Afghanistan, had come and gone. The plot had been undetected for years by the $30-billion-per-year apparatus of American national security, and by the trillion-dollar system of bases around the world. Various threads of the plot had been picked up at various times by NSA signals intelligence, NIMA imagery intelligence, CIA human source intelligence, and other sources such as State Department reporting, and by the FBI in investigating the embassy bombings of 1998 and the USS *Cole* bombing of 2000, and in conducting its normal field intelligence inside the United States. No one, however, had had access to all of the various threads of information.

This failure to share information was not a result of accident or incompetence; it was largely, in fact, the way the system had been designed to work. It was, in Amy Zegart's phrase, a system that was "flawed by design," in the way that much of American government is flawed by design. James Q. Wilson explains: "Many, if not most, of the difficulties we experience in dealing with government agencies arise from the agencies being part of a fragmented and open political system. . . . The central feature of the American constitutional system—the separation of powers—exacerbates many of these problems. The governments of the United States were not designed to be efficient or powerful, but to be tolerable and malleable. Those who devised these arrangements always assumed that the federal government would exercise few and limited powers. As long as that assumption was correct (which it was for a century and a half) the quality of public administration was not a serious problem except in the minds of those reformers (Woodrow Wilson was probably the first) who desired to rationalize government in order to rationalize society."

American government distrusts the concentration of power, and information, in the world of intelligence and law enforcement, is power. It is hardly surprising, then, that agencies like the CIA, the FBI, and the NSA would respect, create, and police vigorously the boundaries between them. Those boundaries were written into the foundational documents creating the CIA, the National Security Council, and the Department of

Defense, and were further amplified over time, in response to perceived abuses. The FBI ensured that Congress, in creating the CIA, gave it no power to gather intelligence domestically; the departments of State, War, and the Navy ensured that they could retain independent intelligence agencies. The competing bureaucracies "sought a central intelligence system that, above all, insulated their own intelligence services from outside interference." They succeeded.

The boundaries between and within departments separated knowledge gained domestically from knowledge gained overseas; knowledge gained through human intelligence from knowledge gained electronically; and knowledge gained through the investigation of criminal conduct from knowledge gained for purposes of situational awareness as general intelligence. Each type of knowledge, moreover, was assigned a security classification that restricted the numbers and types of people who could have access to it. Each of these distinctions created further boundaries, both between departments and within a given department. Each boundary created an obstacle to the sharing of information; these obstacles ranged from inconvenient to insuperable. But each boundary amounted to a fault line, an opportunity for the system to fail.

The results were, in retrospect, absurd. The FBI, investigating the embassy bombings, learns of the importance of a phone in Yemen belonging to Mihdhar's father-in-law; it passes the number along to the NSA and the CIA, which learn of Mihdhar's terrorist ties to Khallad and others by monitoring the number. This information they refuse to pass back to the FBI because of concerns about "the wall" between intelligence and law enforcement. As the various agencies pursued bin Laden and al Qaeda from 1997 to 2001, they would share information even within departments only on a "need to know" basis. The problem with the 9/11 plot, though, was that everyone "needed to know," and that no one knew it.

And so to the final absurdity: In the early morning of 9/11, the FBI intelligence agent who was searching for Mihdhar and Hazmi forwarded a request to the Los Angeles field office. He had learned that Hazmi had arrived in Los Angeles in January 2000. He asked for assistance now in tracking Hazmi and Mihdhar. As he was sending the cable, asking for information that was hopelessly antiquated, the two were waiting at Dulles International Airport to board American Airlines Flight 77.

FAULT LINES

As 9/11 dawned, with America's state-of-the-art, high-tech, fully funded warning systems having failed, the defense of America would be left, in its final hours and minutes, not to the U.S. military's elite Delta Force, or to the Navy with its cruise missiles, or to the Air Force's sophisticated bombers, or to the CIA's "black ops" specialists, or to the FBI's crack terrorism investigators, but to two agencies considered relative backwaters of national security: the Federal Aviation Administration (FAA), and the North American Aerospace Defense Command (NORAD).

How had this happened? In his classic study *Bureaucracy*, James Q. Wilson identified the core of successful government organizations: "All . . . were alike in one sense: incentives, culture, and authority were combined in a way that suited the task at hand." Perhaps the best way to understand the failure of the American national security bureaucracy in detecting or preventing the 9/11 attacks is to view its performance in light of Wilson's criteria for success: (1) a clearly defined mission, or "task at hand"; (2) development of the proper structure and incentives within the organization to fulfill that mission; (3) the cultivation of an organizational culture suited to fulfilling the mission; and (4) exercise of authority commensurate with responsibility, in a way suited to fulfilling the mission. With respect to each of these criteria for success, the American national security bureaucracy proved ineffectual.

THE CENTRAL INTELLIGENCE AGENCY

The CIA was a creature of the Cold War. Formed as part of a "sweeping legislative overhaul of the . . . national security apparatus following

World War II," the CIA, along with the other agencies created in the National Security Act of 1947—the National Security Council and the Department of Defense—had as an overriding purpose the detection and prevention of a surprise attack on the United States.

From its founding in 1947 until the collapse of the Soviet Union in 1991, the primary focus of the CIA had been the prevention of the spread of communism throughout the world. When its principal adversary disappeared, the CIA and the rest of the intelligence community became an agency in search of a mission. Even stalwart defenders of the agency like William Colby advocated a "peace dividend," budget cuts in intelligence so that America could enjoy the social benefits of having defeated communism.

In 1991, President George H. W. Bush ordered a reassessment of the intelligence needs and priorities of the government for the next fifteen years. As a deputy director of Central Intelligence told Tim Weiner of *The New York Times*, the CIA had "lost the simplicity of purpose or cohesion that essentially has driven not only intelligence but has driven this country for forty-plus years." The result of the reassessment, delivered in April 1992, identified no fewer than 176 threats; narcotics and terrorism ranked below nuclear, chemical, and biological weapons as second-tier threats. The reassessment did not result in a shift of existing resources to new priorities so much as it did in a reduction in existing resources. CIA budgets declined from 1991 to 1997.

As the awareness of the increasing threat of terrorism grew, however, so did the awareness that the mission of the Agency—and of the intelligence community as a whole—had to be transformed. As Amy Zegart points out in *Spying Blind*, "Between the fall of the Soviet Union in 1991 and September 11, 2001, no fewer than twelve major bipartisan commissions, governmental studies, and think tank task forces examined the U.S. Intelligence Community and U.S. counterterrorism efforts. All of their reports urged reform within intelligence agencies, across the Intelligence Community, and between the Intelligence Community and other parts of the U.S. government." A 1996 Council of Foreign Relations report summarized the consensus view: "The U.S. intelligence community faces major challenges, including a widespread lack of confidence in its ability to carry out its mission competently and legally. . . . The intelligence community has been adjusting to the changed demands of the post–Cold War world for several years . . . [but] additional reform is necessary. . . . The end of the Cold War has not ushered in an age of peace and security."

Within the CIA itself, as noted, leadership recognized the need to adapt to the mission of combating the growing threat of terrorism in general and bin Laden and al Qaeda in particular. In 1996, when bin Laden was first emerging as a major threat, John Deutch, then director of Central Intelligence, formed the "virtual" station, devoted to gathering intelligence on bin Laden.

This elevation of terrorism generally—and bin Laden specifically—to a high-priority mission of the Agency was reinforced repeatedly. Beginning in 1994, directors of Central Intelligence gave annual threat-assessment briefings to Congress. Terrorism was identified as a significant threat to national security in every annual briefing from 1994 to 2001, and its assessed magnitude increased as the number of attacks and the extent of the real danger increased; by 1998, the year of the embassy bombings, terrorism ranked as a top-tier priority, and by 2001, in the wake of the *Cole* bombing, George Tenet ranked terrorism ahead of nuclear proliferation and weapons of mass destruction as the single greatest danger to national security.

Nor was Tenet's commitment limited to public pronouncements. As we have seen, in the wake of the embassy bombings in 1998, Tenet circulated a memo to his senior staff, making his position unequivocally clear: "We are at war. I want no resources or people spared in this effort." He followed this declaration by issuing the first strategic intelligence plan developed since the Cold War ended. The "DCI's Strategic Intent for the United States Intelligence Community" called for sweeping changes in the way intelligence was gathered and information was shared. It called for aggressive recruiting of first-rate intelligence agents and analysts, and technological upgrades that would enable the creation of data linkages across databases, information sources, and agencies. Finally, he directed that all intelligence community members be issued a standard blue badge to enable them to move freely among agencies located in different facilities, and he ordered that all intelligence officers be required to serve in intelligence agencies outside their own as a condition of promotion. Leadership's endorsement of a transformation in mission could not have been clearer.

Yet Tenet failed to transform the mission in practice. The 9/11 Commission, the Congressional Joint Inquiry, and, most recently, the CIA's own Inspector General have concluded that none of these initiatives succeeded. There was a fundamental disconnect between leadership and the organization it led. The CIA Inspector General's Executive Summary puts it in the starkest terms: "In December 1998, the DCI signed a memorandum in which he declared: 'We are at war.' . . . The Team found that neither the DCI nor the DDCI [deputy director of Central Intelligence] followed up these warnings and admonitions by creating a . . . comprehensive plan to guide the counterterrorism effort at the Intelligence Community level. . . . While CIA and other agencies had individual plans and important initiatives under way, senior officers in the Agency and the Community told the Team that no comprehensive strategic plan for the IC to counter [bin Laden] was created in response to the DCI's memorandum, or at any time prior to 9/11."

A few agency heads outside of the CIA's inner circle received the "declaration of war" memo. All of them ignored it. The lieutenant general who headed the National Security Agency thought that the memo was an internal document and did not apply to him; CIA officers, meanwhile, indicated that they thought the memo applied only to other intelligence agencies outside of the CIA. The Congressional Joint Inquiry and the CIA Inspector General concluded that the memo was ineffective in mobilizing the intelligence community, which remained "fragmented without a comprehensive strategy for combating bin Laden."

As Amy Zegart points out, moreover, the DCI's Strategic Plan "fared even worse." The NSA opposed the director's technology initiative because of the potential loss of "turf, power, and control over their own activities." The blue security badges were issued, but often ignored; some employees refused to carry them, and the agencies all continued to issue their own badges. The directive that analysts and agents work for other intelligence agencies as a condition of promotion was simply ignored; the DCI lacked the authority to enforce such an order in the Department of Defense, which housed the majority of workers in the intelligence community.

The natural recalcitrance in the face of change was reinforced by the organizational structure of the Agency. The Counterterrorism Center, for instance, had been created within the Directorate of Operations, not the Intelligence Analysis section. The Directorate of Operations was "home to people who ran spies, stole secrets, and conducted clandestine operations, not for egghead analysts who sat behind desks piecing together information about future threats." The Counterterrorism Center gave "short shrift to strategic analysis from day one." Because analysts were not highly valued employees on the ops side of the house, moreover, many analysts did not want to work for the Counterterrorism Center.

Perhaps the most serious deficiency in the CIA's efforts to track and capture and kill bin Laden—human intelligence—is traceable directly to the Agency's inability to transform itself institutionally after the Cold War: "Years after the Soviet Union's collapse, clandestine human intelligence operations were still frozen in a Cold War model: most undercover operatives continued working under official covers, posing as U.S. government employees in American embassies around the world and attending diplomatic events and parties where they would recruit foreign military officials, party members, and other bureaucrats to spy for the United States. One veteran clandestine operative described the usefulness of the model this way: 'The guy in the embassy was appropriate for the last fifty years because the secrets you wanted resided in a defense minister's safe or a prime minister's office. They were in governments.'" Thus, the number of so-called nonofficial covers—which could be expected to rise exponentially with the emergence of nonstate terrorist groups like al Qaeda—remained constant from 1990 to 2001. In short, as Amy Zegart concludes, "While terrorism posed extraordinary challenges for any human intelligence service, it proved impossible for one designed decades earlier for a different enemy."

The authority that Tenet sought to exercise to bring about the transformation of his Agency could not, ultimately, overcome the estrangement of the Director of Central Intelligence from the rank-and-file career employees of the Agency and his lack of any authority over employees of the other intelligence agencies. All of the "top-down" edicts in the world about being "at war" with bin Laden would not resonate with a career staff that resisted change from its Cold War paradigm, that resisted cooperating with the FBI and other agencies, and that simply did not recognize his authority.

The assumption was that it would be sufficient for the director to identify broadly the themes and tasks in a "top-down" edict, and that the bureaucracy would then be charged with figuring out how to make his vision a reality. But the assertion of top-down leadership exposed a fundamental disconnect between the executive's vision and the changes that his vision would require in the way that ground-level intelligence employees would go about their jobs. The responsibility for failure resided at the top, with the Director of Central Intelligence, but there was no correspondence between the responsibility he bore and the actual power he wielded to accomplish reform.

THE FBI

Like the CIA, the FBI experienced a radical reconsideration of its mission in light of the end of the Cold War and the rise of the Islamist threat of the 1990s. The Bureau's 1998 strategic plan called for a reorientation of the organization's core mission from solving and prosecuting crimes to preventing acts of terrorism and espionage that would weaken the nation's security. While paying homage to the Bureau's traditional role in domestic law enforcement, the report cited the Cold War's end, concluding that "unprecedented, and in some cases wholly unforeseen, changes in the world over the past five years have dramatically altered the world of international crime. . . . Meeting the strategic goals requires that the FBI supplement its reactive capability with bold and innovative proactive efforts designed to deter and prevent—to the maximum extent feasible—criminal activities that threaten vital American interests." The criminal threats to public safety like terrorism, the report concluded, had become "more sophisticated, creating demands on the FBI to develop strategies to prevent rather than merely respond to new and emerging crime. This will require an intelligence capability far different than that which has supported the FBI's efforts over the past several decades."

As with the CIA, the vision of the FBI's leadership with regard to the needed changes could not have been more clearly stated. Furthermore, as mentioned above, concrete steps were adopted to further this mission: nearly doubling the number of foreign Bureau offices; creating a headquarters-based counterterrorism division; consolidating intelligence into a single Investigative Services Division; and launching MAXCAP 05, an initiative designed to attain "maximum feasible capacity" by 2005 in the investigation of terrorism, so that it could be treated systematically, rather than as a congeries of distinct and unrelated leads, suspects, and cases.

None of it worked. As Amy Zegart puts it, "By September 11, 2001, every reform initiative had failed. The 1998 strategic plan made terrorism a top FBI priority in theory, but never in practice. Between 1998 and 9/11, counterterrorism spending remained flat, 76 percent of all field agents continued to work on criminal investigations unrelated to terrorism, the number of special agents working international terrorism cases actually declined, and field agents were often diverted from counterterrorism and intelligence work to cover major criminal cases."

More important, the reforms failed to address any of the structural fault lines that inhibited the effective discharge of the new mission. The fifty-six field offices continued to operate largely independently; it was the Manhattan field office, not FBI headquarters, that took the lead in investigating terrorism. Intelligence agents within FBI and other intelligence agencies considered themselves barred from communicating with criminal investigative agents, and vice versa, for fear of tainting criminal investigations with incompetent evidence. The separation of functions based on whether the source was foreign or domestic also persisted: "Electronic surveillance of terrorist communications continued to be artificially divided between the National Security Agency, which monitored communications abroad, and the FBI's domestic surveillance of terrorists inside the United States. . . . This divide left no agency responsible for collecting information transmitted between U.S.-based and foreign terrorist cells or considering how a terrorist group might target the United States itself."

The persistence of these boundaries ensured the frustration of Director Freeh's effort to remake the Bureau as a crime-prevention agency. The persistence of the field-office culture assured that the Phoenix memo warning of Islamic extremists learning to become pilots would not be shared with the Bureau as a whole, and thus would not be available to the Minnesota field office when it began to investigate Moussaoui. The division of electronic surveillance between foreign (NSA) and domestic worked to prevent the FBI from learning about the fruits of the NSA's tap of Mihdhar's father-in-law's phone—which connected the embassy bombings to the *Cole* bombing and to the 9/11 conspiracy—despite the fact that the Bureau had discovered the number in the first place. The so-called "wall" between intelligence and criminal investigations kept the agents in Manhattan who knew the most about al Qaeda from learning what the CIA and FBI intelligence agents knew about Mihdhar and Hazmi, or assisting in the search for them in the days leading up to 9/11. To put it starkly, the agents in Arizona working on the flight-schools problem were unaware that agents in Minnesota were investigating Moussaoui, or that agents in New York were looking for Mihdhar and Hazmi, and vice versa. The FBI could not possibly fulfill its new mission of prevention; it was itself prevented from learning the information necessary to prevent the 9/11 attacks.

Like the CIA, the FBI was beset by a fundamental estrangement of its leadership from the rank and file. Nothing illustrates this reality better than the stark fact that, as little as the agents in Arizona, Minnesota, and New York knew about the total picture, FBI director Tom Pickard, during the summer of threat, knew less than any of them. He found out about the Phoenix memo, and the Moussaoui investigation, and the failed search for Mihdhar and Hazmi only after the attacks on September 11, 2001. A former FBI official captured the essential disconnect in an interview with Amy Zegart, when he described a session Director Freeh conducted with the special agents in charge [SACs] to introduce them to the new mission: "Louis rolls out how we have to be more proactive and not reactive . . . [and] the SACs, the senior cardinals of the church, say . . . 'Let me get this right. I'm going to be evaluated in Cleveland on white-collar crime that doesn't take place?' There was absolutely no comprehension." There was no reform, either. The Cold War–era model of law enforcement persisted.

THE DEPARTMENT OF DEFENSE

More than either the CIA or the FBI—more, in fact, than any other department of the federal government—the end of the Cold War prompted the Department of Defense to reexamine its role in defending the United States, as well as its place in American society. The enemy it had been created to counter—communism in general and the Soviet Union in particular—had been vanquished. The Soviet Union withdrew from Afghanistan and announced that it planned to reduce its nuclear arsenal unilaterally; when the Soviet Union dissolved, many of its constituent republics renounced any nuclear arsenal at all, ceding theirs to Russia. Many in America, including the new president, Bill Clinton, spoke openly of a "peace dividend," of redirecting some of the billions of dollars that were being spent on America's nuclear weapons arsenal and on maintaining hundreds of bases around the world to address domestic problems, or to address geopolitical problems in a different manner.

Incoming Clinton administration secretary of defense Les Aspin, as one of his first acts in office, ordered a "Bottom-Up Review" of the entire military/national defense posture in light of the Soviet Union's collapse. He followed this, in autumn 1993, by commissioning a "Nuclear Posture Review," a reassessment of the nuclear arsenal in light of the Soviet collapse.

Significant restructuring was already under way. The number of nuclear warheads in the United States's arsenal had been decreasing steadily since President Reagan's 1987 accord with Premier Gorbachev; under Presidents Reagan and Bush, it would be reduced by nearly 50 percent. Under the Strategic Arms Reduction Treaty I, Soviet long-range nuclear warheads were reduced in number from 11,012 to 6,163; American warheads were reduced from 12,646 to 8,556. START II called for further reductions of the American arsenal to approximately 3,500 warheads. Reagan and Bush also phased out tactical nuclear weapons deployed from ships or on the battlefield, ended testing, and halted B-52 strategic alerts. Furthermore, under President Bush the Defense Department announced in 1990 that the overall size of the American military would be reduced by 25 percent. Secretary Aspin's review was intended to give coherent policy shape to these efforts.

The Pentagon's career military officers greeted the strategic review process with inertia: "At bottom, the military custodians of the strategic forces, and their allies among the Pentagon's 'samurai bureaucrats,' regarded the Clinton-sponsored civilian reviewers as interlopers, typical of the newly arrived zealots that sweep into the Building every time an administration changes. . . . In response to the outsiders' position papers and planning documents, the Pentagon insiders would nod politely as their eyes glazed over. As always, it would simply be a matter of waiting them out."

That didn't take long. Secretary Aspin resigned within a year, blamed widely for the infamous "Black Hawk Down" misadventure in Somalia in October 1993, when a failed mission to kidnap a Somali warlord resulted in the deaths of seventeen American Special Forces soldiers. Because Secretary Aspin had refused the military's request to deploy tanks to the region, the American soldiers who were pinned down by Somali militia were rescued ultimately by armored vehicles from Italy and Pakistan. At the same time, President Clinton's controversial proposal on gays in the military had further alienated the career military from their commander-in-chief. President Clinton ran the real risk, because of these early setbacks, of being outflanked by conservatives on the issue of national defense, of being portrayed successfully as a weak president haunted by the kind of indecision he demonstrated in his flirtation with the National Guard during the Vietnam War.

It is also indisputable that the post–Cold War world appeared more dangerous than anyone had anticipated. As James Carroll notes, "During the first Clinton term, in the chaotic aftermath of Cold War stasis, three dozen wars broke out around the world, some of them exceedingly violent and a few obviously preventable. Terrorism came into its own as a mode of political conflict, with a stunning attack on New York's World Trade Center occurring a little over a month after Clinton took office. Of greater significance than the weight or lightness of Clinton's team was the nation's new situation."

Whatever the reason, or combination of reasons, the bottom line was this: the fundamental reassessment Clinton and Aspin had envisioned of the Pentagon's role in a post–Cold War world, and its attendant peace dividend, never really occurred. If anything, the military's role grew; the Cold War mission was retained virtually intact, but augmented by the need to address emerging missions like regional conflicts and transnational terrorism through the achievement of "global force projection" and "full-spectrum dominance." The reduction in American nuclear forces ceased. In addition to maintaining the hundreds of American military bases around the world, the Clinton administration supported funding for missile defense and for an expanded global military presence. Defense spending, which had been trending downward under President Bush, rose under President Clinton, from $260 billion to more than $300 billion. Lawrence Korb, an assistant secretary of defense under President Reagan, told James Carroll in 1998: "We won the Cold War, but we're still spending at Cold War levels. How the hell did that happen?"

Unlike both the FBI and the CIA, whose leadership produced fundamental reevaluations of their respective missions after the Cold War ended, the Department of Defense, whose mission was called into question most plainly by the demise of the Soviet Union, never undertook seriously to redefine itself. For purposes of the nuclear posture, the Pentagon treated Russia as though it remained the Soviet Union. The long-awaited Nuclear Posture Review cautioned in 1996 that Russia could reemerge as a national security threat; accordingly, it recommended that the United States maintain the nuclear status quo as a "hedge" against that development. The Defense Department also continued its Cold War posture by funding the Missile Defense Initiative, and by actively seeking to expand NATO by including former Soviet bloc nations in the alliance; the latter was greeted with particular alarm in Russia, whose historical paranoia about its borders was reinvigorated. Citing the threat posed by NATO expansion, Russia refused to ratify the START II treaty, and abandoned its commitment never to be the first to fire nuclear weapons.

This state of affairs remained largely unchanged when the Bush administration took office in January 2001. As the 9/11 Commission pointed out, the new administration "focused heavily on Russia, a new nuclear strategy that allowed missile defenses, Europe, Mexico, and the Persian Gulf." The new administration's goal was to maintain American preeminence—in Paul Wolfowitz's terms, "to prevent the emergence of a new rival." This vision would be supported by "not only the maintenance of America's global array of bases but the expansion of it. Not only the maintenance of America's huge defense budget but the expansion of it. Not only the maintenance of the nuclear arsenal, but the expansion of it. The defense industry would continue to boom. The Pentagon would continue to be the very heartbeat of government, the capital of a Pax Americana."

As the Pentagon prepared its 2001 Quadrennial Review—a draft of which was withdrawn quickly and rewritten after the 9/11 attacks—the Bush administration planned to continue more aggressively down the path charted by the Clinton administration. A briefing memo circulated on February 8, 2001, by the Project on Defense Alternatives, questioned this approach, and challenged military planners to address the three "paradoxes" of post–Cold War U.S. policy: first, that "defense spending has remained near Cold War levels . . . and is now rising, despite the continuing decline in the magnitude of military threats to U.S. interests"; second, that "Ten years have passed [since the collapse of the Soviet Union] but our armed forces remain poorly adapted to the challenges and opportunities of the new era"; and third, that the forward projection of American forces around the world, rather than providing stability, have "sown dissent among allies and stimulated anti-Americanism among those outside the western sphere. . . . These dynamics portend a dangerous combination of weakened alliances and increased tensions." Whatever the causes, and however beset with paradoxes, the reality was that, as 9/11 dawned and the attack on America began, the Pentagon was—quite literally, as we shall see—still fighting the Cold War.

As far as terrorism was concerned, the immediate issue for Defense Department policymakers to consider was a possible response to the *Cole* bombing. The White House was presented with the same assessment of the Cole bombing that had paralyzed the Clinton administration; March 2001 CIA briefing slides for the national security advisor still indicated that the judgment that al Qaeda was responsible was "preliminary" and that the CIA lacked "conclusive information on external command and control" responsibility for the attack. Defense Secretary Donald Rumsfeld and his deputy, Paul Wolfowitz, both believed that the time to respond to the *Cole* attack had passed; it was, in Wolfowitz's terms, "stale." The *Cole* bombing went unaddressed.

Because the post–Cold War reassessment of the Department of Defense's mission never really occurred, the institutional and organizational barriers to effective intelligence remained in place throughout the 1990s. Despite the consensus among five major review commissions in the mid-1990s that reforms should be enacted to ensure "greater integration across U.S. intelligence agencies, improvement in setting intelligence priorities, and personnel reforms to enhance information sharing," the secretary of defense's control over the intelligence budget was undisturbed. Indeed, every congressional effort to bolster the power of the Director of Central Intelligence was scuttled at the behest of the Pentagon. As a result, the Cold War model of intelligence—with the secretary of defense controlling 80 percent of the budget for intelligence, and with the various DoD-controlled intelligence agencies observing strict boundaries on sharing information with other interested agencies, specifically the FBI and the CIA—remained intact.

The Clinton and Bush administrations' decision to leave the Cold War structure of the Defense Department largely intact did, however, admit one exception—an exception that is, from the perspective of 9/11, ironic. Created in 1958 to protect the North American continent from the threat of Soviet bombers carrying nuclear bombs, the North American Aerospace Defense Command (NORAD) is a joint U.S.–Canadian command. At one point at the height of the Cold War there were alert sites throughout the United States and Canada; at each alert site, fighter jets sat, armed, with flight crews prepared to intercept aircraft from abroad that might pose a threat to the continent. On October 14, 1961, a NORAD exercise known as Sky Shield II was conducted to test the capabilities of the air defense system. For twelve hours that day, the civilian aviation system was grounded. More than a thousand fighter jets were on full alert for the exercise, and four hundred Strategic Air Command bombers and tankers were deployed within fifteen minutes. Forty years later, when civilian air traffic was halted again, on 9/11, NORAD had fourteen fighter jets on alert.

How had this force erosion happened? As the Cold War progressed, the superpowers came to rely less and less upon intercontinental bombers and more on intercontinental ballistic missiles; accordingly, the threat from a bomber attack over the North Pole diminished even before the Cold War subsided. The number of fighter jets under NORAD command was gradually phased down, from 750 in 1959, to 325 in 1976, to 200 in 1990, to 175 in 1997, to 14 in 2001. When the Cold War ended, Pentagon analysts recommended in 1992 that NORAD's mission be phased out entirely.

What followed was a rearguard action by a succession of NORAD commanders throughout the 1990s to preserve NORAD by redefining its mission. NORAD commanders argued successfully for a supporting role in the war on drugs, offering to assist the Drug Enforcement Administration and the FBI by interdicting flights smuggling narcotics and other contraband into the United States. Furthermore, NORAD had played a role historically in responding to hijacked flights, assisting the Federal Aviation Administration by identifying the hijacked plane and tailing it until it landed safely. As the 1990s progressed, and the threat of terrorism escalated, NORAD's commanders seized upon this growing "asymmetric threat" to the homeland to argue for the preservation of their command. NORAD commanding general Ralph Eberhart told the 9/11 Commission that there was "an ongoing debate after the implosion of the Soviet Union and the fall of the wall, and that centered on was NORAD a Cold War relic . . . that we did not need, because the Soviet Union was no longer our enemy[?]. . . . There were great debates during the 90s, and we came close to having zero airplanes on alert. . . . And that was one of the options . . . that almost went to the end game."

Air Force General Larry Arnold, who had been part of the air defense mission for much of his career and commanded the Continental U.S. Region (CONR) for NORAD on 9/11, recalled that "When I became the 1st Air Force vice commander in January 1997, the Department of Defense had just released its Quadrennial Defense Review [QDR]. This document indicated that the Air Force would provide only four fighter alert sites for a 'four corners' defense. It was a familiar basketball strategy that had no place in the air sovereignty mission." NORAD commanders thought the "four corners" idea was "ridiculous but it became popular. So there was a fight just to maintain the number of alert sites that we had. We felt that we could operate fairly reasonably with about 10 sites and thought eight was the absolute highest risk we could take. We ended up with seven. I didn't feel particularly comfortable with seven because there are large distances between the alert sites."

Desperate to demonstrate to the Pentagon bureaucracy the necessity of its air sovereignty mission, in 1999 NORAD formed a "Roles and Missions" team to study the viability of the air defense mission. As General Arnold explained, "I wanted a study before the next [2001] QDR that said, 'Here's how we do the mission now, here's alternative ways to do the mission. . . . I wanted a team to talk to the commanders of NORAD and ACC [Air Combat Command] and the leadership all over the Air Force and find out . . . if there's no mission. And I said, 'If there's no mission, we'll shut down now.'" The Roles and Missions team comprised both proponents and detractors of NORAD's air defense mission. As the team began its work, Arnold recalled, "the Hart-Rudman study had indicated that the biggest threat to the United States in the aftermath of the Soviet Union was from rogue nations or terrorists. Our focus then was, What can we do to thwart a terrorist attack from outside the borders? . . . So we were focused on the terrorist threat, but we certainly weren't focused on the terrorist threat in the way that it came down on 9/11."

Retired Colonel William Scott, who was active at the time, recalled, "A number of papers were published as we were struggling for survival. People did studies, including the Hart–Rudman study, that said we would get hit by terrorism in the next five years. This debate was going on in the mainstream of the Department of Defense as we were struggling for survival. What we picked up from that debate was this: 'We need to define those asymmetric threats as they pertain to our mission.' We thought that the primary threat was some sort of poor-man's cruise missile . . . from a commercial ship off the coast, maybe some old rickety freighter out in the Gulf. And in one of our briefings, we pointed out that for $83,000 you can buy an Unmanned Aerial Vehicle with GPS navigation. These guys weren't looking for pinpoint accuracy. If you launch it into a metropolitan area, that's good enough. The objective is to kill Americans, as many as you can." NORAD's mission brief was revised to reflect the emerging threat posed by terrorism in general and Osama bin Laden in particular: "As we started talking about Osama bin Laden, the examples we gave in our mission brief were the first World Trade Center bombing, the Tokyo subway, Oklahoma City bombing, and Atlanta Olympics. What we did was connect those dots. The conclusion we drew was that we had a viable threat." The Roles and Missions team "made some pretty bold predictions in our briefing," recalled Major General Mike Haugen of the North Dakota National Guard, a team member. "We didn't predict how the terrorists would strike, but predicted they would strike."

NORAD was not scuttled, but its rearticulated mission of combating terrorism was not embraced fully either. The number of alert sites was scaled back still further, decommissioning such tactically critical sites as Atlantic City, the closest alert site to New York City. On 9/11, there were seven remaining alert sites; Pentagon plans still called for an eventual reduction to four sites. By 2001, then, NORAD had survived, but just barely. Upon assuming command of NORAD in 1998, General Richard Myers "told the chairman of the Joint Chiefs of Staff that he could provide air sovereignty in name only. He didn't get any more forces."

The failure of the FBI and CIA directors to implement their vision of a transformed mission was replicated at NORAD. Like the FBI and the CIA, the NORAD commanders' vision of a mission transformed to meet the challenge posed by asymmetric threats like terrorism suffered from a radical disconnect between the commanders' articulation of that mission and the measures undertaken to assure its achievement. The reduction of NORAD alert sites left successive commanders Richard Myers and Ralph Eberhart, and veteran air defense experts like General Arnold, doubting openly whether NORAD was left with the means necessary to defend the homeland; the reduction in alert sites, coupled with the transfer of the command and control of NORAD fighters to the Air National Guard from the "regular" Air Force, underscored the marginalization of the NORAD mission.

Furthermore, although accepting the threat of domestic terrorist attacks as a principal reason for retaining NORAD, the Department of Defense did little if anything to reconfigure the agency to meet its new mission. In 2000, for instance, planners rejected a proposed NORAD training exercise, known as Positive Force, which took as its premise that a hijacked plane would be involved in a suicide attack on the Pentagon. Chairman of the Joint Chiefs Richard Myers, who at the time was the NORAD commander, explained to the 9/11 Commission: "Exercising alone is not enough, if you look at all . . . the policy that we've gotten through the 90s into early 2000, 2001, and all the policy guidance was that we treat terrorism primarily as a criminal event. And the role of the Defense Department was to defend our forces, primarily, it was force protection, anti-terrorism, not counterterrorism—counterterrorism responsibilities . . . domestically were the FBI, externally were the CIA." Thus, mission boundaries similar to those that hampered the FBI and CIA in thwarting the al Qaeda plot also beset NORAD.

General Myers's point was that merely conducting an exercise involving a hypothetical hijacked plane heading for the Pentagon would not have been sufficient to reorient the organization; its sense of mission was too deeply ingrained: "There was an exercise, and . . . the idea was to stress the continuity of command . . . but it was an exercise focused on Korea, and that's why the scenario was rejected, because it did not . . . contribute to the exercise at hand. . . . It's more—it's the way we were directed to posture, looking outward. Those were the orders that NORAD had, and it's had for, ever since the end of the Soviet Union when we had, at that time, I think it was 26 alert sites around the United States, and we'd gone down to seven. So it would have . . . required more than exercising if you wanted to be effective, and it would have been not just the military, because civilian agencies had . . . the major role." These views were confirmed in 9/11 Commission staff interviews, recently made public by the National Archives, with NORAD personnel who designed the exercises. In particular, Larry Merchant, who was the exercise director within the NORAD Battle Staff on 9/11, stated that "NORAD must use Russia in its exercises at the strategic level since no other country poses a great enough threat to NORAD's capabilities and responsibilities. . . . As far as emerging threats, Merchant noted that they received scenarios involving crop dusters, Unmanned Aerial Vehicles (UAVs) and 'poor man's cruise missiles.' Merchant noted that though the commander stressed that 'the cold war is over' and that they should develop 'more real scenarios,' they still had a concept plan—and that plan still necessitated training for over-water events."

This explanation did not satisfy 9/11 Commissioner John Lehman, who pressed the issue with General Myers: "I understand that there was a great argument during the period before 9/11 about whether NORAD should exist at all, and the reduction from 23 [*sic*] to seven sites. Why, given the increasing threat discussion of the possibility of hijackings and the intentions of al Qaeda, was this such a big issue?" General Myers responded: "I think it's because the threat was not perceived to be so evident, and we were following the same guidance that we got right after the fall of the Soviet Union: 'Where is the dividend from this?' And so forces were scaled down. Alert facilities, which are expensive to maintain, were closed. And we wound up with those seven sites." Myers continued: "It's the priorities that the Defense Department goes through to balance risk. And, again, the threat perception was not there to balance that risk."

NORAD commanders considered the most likely form of terrorist attack to be a cruise missile from offshore, but such missiles usually fly below the radar coverage, and thus would remain undetected by NORAD, which had no way other than radar available to detect incoming flying objects. They were not alone in this perception. A February 8, 1999, analysis of post–Cold War threats to U.S. security in the journal *Policy Analysis* stated: "A more likely threat [than a ballistic missile from a rogue nation or terrorist group] would be a cruise missile with a nuclear, biological, or chemical warhead launched by a rogue state or terrorist group from a ship off the U.S. coast. Defense against cruise missiles, which fly low under radar surveillance, is difficult. In addition, it would probably be more difficult to trace the origin of such an attack than it would be to do so for a ballistic missile launched from the territory of a rogue state. Yet less emphasis has been placed on defending the American homeland from cruise missile attacks—something that perhaps needs to be rectified." No funding was obtained to counter the threat that NORAD considered most credible; NORAD was fully occupied just trying to survive.

With respect to any threats arising domestically, NORAD was inhibited in responding by the law of posse comitatus, a statute dating to Civil War Reconstruction that limits severely the ability of the military to be involved in domestic law enforcement. As General Myers explained to the 9/11 Commission, "What we try to do is follow the law, and the law is pretty clear on Posse Comitatus and that is whether or not the military should be involved in domestic law enforcement. . . . Again, at the time terrorism was viewed as a criminal act."

In addition, NORAD was hampered in responding to any internally arising threat by a stark reality: it couldn't see large areas of the continental United States on its radar. The extensive system of radar detection that had been constructed during the height of the Cold War in the 1950s and early 1960s had been allowed to erode along with NORAD's mission. On October 25, 1999, when golfer Payne Stewart's flight from Orlando to Dallas strayed off course, NORAD deployed fighter jets and helped to escort the plane, which had lost cabin pressure and eventually crashed. "The significant thing," recalled General Arnold, "was, we could not see that aircraft and the sectors worked with the FAA to track the airplane and feed information to us. Using the FAA radar and FAA positioning in order to use our fighters, we were able to divert them from training missions . . . to escort the plane. What this proved to us is that we couldn't see and couldn't talk to each other over the central part of the United States." Colonel Scott concluded that the Stewart tragedy "led the public to believe we were much more ready than we were."

Like the other federal agencies, then, NORAD responded to the emerging terrorist threat by redefining its mission to accommodate that threat. In some ways, that redefinition salvaged NORAD. Also like the other agencies, however, NORAD continued to function as it always had, as a Cold War entity subject to all of the Cold War rules, modes of operation, and restrictions. In the context of NORAD's mission, these rules meant that because domestic terrorist attacks were considered criminal acts, NORAD's focus had to remain what it had been during the Cold War, focused on the terrorist attack that would come from abroad. Even in that circumstance, however, NORAD lacked the capability to thwart the external threat it viewed as most credible: a low-flying missile attack from offshore by a rogue nation or terrorist group. The disconnect between the vision of the mission held by the agency heads and commanders and its execution was as vast in NORAD as it had been at the CIA and the FBI.

And so it was that on the morning of 9/11, the Northeast Air Defense Sector in Rome, New York, stood up at full alert, not in preparation for a terrorist attack but in preparation for an exercise in which Russian planes would fly over the North Pole to bomb the United States, a scenario that had been described as outdated as long ago as 1966 by Defense Secretary Robert McNamara. At 8:37:52, as the exercise was about to begin, the phone at Staff Sergeant Jeremy Powell's desk began to ring:

> FAA: Hi. Boston Center TMU [military liaison]. We have a problem here. We have a hijacked aircraft headed towards New York, and we need you guys to—we need someone to scramble some F-16s or something up there, to help us out.
>
> NEADS: Is this real-world or exercise?
>
> FAA: No, this is not an exercise, not a test.

The plot that had been hatched five years earlier in a cave in Afghanistan was now airborne over America. It had evaded the most sophisticated and expensive worldwide early-warning system of human and electronic intelligence, law enforcement, and military force projection ever devised. For all of the trillions of dollars expended since the

Cold War ended, the agencies principally responsible for detecting and interdicting the plot had failed to adjust the way they worked to meet the new threat of terrorism that they all recognized. That left NORAD, the unlikeliest of agencies. As General Eberhart would state later: "NORAD is not the right way to work this problem. It is a force of last resort. If you use us . . . everybody on that airplane will die. . . . Where we really need to focus is destroying those terrorist networks, not allowing them into our country—don't allow them into our airports. Don't allow them on our aircraft. If they get on our aircraft, don't let them take control of the airplane."

By 9/11, it was too late. The defense of the country rested on NORAD, because every other (more prominent and better-funded) agency had failed, and in precisely the same ways. As a consequence, the terrorists had trained in Afghanistan and traveled to the United States. They had gotten into the country. They had learned to fly here. They had gotten into the airports, through security, and onto the airplanes. They had taken control of the airplanes, and were flying them toward their targets. NORAD would now attempt, in the next ninety minutes, to do what agencies like the CIA and the FBI and DoD as a whole had failed throughout the 1990s to do: adapt its operations to a new kind of war. It was now up to NORAD, a backwater Cold War agency that was being phased down, to try to stop al Qaeda.

PART THREE

DAY OF DAYS

HOURS

PREDAWN TO 8:00 A.M.

The attacks on September 11 ended by exploding into a cloudless blue sky on a nearly windless morning. They began, however, hours earlier, in predawn darkness. As the earth's shadow passed slowly over the East Coast and the horizon's rim began to brighten, thousands of government personnel dedicated to defending America were working the "night shift" around the world: military assigned to the more than seven hundred bases and to Navy fleets at home and abroad; intelligence agents embedded in foreign embassies and in private-sector employment; law enforcement officers on the streets of American towns and cities; personnel at the National Security Agency manning the technology that would intercept billions of messages from every continent; signals experts scrutinizing satellite data. In Rome, New York, at NORAD's Northeast Regional Defense Sector, the overnight skeleton crew sat bathed in the dim green lights of their radar screens, watching the skies. The day shift had already started to drift in because of a large-scale exercise planned for that morning, a classic Cold War simulation of a Soviet—now Russian—bomber offensive over the North Pole.

Shortly before 6:00 a.m., the commander-in-chief of this formidable defense structure, President George W. Bush, awoke at the Colony Beach Resort in Sarasota, Florida, and pulled on an old T-shirt, shorts, and his running shoes. Joined by a Secret Service agent and a reporter, the president went for a four-mile run in the cool half-light, starting at 6:30.

Just as the president was awaking, at 5:40 a.m., Mohammed Atta and Abdul Aziz al Omari pulled into the Portland, Maine, International Jetport parking lot. Three minutes later, they checked in at the US Airways counter for the Colgan Air Flight 5930 to Boston. Atta checked two bags; Omari checked none. When he was given his boarding pass for the flight to Boston, Atta asked the agent why he was not provided a boarding pass for his connecting flight on American Airlines Flight 11 from Boston to Los Angeles. He was informed that he would have to check in again with American Airlines in Boston to obtain his boarding pass. Atta clenched his jaw, appeared to fight back anger. He "stated that he was assured he would have 'one-stop check-in.'" The agent told him that they had better hurry if they planned to make their flight. Atta turned back, paused as if to respond, then decided to let it drop. He proceeded to the security checkpoint.

Atta, Omari, and their seventeen comrades would directly encounter no part of the trillion-dollar frontline American defense infrastructure that morning. Instead, they would encounter, confront, and largely defeat a largely civilian agency, the Federal Aviation Administration, whose role in providing for national security was considered so inconsequential that the FAA was not even included as a participant in the Pentagon's Air Threat Conference Calls.

Founded in the late 1950s, after a deadly midair passenger plane collision in 1956 revealed the inadequacy of the air traffic control system, the FAA's primary mandate has been to regulate the safety and security of civil aviation. On 9/11, this was accomplished before takeoff through a multilayered security system designed to ensure that passengers posing a security risk were not allowed to board. After takeoff, the FAA assured flight safety by employing a sophisticated system that regulated the flow of air traffic.

The FAA's security system was guided, at least in theory, by the FAA intelligence bureau's assessment of the current threats to civilian aviation. FAA intelligence was supposed to inform the security procedures relating to airport access control, passenger prescreening, passenger checkpoint screening, checked baggage screening for explosives, and onboard security. FAA Administrator Jane Garvey summarized the agency's pre-9/11 posture in testimony before the 9/11 Commission:

> On September 10 we were not a nation at war. On September 10, we were a nation bedeviled by delays, concerned about congestion, and impatient to keep moving. . . . Based on intelligence reporting, we saw explosive devices on aircraft as the most dangerous threat. We were also concerned about what we now think of as traditional hijacking, in which the hijacker seizes control of the aircraft for transportation, or in which passengers are held as hostages to further some political agenda.

This was true, to an extent. The FAA certainly had no knowledge or intelligence information suggesting that al Qaeda or any other terrorist group was planning to hijack commercial airliners in the United States and use them as weapons against American landmarks. Nonetheless, in both 1998 and 1999, the FAA's intelligence unit had produced reports about the hijacking threat posed by bin Laden and al Qaeda. Those reports had discussed the possibility that al Qaeda might "try to hijack a commercial jet and slam it into a U.S. landmark." These reports concluded, however, that such an "unlikely" scenario constituted a "last resort."

Similarly, in the spring of 2001, FAA intelligence distributed a CD-ROM briefing to air carriers and airports, including Logan, Newark, and Dulles, titled "2001 Terrorism Threat Prevention to Aviation Security Personnel at Airpots and Air Carriers"; that briefing discussed, in slide 24, the possibility that terrorists might conduct suicide hijackings, but concluded that "we have no indication that any group is currently thinking in that direction."

This was followed on July 17 by a notice published by FAA in the Federal Register that stated:

Terrorism can occur any time, anywhere in the United States. Members of foreign terrorist groups, representatives from State sponsors of terrorism and radical fundamentalist elements from many nations are present in the United States. . . . Thus an increasing threat to civil aviation from both foreign and potentially domestic [terrorists] exists and needs to be prevented and countered.

In sum, between 1993 and 2001 the FAA opened more than 1,200 intelligence case files to track potential threats to commercial aviation. Daily intelligence summaries derived from these case files were distributed to the FAA's top policymakers, including the Security Directive Working Group, set up to advise whether the enhancement of civil aviation security should be ordered. Between April 1 and September 10, 2001, 105 daily summaries were issued by FAA intelligence, based on information gleaned from other intelligence agencies, primarily the FBI and CIA. Fifty-two of those summaries mentioned bin Laden, al Qaeda, or both, mostly in connection with overseas threats. Five summaries mentioned hijacking as an al Qaeda capability; two mentioned suicide attacks, but not in connection with crashing airplanes. One of the summaries discussed air defense measures being taken in Genoa, Italy, in connection with an economic summit; these measures were designed, in part, according to the daily summary, to protect the event from possible air attack from terrorists. One scenario anticipated was the use of an explosives-laden aircraft as a weapon.

Between March 14 and May 15, 2001, the FAA's Office of Civil Aviation Intelligence conducted a series of classified briefings for security officials at nineteen of the nation's busiest airports, including Newark, Logan, and Dulles. The briefing discussed the threat posed by terrorism generally and bin Laden and al Qaeda in particular, including the groups' renewed interest in hijacking. In particular, the briefing stated that "a domestic hijacking would likely result in a greater number of American hostages but would be operationally more difficult. . . . We don't rule it out. . . . If, however, the intent of the hijacker is not to exchange hostages for prisoners, but to commit suicide in a spectacular explosion, a domestic hijacking would probably be preferable."

Notwithstanding the efforts of the FAA's twenty-four-hour, seven-day-a-week intelligence operation, none of its extensive reporting to FAA management, to the airlines, or to airport security in the years, months, and weeks leading up to 9/11 resulted in enhancement of security at the nation's airports as of September 11, 2001. Although FAA Administrator Garvey told the 9/11 Commission that she was aware of the heightened threat during the summer of 2001, her closest deputies denied knowing of the heightened threat environment, and the airlines were not informed of it. The closest the FAA came was in an information circular issued July 31, alerting the aviation security community to "reports of possible near-term terrorist operations . . . particularly on the Arabian Peninsula and/or Israel." The circular advised:

> The FAA does not have any credible information regarding specific plans by terrorist groups to attack U.S. civil aviation interests. Nevertheless, some of the currently active groups are known to plan and train for hijacking and have the capability to construct sophisticated IEDs. . . . The FAA encourages all U.S. carriers to exercise prudence and demonstrate a high degree of alertness.

The FAA's lack of urgency is usually explained by noting that before 9/11, it had been over a decade since the last domestic hijacking. This led to a belief among FAA regulators and airline carriers that the existing system of checkpoint screening was working well and that, in effect, "the nation had won the battle against hijacking." This view is difficult to reconcile, however, with the volume of intelligence reporting warning of both the presence of terrorist operatives in the United States and the renewed interest of terrorist groups in general, and al Qaeda in particular, in hijacking. Indeed, on July 17, 2001, the FAA expressly cited, as justification for its proposed rules, both the presence of terrorists in the United States and their interest in targeting the transportation infrastructure.

The more likely culprit in the FAA's lack of urgency is the familiar one, the one that beset the DoD, the FBI, and the CIA: it was a function of the way that government works. As in other agencies, despite the awareness within the FAA's intelligence unit of the growing domestic threat posed by terrorists, of the direct threat to the airline industry that Osama bin Laden had issued, and of the surge of interest among terrorists, including al Qaeda, in hijacking and suicide missions, there was a fundamental disconnect between the threats the unit (and others) identified and the measures taken to calibrate the existing security system to meet those threats.

In 1997, for instance, the Gore Commission, created by President Clinton in response to the explosion of Pan Am Flight 800, had concluded that "the threat against civil aviation is changing and growing, and . . . the federal government must lead the fight against it." The Gore Commission Report voiced the consensus of American intelligence agencies: namely, that "the threat of terrorism is changing in two important ways. First, it is no longer just an overseas threat from foreign terrorists. . . . The second change is that . . . it is becoming more common to find terrorists working alone or in ad hoc groups, some of whom are not afraid to die in carrying out their designs." The Gore Commission recommended that security measures be adopted that were commensurate with the evolving threat it had identified: "It is important to improve security not just against familiar threats, such as explosives in checked baggage, but also to explore means of assessing and countering emerging threats." Among other things, the commission recommended that, consistent with civil aviation's becoming a national security priority, the FAA work closely with the FBI, CIA, DoD, State Department, and other law enforcement and intelligence agencies to ensure that its security measures evolved along with the nature of the threat.

That effort largely failed, for several familiar reasons. The FAA had no independent intelligence capability but depended upon the capabilities of other federal agencies and their willingness to share intelligence. Domestic intelligence sharing was hampered, according to FAA officials, by the fact that "although the FBI was the lead government agency on counterterrorism issues, its primary focus was on collecting evidence for criminal cases, not on the collection and dissemination of intelligence." Indeed, evidence collected for use in criminal cases could not be shared with other agencies without violating federal law relating to grand jury secrecy. The CIA, on the other hand, was focused on threats overseas. This left a gap in the quantity and reliability of intelligence shared. A senior FAA security official repeated to the 9/11 Commission his constant complaint to the federal intelligence community before 9/11: "You guys can tell us what's happening on a street in Kabul, but you can't tell us what's going on in Atlanta."

Even where intelligence information could have been shared, it wasn't. The FAA was never notified, for instance, of the FBI's concern, in 1998, and again in 2001, about Middle Eastern men undertaking flight training, despite the fact that, as the regulator of flight schools nationwide, the FAA would have been well situated to assist in an investigation.

More egregious, FAA intelligence was never provided with, or even informed about, the State Department's list of known or suspected terrorists. Thus, there was a tremendous disparity between the FAA's "no-fly" list, which on 9/11 comprised twelve names, including Khalid Sheikh Mohammed, and the State Department's TIPOFF list, which included some 60,000 names. In fact, the FAA's former head of civil aviation security, Cathal "Irish" Flynn, testified before the 9/11 Commission that he had never heard of the State Department's TIPOFF list until the Commission's hearing on the subject in January 2004.

This prompted the following exchange between Commissioner Tim Roemer and the FAA's Claudio Manno:

> MR. ROEMER: There is a TIPOFF list at the State Department that you don't know about until yesterday, that you don't know about that exists before September 11. Mr. Manno, this list has approximately 61,000 names of people around the world that are prevented from flying, that are picked out by the

State Department at that point and they're picked out because they're dangerous and they shouldn't be on airplanes, 61,000 names.

Your list, according to what you just said, or what our staff has told me, is twelve people. So there's a difference of 60,988 names, a difference of 60,988 names between what's been accumulated at the State Department as dangerous people, shouldn't be flying, and what you have with your twelve people. Now, I can't understand why there are not more efforts in liaison activities to reach out to State Department and start to bring some of those names over and prevent those people from flying.

MR. MANNO: Well, again the process at the time was to include in the security directive names of people where there was specific and credible information that they posed a threat. Part of that process required, because a lot of times the information was classified, that it be declassified because the information circulars in the security directives were not classified documents that went out to the industry. And it was simply very difficult to get clearance from the community in cases where there wasn't a direct connection to civil aviation for them to get the release information. We had to justify that in each case. Now, did we do it? Did we go in and say we want all 61,000 of these names? No, that was not—we didn't do that. We focused on the information, again, that was specific to aviation at the time.

Two of the 9/11 hijackers, Nawaf al Hazmi and Khalid al Mihdhar, had been placed on the TIPOFF list by the FBI in late August as the search for them intensified. But the FBI never contacted the FAA to place the names on its no-fly list, so their ability to fly on 9/11 remained unimpaired.

Underlying these failures of communication was what FAA intelligence officials considered to be a certain level of bureaucratic condescension from their sister agencies. Cathal Flynn testified that "We [were] told because [we] pushed on it frequently, 'Don't worry about it, we're not going to give you raw intelligence, we're not going to give you processed intelligence. If there is a threat to aviation, we'll tell you.'"

But the FAA itself was far from blameless. At the sentencing trial of Zacarias Moussaoui, the manager of the Arizona flight school where Hani Hanjour had trained testified that she had called the FAA to discuss her concerns about Hanjour long before the attacks. She informed the FAA that he lacked the English proficiency necessary to become a pilot, and noted that it had taken him eight hours to complete a two-hour test. Margaret Chevette was told "not to worry," she testified; Hanjour could use an interpreter in the cockpit. Similarly, a flight-school instructor from Florida testified that Mohammed Atta and Marwan al Shehhi once left a small plane on a runway at Miami International Airport after a lesson, a breach in protocol that should have triggered an interview with the FAA. To his knowledge, neither man was ever interviewed.

Whether the FAA's knowledge of the heightened threats should have been sufficient to cause an adjustment in security measures, and whether the information it lacked was critical, are matters for conjecture. What is clear is that, as Commission staffer John Raidt testified, "FAA documents including agency accounts published in the Federal Register on July 17th, 2001, expressed the FAA's understanding that terrorist groups were active in the United States and maintained an historic interest in targeting aviation, including hijacking. While the agency was engaged in an effort to pass important new regulations to improve checkpoint screener performance, implement anti-sabotage measures and conduct ongoing assessments of the system, no major increases in anti-hijacking security measures were implemented in response to the heightened threat levels in the spring and summer of 2001, other than general warnings to the industry to be more vigilant and cautious."

At 5:45 a.m. on 9/11, then, as Mohammed Atta and Abdul Aziz al Omari took their tickets and proceeded to the checkpoint screening at

Portland's Jetport, the aviation security system was configured to guard against two perceived security threats: sabotage by explosives, and hijacking for a purpose that usually included a political negotiation. Several layers of security checks were put into place to assure security against these threats.

The first layer was passenger prescreening. Mohammed Atta triggered the prescreening system.

When he checked in, Atta was selected for additional screening by the Computer Assisted Passenger Prescreening System (CAPPS). The CAPPS system was designed to apply a computer algorithm to identify potential security risks; it replaced, in the late 1990s, a prior system of manual review that had been, in the view of FAA management, too subjective. The CAPPS system would automatically assess each passenger's security risk according to a series of predetermined "factors" and "weights"; those deemed most likely to pose a security threat were chosen for extra screening. In addition, the system randomly selected a certain number of additional passengers on each flight for screening.

The consequences of selection, however, bore no relation to the threat posed by a hijacker like Mohammed Atta. First, although Aviation Security Alert Level III, which was in effect on September 11, directed airport screeners to search physically or screen with an approved device the person and carry-on items of all CAPPS selectees, that procedure had not been followed for some time. Instead, by September 11, 2001, CAPPS selection meant simply that Atta's checked luggage would be either screened for explosive devices by machine, or held off the airplane until Atta himself had boarded; the assumption, which ignored the trend toward suicide martyrdom, was that no one would bomb a plane on which he planned to be a passenger. Because the Portland Jetport had no explosives-detection devices, Mohammed Atta's checked luggage was held off the flight to Boston until he boarded. CAPPS selection resulted in no further screening of Atta or his carry-on bags at the security checkpoint. Perhaps more egregious, CAPPS screening did not result even in holding Atta's checked bags when he transferred flights in Boston; the bags were simply checked through.

The next layer of security was the X-ray and metal-detection checkpoint. On 9/11, these checkpoints were operated by the airlines, under the direction of the FAA; services were usually performed by subcontractors. Atta and Omari reached the security checkpoint at 5:45 a.m. Each passenger's carry-on bags passed through an X-ray machine; the purpose of this screening was to identify and confiscate weapons and other prohibited items. The passengers themselves walked through a metal detector calibrated to detect items with the metal content of a small-caliber handgun. The men walked through the metal detector, and their bags passed through the X-ray machine, without incident, in twelve seconds. Atta and Omari both claimed black shoulder bags; in addition, Omari carried a smaller black case resembling a camera or camcorder case. They boarded the 6:00 a.m. flight to Boston, along with eight other passengers; the Beechcraft 1900 plane held up to nineteen. They were the last to board, and occupied the last row of the aircraft. The flight departed on time and arrived at Gate B9A at Boston's Logan Airport at 6:45 a.m.

Waiting for them at Logan Airport were their fellow passengers for American Airlines Flight 11, Wail al Shehri, Waleed al Shehri, and Satam al Suqami, who parked their rental car at Logan Airport's central parking facility at 6:45 a.m. All three men were selected by the CAPPS system for additional security screening; their luggage was screened by an explosives-detection monitor and then loaded onto the plane. As with Mohammed Atta, their selection by CAPPS required no additional screening of their persons or carry-on bags. All five of the men passed through the security checkpoint at Logan Airport without incident.

At 6:52 a.m., as President Bush was completing his run, a phone call was placed to Atta's cell phone from a pay phone in Logan Airport. That pay phone was located in Terminal C, the departure terminal for United Airlines Flight 175, between the screening checkpoint and the departure gate. All of the United Flight 175 hijackers checked in between 6:20 and 6:53 a.m. None of them was selected for heightened security screening by the CAPPS system. It is a reasonable inference that the call was placed to confirm for Atta that the United 175 hijackers were in place. The men passed through a security checkpoint operated by a subcontractor for United Airlines; none of the checkpoint operators on duty that morning recalled anything unusual about any of the men.

Mohammed Atta and Abdul Aziz al Omari boarded American Airlines Flight 11 at 7:39 a.m. Wail and Waleed al Shehri had boarded at 7:31. The final hijacker, Satam al Suqami, boarded at 7:40. Waleed and Wail al Shehri sat in first class, seats 2A and 2B; the other three sat in business class, Atta and Omari in seats 8D and 8G, and Suqami in seat 10B.

All five hijackers boarded United Airlines Flight 175 between 7:23 a.m. and 7:28 a.m. Like the American 11 hijackers, their seats were clustered in first class (seats 2A and 2B), and business class (seats 6C, 9C, and 9D).

The cell that had traveled from Paterson, New Jersey, to board American Airlines Flight 77 had substantially more difficulty navigating the multilayered security system at Dulles International Airport in Virginia. At 7:15 a.m., Khalid al Mihdhar—one of the subjects of the FBI's manhunt, who had been placed on the State Department's TIPOFF list of suspected terrorists—checked in at the American Airlines ticket counter at Dulles, along with Majed Moqed. Nearly fifteen minutes later, Nawaf al Hazmi—the other subject of the FBI search who had been added to the TIPOFF list—checked in with his brother, Salem. The fifth hijacker, Hani Hanjour, followed shortly thereafter.

All five were selected for enhanced security by the CAPPS system. Hanjour, Mihdhar, and Moqed were selected by the computer algorithm; Nawaf and Salem al Hazmi were selected at the discretion of the American Airlines customer-service representative who checked them in. The customer-service representative recalled that one of the men presented identification with no photograph and did not seem to understand English; he felt that both men were suspicious, and so he designated both for enhanced screening.

As with Mohammed Atta in Portland, however, the CAPPS selection of the men as potential security risks had little practical effect. Salem al Hazmi and Majed Moqed, who checked bags, had their checked bags held off American Flight 77 until they had boarded. The other three passengers, who did not check any bags, suffered no enhanced security consequences as a result of their CAPPS selection.

The five also caused a stir at the security checkpoint. Hani Hanjour and Salem al Hazmi passed through the magnetometer and the X-ray screening without incident; the other three, however, all set off the metal detector and were subject to additional screening. The system at Dulles International Airport called for passengers who set off the alarm to proceed to a second metal detector; Mihdhar did not set off the second metal detector, and was allowed to pass. Moqed and Nawaf al Hazmi, however, did set off the second metal detector as well, and were, as a consequence, screened by security personnel using a hand-held metal-detection wand. In addition, Nawaf al Hazmi's shoulder bag was swiped by an explosive trace detector. Both passed this cursory inspection and were allowed to proceed.

Moqed and Mihdhar boarded American Flight 77 at 7:50 a.m., and sat in seats 12A and 12B in coach class. Hanjour boarded two minutes later and occupied seat 1B in first class. Nawaf and Salem al Hazmi boarded at 7:55 a.m. and occupied seats 5E and 5F in first class.

The final group of hijackers, holding tickets for United Airlines Flight 93 out of Newark, had a much easier time. The men checked in at the United Airlines counter between 7:03 and 7:39 a.m. Only one of the four hijackers, Ahmad al Haznawi, was selected by the CAPPS system for enhanced screening. His bag was held off the plane until he boarded. All four men passed through the security checkpoint without incident. Two men—Saeed al Ghamdi and Ahmad al Haznawi—boarded United 93 at 7:39 a.m. and sat in seats 6B and 3D, both in first class. Ahmed al Nami boarded at 7:40 and sat in 3C, in first class. At 7:48, Ziad Jarrah boarded and sat in 1B, also in first class.

By 8:00 a.m. on 9/11, then, the nineteen al Qaeda hijackers sat innocuously among 213 other passengers aboard four transcontinental flights on two airlines, American and United. Those flights—American 11 from Boston to Los Angeles; United 175 from Boston to Los Angeles;

American 77 from Washington Dulles to Los Angeles; and United 93 from Newark to San Francisco—were four flights among several thousand scheduled to take off that morning leaving or bound for the East Coast. On a daily basis, the civil aviation security system was responsible for safeguarding 1.8 million passengers aboard more than 25,000 flights.

American Airlines Flight 11 pushed back from its gate at 7:40 a.m. and taxied to its runway. The flight took off at 7:59 a.m., just as United Flight 175 was pushing back from its gate. American Flight 77 and United Flight 93 were closed to further passenger boarding but sat at their gates at 8:00.

As American Airlines Flight 11 lifted into the sky, only two security barriers stood between the hijackers and the completion of their mission: onboard security measures—the reaction of the passengers and crew to their attacks—and the response of the FAA air traffic controllers and, ultimately, NORAD to the news of the hijackings.

On the basis of the two agencies' posture on 9/11, neither was a good candidate to succeed in thwarting the hijackings. The system of onboard security for civilian aircraft called for response to hijacking in accordance with a "Common Strategy." Developed as a result of decades of experience in dealing with hijackings, the Common Strategy called for flight crews "to refrain from trying to overpower or negotiate with hijackers, to land the aircraft as soon as possible, to communicate with authorities, and to try delaying tactics." As FAA administrator Garvey would testify, "Our aviation system's policy was to get the passengers on the ground safely and that meant negotiation, not confrontation." Despite the FAA's awareness of the increased possibility of suicide hijacking, the 9/11 Commission noted, "The FAA-approved training for commercial flight crews contained no guidance on how to respond if hijackers were bent on suicide, resorted to violence on the aircraft, or attempted to unseat the flight crew from the cockpit."

Other potential sources of onboard security were also lacking. There were no armed and trained air marshals aboard any of the flights; there were only thirty-three air marshals system-wide on 9/11, and they were assigned to international flights. The number of air marshals had been phased down from several hundred in the 1970s because of the perceived success of checkpoint screening and the higher priority accorded other FAA initiatives.

Although cockpit doors were supposed to be kept locked during flight, one key opened all cockpit doors on Boeing aircraft, and every flight attendant carried a copy. Any kind of locked or hardened cockpit door would in any event likely prove ineffective, given the Common Strategy to cooperate with hijackers. The chairman of the Air Line Pilots Association's Security Committee, in responding to proposals in January 2001 to install reinforced cockpit doors, stated the prevailing view of commercial airline pilots as 9/11 loomed: "Even if you make a vault out of the door, if they have a noose around my flight attendant's neck, I'm going to open the door."

It was 8:00 a.m. American Airlines Flight 11 cleared the tower at Boston's Logan Airport and headed west.

RUSH HOUR

8:00 TO 9:03 A.M.

As American Airlines Flight 11 cleared the Logan Airport tower and climbed, its pilots were following the directions of area air traffic controllers, who monitored direction, altitude, and velocity, and positioned aircraft accordingly, to one another to maintain a safe distance between them.

In the immediate vicinity of Logan Airport, the flight's movements were guided initially by controllers in the tower, who then passed the flight to the local Terminal Radar Approach Control (TRACON), located in proximity to Logan, a major metropolitan airport. Once an aircraft is approximately thirty miles from its point of departure, TRACON controllers hand the aircraft off to the corresponding Air Traffic Control Center whose airspace the plane will enter next.

Communications with American 11 were normal as it climbed past 10,000 feet, heading west. Across the country, the tower and TRACON controllers were responsible for maintaining more than 200,000 take-offs and landings per day in the United States, more than 73 million per year.

American Flight 11 climbed quickly, and was passed from the TRACON to Boston Center. Located in Nashua, New Hampshire, Boston Center was one of twenty-two Air Traffic Control Centers. Controllers at the Centers guided aircraft on a regional basis and at higher altitudes.

On 9/11 the Air Traffic Control system used two primary technologies to track aircraft: radar and transponder beacon codes. The radar system, which had been in place for decades, had been constructed jointly with the military in the 1950s and 1960s, but with the emergence of satellite technology many in the FAA believed that the radar system was antiquated. Accordingly, it had been only sporadically maintained, and was used, in the years immediately preceding 9/11, primarily as a backup system—in situations where, for whatever reason, a plane's transponder malfunctioned.

As controllers tracked a typical flight, what appeared on their screen was not a radar track but a flashing transponder signal that identified both the location and the identity of the flight. If, as happened on occasion, an aircraft's transponder shut down or malfunctioned, the controller could switch his scope to display the flight's primary radar tracks. These were not flight-specific, however; in a sky crowded with as many as four thousand planes at any given hour, it could be exceedingly difficult to isolate a specific flight just by means of primary radar. In addition, there was no way to determine a plane's altitude from its primary radar track. In such circumstances, controllers also relied on radio contact with the flight to assure themselves of its location.

Circumstances where flights were both not transponding and out of radio contact—or "NORDO," as loss of radio contact was called—were extremely rare. Controllers told the 9/11 Commission staff that such a combination of malfunctions would be taken by them to indicate a catastrophic failure of some sort.

Many within the FAA believed that, with the emergence of global positioning technology, radar could be phased out entirely; when the military objected to such proposals because of NORAD's continuing need for radar, a dispute arose about which agency should pay to maintain the radar system. That funding dispute remained unresolved; as a consequence, NORAD utilized only radars located around the perimeter of the United States, and was not capable of seeing much of the nation's interior.

At 8:09, the Logan Airport and TRACON air traffic controllers had passed control of American Flight 11 to controller Pete Zalewski at Boston's en route center. He made routine contact with the plane as it reached 26,000 feet, telling the pilot to "climb maintain flight level two eight zero [i.e., 28,000 feet]." Shortly before 8:14 a.m., Zalewski radioed: "American 11 turn twenty degrees right." In addition to the dozens of flights departing Logan Airport and heading west, controllers had to contend with dozens of flights heading east toward Boston. A controller could have as many as twenty flights under his control at any given time. American 11 responded: "Twenty right American 11." At 8:14, Zalewski instructed the flight to climb to 35,000 feet. There was no response.

Zalewski tried again: "American 11, do you copy?" Again no reply. He tried repeatedly over the next five minutes, to no avail. Zalewski thought, "Maybe the pilots weren't paying attention, or there's something wrong with the frequency."

At 8:19 a.m., Betty Ong, one of the flight attendants assigned to American Flight 11, called the American Airlines Southeastern Reservations Office in Cary, North Carolina, via AT&T Airphone. She stated: "The cockpit is not answering, somebody's stabbed in business class—and I think there's mace—that we can't breathe—I don't know, I think we're getting hijacked."

The hijackers had moved at 8:14. As Mohammed Atta and Abdul Aziz al Omari rushed the cockpit, a passenger seated directly behind them, in 9B, who had served for four years as an officer in the Israeli military, may have tried to stop them. He was seated one row ahead of Suqami. He was stabbed repeatedly and left in the aisle. Two stewardesses were also stabbed. The hijackers sprayed mace toward the back of the plane to keep the passengers and other flight crew members at bay, then took control of the cockpit.

In Boston Center, Zalewski tried nine more times to radio the cockpit, then tried to raise American 11 on an emergency frequency. Neighboring controllers moved incoming flights out of the plane's way. At 8:21 a.m., the transponder signal vanished. American 11 disappeared. The controllers switched their scopes and continued to follow the flight on primary radar.

Zalewski "very quietly turned to the supervisor" and said, "Would you please come over here? I think something is seriously wrong with this plane. I don't know what. It's either mechanical, electrical, I think, but I'm not sure."

The supervisor advised Zalewski to follow standard operating procedures for handling a NORDO flight. Zalewski checked the working condition of his own equipment, then attempted to raise the flight on an emergency frequency. He attempted to contact American Airlines to establish some communication with the flight.

Controllers contacted other planes from American Airlines in an attempt to have them make contact with American 11, and frantically cleared the airspace in front of American 11 from 35,000 feet to the ground. The flight began to move through the arrival route for Logan Airport, and then toward another air traffic sector's airspace.

On board the aircraft, Betty Ong told American Airlines officials at 8:22: "I think the guys are up there. They might have gone there, jammed their way up there, or something. Nobody can call the cockpit. We can't even get inside." One minute later, the American Airlines flight dispatcher sent an Aircraft Communications and Reporting System (ACARS) text message to American 11. The ACARS system allowed for rapid communication between the airlines and the flights via e-mail. The airline's message stated: "Good morning. . . . ATC [air traffic control] looking for you on [radio frequency] 135.32."

At 8:24 a.m., American 11 took a dramatic turn toward the south. "Zalewski heard two clicks over the frequency assigned to the flight, and radioed: 'Is that American 11 trying to call?'" The following transmission came from American 11: "We have some planes. Just stay quiet and you'll be okay. We are returning to the airport." Controller Zalewski "wasn't quite sure what it—what it was, because it was just a foreign voice. . . .

To me, it sounded almost Middle Eastern. And I asked—'American 11, is that you? American 11, are you trying to call me?' And then came the next transmission," at 8:24:57 (that is, 8:24 and 57 seconds): "Nobody move. Everything will be okay. If you try to make any moves, you'll endanger yourself and the airplane. Just stay quiet."

Controller Zalewski could not make out the first transmission, but he heard the second clearly. He "immediately stood up and yelled at the supervisor . . . 'Get over here immediately, right now,' and I can just remember everybody in that building, and they were all just looking at me, like, 'What's wrong with you?'" He "felt, from those voices, the terror. For some reason, I knew something was—seemed worse than a normal hijack."

Aboard the flight, Betty Ong reported to the airline that there had been no communication from the cockpit; the radio transmission to Air Traffic Control seems, therefore, to have been a mistaken attempt to communicate with the restive passengers and remaining flight crew.

The Boston supervisor assigned a senior controller to assist Zalewski in handling American 11, which was continuing south in the direction of New York City at close to 600 miles per hour at an unknown altitude. Betty Ong reported to her airline at 8:26 that the plane was flying erratically.

Because the initial transmission wasn't heard clearly, the Boston Center manager ordered the Center's Quality Assurance Specialist to "pull the tape," listen closely to it, and report what he had heard. Then, at 8:25, Boston Center began to inform the chain of command at the FAA of the hijacking.

The FAA's twenty-two Traffic Control Centers, such as Boston Center, are grouped under seven regional facilities that help manage and oversee operations within their airspace. The Traffic Control Centers also operate in close coordination with the Air Traffic Control System Command Center ("Command Center"), located in Herndon, Virginia. Command Center's responsibility is to oversee day-to-day operations within the entire airspace system, and to manage traffic levels for controllers working at en-route centers like Boston.

The regional centers report to FAA Headquarters in Washington, D.C. A Washington Operations Center (WOC) located at FAA Headquarters is charged with receiving notifications from the en-route centers and the regions of incidents affecting the National Air System, including accidents and hijackings.

At 8:25, Boston Center notified New England Region's Operations Center, the Herndon Command Center, and the Boston Center Air Traffic Manager that American 11 had been hijacked. This message was reinforced at 8:28, when a manager from Boston Center called the Command Center in Herndon to advise that American 11 had been hijacked and was heading for New York airspace. The Command Center established a teleconference between Boston, New York, and Cleveland Centers to assure coordination in handling the hijacking.

The Washington Operations Center was notified of the hijacking of American 11 at 8:32 a.m. by the Command Center in Herndon. The Command Center was informed that the Washington Operations Center had begun discussing the situation on a conference call with New England Region.

At that moment, on board American 11, Betty Ong and a fellow flight attendant, Amy Sweeney, sat in the back of the plane, each on the phone with someone from American Airlines. Sweeney told the flight service manager at Logan Airport, Michael Woodward, in a voice he later described as "calm," that the plane had been hijacked; that a passenger in first class had had his throat slashed and was dead; that two flight attendants had also been stabbed; that one flight attendant's wounds were serious and she was on oxygen, while the other's were minor; that a doctor had been paged; that the crew was unable to contact the cockpit; and that there was a bomb in the cockpit. Betty Ong confirmed, in her separate conversation at 8:34, that "one of our passengers, possibly in 9B, Levin or Lewis, might have been fatally stabbed."

At that moment, a third transmission came to Boston Center from American 11: "Nobody move, please. We are going back to the airport. Don't try to make any stupid moves." This third transmission, coupled with the observation that the plane was losing velocity quickly, and thus might be descending, galvanized the Boston controllers. They called out to other flights to ask whether any had seen American 11 and, if so, at what altitude it was flying. They also decided that American 11, wherever it was, needed a fighter escort. Someone would have to contact the military.

There were established protocols in place on 9/11 for the interaction of the FAA with the military. Those protocols had been developed in response to the hijackings of the 1970s and 1980s, which typically resulted in hostage negotiations, and although they had been revised at Secretary of Defense Rumsfeld's direction to increase his authority over the process, those revisions to the protocols reflected none of the intelligence reporting with respect to the increased domestic hijacking threat or the growing prevalence of suicide terrorist attacks.

The protocols in place called for the officials in the FAA's Washington Operations Center to notify FAA's senior leadership, specifically the FAA "hijack coordinator," who was "the Director of the FAA Office of Civil Aviation Security or his or her designate." The FAA's hijack coordinator, in turn, was required to make "direct contact" with the National Military Command Center (NMCC) at the Pentagon and "request the military to provide an escort aircraft."

The purpose of the military escort, under the protocols existing on 9/11, was to "follow the flight, report anything unusual, and aid search and rescue in the event of an emergency." Once the official request was received from the FAA, the NMCC was required to seek approval from the Office of the Secretary of Defense (OSD) to provide military assistance.

Once the secretary of defense's office had granted approval, the order worked its way back down the chain of command. The approval would be communicated to the NMCC, which would contact the commander-in-chief (CINC) of NORAD in Colorado to inform him of the approval. NORAD headquarters would then notify the appropriate region where the hijacked flight was located of the need for a fighter escort. If the hijacked aircraft was located in the continental United States, NORAD would notify its Continental Region (CONR) in Panama City, Florida, which would, in turn, identify the appropriate NORAD sector; if the flight was located in the northeast region of the United States, as American 11 was, the appropriate sector was the Northeast Air Defense Sector (NEADS), located in Rome, New York. NORAD Headquarters officials would then contact the NMCC at the Pentagon and advise them that NEADS was the defense sector tasked with providing the fighter escort.

The NMCC was then supposed to advise the FAA hijack coordinator of which squadron would be tasked with providing the escort. NMCC would then, finally, authorize direct coordination between FAA and the designated military unit. The FAA en-route center that was tracking the hijacked aircraft—in this case, Boston Center—was then authorized to coordinate the military response with NEADS.

The fighter escort, once scrambled and launched, was prepared and trained to (1) approach and identify the target, and (2) provide a covert escort, "vectored to a position five miles directly behind the hijacked aircraft," until the flight had landed safely. In sum, as the 9/11 Commission concluded:

> The protocols in place on 9/11 . . . presumed that the hijacked aircraft would be readily identifiable and would not attempt to disappear; there would be time to address the problem through the appropriate chain of command; and the hijacking would take the traditional form; that is, it would not be a suicide hijacking designed to convert the aircraft into a guided missile. On the morning of 9/11, the existing protocol was unsuited in every respect for what was about to happen.

Boston Center officials, unable to learn the altitude of American 11 and observing a dramatic reduction in speed, decided not to wait for the protocols to work. Beginning at 8:34, they decided to contact the military directly. Center managers tried to call Otis Air Force Base on Cape Cod and an old NORAD alert site in Atlantic City, New Jersey, that no longer functioned as such; these efforts were unsuccessful. Finally, at 8:38, Boston Center reached the Northeast Air Defense Sector and requested fighter assistance for the hijacked American 11.

> FAA: Hi. Boston Center TMU. We have a problem here. We have a hijacked aircraft headed towards New York, and we need you guys to—we need someone to scramble some F-16s or something up there, to help us out.
>
> NEADS: Is this real-world or exercise?
>
> FAA: No, this is not an exercise, not a test.

Flight identification technicians at NEADS then tried to ascertain the location of American 11. (In the time stamps that appear throughout the transcripts of the data files, the hours were given as 12, 13, 14, and so on, although the minutes and seconds correspond to real time after 8:00 a.m. and match the log notations; for clarity's sake I have rendered the hours accordingly, i.e., 8 rather than 12, 9 rather than 13, and so on.)

> NEADS:
> 8:38:36 We're checking to get some information from you if we could.
>
> BOSTON CENTER:
> 8:38:39 Okay, what would you—what do you need?
>
> NEADS:
> 8:38:40 Type of aircraft?
>
> BOSTON CENTER:
> 8:38:42 It's a—American 11.
>
> BOSTON CENTER:
> 8:38:43 What's that?

NEADS:

8:38:44 American 11?

BOSTON CENTER:

8:38:45 Type aircraft is a 767. [NOISE]

NEADS:

8:38:49 And tail number, do you know that?

BOSTON CENTER:

8:38:52 I—I don't know—hold on. Hey, Dan, you got—we got souls on board and all that information?

BOSTON CENTER:

8:38:57 We don't have any—

[OVERTALK]

BOSTON CENTER:

No, we—we don't have any of that information.

NEADS:

8:38:59 You don't have any of that?

BOSTON CENTER:

8:39:00 They—

NEADS:

Okay.

BOSTON CENTER:

8:39:01 —position's about 40 miles north of Kennedy.

NEADS:

8:39:03 Forty miles north of Kennedy?

BOSTON CENTER:

8:39:04 Right.

NEADS:

8:39:05 Do you have a mode three [transponder code]?

BOSTON CENTER:

8:39:07 No, we don't. We have the primary target only.

NEADS:

8:39:09 Primary target only?

BOSTON CENTER:

8:39:11 Yup.

NEADS:

8:39:12 Okay. And you don't know where he's coming from or the [UNINTELLIGIBLE]?

BOSTON CENTER:

8:39:15 No idea. He took off of Boston originally heading for—Los Angeles. So he's—

NEADS:

8:39:20 Boston to Los Angeles?

BOSTON CENTER:

8:39:22 That was his original destination. Yeah.

NEADS:

8:39:24 And they [UNINTELLIGIBLE]. And where are they going now, do you know?

BOSTON CENTER:

8:39:27 No idea.

NEADS:

And—

BOSTON CENTER:

8:39:28 He's heading towards Kennedy. It looks like his speed is decreasing. I'm not exactly sure where—nobody really knows.

NEADS:

8:39:33 Are you the controlling agency—

BOSTON CENTER:

8:39:35   Boston—

[OVERTALK]

NEADS:

—or is New York? Boston Center—

BOSTON CENTER:

8:39:36   —right now we are. He's heading right for New York center. . . .

NEADS:

8:39:49   But you don't have a—you don't have any modes or codes on him?

BOSTON CENTER:

8:39:53   No, right now I'm—right now it's just . . .

NEADS:

8:39:58   Is he inbound to JFK?

BOSTON CENTER:

8:40:00   We—we don't know.

NEADS:

8:40:01   You don't know where he is at all?

BOSTON CENTER:

8:40:03   He's being hijacked. The pilot's having a hard time talking to the—I mean we don't know. We don't know where he's goin'. He's heading towards Kennedy. He's—like I said, he's like 35 miles north of Kennedy now at 367 knots. . . .

8:40:22   Okay. Right now, I guess we're trying to work on—I guess there's been some threats in the cockpit. The—the pilot—

NEADS:

8:40:27   There's been what? I'm sorry.

BOSTON CENTER:

8:40:33   We'll call you right back as soon as we know more info.

[UNHEARD QUESTION]

8:40:34   Thank you.

NEADS conducts operations from a Sector Operations Command Center (SOCC) in Rome, New York. Like the facilities at NORAD Headquarters in Cheyenne Mountain, Colorado, the Rome facility is a Cold War relic. As Michael Bronner describes it, "NEADS is a desolate place, the sole orphan left behind after the dismantling of one of the country's busiest bomber bases—Griffiss Air Force Base, in Rome, New York, which was otherwise mothballed in the [mid-1990s]." The restaurants in Rome bear photographs of the New York town in its glory, at the height of the Cold War: dignitaries from around the world, including President Eisenhower, being feted at Griffiss in its, and the town's, heyday. The facility in which NEADS operates is "an aluminum bunker tricked out with antennae tilted skyward. It could pass for the Jetsons' garage."

In normal day-to-day operations, the SOCC is led by a Mission Crew Commander (MCC). On 9/11 the MCC was Major Kevin Nasypany. The MCC monitors the SOCC floor, receives reports from numerous watchstanders manning radar consoles, and makes tactical decisions based on those reports. Identification technicians attempt to identify the type and location of unknown aircraft. Surveillance officers man radarscopes to look for potential target aircraft. Weapons controllers serve as air traffic controllers for military aircraft.

Normally, the MCC also directs the updating of CONR (Continental U.S. Region) and NORAD headquarters through a secure computer terminal communication called a "chat log." Every critical decision and piece of incoming information is recorded in real time by an assistant to the MCC. During exercises or real-world operations, a battle commander assumes the highest authority at NEADS, oversees the MCC and the SOCC, and communicates directly with the commander at CONR.

Because an exercise was scheduled for the morning of 9/11, the battle commander, Colonel Robert Marr, was present.

CONR is responsible for coordinating the sector commands and the air defense for the continental United States. The CONR commander is the highest-ranking military authority at CONR, and reports to NORAD. On 9/11, the operations center at CONR was called the Regional Air Operations Center (RAOC). The highest authority at CONR is the CONR battle commander (CONR BC). On 9/11, the RAOC floor, unlike sector operations centers, did not utilize radarscopes or any direct-feed radar data from the FAA or NORAD radar sites. Instead, it used computer terminals, and communicated with the sectors by both secure and unsecure phone lines and the chat log.

NORAD headquarters (HQ) exercises command authority over NEADS via CONR. NORAD HQ operations were then run from the Cheyenne Mountain Operations Center (CMOC), located in Cheyenne Mountain, Colorado. NORAD's command director runs the CMOC and is responsible for deciding the appropriate level of response from NORAD assets, and for communicating with the National Military Command Center (NMCC), which is located at the Pentagon. CMOC did not possess direct radar picture feeds from either FAA or NORAD radar facilities.

At NEADS, the report that American Airlines Flight 11 was hijacked was relayed immediately to Battle Commander Colonel Robert Marr, who was stationed in the glassed-in "battle cab," located behind the operations floor, in preparation for the scheduled exercise. He communicated with the MCC position via headphones. Marr asked the same question—confirming that the hijacking was "real-world"—then ordered fighter pilots at Otis Air Force Base in Massachusetts to battle stations. The time was 8:41.

Aboard American 11, Betty Ong and Amy Sweeney continued to report to their airline on the status of the flight. Sweeney told American officials that the hijackers were Middle Eastern men seated in the front of the plane; that one spoke excellent English and one spoke very little English; and that she did not know how they gained entry to the cockpit. She advised that the plane was in a rapid descent. At 8:44, Ong's telephone connection was lost. Sweeney reported: "Something is wrong. We are in a rapid descent . . . we are all over the place." American Airlines officials asked her to look out the window to see if she could tell where they were. She said, "We are flying low. We are flying very, very low. We are flying way too low. Oh my God we are way too low." Then they lost the connection.

At the FAA, control of American 11 had been passed to New York Center at 8:41. Air traffic controller Dave Bottiglia received the handoff of the primary radar signal, moments after also receiving the handoff of another flight, United 175. When United 175 entered his airspace, Bottiglia recalled, "The first thing [the pilot] said to me was, 'We heard threatening communication being broadcast by the American.'" Specifically, the United 175 pilot stated: "We figured we'd wait till we got to you, Center, ah, we heard a suspicious transmission on our departure out of Boston, ah, with someone, ah, sound like someone, sound like someone keyed the mike and, ah, said, ah, Everyone, ah, stay in your seats." Bottiglia said he would pass the information on.

The pilot of United 175 told Bottiglia that he had heard someone say, "Everyone stay in your seats." He told Bottiglia that he had waited until he was in New York Center's airspace to relay the information because he did not want the hijackers to overhear him. United Airlines allowed, and still allows, passengers to listen to air traffic control transmissions on Channel 9; had any of the hijackers aboard United 175 been listening, they would have overheard their plane's pilot discussing the hijacking of American 11. Almost immediately after this transmission, the United 175 hijackers stormed the cockpit.

The report from United 175 heightened the controllers' concern about American 11. The controller next to Bottiglia "walks over to me and he says, 'You see this target here?' He says, 'This is American 11. Boston Center thinks it's a hijack.'" Bottiglia tracked the primary radar, knowing that "he was descending at a rapid pace, but we had no altitude or anything on him." Bottiglia followed the track of American 11 as it disappeared from his screen over Lower Manhattan.

Military air traffic controllers at NEADS were not as fortunate as the FAA in locating the flight. They searched frantically for it in a sea of primary radar tracks:

> **NEADS:**
>
> Yeah, Huntress [NEADS]. Just calling you back real quick. Just—did you guys have a mode three [a transponder beacon code] at all on—
>
> **BOSTON CENTER:**
>
> 8:41:50   Oh—
>
> **NEADS:**
>
> —American 11?
>
> **BOSTON CENTER:**
>
> 8:41:51   —last—last altitude we saw him, he's—was descending to point 0290.
>
> **NEADS:**
>
> 8:41:56   Did you have a—I'm sorry, a prior mode three for American 11?
>
> [OVERTALK]
>
> **NEADS:**
>
> 8:42:02   —a mode three—file anything? Any information for mode three? 'Cause we locate him on the scope if so.
>
> **BOSTON CENTER:**
>
> 8:42:09   Well—
>
> **NEADS:**
>
> Boston to Los—that was—
>
> **BOSTON CENTER:**
>
> 8:42:12   —la—last known altitude was flight level 290. Before that he was requesting—hold on—it looks like he was requesting level 350.

NEADS:

8:42:19   Okay, all we're asking is your mode three.

BOSTON CENTER:

8:42:22   What?

NEADS:

8:42:23   Your mode three. Did you assign any mode three to that aircraft?

BOSTON CENTER:

8:42:28   It—original—original was—

NEADS:

8:42:30   —that would be [UNINTELLIGIBLE] 350, but last known was 290—

BOSTON CENTER:

8:42:34   —hold on—we're—working with the—

NEADS:

8:42:37   —returning from the mode three—

BOSTON CENTER:

8:42:41   We still should be able to get it without 53.

NEADS:

8:42:43   We have to file with—we have to file—

[OVERTALK]

BOSTON CENTER:

8:42:48   I—we don't have any mode three right now—

NEADS:

8:42:49   Nothing you guys—

BOSTON CENTER:

8:42:50   —the primary target only. I don't even know what his original— I could try and find his original mode three.

NEADS:

8:42:55 —yeah, that's all we need.

BOSTON CENTER:

8:42:56 Hold on.

NEADS:

8:43:00 We don't know yet— They don't know. They don't have a mode three.

8:43:04 He's gonna try to give us [UNINTELLIGIBLE] with a mode three, though?

NEADS:

8:43:07 —American 11. Yeah.

NEADS:

8:43:11 He—he's having a rough time talking to—because they are making threats in the cockpit—

[OVERTALK]

NEADS:

8:43:17 You know what? I have [UNINTELLIGIBLE]. So ask him if—he's got anybody in the air, like near the aircraft [UNINTELLIGIBLE] aircraft there—

NEADS:

8:43:24 Okay. . . .

BOSTON CENTER:

8:43:40 Hello?

NEADS:

Yes, go ahead.

BOSTON CENTER:

8:43:41 His original code was 1443.

NEADS:

8:43:43 Fourteen forty-three. Copy that. Thank you, sir.

BOSTON CENTER:

8:43:45   Okay.

NEADS:

8:43:46   And we're—one more question.

BOSTON CENTER:

8:43:47   Yup?

NEADS:

Any aircraft close by him that—you can get the—a mode three? . . .

BOSTON CENTER:

8:43:55   I think we're working on that. I—I—I don't have anybody next to him right now. But—

8:44:02   —his speed is slowing down now. He's turning southwest now. So we don't have anybody close to him.

NEADS:

8:44:07   Yup. Okay, thank you, sir.

BOSTON CENTER:

8:44:08   Okay.

NEADS:

8:44:12   None.

8:44:13   —we're coming up on a one four—

[OVERTALK]

8:44:16   —1443—

NEADS FEMALE VOICE:

8:44:18   —the scope up there is approximately—

NEADS MALE VOICE:

8:44:21   —last known position?

NEADS FEMALE VOICE:

8:44:22 He said nobody—should have surveillance hit up everybody in that area and bring up—it looks like they are, though—

NEADS MALE VOICE:

8:44:34 You know what? Just starting hitting up tracks.

The Mission Crew Commander explained to Colonel Marr:

> Okay, what—what we're doing, we're tryin' to locate this guy. We can't find him. . . . What we're gonna do, we're gonna hit up every track within a 25-mile radius of this—the Z point that we put on the scope. Twenty-nine thousand heading 1-9-0. We're just gonna do—we're gonna try to find this guy. They can't find him [UNINTELLIGIBLE] there's been—supposedly there's threats in the cockpit. So, we're just—we're doing the thing.

On the basis of the information that the flight was heading toward Kennedy Airport, NEADS identification technicians called New York Center to try to coordinate:

NEADS FEMALE VOICE:

8:44:50 —who's talking to New York, giving them a heads-up? Anybody called New York, given them a heads-up? . . .

NEADS FEMALE VOICE:

8:45:02 It's around there, Steve. New York, Huntress ID. New York . . . are you aware of the—possible hijack of American 11?

NEW YORK CENTER:

8:45:14 No, I'm not—

NEADS:

8:45:15 —Boston center, ma'am, we just got information there is a real-world hijack, American 11. He is headed—he was 40 miles north of JFK headed towards JFK . . .

8:45:27 We're trying to find out any information that we possibly can.

Apparently the pilot was having a rough time, because there have been threats on the cockpit. . . .

8:45:46 And we're trying to locate any information as far as the location where he is currently on mode three. Do you have any information whatsoever?

NEW YORK CENTER:

8:45:54 I—do not. Hold on one second.

NEADS FEMALE VOICE:

8:46:00 Keep trying to [UNINTELLIGIBLE] locate that—mode three.

NEADS MALE VOICE:

8:46:03 We got nothing. Try it again—1443, [UNINTELLIGIBLE] three—not—

[OVERTALK]

NEADS FEMALE VOICE:

8:46:14 Yes. New York, [UNINTELLIGIBLE] hold on. You—you heard that, right?

NEADS FEMALE VOICE:

8:46:20 Yup.

NEADS FEMALE VOICE:

—you—you—you—

NEADS FEMALE VOICE:

8:46:23 —man—

NEADS FEMALE VOICE:

8:46:34 —come on, New York—

NEADS FEMALE VOICE:

8:46:37 Airborne—

NEADS FEMALE VOICE:

8:46:38 Hey, you know what—

NEADS MALE VOICE:

8:46:39 —we're gonna—

NEADS FEMALE VOICE:

8:46:40 —you know what?

NEADS MALE VOICE:

—crash—

NEADS FEMALE VOICE:

8:46:41 Let's get a tail number off of it for American 11.

NEADS FEMALE VOICE:

8:46:45 —call Boston, American 11 tail number—

NEADS FEMALE VOICE:

8:46:47 Tell him we need the tail number of the aircraft. . . .

NEW YORK CENTER:

8:46:52 Right now he's primary only.

NEADS:

8:46:55 Do you have no mode three or anything? Or a location—

NEW YORK CENTER:

8:46:59 I'm not showing anything. No.

[UNHEARD QUESTION]

8:47:01 Do you have a—

[OVERTALK]

NEW YORK CENTER:

8:47:02 Hold on. I can get a—a lat-long [i.e., a position fix in *lati*tude and *long*itude]. Hold on a second.

NEADS:

8:47:05 All right, that's good. We're gonna get an updated lat-long now. . . .

NEADS FEMALE VOICE:

8:47:12   We called Boston. His filed one was four—1443. But he's not—

8:47:17   —he's not working that. . . .

8:47:19   He's on primary only. We're getting an updated lat-long position. And I'm going—

[OVERTALK]

NEW YORK CENTER:

8:47:22   —okay, I'm showing—4039 north.

NEADS:

8:47:26   Forty thirty-nine north.

NEW YORK CENTER:

8:47:27   And 7403 west.

NEADS:

8:47:29   Seventy-four oh three west . . .

While the Identification Technicians were trying to learn the plane's location, and the Weapons and Surveillance desks were searching for the primary track on radarscopes, Colonel Marr was consulting with Major General Larry Arnold, the commanding general of the First Air Force and CONR. Marr advised him of the situation and sought authorization to scramble the Otis fighters in response to the reported hijacking.

Major General Arnold instructed Colonel Marr to "go ahead and scramble the airplanes and [we'll] seek the authorities later," as he told the 9/11 Commission. "And the reason for that is that the procedure . . . if you follow the book, is they [law enforcement officials] go to the duty officer of the national military center, who in turn makes an inquiry to NORAD for the availability of fighters, who then gets permission from someone representing the Secretary of Defense. Once that is approved then we scramble an aircraft. We didn't wait for that." General Arnold then picked up the phone and talked to the operations deputy up at NORAD and said, "'Yeah, we'll work with the National Military Command Center [NMCC]. Go ahead and scramble the aircraft.'"

The scramble order was passed from Battle Commander Colonel Marr to Mission Crew Commander Major Nasypany, who passed the order to Weapons director Major James Fox. Almost immediately, however, a problem arose. Fox asked: "MCC, I don't know where I'm scrambling these guys to. I need a direction, a destination." As the scramble order was passed, NEADS personnel continued to try to find the plane:

NEADS MALE VOICE:

8:47:57 —four six scramble? [This reflects the time of the scramble, 8:46, which was to be memorialized in NEADS and NORAD logs.]

NEADS FEMALE VOICE:

8:47:58 Four six scramble? . . .

NEADS FEMALE VOICE:

8:48:17 Let's bring it up and find a—

NEADS MALE VOICE:

8:48:19 Yeah—

NEADS FEMALE VOICE:

—a primary.

NEADS MALE VOICE:

All right.

[OVERTALK]

NEADS MALE VOICE:

8:48:22 While we're looking to see for a search target, after all they have is primary. I don't see . . .

NEADS FEMALE VOICE:

8:48:34 Tell him—hey, call—call her back and tell her that we want—

NEADS MALE VOICE:

8:48:40 —five miles—

NEADS FEMALE VOICE:

—if it's possible if she's not too busy, that we need—updates every—

NEADS FEMALE VOICE:

8:48:46 —New York—

NEADS FEMALE VOICE:

8:48:47 —three to five minutes—

NEADS MALE VOICE:

8:48:48 Yeah—

NEADS FEMALE VOICE:

8:48:49 We need lat-long updates. . . .

NEADS:

8:48:53 Is there any way, ma'am, that we can [get] updates as far as the—lat-longs of that aircraft? You know, as often—

[OVERTALK]

NEW YORK CENTER:

8:48:58 Actually, I'm showing it's tracking coast right now. So I—

NEADS:

8:49:02 Tracking coast, [NOISE] what does that mean? Is he northbound?

NEW YORK CENTER:

8:49:03 It—it means we—I—as far as what I'm showin' here, they've lost track on it. Let me see if I can find out, and I'll—

NEADS:

8:49:10 Yeah.

"Tracking coast," in FAA parlance, meant that the track appearing on the FAA's radarscopes did not correspond to a real-world primary radar return. It was, instead, a computer projection of where the plane would be if it were continuing in the same direction it was heading when it was lost on radar. It meant, in other words, that the FAA had now lost even the primary radar track.

The military, however, had by 2001 evolved its own air traffic terminology and procedures. Even its radarscopes were configured differently from the scopes used by FAA controllers, which made coordination a challenge. When the FAA reported that the plane was "tracking coast," military controllers started looking along the East Coast for the plane. Communication difficulties mounted as the NEADS air defenders searched for the plane; the military air defenders were still trying to learn the meaning of the term "tracking coast" when news reached the floor that a plane had crashed into the World Trade Center.

NEW YORK CENTER MILITARY LIAISON:

8:49:10 Yes, hi. Good morning. This is New York military calling at New York center.

NEADS:

8:49:14 Yeah, how you doin'?

NEW YORK CENTER:

Good, good. Our—watch supervisor needs a number for a possible hijacking. He wants to call somebody in case they need some assistance with the [UNINTELLIGIBLE] fighter jets.

NEADS:

8:49:24 All righty. Our phone number is gonna be—DSN or commercial?

NEW YORK MILITARY MALE VOICE:

8:49:28 It would be commercial out there. . . .

NEADS FEMALE VOICE:

8:50:24   They—they showed him heading—what did—she showing? [NOISE] North—

NEADS MALE VOICE:

8:50:27   —American Airlines—

NEADS FEMALE VOICE:

8:50:28   —coastal. I didn't know what that meant. [NOISE]

8:50:29   You—you said that they—he—they showed him heading coastal now. [NOISE] . . .

8:50:35   We—we ask that you explain that . . .

NEADS FEMALE VOICE:

8:51:11   A plane just hit the World Trade Center?

NEADS FEMALE VOICE:

8:51:13   What?

NEADS FEMALE VOICE:

   No, sir—

NEADS FEMALE VOICE:

8:51:16   —was a 737?

NEADS MALE VOICE:

8:51:18   Hit what?

NEADS FEMALE VOICE:

   Like the World Trade Center—

NEADS FEMALE VOICE:

8:51:19   Who are you talking to?

NEADS FEMALE VOICE:

8:51:21   Oh!

NEADS FEMALE VOICE:

8:51:23   Get patched—patch it to them—

[OVERTALK]

NEADS MALE VOICE:

8:51:29 —one one—

NEADS FEMALE VOICE:

8:51:31 Oh my God.

NEADS MALE VOICE:

8:51:32 Three one one.

NEADS FEMALE VOICE:

8:51:34 Oh God.

NEADS FEMALE VOICE:

8:51:37 —three one one—

NEADS FEMALE VOICE:

8:51:39 Oh my God.

NEADS FEMALE VOICE:

8:51:42 —saw it on the news. It's— [UNINTELLIGIBLE] plane just crashed into the World Trade Center.

NEADS FEMALE VOICE:

8:51:49 —New York—

NEADS FEMALE VOICE:

8:51:52 New York [UNINTELLIGIBLE] center [UNINTELLIGIBLE]?

NEADS FEMALE VOICE:

8:51:55 See if they lost altitude on that plane altogether.

NEW YORK CENTER:

8:51:58 New York.

NEADS:

Yes, ma'am. Did you just hear the information regarding the World Trade Center?

NEW YORK CENTER:

8:52:01 No.

NEADS:

8:52:02 Being hit by an aircraft?

NEW YORK CENTER:

8:52:03 I'm sorry?

NEADS:

8:52:04 Being hit by an aircraft.

NEW YORK CENTER:

8:52:06 You're kidding.

NEADS:

It's on the world news.

NEADS FEMALE VOICE:

8:52:07 Ask 'em if he—they still have altitude—

NEADS:

8:52:09 Do you still have altitude on that aircraft that you have—

[OVERTALK]

NEW YORK:

8:52:11 No, like I—like I—I said I'm—I don't work a radar here.

NEADS:

8:52:14 Yeah, you lost—

NEW YORK CENTER:

8:52:15 Who—

NEADS:

—you said you lost contact, though?

NEADS FEMALE VOICE:

8:52:17 —call this number again. Call this number right here again—

NEADS FEMALE VOICE:

8:52:19 No, it won't go through.

NEADS FEMALE VOICE:

8:52:20 Tell her that we can't get—

[OVERTALK]

NEADS:

8:52:22 —one, ma'am, four six eight—

NEW YORK CENTER:

8:52:24 —five nine five nine?

NEADS:

8:52:25 —we cannot get through to that number. Is there any other number? Is that—New York Military?

NEW YORK CENTER:

8:52:30 No, it's not. That's the only number I have for operations there.

NEADS:

8:52:34 Okay, well, just wanna give you a heads-up that—there is an aircraft that did hit the World Trade Center just a few minutes ago. But that, incidentally, is that—not—not that guy—

NEW YORK CENTER:

8:52:42 —not that guy? . . .

NEADS:

8:52:47 We're just trying to find out what we can, ma'am. We're trying to sort it out.

NEW YORK CENTER:

8:52:49 Yes—

NEADS:

But that phone number that you—

NEW YORK CENTER:

8:52:50 —we—

NEADS:

—gave us, I can't—

NEW YORK CENTER:

8:52:51 —he doesn't have—

NEADS:

—reach anybody.

8:52:52 —we need to find out who's tracking this guy on his scope . . .
in New York center and get . . . and see if he still has an altitude. If he doesn't have an altitude—

The NEADS ID technicians ultimately reached an air traffic controller
at New York Center.

NEW YORK CENTER MALE VOICE:

8:53:02 Hello.

NEADS:

8:53:03 New York center. Huntress ID—
8:53:06 —is anyone tracking the hijacked American 11?

NEW YORK CENTER MALE VOICE:

8:53:09 I'm sorry. Start over again. What about American 11?

NEADS:

8:53:12 The hijacked aircraft, American 11, is anyone tracking from
New York center, that aircraft?

NEW YORK CENTER MALE VOICE:

8:53:17 We had a primary target on him. We are trying to follow him as best we can. He is not squawking a beacon code whatsoever—

[OVERTALK]

NEADS FEMALE VOICE:

8:53:24 —primary—And he's still tracking primary?

NEW YORK CENTER MALE VOICE:

8:53:28 No, I do not see a primary target at this moment.

NEADS:

8:53:31 There—

NEW YORK CENTER MALE VOICE:

However, he's not in my airspace. So—

NEADS:

8:53:32 Okay, I just wanted to give you a heads-up, New York. I don't know if you know, but the World Trade Center's just been hit by a—

NEADS FEMALE VOICE:

8:53:36 He has primary on this guy—

NEADS:

8:53:38 —real world—

NEW YORK CENTER MALE VOICE:

8:53:40 You have—you that confirmed?

NEADS:

8:53:41 That is on the news, sir, right now.

NEW YORK CENTER MALE VOICE:

8:53:43 Hmmm. Okay.

NEADS:

8:53:46 We have no confirmation—that's on the news—

NEADS MALE VOICE:

8:53:49 —the World Trade Center—

NEW YORK CENTER MALE VOICE:

8:53:50 I'm sorry, there's too much—there's too many p—people talking at once.

[UNHEARD QUESTION]

8:53:53 Yeah, I hear that, too. Thank you. If there's any [UNINTELLIGIBLE] we'll give you a call.

NEW YORK CENTER MALE VOICE:

8:53:56 Okay, thank you.

[UNHEARD QUESTION]

8:53:57 Sure.

AMERICAN AIRLINES FLIGHT 11 had disappeared from air traffic controller Bottiglia's scope at 8:46, as it crashed into the North Tower of the World Trade Center at 8:46:40 a.m. At almost precisely the same moment, unaware of the location of American 11, NEADS commanders issued the scramble order to the F-15s at Otis Air Force Base. Although it would not be noticed for several minutes, virtually simultaneously with the crash of American 11 into the North Tower, United Flight 175's assigned transponder code switched from 1479 to 3020, and then switched again to 3321.

That flight too, officials would discover, was under attack. Moments before the transponder code shift, the pilot of United 175 had radioed New York Center with the information about American 11: "We figured we'd wait till we got to you, Center, ah, we heard a suspicious transmission on our departure out of Boston, ah, with someone, ah, sound like someone, sound like someone keyed the mike and, ah, said, ah, Everyone, ah, stay in your seats." Had the hijackers aboard United 175 been listening to Channel 9, as United allows to this day, they would have learned that the first attack of the morning had occurred.

The interplay of the FAA and NEADS regarding American Airlines Flight 11 prefigured, in many respects, their interactions throughout the critical morning hours of 9/11. First, and most important, both entities immediately disregarded the established protocols for reporting and requesting assistance for a hijack event. Rather than reporting the hijack up through the FAA Herndon Air Traffic Services Command Center and FAA Washington Headquarters so that it could request assistance through the National Military Command Center and the secretary of defense, Boston Center elected to request assistance directly from the Northeast Air Defense Sector. When the request reached NEADS, moreover, the battle commander and the CONR commander, rather than seeking authorization to scramble aircraft through the chain of command and, ultimately, from the secretary of defense, chose to authorize the action on their own and, as General Arnold put it, "seek the authorities later."

It is impossible to fault either decision. Given the emergent nature of the situation, the reports of "trouble in the cockpit," and the fact that there was no easily identified transponder signal emitted from the aircraft, the necessity to shortcut the hijack protocols is apparent. It is clear, moreover, that the protocols themselves were ill-suited to the American 11 event; the multilayered notification and approval process assumed a "classic" hijack scenario in which there is ample time for notice to occur, there is no difficulty in locating the aircraft, the hijackers intend to land the aircraft somewhere, and the military's role is limited to identification and escort of the aircraft.

Bypassing the established protocols for air emergencies, however justified in the case of American 11, may have had an unintended consequence as the day wore on; leadership at the national levels at the FAA and DoD were not involved—or were involved only after the fact—in the critical decision making and the evolving awareness of American 11's situation. They would remain largely irrelevant to the critical decision-making and unaware of the evolving situation "on the ground" until the attacks were completed.

The critical information NEADS received would continue to come from Boston Center, which relayed information as it was overheard on FAA teleconferences. Indeed, at one point that morning the mission crew commander, in the absence of regular communication from anyone else at FAA, encouraged the Military position at Boston Center to continue to provide information: "If you get anything, if you—any of your controllers see anything that looks kind of squirrelly, just give us a yell. We'll get those fighters in that location." Frustrated by the lack of information from Washington Center, the NEADS ID technicians would complain repeatedly that morning that "Washington has no clue what the hell is going on. . . . Washington has no clue." The Boston Military FAA representative, when interviewed, expressed astonishment that he had been the principal source of information for NEADS personnel on the morning of 9/11; he had believed, he said, that he must have been one of several FAA sources constantly updating NEADS that morning. No open line was established between NEADS and CONR and either FAA Headquarters or the Command Center at Herndon until the attacks were virtually over.

It is clear that, as the order to scramble came at 8:46 a.m., just as American 11 was hitting the World Trade Center, the military had insufficient notice of the hijacking to position its assets to respond. This reality would also be repeated throughout the morning. Indeed, the eight minutes' notice that NEADS had of American 11 would prove to be the most notice the sector would receive that morning of any of the hijackings, and the sector's inability to locate the primary radar track until the last few readings would also recur.

The two F-15 fighter jets ordered scrambled at 8:46 were airborne at 8:52. At the FAA's New York Center, Controller Dave Bottiglia, who had been concentrating on searching for American 11 since it disappeared from primary radar at 8:46, noticed that the plane he believed was United 175, which was also on his scope, was using the wrong transponder code. He asked United 175 to "recycle" its transponder code to the correct number. There was no response. He noticed that the plane was deviating from its flight path, and tried five times between 8:52 and 8:55 to communicate with the pilots of United 175 but received no response. He handed off the other flights on his scope to other controllers, saying, "I've got some handoffs for you. We got some incidents going over here." Bottiglia watched as the aircraft he thought was United 175 moved southwest and continued off course.

Just as Controller Bottiglia noticed the transponder change and tried to contact United 175, passenger Peter Burton Hanson called his father, Lee Hanson, and told him the plane had been hijacked. "I think they've taken over the cockpit—an attendant has been stabbed—and someone else up front may have been killed. The plane is making strange moves. Call United Airlines—tell them it's Flight 175, Boston to L.A."

A male flight attendant aboard United 175 called Marc Policastro, a United Airlines employee in San Francisco, also at 8:52. He told Policastro that the plane had been hijacked, that both pilots had been murdered, that a flight attendant had been stabbed, and that he believed the hijackers were flying the plane.

On the floor at NEADS, the mission crew commander coordinated the direction in which the fighters would be scrambled with Major James Fox, the Weapons commander, and Colonel Marr.

MAJOR NASYPANY (TO COLONEL MARR):

8:53:11   This is what I got. [UNINTELLIGIBLE PHRASE] possible news a 737 just hit the World Trade Center. This is a real-world.

8:53:18   And we're trying to confirm this.

MAJOR NASYPANY (TO MAJOR FOX):

8:53:21   Okay. Continue taking the fighters down to the New York City area, JFK area, that's if you can. Make sure that the FAA clears it—your route all the way through. Do what we got to do, okay? Let's press with this. It looks like—it looks like this guy could have hit the World Trade Center. . . .

8:53:42   We want to get him heading in that direction. Help us out. All right, thanks. . . .

MAJOR FOX:

8:53:50   Until we're confirmed, it's gonna be a lot easier for me to get down to this area if I bring 'em out like this [over the ocean] rather than through all this crap that . . .

8:53:57   Until that's confirmed do you want me to bring 'em down this way—

MAJOR NASYPANY:

8:54:00   Work with FAA. Just tell 'em to clear you a route. Clear you a route.

MAJOR FOX:

8:54:04   Yes, sir.

NEADS MALE VOICE:

8:54:05   Weapons, sorry, 5-2 airborne? [confirming the time for purposes of record-keeping]

8:54:06   5-2 airborne. . . .

8:54:28   MCC, he just crashed into the World Trade Center.

NEADS MALE VOICE:

8:54:33   That was the last call.

MAJOR NASYPANY:

8:54:36   Right there?

MAJOR FOX:

8:54:46   All right, our last actual report [UNINTELLIGIBLE] if he didn't crash into the World Trade Center, it's 20 miles south of JFK.

MAJOR NASYPANY:

8:54:53   So, I want you to take him down into this area [military airspace over the ocean]. Put them in—hold as needed. Whatever altitude they need to go for Center to make that work is fine with me. But—that's the area I want 'em to go and hold. Right in that little gap there.

8:55:08 That last Z point, making sure FAA clears out a route.

MAJOR FOX:

8:55:11 All right, this is what we're doin'. Takin' 'em down in this area. Then hold for now. Whatever altitude Center needs for them to do that is fine. But—

MAJOR NASYPANY (TO MARR):

8:55:21 So you want me—to have Center have 'em hold?

MAJOR NASYPANY:

8:55:25 Their Weapons teams should have them. The fighters should be talkin' to Center. They're gonna pass that through the fighters exactly what we want them to do. Now—okay, now—

MAJOR NASYPANY:

8:55:34 Foxy?

MAJOR FOX:

8:55:35 Yeah . . .

MAJOR NASYPANY:

Okay. [UNINTELLIGIBLE] If you can, hand the fighters over directly to FAA so they—

MAJOR FOX:

They're still under FAA control. We're never gonna take 'em.

MAJOR NASYPANY

Just take 'em all the way. Work with 'em, coordinate with them just best that you can with that. Take 'em to the area and let them handle that airspace.

8:56:05 Okay, another heads-up . . .

8:56:48   So, w—what did they say about the aircraft that hit the building? The World Trade Center? . . .

8:57:00   Okay, Boston just talked to us. Just called up on—and they said, he doesn't want to confirm this or not, but they're pretty sure that that is—that was an aircraft. . . .

8:57:11   Unconfirmed from Boston, yeah. They're pretty doggone sure it is him. Yup.

MISSION CREW COMMANDER NASYPANY'S initial instinct, to vector the fighters right toward New York's JFK International Airport, was complicated by the volume of air traffic along the eastern seaboard that morning. Weapons Director Fox pointed out that, given the difficulties associated with navigating through the heavy traffic, it would be quicker to send the fighters out over the ocean toward airspace reserved for military use in the Atlantic Ocean and have them hold there until the situation could be clarified and a target could be identified. At this point, given the distinct possibility that the hijackers of American 11 had flown the plane into the World Trade Center, the absurdity of conducting a Cold War–era exercise involving hypothetical Russian bombers flying over the Pole hit home with Major Nasypany. He commented to Colonel Marr: "Think we put the exercise on hold. What do you think? [LAUGHTER]"

At 8:57, United 175 turned to the northeast and leveled off at 28,500 feet. One minute later, it turned toward New York City. Seeing the turn, Bottiglia told another controller, "We may have another hijack over here, two of them." Controllers followed United 175 as it headed at over 600 miles per hour from the skies over Allentown, Pennsylvania, into western New Jersey airspace. They realized it was heading straight toward Delta Airlines Flight 2315 en route to Tampa, Florida, from Connecticut. Normal controller calm was replaced with urgency, as the controllers warned the Delta pilot: "Traffic, 2:00. Ten miles. I think he's been hijacked. I don't know his intentions. Take any evasive action necessary."

Aboard United 175, the situation was becoming desperate. At

9:00, Peter Hanson called his father: "It's getting bad, Dad—A stewardess was stabbed—They seem to have knives and mace—They said they have a bomb—It's getting very bad on the plane—Passengers are throwing up and getting sick—The plane is making jerky movements—I don't think the pilot is flying the plane—I think we are going down—I think they intend to go to Chicago or someplace and fly into a building."

The flight continued to bore in on New York City. A minute later, a manager from New York Center, on the phone with the Command Center in Herndon, stated:

> We have several situations going on here. It's escalating big, big time. We need to get the military involved with us. . . . We're we're involved with something else, we have other aircraft that may have a similar situation going on here.

No call to the military resulted from this exchange.

At 9:01, New York Center called New York Terminal Approach and asked for its assistance in tracking the flight they believed was United 175. At 9:02, New York Terminal Approach located the unidentified plane descending rapidly into New York City and told New York Center:

> TERMINAL: Got him just out of 9,500–9,000 now.
>
> CENTER: Do you know who he is?
>
> TERMINAL: We're just, we just don't know who he is. We're just picking him up now.
>
> CENTER: Alright. Heads-up, man, it looks like another one coming in.

At 9:03 a.m., in Boston Center, Manager Terry Biggio announced to an FAA regional representative that Boston Center had deciphered the tape of the initial transmission from American 11.

BOSTON CENTER: Hey . . . you still there?

NEW ENGLAND REGION: Yes, I am.

BOSTON CENTER: . . . as far as the tape, Bobby seemed to think the guy said that 'we have planes.' Now, I don't know if it was because it was the accent, or if there's more than one, but I'm gonna, I'm gonna reconfirm that for you, and I'll get back to you real quick. Okay?

NEW ENGLAND REGION: Appreciate it.

FEMALE VOICE: They have what?

BOSTON CENTER: Planes, as in plural.
BOSTON CENTER: It sounds like—we're talking to New York—that there's another one aimed at the World Trade Center.

NEW ENGLAND REGION: There's another aircraft?

BOSTON CENTER: A second one just hit the Trade Center.

NEW ENGLAND REGION: Okay, yeah, we gotta get—we gotta alert the military quick on this.

Even as Boston Center and the New England Region discussed the situation, New York Center informed NEADS that there was a second hijacked aircraft.

NEADS FEMALE VOICE:

9:03:17   They have a second possible hijack . . .

9:04:11   Oh God.

9:04:12   I know. . . .

9:04:21   United 175?

9:04:26   —one seven five—

9:04:27   —twenty-one—

9:04:29   What is it? [NOISE]

9:04:32   United 175 is the other aircraft . . .

9:04:37   Mode three, 3321.

NEADS MALE VOICE:

9:04:39   Three-three-two-one?

NEADS FEMALE VOICE:

9:04:41   —two-one . . .

9:04:50   Oh my God. They say it's pretty serious. Stacia [Rountree, an ID tech], what were you talking to?

9:04:59   I was talking to New York—[NOISE]

9:05:08   —is 175—[NOISE]

9:05:12   —who—who's that from?

BOSTON CENTER:

9:05:13   Scoggins. Boston's Center TMU Military.

NEADS:

9:05:15   Boston, Huntress ID calling you back. Do you have any information on a United 175 aircraft at all?

BOSTON CENTER:

9:05:20   Stand by. Is that the call sign you have?

NEADS:

9:05:22   We have a United 175, possibly a hijack—

BOSTON CENTER:

9:05:25   United—

NEADS:

9:05:26   —also.

BOSTON CENTER:

—United 175?

NEADS:

9:05:27   Yes. So we need—

BOSTON CENTER:

Hold—[UNINTELLIGIBLE PHRASE] you wanna check anything on that if you can . . .

9:05:32   What was your request on that?

NEADS:

9:05:34   Request for United 175, possible hijacked aircraft also. We're looking for—we have a mode three of 3321. We're looking for—

BOSTON CENTER:

9:05:41   Three-three—

NEADS:

—any information—any information regarding a tail number or anything that you have. Do you have any information on that?

BOSTON CENTER:

9:05:47   Okay, I will check on that. Mode three, 3321, United 175. Do you know its departure point or destination by any chance? We're looking into it now.

NEADS:

9:05:55   Negative. We just found out from New York Center, possible crash also—

BOSTON CENTER:

9:05:59   Okay.

NEADS:

—you heard about the first?

BOSTON CENTER:

9:06:00   Yes.

NEADS:

9:06:01 Okay. Possibly a second—

BOSTON CENTER:

9:06:02 We're checking on that—

NEADS:

9:06:03 —hijack—

BOSTON CENTER:

9:06:04 —flight plan now if you wanna hold on one second.

NEADS:

9:06:05 Thank you.

Lee Hanson got off the phone with his son at 9:03. He turned on his television as United 175 banked over Lower Manhattan and slammed into the South Tower. The time was 9:03:11. America was under attack.

MINUTES

9:03–9:37 A.M.

An hour after the first flight, American 11, took off from Logan Airport, the "planes conspiracy" that had been hatched years before in the remote mountain wilderness of Afghanistan was halfway to triumphant completion. American 11 had crashed at 8:46 into the upper floors of the World Trade Center's North Tower, blowing through floors 93 to 99. All three of the building's stairwells became impassable from the ninety-second floor up. Hundreds were killed instantly by the impact; hundreds remained alive but trapped above the crash site. By 8:57, the New York Fire Department chiefs on site had instructed the Port Authority of New York and New Jersey Police and the Trade Center building personnel to evacuate both towers because of the extent of the damage to the North Tower. At 9:02, a minute before United 175 hit the South Tower, an announcement over the public-address system in that building advised that an orderly evacuation could begin, if conditions warranted.

United 175 hit the South Tower from the south, banking into the seventy-seventh through eighty-fifth floors, killing everyone on board and hundreds of people on those floors, but leaving one of its three stairwells passable, at least initially, from the ninety-first floor down. As *The 9/11 Commission Report* stated, "What had been the largest and most complicated rescue operation in [New York] city history instantly doubled in magnitude."

The second crash resonated far beyond New York City. Seen live on television by millions, the deliberate banking and acceleration of United 175 into the South Tower was unmistakably malevolent; the country was, without question, under attack. The explosion blew out the back of the Tower in a mammoth orange-and-black fireball. People could no longer calibrate their day in hours; now, for millions, the day was counted off in minutes. For the first time, national leadership was engaged from the top down.

President Bush, in Sarasota, Florida, for a reading event at Booker Elementary School, had been informed before his 9:00 a.m. event by senior advisor Karl Rove and chief of staff Andrew Card that "a small, twin-engine plane had crashed into the World Trade Center. The president's reaction was that the incident must have been caused by pilot error." He spoke to National Security Advisor Condoleezza Rice in Washington at 8:55; she recalled telling him first that a twin-engine plane had hit the Trade Center, and then, as information developed, that a commercial aircraft had hit the Trade Center. She said, "That's all we know now, Mr. President," as President Bush entered the classroom at 9:00.

Chief of Staff Andrew Card entered the classroom where President Bush was seated at 9:05. He bent to the president's ear and whispered, "A second plane hit the second tower. America is under attack." The president, intending to project an image of calm, remained in the classroom another five to seven minutes, while the children continued reading to him.

At the White House, Vice President Cheney was interrupted during a meeting by an assistant who told him to turn on his television because a plane had struck the World Trade Center. He was wondering, "How the hell could a plane hit the World Trade Center?" when he saw the second plane hit the South Tower. The Secret Service moved immediately to enhance security around the White House.

Donald Rumsfeld, the secretary of defense, had had breakfast that morning with members of Congress. Despite hijacking protocols that called for his notification and approval before scrambling fighter jets, Rumsfeld was not aware of the hijacking of American 11 or of the scrambling of the Otis fighters. An aide interrupted his daily intelligence briefing to inform him of the second plane crashing into the World Trade Center. There is no indication that he asked whether fighters had been deployed; he did not order them deployed himself at that point. He did not seek to contact NORAD or the FAA. He resumed his daily briefing while awaiting further information.

CIA Director George Tenet was having breakfast a few blocks from the White House with former senator David Boren, one of his mentors from his days as a legislative staffer, when he learned of the Trade Center crash. Boren recalled that he was "struck by the fact that [the aide] used the word 'attacked.'" Tenet made several phone calls, then resumed his breakfast. "You know," he said to Boren, "this has bin Laden's fingerprints all over it."

At the FAA's Boston Center and NORAD's Northeast Air Defense Sector, the response to the second crash was immediate. Terry Biggio, the FAA's Boston Center manager, updated the FAA's New England Region, and advised the New England Region that Boston Center was going to stop all aircraft scheduled to depart from any airport within Boston Center. At 9:05 a.m., Boston Center confirmed for both FAA Command Center and New England Region that the hijackers aboard American Flight 11 said, "We have *planes.*" At exactly the same time, New York Center declared "ATC zero." The impact of this declaration was that aircraft were not permitted to depart from, arrive at, or travel through New York Center's airspace until further notice.

Within minutes of the second impact at the WTC, Boston Center's operations manager instructed all air traffic controllers in his center to use their radio frequencies to inform all aircraft in Boston Center of the events unfolding in New York and to advise the aircraft to heighten cockpit security in light of those events.

At approximately 9:15 a.m., another Boston Center manager asked

Command Center to relay the message to all FAA centers in the country to use heightened cockpit security.

> **BOSTON CENTER:** Hi, Boston. Listen, both of these aircraft departed Boston, both were 76's, both heading to L.A., and I'm looking out on the TSD (traffic situation display), and I think that all departures out of Boston should have heightened cockpit security. Is there any way you can ring every center in the country and relay that message, so that they can tell the aircraft, that are out there flying right now, to increase the cockpit security, vigilance on this day?
>
> **COMMAND CENTER:** I'll get the message out.
>
> **BOSTON CENTER:** Thank you very much.

There is no evidence to suggest that Command Center managers acted on Boston's request to issue a nationwide alert to aircraft. One Command Center manager told the 9/11 Commission staff that the FAA would not have relayed this message directly to all pilots. She said the FAA would pass situational awareness to the airline company representatives, who, in turn, would determine if such action was necessary. If necessary, the airlines would pass the warning via ACARS text-messaging to the cockpits of its carriers.

At NEADS, Major Nasypany (the mission crew commander), consulting with Colonel Marr, moved decisively to position the Otis fighters.

> **MAJOR NASYPANY:**
>
> 9:05:14 Boston's is now grounding all—all aircraft out of Boston. FAA—FAA Center . . .
>
> 9:05:19 Okay. New York Center is who you need to get a hold of.
>
> **NEADS MALE VOICE 1:**
>
> 9:05:22 Okay, sir. I'll do that.

9:05:26   [TO FLOOR] I got—Team 2-3 and Team 2-4 airborne. In New York Center airspace. They're northeast of New York right now. Two DC-10s. They got a lotta gas.

MAJOR NASYPANY:

9:05:35   Okay.

9:06:02   Somebody—! . . .

9:06:33   Two planes?

MALE VOICE:

He was in Whiskey 105 [i.e., military airspace]. . . .

MAJOR NASYPANY:

Get the fuck out . . .

MALE VOICE:

9:06:43   United 1-7-5.

9:06:45   [OFF-MIC CONVERSATION]

MALE VOICE:

9:06:50   And American was 1-1?

9:06:52   [OFF-MIC CONVERSATION]

MAJOR NASYPANY:

9:07:20   Okay, Foxy. Plug in. I want to make sure this is on tape.

9:07:33   Okay, Foxy. This is what—this is what I foresee that we probably need to do. We need to talk to FAA. We need to tell 'em if this stuff's gonna keep on going, we need to take those fighters on and then put 'em over Manhattan, okay? That's the best thing. That's the best play right now. So, coordinate with the FAA. Tell 'em if there's more out there, which we don't know, let's get 'em over Manhattan. At least we got some kind of play.

Discussion then ensued about whether and how to deploy NORAD's other East Coast assets, F-16s on alert at Langley Air Force Base in Virginia. The mission crew commander (Major Nasypany) favored sending them directly to New York to support the Otis fighters, but he was over-ruled by Colonel Marr.

NEADS MALE VOICE:

9:08:27   Second suspected aircraft is United 1-7-5. I just—

NEADS MALE VOICE:

9:08:30   Okay, here's a—

9:08:31   [OFF-MIC CONVERSATION]

MAJOR NASYPANY (TO COLONEL MARR):

9:08:33   Okay, we can do that. Okay. [TO THE WEAPONS SECTION] Yeah. Okay, this is what I got goin'. Tell Foxy to scramble Langley, send 'em in same location.

[INAUDIBLE INSTRUCTION FROM COLONEL MARR]

MAJOR NASYPANY:

9:08:43   [TO COLONEL MARR] Bat—battle—battle stations or scramble? [TO WEAPONS] Battle stations only at Langley.

9:08:49   Okay, this is—who's up there?

MALE VOICE [BACKGROUND]:

9:08:50   Battle stations only at Langley?

MAJOR NASYPANY:

9:08:51   Okay, you're listening? What I told the SD so far, we need to get those fighters scram—over Manhattan because we don't know how many guys are out of Boston wanting [or waiting] to do the same thing again.

9:09:01   Could be just these two—could be more.

9:09:03   [INAUDIBLE REPLY FROM COLONEL MARR]

MAJOR NASYPANY:

9:09:04   I don't know.

9:09:05   [INAUDIBLE REPLY FROM COLONEL MARR]

MAJOR NASYPANY:

9:09:07   Just in case. Not down in Whiskey 1-0-5 [military airspace] where they want—FAA wants to hold 'em to Whiskey 1-0-5. They want to hold 'em in Whiskey 1-0-5.

9:09:17   We need to do more than fuck with this.

The order to place the Langley fighters on battle stations was passed from the Weapons controllers and confirmed down the chain of command.

WEAPONS CONTROL:

9:09:27   Huntress placing Quit 2-5 2-6 [the Langley fighters] on battle stations. Time 1-3-1-0. Authenticate Sally Victor. That's Quit 2-5 2-6 on battle stations. All parties acknowledge with initials: Langley? . . . Command Post? . . . Giant Killer? . . .

By 9:20, then, the FAA's centers in Boston and New York had shut down their airspace; no more planes would be allowed to take off or land. NEADS had ordered the two fighters from Otis Air Force Base, which had been in a holding pattern over the Atlantic Ocean, awaiting the location of a target to intercept, to fly directly to New York City and fly a combat air patrol (CAP) over the city. Not knowing what else might happen, NEADS had also placed its other two assets on the East Coast, a pair of F-16s at Langley Air Force Base in Virginia, on battle stations, which meant that the fighters would sit at the ready with pilots on board, awaiting orders to scramble. Unknown to the FAA in Boston and New York, to the Herndon Command Center and Headquarters, and to NORAD and the Department of Defense, the FAA's Indianapolis Center was desperately trying to locate a third plane, American 77, a flight from Dulles International Airport in Virginia that had disappeared completely from radar.

American Airlines Flight 77 had begun its takeoff roll from Dulles at 8:20 a.m. The flight proceeded normally through airspace controlled by the Washington Air Traffic Control Center, and was handed off to Indianapolis Center at approximately 8:40 a.m. Radio contact was routine.

American 77 was acknowledged by the controller, who had fourteen other planes in his sector at the time. He later instructed American 77 to climb to 35,000 feet and to turn right ten degrees. At 8:50 a.m., American 77 acknowledged a routine navigational clearance instruction. This was the last transmission from American 77.

Sometime between that transmission and 8:54, the hijackers brandished knives and box-cutters. They forced the passengers and crew in first class to the back of the plane, then moved to secure control of the cockpit.

At 8:54 a.m., the flight began a left turn toward the south without authorization. Shortly after it began the turn, the aircraft was observed descending. At 8:56 a.m., as the plane continued to deviate slightly to the south from its flight plan, it was lost from radar completely; not only was the transponder signal gone, but the plane also disappeared as a primary target. The controller stated over his frequency: "This is Henderson [sector]. American 77—I don't know what happened to him. I'm trying to reach somebody; look[s] like he took a turn to the south and now I'm, uh, I don't know what altitude he's at or what he's doing last [UNINTELLIGIBLE] ah, heading towards Falmouth at 35 [i.e., 35,000 feet]."

The controller tried repeatedly to contact American 77, to no avail, and then contacted American Airlines in an attempt to have the airline contact the flight. In addition, the controller reached out to controllers in other sectors at Indianapolis Center to advise them of the situation. The controllers agreed to "sterilize the airspace" along the flight's projected westerly route so that other planes would not be affected by American 77: "We're just gonna treat him like nonradar and we've already told the next sector they're gonna have to sterilize for him until we find out." At 8:59 a.m., Indianapolis Center began to work with controllers in other centers to protect the airspace of American 77's projected flight path to the west.

After several minutes of searching, Indianapolis controllers once again tried to contact the airline. They were still unaware of the events in New York City. At 9:09 a.m., Indianapolis Center reported to the Great Lakes Regional Operations Center a possible aircraft accident involving American 77 because of the simultaneous loss of radio communications and radar identification.

Aboard American 77, the hijacking was complete. At 9:11, Renee May, a flight attendant who had been working in first class, tried to call her parents from the plane. That call didn't go through, but a second attempt was successful. She told her mother at 9:12 that the flight was being hijacked "by six individuals who had moved them—her mother was not sure whether she meant all the passengers or just the crew—to the rear of the plane." She gave her mother contact numbers for American Airlines and asked her to call and make sure they knew about the hijacking. Renee's mother reached an American Airlines employee and passed the information. The employee thought Mrs. May was talking about the plane that had crashed into the World Trade Center, but Mrs. May assured her that American 77 was still in the air. According to the employee, she informed an American Airlines flight services manager.

At Indianapolis Center, controllers believed that American 77 had crashed. At 9:15 a.m., the Indianapolis Center's operations manager requested the Traffic Management Unit to notify Air Force Search and Rescue in Langley, Virginia, of a possible crash of American 77. The operations manager also contacted the West Virginia State Police to advise them of the missing aircraft and ask whether they had any reports of a downed aircraft.

At 9:16, an American Airlines air traffic control specialist called the FAA's Herndon Command Center to ask about the status of New York air traffic. He told Herndon that the airline believed that American 11 had crashed into the World Trade Center and that American 77 was "missing." As he made this report, he received an update from American's management that American 77 might also have crashed into the Towers.

Herndon replied that it doubted the second crash was American 77 because "we have another call sign" (meaning, United Airlines 175) for that incident.

Barbara Olson, a passenger in first class aboard American 77, called her husband, Solicitor General Ted Olson, at about 9:16. They spoke for about a minute before the call was cut off. She told him that the flight had been hijacked and that the hijackers were armed with knives and box-cutters. She said all of the passengers had been forced to the back of the plane. Neither she nor Renee May mentioned any stabbings or use of violence by the hijackers in taking over the plane. She told her husband that the hijackers were not aware that she was placing the phone call. Ted Olson tried unsuccessfully to reach Attorney General John Ashcroft, who was out of town; he then called the Justice Department's Command Center and told them that his wife's flight, American 77, had been hijacked. That information does not appear to have left the Justice Department.

By 9:18, awareness of events was spreading through the FAA. The Air Route Traffic Control Centers in Indianapolis, Cleveland, and Washington were now aware that American 77 was lost and that two planes had crashed into the World Trade Center. This news led Indianapolis Center to doubt its conclusion that American 77 had crashed because of mechanical failure. Indianapolis managers wondered openly on the phone with the Command Center in Herndon whether American 77 might be a hijack.

The air defenders at NEADS were trying to coordinate more closely with the FAA. Mission Crew Commander Nasypany got on the phone with Colin Scoggins, Boston Center's military liaison, at 9:17.

COLIN SCOGGINS:

9:17:19   Yes, Colin Scoggins, Boston Center Military.

MAJOR NASYPANY:

9:17:21   Hey, how you doin'. It's Major Nasypany.

COLIN SCOGGINS:

9:17:23   How you doin'. We have a—could we shut every—nobody is departing Boston—in the whole airspace, Boston Center. We've shut all the aircraft down. And we're rerouting New York Metro airports. Our only concern is that there are aircraft in the sky. And in case any more of 'em divert or start—turning or whatever they're gonna do, I—we were just wondering, do you have people on alert that we—

[OVERTALK]

MAJOR NASYPANY:

9:17:43   I got fight—I got fighters in Whiskey 105 right now. I have a tanker there as well. I got other aircraft on alert down at Langley.

COLIN SCOGGINS:

9:17:49   Okay.

MAJOR NASYPANY:

And I'm getting ready to—and I have trackers—over JFK, over Boston, and in that area right now just looking for anything suspicious.

COLIN SCOGGINS:

9:17:57   Anything suspicious. Okay. And—we'll let you know about the internationals. We're not sure what we're doing with them yet at this time. But—

MAJOR NASYPANY:

9:18:02   Okay, well J—JFK and Boston are shut down, correct?

COLIN SCOGGINS:

9:18:05   We've shut down Boston. I'm not sure if New York Center's [UNINTELLIGIBLE], but we are—are rerouting all our—any aircraft that's bound for New York we are rerouting and putting 'em somewhere else.

MAJOR NASYPANY:

9:18:12   Okay—

NEADS FEMALE VOICE:

9:18:13   Great.

MAJOR NASYPANY:

—and if you get anything—if you . . .—any—any of your controllers . . . see anything that looks—

COLIN SCOGGINS:

9:18:16   Yup—

MAJOR NASYPANY:

9:18:17   —kind of squirrelly . . . just give us a yell. We'll get those fighters in that lo—location.

COLIN SCOGGINS:

9:18:22   Okay, all righty. Thank you—

Major Nasypany (the mission crew commander) told Colonel Marr he had spoken to the FAA's Boston Center, then raised for the first time that morning a previously unthinkable proposition: that NORAD might be forced to shoot down a hijacked plane, if there was another one.

MAJOR NASYPANY [SPEAKING TO COLONEL MARR, WHO IS NOT HEARD HERE]:

Boston Center, or Boston has just shut down Boston Airport. And, anything that's in the air, they're diverting out. And, I've been talking with—Mr. Scoggins there from Boston Center. He just wanted to know if we had any aircraft. I told him about the aircraft in the area that we have. Our fighters. Our fighters in the area, tankers, and also—okay. Also—we're in close contact. So, if he sees anything squirrelly, he's gonna give us a yell. And—we're gonna press.

9:19:21   Yeah.

9:19:22   Battle stations. They're, ah, sittin' at battle stations right now. . . .

9:19:44   The—the 15s [the fighters from Otis] are 0 by 2 by 2 by gun.
My recommendation, if we have to take anybody out, large
aircraft, we use AIM-9s in the face. . . . If need be . . . And,
that's my recommendation is from earlier tests Okay? . . .

9:20:52   Yeah, ask the question. Probably put the—you know what?
Put slammers—if—if need be, put slammers and heaters.
Okay? Bye . . .

9:21:11   Can somebody get me a cup of coffee? [LAUGHTER]

At 9:20 a.m., Barbara Olson reached her husband again from American 77. She told him that the pilot had announced that the plane had been hijacked. She asked him what she should tell the pilot to do. Ted Olson asked for her location. She said they were flying over houses. Another passenger told her they were heading northeast.

At the same time, the FAA Headquarters Security personnel set up a hijacking teleconference with several agencies, including the Defense Department. Although it is unclear which agency personnel participated at what times on this call, it is undisputed that no critical information concerning any of the hijackings was passed on this call.

By no later than 9:21 a.m., FAA's Command Center in Herndon, some FAA field facilities, and American Airlines had started to search for American 77 and feared it had been hijacked. Four minutes later, at 9:25 a.m., Command Center reported to FAA Headquarters that contact with the plane had been lost, that it could not be located even on primary radar, and that it was a suspected hijack. No one from FAA Headquarters contacted the military with this information.

At this point, the military was completely unaware that the search for American 77 had begun. In fact, the military officers would hear once again about American 11 before they received any notification that American 77 was lost.

On the floor at NEADS, the identification technicians received a call from Boston Center at 9:21:

BOSTON CENTER MILITARY:

Military, Boston Center. I just had a report that American 11 is still in the air, and it's on its way towards—heading towards Washington.

NEADS ID:

Okay. American 11 is still in the air?

BOSTON CENTER MILITARY:

Yes.

NEADS ID:

On its way towards Washington?

BOSTON CENTER MILITARY:

That was another—it was evidently another aircraft that hit the tower. That's the latest report that we have.

NEADS ID:

Okay.

BOSTON CENTER MILITARY:

I'm going to try to confirm an ID for you, but I would assume he's somewhere over, uh, either New Jersey or somewhere further south.

NEADS ID:

Okay. So American 11 isn't a hijack at all, then, right?

BOSTON CENTER MILITARY:

No, he is a hijack.

NEADS ID:

He—American 11 is a hijack?

BOSTON CENTER MILITARY:

Yes.

NEADS ID:

And he's heading into Washington?

BOSTON CENTER MILITARY:

Yes. This could be a third aircraft.

This news electrified the operations floor at NEADS. The mission crew commander acted instantly to meet the new threat:

NEADS ID [TO MAJOR NASYPANY]:

9:21:37   Another hijack, it's headed towards Washington.

MAJOR NASYPANY:

9:21:41   Shit. Give me a location. . . .

MALE VOICE:

9:21:46   Third aircraft. Hijack. Heading towards Washington.

MAJOR NASYPANY [TO COLONEL MARR]:

9:21:50   Okay. American Airlines is still airborne. Eleven, the first guy? He's heading towards Washington. Okay, I think we need to scramble Langley right now. And, I'm—I'm gonna take the fighters from Otis and try to chase this guy down if I can find him. . . .

9:22:07   You sure?

9:22:10   Okay. He's heading towards Langley, or, I should say, Washington. American 11. The original guy who's still airborne. [NOISE] We're still g—still gettin' a—a—we're gettin' a position.

9:22:25   [to NEADS ID] You got a position?

MALE VOICE [IN BACKGROUND]:

9:22:26   We got, like, a couple of hijacks on the go. Real-world. Got to go. [NOISE]

MAJOR NASYPANY:

9:22:35   Foxy, scramble Langley. Head 'em towards the Washington area.

MAJOR FOX:

9:22:38   Roger that. . . .

NEADS ID:

9:22:45   We're trying to get a code right now.

MAJOR NASYPANY:

9:22:47   We're trying to get a code on this guy right now.

NEADS ID:

9:22:49   We do have a tail number—

MAJOR NASYPANY:

We do have a tail number. . . .

9:23:12   If we can't find him—we—yeah, we're gettin'—we're tryin' to get—we're—we're trying to get the mode to try and get position on this guy. So, if this is him, we'll run on him. Yup. Okay. Bye. Okay.

Major Nasypany's strategy was to send two fighters from Langley Air Force Base to the Washington area, and to use the Otis fighters to chase down American 11 from the north. The order to scramble the fighters from Langley was issued at 9:24 a.m. Major Fox gave the direction.

MAJOR FOX:

They're gonna be getting Quit 2-5 2-6 [the Langley F-16s], 0-1-0 heading [a one-o'clock direction], flight level 2-9-0 [altitude 29,000 feet]. . . . He'll have to maintain comms with FAA. . . . Your mission will be to bring him up north. For right now, just head 'em to Baltimore Washington International. Tell them to coordinate with Center that NORAD wants them to CAP and hold in the Baltimore Washington International area.

MALE VOICE:

I got you. Coordinate with Center. No problem.

At 9:24 a.m., Great Lakes Regional Operations Center notified FAA Headquarters of the simultaneous loss of radio communications and radar identification for American 77. No one from headquarters contacted the military with this information.

A White House videoconference led by Richard Clarke was organized at 9:25 and eventually included the CIA, the FBI, the departments of State, Defense, and Justice, and the FAA. It took at least ten minutes for the call to begin in earnest. No information relating to American 77 was passed on this call.

The Otis Air Force Base F-15s arrived over New York City and formed a combat air patrol at 9:25. On the ground in New York, many thought that their arrival signified a new attack.

The FAA's Command Center was coordinating the search for American 77, to no avail. At 9:25, acting on his own initiative, Ben Sliney, the Herndon Command Center National Operations Manager, ordered a "nationwide ground stop," which "prevented any aircraft from taking off in the United States."

On the floor at NEADS, Colonel Marr weighed in with Mission Crew Commander Nasypany on the tactic of chasing the reported American 11 with the Otis fighters.

MAJOR NASYPANY [TO LOG KEEPER]:

9:24:10   Okay, Langley, call sign birds are Quit 2-5 2-6. . . . Quit—Quebec, Uniform, India, Tango—2-5 2-6.

MALE VOICE:

9:24:24   Got it. A-firmative.

MAJOR NASYPANY:

9:24:33   Okay, right now what we're running with out there is 2 by zero by 2 by gun for Langley. . . .

9:24:43   Okay, also we have the Panta 4-5 4-6, zero by 2 by 2 by gun. We're gonna try and turn it into a tail chase on this American one heading towards Washington if we can find him . . .

9:25:15   2-2 and 2-3. Two KC 10's. I'm stickin' 'em in—Whiskey 1-0-7. Yeah. And, did you get the word that Langley got scrambled? . . .

9:25:29   Yeah, he just got scrambled—about two minutes ago. . . .

9:25:35   [TO MAJOR FOX] DO [i.e., Colonel Marr] says forget the tail chase.

MALE VOICE:

9:25:37   Even though we couldn't find 'em.

MAJOR NASYPANY:

9:25:42   Yeah, great. That's great.

The mission crew commander, Nasypany, summarized the situation at 9:27: "Three planes unaccounted for. American Airlines 11 may still be airborne, but the flight that—United 175 to the World Trade Center. We're not sure who the other one is."

At 9:29, President Bush addressed the nation from the Booker Elementary School in Sarasota. He said:

Ladies and gentlemen, this is a difficult moment for America. . . . Today we've had a national tragedy. Two airplanes have crashed into the World Trade Center in an apparent terrorist attack on our country. I have . . . ordered that the full resources of the federal government go to help the victims and their families, and to conduct a full-scale investigation to hunt down and to find those folks who committed this act. Terrorism against our nation will not stand.

As he was speaking, the Langley Air Force Base F-16s lifted off and headed east over the Atlantic to avoid other aircraft. American Airlines 77 was flying at 7,000 feet, heading east, thirty-eight miles west of the Pentagon, unknown to air traffic control supervisors and unknown to the military.

At the Pentagon, the deputy director of operations at the National

Military Command Center called for a "significant event" conference call. That call began at 9:29. The FAA was asked to provide an update, but it had not been added to the call. At 9:30, the deputy director stated that it had just been confirmed to him that American 11 was still airborne and headed for Washington, D.C. NORAD confirmed that American 11 was still airborne and headed for Washington. Thus, the mistaken report that American 11 has not hit the Tower had now percolated to the highest levels of the Pentagon. The call ended at 9:34, and a new call—an Air Threat Conference Call—began at 9:37. The FAA was not on the line for that call either, and would not join until 10:17.

On the phone with his wife, Ted Olson told her about the two hijacked planes that had crashed into the World Trade Center. Barbara Olson took the news calmly, with no hint of panic. He lost her call at 9:31.

At 9:32, air traffic controllers at Dulles International Airport Terminal Approach observed "a primary radar target tracking eastbound at a high rate of speed." They called Reagan National Airport and told officials there of the approaching aircraft.

"The tower supervisor at Reagan picked up a hotline to the Secret Service and told the Service's Operations Center," at 9:33, that "we've got an aircraft coming at you and not talking with us." The Secret Service agent who took the call was "about to push the alert button [to evacuate the vice president] when the tower advised that the aircraft was turning south and approaching Reagan National Airport."

A NEADS ID technician searching for American 11 decided to call the FAA's Air Route Traffic Control Center in Washington to find out whether that center was tracking American 11:

WASHINGTON CENTER OPERATIONS MANAGER:

9:32:24   Huntress ID, this is Washington Center, the Operations Manager.

NEADS ID:

9:32:27   Go ahead, sir.

WASHINGTON CENTER OPERATIONS MANAGER:

9:32:28　Okay. I guess you had called here a couple times. You never talked to me. But—if there's anything you need or anything I can help you with, let—let me know what it is right now, please.

NEADS ID:

9:32:36　Okay. Do you want me to let you know what we have going on, sir?

WASHINGTON CENTER OPERATIONS MANAGER:

9:32:39　I would appre—yes.

NEADS ID:

9:32:40　Okay.

WASHINGTON CENTER OPERATIONS MANAGER:

But I have a pretty good idea, but yes.

NEADS ID:

9:32:41　Okay. There are three aircraft missing out of Boston. I just spoke with Boston. And they said that they're not sure of the third aircraft call sign, but they do have two. One is United 175. The other is American 11.

WASHINGTON CENTER OPERATIONS MANAGER:

9:32:51　Right.

NEADS ID:

9:32:52　They thought that the American 11 was the aircraft that crashed into the World Trade Center with the United 175. However, American 11 is not the aircraft that crashed.

WASHINGTON CENTER OPERATIONS MANAGER:

9:33:00　[UNINTELLIGIBLE]—

NEADS ID:

He said the pilot on American 11 was talking to him, having a rough time telling him what's going on. There was threats in

the cockpit being made. This was the initial—hijack information that we got on American 11, the 767 from Boston to Los
Angeles. Proposed route—he was headed towards JFK at the
time that they lost contact. But that was not the aircraft
headed—into the World Trade Center, that hit it—

WASHINGTON CENTER OPERATIONS MANAGER:

9:33:23 Okay.

NEADS ID:

—is what Boston's saying. He—the last known—and I'm
not sure where we heard it through the grapevine, people calling—is that American 11 was headed towards Washington—

[OVERTALK]

FEMALE VOICE:

9:33:31 —the aircraft—

NEADS ID:

9:33:32 —and that's the only thing—

MALE VOICE:

—American—

WASHINGTON CENTER OPERATIONS MANAGER:

9:33:33 Was headed toward where?

NEADS ID:

9:33:34 Washington.

WASHINGTON CENTER OPERATIONS MANAGER:

9:33:35 Okay.

NEADS ID:

9:33:36 . . . And I just wanted to give you a heads-up.

WASHINGTON CENTER OPERATIONS MANAGER:

9:33:39 Okay. Now—

NEADS ID:

The last—

WASHINGTON CENTER OPERATIONS MANAGER:

—is there—okay, go ahead.

NEADS ID:

9:33:40 —the last known lat-long that we had, primary target only was 4038 north, 07403 west, on American 11.

[OVERTALK]

MALE VOICE:

9:33:52 —workin'—

WASHINGTON CENTER OPERATIONS MANAGER:

9:33:52 Okay.

NEADS ID:

But again, remember nothing has been confirmed as far as with the aircraft that hit the World Trade Center. But the other one, we have its information, headed towards Washington.

There was a brief pause as the FAA's Washington Center Manager absorbed the news from NEADS, then the Washington Center representative dropped his own bombshell.

WASHINGTON CENTER OPERATIONS MANAGER:

9:34:01 Okay. Now let me tell you this. I—I'll—we've been looking. We're—also lost American 77.

FEMALE VOICE:

9:34:06 Hey—

NEADS ID:

American 77?

NEADS ID [TO NEADS FLOOR]:

9:34:07 —American 77's lost—

NEADS ID [TO FAA]:

9:34:08 Where was it [UNINTELLIGIBLE], sir?

WASHINGTON CENTER OPERATIONS MANAGER:

9:34:10 Excuse me?

FEMALE VOICE:

—American 77—

NEADS ID:

9:34:11 Where was it supposed to head, sir?

WASHINGTON CENTER OPERATIONS MANAGER:

9:34:12 Okay. He was goin' to L.A. also—

[OVERTALK]

FEMALE VOICE:

9:34:15 —he was also—

NEADS ID:

—going to LAX—

FEMALE VOICE:

—going to L.A.—

WASHINGTON CENTER OPERATIONS MANAGER:

9:34:16 Now—

NEADS ID:

9:34:17 From where, sir?

WASHINGTON CENTER OPERATIONS MANAGER:

9:34:19 I think he was from Boston also.

FEMALE VOICE:

9:34:21   Boston to L.A.—

WASHINGTON CENTER OPERATIONS MANAGER:

Now—now let me tell you this—this story here. The In—Indianapolis Center was working this guy—

NEADS ID:

9:34:27   What guy?

WASHINGTON CENTER OPERATIONS MANAGER:

9:34:28   American 77.

NEADS ID:

9:34:29   Okay.

WASHINGTON CENTER OPERATIONS MANAGER:

9:34:30   At flight level 350. However . . .

9:34:33   —they lost radar with him. . . .

9:34:35   They lost contact with him. They lost everything. And they don't have any idea where he is or what happened. So what we've done at the round—surrounding centers here, is to tell everyone to look out for limited codes, primary targets, or whatever the case may be.

NEADS ID:

9:34:49   Okay.

WASHINGTON CENTER OPERATIONS MANAGER:

And that was the last time—that was about 15 minutes ago since I talked to the—

NEADS ID:

9:34:54   Type—

WASHINGTON CENTER OPERATIONS MANAGER:

9:34:55   —Indianapolis Center—Operations Manager.

NEADS ID:

9:34:57 —do you have the type aircraft, sir?

WASHINGTON CENTER OPERATIONS MANAGER:

9:34:59 That was a 767, I believe.

FEMALE VOICE:

9:35:01 A 767—

NEADS ID:

Okay. And . . . all I need is the lat-long, last known position of
the 767.

WASHINGTON CENTER OPERATIONS MANAGER:

9:35:13 Well, I don't know. That was [UNINTELLIGIBLE]—that was Indy
Center. But they said somewhere—it was the last time I talked
to them, they said it was east of York. And I don't even know
what that state that is.

NEADS ID:

9:35:21 Okay, sir. Well, I'm gonna go ahead and just give them a call.

WASHINGTON CENTER OPERATIONS MANAGER:

9:35:24 Okay.

[UNHEARD QUESTION]
Thank you, sir.

WASHINGTON CENTER OPERATIONS MANAGER:
Thanks.

Controllers at Reagan National Airport, having learned of an unidentified fast-moving aircraft heading toward them, directed an unarmed
National Guard C-130H cargo aircraft, which had just taken off en route
to Minnesota, to identify and follow the plane identified by Dulles International Airport. The C-130H pilot spotted it, identified it as a Boeing
757, and observed it making a 330-degree turn to the south. At the end

of the turn, the plane descended through 2,200 feet and flew toward the Pentagon or White House. When the tower advised the Secret Service of this turn, the Service ordered the immediate evacuation of the vice president at 9:36. Agents lifted the vice president from his chair and propelled him to the bunker. He entered the tunnel leading to the shelter at 9:36.

NEADS received another call from Boston Center at 9:36.

> **BOSTON MILITARY:**
>
> Latest report. Aircraft VFR [visual flight rules] six miles southeast of the White House. . . . Six, southwest. Six, southwest of the White House, deviating away.

The mission crew commander reacted instantly:

> **MAJOR NASYPANY:**
>
> 9:36:23   Okay, Foxy. I got a aircraft six miles east of the White House! Get your fighters there as soon as possible . . .
>
> 9:36:28   [OFF-MIC CONVERSATION]
>
> **MALE VOICE:**
>
> 9:36:34   That came from Boston?
>
> **MAJOR NASYPANY:**
>
> 9:36:35   We're gonna turn and burn it—crank it up—
>
> **MALE VOICE:**
>
> Six miles!?!
>
> 9:36:37   [OFF-MIC CONVERSATION]
>
> **MAJOR NASYPANY:**
>
> 9:36:38   All right, here we go. This is what we're gonna do— We got an an aircraft deviating eight miles east of the White House right now. . . . Take 'em and run 'em to the White House! . . . These guys are smart.

MAJOR NASYPANY [TO COLONEL MARR]:

9:36:54   Authorizing AFIO [Authorization for Interceptor Operations, when the military takes control of the airspace] right now? You want to authorize it?

9:36:55   [OFF-MIC CONVERSATION]

WEAPONS CONTROLLER:

9:36:56   I can't get through—

MALE VOICE:

Yeah, we're hearin' 'em loud and clear.

9:36:58   [OFF-MIC CONVERSATION]

MAJOR FOX:

Doesn't matter. . . . You turn 'em right now. . . .

MALE VOICE:

9:36:59   What are we doin'?

MALE VOICE:

We're going direct DC? AFIO?

MAJOR FOX:

We're goin' AFIO. . . .

9:37:07   [OFF-MIC CONVERSATION]

WEAPONS CONTROLLER:

9:37:10   Giant Killer, Huntress 9-2-4, reference Whiskey 3-86—

FEMALE VOICE:

9:37:14   Go ahead.

WEAPONS CONTROLLER:

Ma'am, we are going AFIO right now with Quit 2-5. They are going direct Washington. . . .

Having seized control of the airspace, the NEADS crew searched for the primary radar target over Washington.

MALE VOICE:

9:37:34   That's the radar-only guy right there.

MALE VOICE:

9:37:36   Radar only.

MALE VOICE:

9:37:38   This guy right here? Bravo 0-1-3?

9:37:41   [OFF-MIC CONVERSATION]

MALE VOICE:

9:37:42   Bravo 0-3-2—

9:37:44   [OFF-MIC CONVERSATION]

MALE VOICE:

9:37:45   Oh, this dude right here?

9:37:47   [OFF-MIC CONVERSATION]

MALE VOICE:

9:37:52   0-3-2—

MALE VOICE:

Losing altitude, eh? No altitude on him.

9:37:53   [OFF-MIC CONVERSATION]

MALE VOICE [POINTING AT RADAR TRACKS]:

9:37:56   Right here, right here, right here. I got him. I got him.

MALE VOICE:

9:37:58   Bravo—

9:37:59   [OFF-MIC CONVERSATION]

MAJOR NASYPANY:

9:38:03   Yeah, we just lost track. Just—just—

MALE VOICE:

9:38:05   Get a Z point.

MAJOR NASYPANY:

9:38:06   Get a Z point on that.

The NEADS trackers located the primary radar track, but the track faded over Washington before they could forward the information to the Cheyenne Mountain Operations Center. Major Nasypany then turned to where the Langley fighters were, and found that they had flown directly east and were over the ocean, some 150 miles away.

MAJOR NASYPANY:

9:38:10   Yeah, we just did, too [lose the primary radar track]. Okay, we
           got guys lookin' at 'em. Hold on . . . Where's Langley at?
           Where are the fighters?

9:38:19   [OFF-MIC CONVERSATION]

MALE VOICE:

9:38:20   Keep squawkin'.

MALE VOICE:

9:38:21   Goin' AFIO . . .

9:38:35   Okay, they're in 3-86 and goin' up north.

9:38:38   [OFF-MIC CONVERSATION]

MAJOR NASYPANY:

9:38:50   We need to get those back up there—

           [OFF-MIC CONVERSATION]

MALE VOICE:

9:38:55   Okay.

9:38:56   [OFF-MIC CONVERSATION]

MAJOR NASYPANY:

9:38:59   I don't care how many windows you break. . . .

MALE VOICE:

9:39:31   I got to—to find that track.

9:39:34   [OFF-MIC CONVERSATION]

MAJOR NASYPANY:

9:39:36   Why they'd go up there?

MALE VOICE:

9:39:37   'Cause Giant Killer sent 'em up there.

MAJOR NASYPANY:

9:39:38   Goddamnit! Okay. Push 'em back!

By the time American 77 crashed into the Pentagon, at 9:37 a.m., most of the top officials in the critical government agencies were involved in the numerous teleconferences that had been convened to discuss the crisis. Upon arriving at the White House, shortly after the second plane hit the World Trade Center, Richard Clarke instructed his deputy, Lisa Gordon-Hagerty: "I want the highest-level person in Washington from each agency on-screen now, especially FAA." According to Richard Clarke's account, the videoconference began shortly after 9:20 with a briefing from FAA Administrator Jane Garvey:

"Okay," I began. "Let's start with the facts. FAA, FAA, go." I fell in to using the style of communication on tactical radio so that those listening in the other studios around town could hear who was being called on over the din in their own rooms.

Jane Garvey, the administrator of the Federal Aviation Administration, was in the chair. "The two aircraft that went in were American Flight 11, a 767, and United 175, also a 767. Hijacked. . . . We have reports of eleven aircraft off course or out of communications, maybe hijacked." . . .

"Eleven," I repeated. "Okay, Jane, how long will it take to get all

aircraft now aloft onto the ground somewhere? . . . Are you prepared to order a national ground stop and no fly zone?"

"Yes, but it will take a while." . . .

I turned to the Pentagon screen. "JCS, JCS. I assume NORAD
has scrambled fighters and AWACS. How many? Where?"

"Not a pretty picture, Dick." Dick Myers, himself a fighter pilot,
knew that the days when we had scores of fighters on strip alert
had ended with the Cold War. . . . "Otis has launched two birds
toward New York. Langley is trying to get two up now. . . ."

"Okay, how long to CAP over D.C.?" . . .

"Fast as we can. Fifteen minutes?" Myers asked, looking at the
generals and colonels around him. It was now 9:28.

This account does not square in any significant respect with what occurred that morning. The videoconference was logged in the White House
Situation Room as initiated at 9:25, but the FAA and CIA did not join
until 9:40, after the Pentagon had been hit. Not surprisingly, then, the
conference's first agenda item was not a briefing from the FAA, which
had not yet joined, but the security of the president and the vice president, and federal agencies. This was being discussed at 9:40, when the
conference learned that the Pentagon had been hit. Furthermore, Jane
Garvey, the FAA administrator, could not have briefed the videoconference, even at 9:40, that the planes that had hit the World Trade Center
were American 11 and United 175; there was confusion within her own
agency about which flights had crashed where. In fact, the FAA had reported that American 11 was still airborne and heading for Washington
at precisely the same moment that Richard Clarke recalls Administrator
Garvey telling the videoconference that American 11 had hit the WTC.

Furthermore, Clarke's recollection that Garvey reported eleven flights
off course or out of communication before 9:30 is belied not only by the
fact that the FAA was not yet on the conference but by the contemporaneous log of the conference, which records that at 10:03 the conference received reports of other missing aircraft: "2 possibly 3 aloft." His

recollection, however, that the number "eleven" was reported into the conference squares with the reality of that morning: the report that American "eleven" was still flying and en route to Washington, D.C.

The decision to order a national ground stop was in fact initiated by the national operations manager at the FAA's Herndon Command Center, Ben Sliney, on his own authority, not as a consequence of the videoconference. Similarly, the decision to form a combat air patrol over Washington was made by Major Nasypany at NEADS and verified up the chain of command, not prompted by the conversation on the videoconference. The White House videoconference "learned of a combat air patrol over Washington" at 10:03. In fact, General Myers was almost certainly not on the White House videoconference at 9:28; he was on his way back from Capitol Hill. As the 9/11 Commission put it: "We do not know who from Defense participated, but we do know that in the first hour none of the personnel involved in managing the crisis did. And none of the information conveyed in the White House video teleconference, at least in the first hour, was being passed to the National Military Command Center." In fact, "The White House video teleconference was not connected into the area of the NMCC where the crisis was being managed [via the air threat conference call]. Thus the director of the operations team—who was on the phone with NORAD—did not have the benefit of information being shared on the video teleconference. . . . Moreover, when the Secretary and Vice Chairman [of the Joint Chiefs of Staff] later participated in the White House video teleconference, they were necessarily absent from the NMCC and unable to provide guidance to the operations team." Clarke's memoir of the day is remarkable, ultimately, not as an artifact of history but as an indication of how little-understood the events of the morning remained years later, even—and perhaps especially—to national leaders. They honestly believed that their actions in those critical moments made a difference; the records of the day say otherwise.

The other teleconferences were similarly ineffectual. The air threat conference call, operated by the Pentagon, was still trying to include the FAA by 9:40, and so was obtaining whatever operational information it had from NEADS through the chain of command at NORAD. NEADS, in turn, was acquiring information on an ad hoc basis from FAA centers, notably Boston Center, which, in turn, were acquiring information by listening in on FAA teleconferences being conducted from FAA Headquarters, from the Command Center in Herndon, and by the New England Region.

To its great frustration, the 9/11 Commission staff was never able to pinpoint the source of the pivotal report of the morning: the mistaken report that American 11 was still airborne and heading for Washington. It was reported to NEADS by the military liaison at the FAA's Boston Center, who heard it reported on one of the teleconferences. FAA officials at headquarters and the Command Center also recalled hearing the report, but no one could recall its source. There is no question, however, about the report's significance that morning. In response to it, NEADS scrambled the Langley fighters and reported the news about American 11 up the chain of command in NORAD. NORAD's repetition of the report concerning American 11 to the NMCC triggered the air threat conference call.

Given the number of conference calls occurring at that time, the extremely tenuous connections between them, and the introduction of the news that American 77 was missing, what seems to have occurred was a continent-wide game of telephone, in which the news that American 77 was missing was somehow, through the alchemy of repetition, transmuted to the news that American 11 was still airborne; if American 11 was still airborne, moreover, it must be heading for Washington. What is clear is that at the highest levels of government, during these critical moments, the top officials were talking mainly to themselves. They were an echo chamber. They were of little or no assistance to the people on the ground attempting to manage the crisis.

The NEADS air defenders would never reacquire their primary radar target. At 9:37:46, American 77 crashed into the Pentagon at a speed of 530 miles per hour. All on board, plus 125 civilian and military people in the Pentagon, were killed.

The president's motorcade was racing to the airport. The vice president was rushing into the bunker deep below the White House. Secretary of Defense Rumsfeld felt the impact of the crash and made his way to the Pentagon parking lot to assist. The Pentagon air threat conference call was trying to connect with the FAA. NEADS was looking for the missing flight over Washington, while the Langley Air Force Base fighters were flying at maximum subsonic speed toward Washington.

Most ominous, FAA Headquarters was responding to the news it had received, at 9:34, that a fourth aircraft had been hijacked over Ohio. The pilot and copilot and a flight attendant aboard that flight, United 93, had been murdered. The passengers aboard that fourth aircraft, United 93, were learning what was happening everywhere else and discussing desperately what they should do. The morning was being lived now not in hours or even minutes, but in seconds.

SECONDS

9:37–10:30 A.M.

Unlike the other hijacked flights that morning, United 93 had not taken off on time; its departure from Newark Airport was delayed until 8:40 a.m. because of the usual morning traffic congestion leaving that airport. The flight was passed routinely from the terminal approach controllers to New York Center, and then to Cleveland Center.

Only four hijackers were on board, perhaps because the fifth, Mohamed al Khatani, had been turned away at Orlando airport on August 4; Khatani would be captured after 9/11 in Afghanistan. United 93 was also unlike the other hijacked flights in that significant time had elapsed with no attack from the hijackers. It is possible that the delayed takeoff confused the sequencing of the attack, and that the hijackers hesitated because the delay had disrupted their plans. It is also possible that the hijackers hesitated because their pilot, Ziad Jarrah, had misgivings about proceeding: he was, after all, more immersed in the Western lifestyle than the other hijackers, and had a close relationship with his German girlfriend. He had, in fact, already jeopardized mission security by traveling to see her. We will never know.

The flight had been airborne for more than forty minutes when United 93's pilot, Jason Dahl, sent an ACARS message to United's dispatcher: "Good mornin'.... Nice climb outta EWR [Newark Airport] after a nice tour of the apt [apartment] courts y [and] grnd cntrl. . . . At 350 occl lt [occasional light] chop. Wind 290/50 ain't helping." At 9:22, climbing to 35,000 feet, the captain radioed in: "United 93, starting to pick up some light chop at 35; any ride reports?"

The Cleveland controller responded: "Ah, first complaint I've had and United 93 contact Cleveland Center on one three three point zero seven [radio frequency]." Before the flight could resume its dialogue with the controller, it received the following ACARS text message from United Airlines at 9:23:

BEWARE ANY COCKPIT INTRUSION. TWO AIRCRAFT IN NY HIT TRADE CENTER BLDS.

At 9:24:20, United 93 checked in with a new Cleveland controller: "Good morning, Cleveland. United 93 is with you at three five oh intermittent light chop." There was no immediate response; the Cleveland controller was managing sixteen other flights on his scope and issuing new routes to several aircraft on the basis of decisions to ground-stop all flights in New York and Boston. When United 93 tried again at 9:25, checking in again at 35,000 feet; the controller replied, "United 93, Cleveland, roger." The controller then engaged in conversations with several aircraft about the "serious" situation that had occurred in New York City, and discussed landing flights in Philadelphia. At the same time (9:26), United 93's pilot sought confirmation of the ACARS message from his airline: "Ed [Ballinger, the United Airlines dispatcher] confirm latest mssg plz—Jason."

At 9:27:25, the Cleveland controller advised United 93 of potential traffic as a consequence of rerouting so many planes: "United 93, that traffic for you is one o'clock, twelve miles eastbound, 370." United 93 responded: "Negative contact, we're looking. United 93."

At 9:28:16, the hijackers breached the cockpit; over the radio, amid crashing sounds and static, came the words "Mayday mayday . . . Hey, get out of here!" Thirty seconds later, at 9:28:46, the words were repeated: "Get out of here! . . . Get out of here!" Because the Cleveland controller was unsure which of the flights under his control was the source of the transmission, he said: "Somebody call Cleveland?" He then noticed that United 93 had dropped dramatically in altitude, losing 685 feet in a matter of seconds. He tried United 93 at 9:29:14: "United 93, verify three five zero." He tried again four more times in the next minute before radioing at 9:30:03: "United 93, if you hear Cleveland Center, ident, please." He repeated this request at 9:30:58, but there was no answer. The controller began to poll the other flights on his frequency, asking whether they had heard the screaming; several said that they had.

An abiding mystery surrounding United 93 is why the hijackers waited so long to attack, and what triggered the attack when it did occur at 9:28. Although the answer will never be known, the circumstances that immediately preceded the attack suggest two possibilities. First, the flight had started to experience light chop; it may be that the pilot had decided to require the passengers to return to their seats and fasten their seat belts. This order, and the uncertainty over how long the "Fasten seat belt" sign would remain illuminated, may have prompted the hijackers to overcome whatever hesitation they may have been feeling, and compelled them to act. A second possibility, made the more intriguing when one considers the circumstances, discussed earlier, leading to the hijacking of the other United flight, 175, is that the hijackers (and other passengers) were listening on their headphones to the air traffic control transmissions on Channel 9, as United flights allowed.

The attack on United 175 followed immediately that flight's pilot's transmission to the FAA's New York Center, quoted earlier: "We figured we'd wait till we got to you, Center, ah, we heard a suspicious transmission on our departure out of Boston, ah, with someone, ah, sound like someone, sound like someone keyed the mike and, ah, said, ah, Everyone, ah, stay in your seats." Given that the attacks in New York and Washington were sequenced, with the United flights intended to follow the American flights in each case, it is reasonable to speculate that the United flights were picked because of the ability they afforded to monitor air traffic control, and thus potentially to learn the fate of prior flights. In any case, immediately before the attack on United 93, passengers listening on Channel 9 to the air traffic control transmissions would have heard the controller discussing the "serious situation in New York" and the need to divert flights. This discussion could have prompted otherwise hesitant hijackers to believe that their window to act was closing.

At 9:31:55, the Cleveland controller heard a foreign voice over his frequency: "Please sit down. Keep remaining seating. We have a bomb on board."

The controller responded at 9:32:05: "Uh, calling Cleveland Center, you're unreadable. Say again slowly." He then heard the following transmission from the flight: "Ladies and gentlemen, here the captain, please sit down, keep remaining sitting. We have a bomb on board. So, sit." In the cockpit, a flight attendant pleaded with the hijackers not to kill her; the cockpit voice recorder picked up the sounds of her murder.

The FAA's Cleveland Center reported immediately to the FAA's Herndon Command Center the news that United 93 might have a bomb on board. The Command Center relayed that information at 9:34 to FAA Headquarters and, between 9:34 and 10:08 a.m., a Herndon Command Center manager provided several updates on the progress of the flight as it turned south and east. FAA Headquarters did not contact the military; it did not request that fighters be scrambled; it did not share the information it received concerning United 93 with any other agency from 9:34 to 10:08.

The Cleveland controller followed by requesting, at 9:35:36: "United 93, if able, squawk trip, please." The controller was, in effect, asking United 93 to confirm—"squawk trip"—that it had been hijacked. He had noticed United 93 climbing to 40,700 feet, and had moved several aircraft out of its way. The flight continued to climb, and the controller moved several more aircraft out of harm's way as the flight deviated.

At 9:36, a flight attendant contacted United Airlines and spoke with a manager at United's maintenance facility in San Francisco. She told him she was calling from the back of the plane. She said the plane had been hijacked, and that the hijackers were in the first-class cabin, behind the curtain, and in the cockpit. They had announced that they had a bomb on board. They had pulled a knife; they had killed a flight attendant.

Cleveland's FAA Center called the Herndon Command Center at 9:36 and asked if anyone had launched fighter aircraft to intercept United 93. Cleveland Center indicated that it was prepared to call a nearby military base to request fighter aircraft assistance. The Command Center told Cleveland that "personnel well above them in the chain of command" were responsible for making that decision and were working on it.

At 9:39, the Cleveland controller heard a fourth transmission from United 93: "Uh, this is the captain. Would like you all to remain seated. There is a bomb on board and are going back to the airport, and to have our demands [UNINTELLIGIBLE]. Please remain quiet." The controller radioed back: "United 93, understand you have a bomb on board. Go ahead." There was no response.

The Northeast Air Defense Sector crew was not aware at 9:40 that United 93 had been hijacked; in fact, NEADS was not even aware yet that the Pentagon had been hit, or that the unknown aircraft circling toward the Pentagon and White House had crashed. Having lost that plane's primary radar track, the ID technicians reached out to the FAA's Washington Center to try to learn its location.

FAA WASHINGTON CENTER:

9:38:35   Washington.

NEADS ID:

Washington, Huntress. Boston just called us. They said that they had information about some aircraft that was six miles southwest of the White House but appears to be deviating. Because of—

FAA WASHINGTON CENTER:

9:38:45   Boston does?

NEADS ID:

9:38:46 —Boston called and said that I'd have to get the information from you on it. They don't [have] a call [sign for the] aircraft, they don't have any codes for the aircraft. They just know that there's one that's six miles southwest of the White House.

FAA WASHINGTON CENTER:

9:38:54 Okay. Well, Boston's airspace doesn't even come close to that. I don't know how they got that information. But—we don't—hey. . . .

9:39:13 Okay. We—we don't know anything about that.

NEADS ID:

9:39:16 Okay. You don't know anything about that.

FAA WASHINGTON CENTER:

9:39:17 No, we do not. And it's probably just a rumor. But—you—you might wanna call—National or Andrews, somebody—somebody like that and find out. But we don't know anything about that.

NEADS ID:

9:39:29 Copy, thanks.

FAA WASHINGTON CENTER:

Okay, bye.

While the military controllers continued to search the radar around Washington for the lost primary radar track, the ID techs received another call from the FAA's Boston Center:

FAA BOSTON CENTER:

9:39:33 Colin Scoggins, Boston Center Military.

NEADS ID:

9:39:35 Yes, sir.

FAA BOSTON CENTER:

9:39:36 Another aircraft Delta 1989.

NEADS ID:

9:39:37 Okay.

[OVERTALK]

9:39:39 Delta 1989.

9:39:40 Okay. Type aircraft?

FAA BOSTON CENTER:

9:39:42 Type aircraft?

NEADS ID:

9:39:43 Yes, sir.

FAA BOSTON CENTER:

9:39:45 Code—can I give you a code?

NEADS ID:

9:39:46 Yes, give me the code.

FAA BOSTON CENTER:

9:39:47 One-three-zero-four presently due south of Cleveland.

NEADS ID:

9:39:50 Okay. Presently due south of Cleveland.

FAA BOSTON CENTER:

9:39:53 Heading westbound, destination Las Vegas.

NEADS ID:

9:39:55 Heading westbound, destination Las Vegas. And is this one a hijack, sir?

FAA BOSTON CENTER:

9:39:59 We believe it is.

NEADS ID:

9:40:00 You believe it is. . . .

FAA BOSTON CENTER:

It's squawking 1304 now, if you wanna try to track him up.

NEADS ID:

9:40:07 Okay.

9:40:08 The type aircraft is what, sir?

FAA BOSTON CENTER:

9:40:10 Type aircraft on that Delta, Delta 1989, I think it's on there, 767.

NEADS ID:

9:40:18 Seven-sixty-seven. And—

FAA BOSTON CENTER:

9:40:20 And altitude?

NEADS ID:

9:40:21 Yes, please.

FAA BOSTON CENTER:

9:40:24 Three-five-oh.

NEADS ID:

Three-five-oh, okay, copy that.

9:40:26 And where—where did he take off out of, sir?

FAA BOSTON CENTER:

9:40:28 Took off outta Boston.

FEMALE VOICE:

9:40:29 Boston? Okay.

Having experienced the two hijackings from Logan Airport earlier in the morning, and having heard the reports of a third missing aircraft, Boston Center decided to try to anticipate the hijackers' next move. The Center identified other transcontinental large commercial aircraft that had already taken off from Boston and might be candidates for hijacking. Boston Center attempted to contact those flights to ensure that everything was normal. One flight in particular, Delta 1989, from Boston to Las Vegas, attracted Boston Center's attention. Like American 11 and United 175, Delta 1989 departed Boston from Logan Airport, was a jumbo jet, and was headed for the West Coast. Boston Center then discovered that Delta 1989 was in Cleveland Center's airspace. Boston Center called Cleveland Center to advise them to pay careful attention to the communications with Delta 1989, and to its flight path. A report over one of the FAA teleconferences that the flight had deviated from its course and was not communicating led to the call to NEADS.

This latest information added to the strain on the NEADS floor, which was struggling to clear the airspace to Washington for the Langley fighters and give them a point in space around which to form the combat air patrol. It had been decades since the military had declared "AFIO" (Authorization for Interceptor Operations) and seized control over continental airspace; there was uncertainty on the floor over the mechanics of that process. Meanwhile, controllers were also trying to maintain the CAP over New York City with the Otis fighters, and locate the aircraft whose primary radar track had faded over Washington.

NEADS MALE VOICE:

9:39:59   All right, Giant Killer [military air traffic control]? Who do they need to contact [to seize control of the airspace between Langley and Washington]?

FEMALE VOICE:

9:40:03   [The FAA's Herndon] Command Center.

MALE VOICE:

9:40:04   Command Center.

Controllers searched the skies over Washington for the primary radar tracks that had faded over the city, and NEADS personnel sought clarification of the current hijacking situation.

MALE VOICE:

9:40:09   [UNINTELLIGIBLE] 0-3-2 data faded.

9:40:10   [OFF-MIC CONVERSATION]

MALE VOICE:

9:40:12   —3-86.

MALE VOICE:

9:40:13   Hunter—

MALE VOICE:

9:40:14   [UNINTELLIGIBLE] what altitude's he gonna [UNINTELLIGIBLE]? . . .

MALE VOICE:

9:40:22   Four?

MALE VOICE:

9:40:23   No, we've heard three now—

MALE VOICE:

9:40:24   Three.

MALE VOICE:

United 1-7-5, American Airlines 11, and American 7-7.

MALE VOICE:

9:40:28   Giant Killer, just push him in there. Whatever altitude he's at, fine . . .

MALE VOICE:

9:41:45   —six miles outside of Washington, okay?

LANGLEY PILOT:

9:41:46   Copy. And, that was CAP over Washington. Do you have a specific point for us over Washington?

9:41:52   [OFF-MIC CONVERSATION]

MALE VOICE:

Stand by. And, we're gonna continue—its current heading.

MALE VOICE:

9:41:54   Holy shit.

MALE VOICE:

Is that the White House or the Pentagon? I'm gonna need to guess, right? . . .

MALE VOICE:

This is bad, man. . . .

MALE VOICE:

9:42:23   Quick 2-5, mission to establish CAP, Bra 3-2-0 hundred and 12.

9:42:29   [OFF-MIC CONVERSATION]

LANGLEY PILOT:

Copy, 3-2-0 a hundred and 12.

9:42:31   [OFF-MIC CONVERSATION]

MALE VOICE:

9:42:38   Attention all players, all teams, contact Huntress 2-3-5 point 9.

FEMALE VOICE:

9:42:44   I can't. I—

9:42:45   [OFF-MIC CONVERSATION]

MALE VOICE:

9:42:49   They can't get in touch with Quick 2-5?

9:42:50   [OFF-MIC CONVERSATION]

MALE VOICE:

9:42:54   Yeah.

NEADS MCC:

Still got those guys there.

We got Langley going to D.C. . . .

MALE VOICE:

9:42:58   Quick 2-5, airline traffic Bra 0-1-0-19 22,000. . . .

With the report that Delta 1989 might be a hijack, Mission Crew Commander Nasypany directed the crew to contact fighter wings in Selfridge, Michigan, and Toledo, Ohio, to see if they had fighters available to scramble.

NEADS MCC:

9:43:40   Okay, they got another aircraft spotted near the Pentagon. Also—did you get the word? I got a Delta 8-9er south of— excuse me—south—southeast of Toledo. I have my folks tracking him right now, see if we can bring him up . . .

9:43:50   [OFF-MIC CONVERSATION]

NEADS MCC:

9:44:05   Yeah, I got a special track on that guy.

9:44:06   [OFF-MIC CONVERSATION]

NEADS MCC:

9:44:07   Okay? Go!

9:44:08   [OFF-MIC CONVERSATION]

NEADS MCC:

9:44:09   No, we're searchin' for it now.

9:44:10   [OFF-MIC CONVERSATION]

MALE VOICE [TO LANGLEY PILOTS]:

9:44:12   Quick 2-5, Huntress, have you on loud and clear. Maintain current heading. Stay at Angels 2-3.

9:44:18   [OFF-MIC CONVERSATION]

PILOT:

Okay, we're at Angels 2-3 and we are stayin' at— [UNINTELLIGIBLE PHRASE]

9:44:25   [OFF-MIC CONVERSATION]

MALE VOICE:

9:44:26   Are you copy?

9:44:27   [OFF-MIC CONVERSATION]

MALE VOICE:

9:44:30   [UNINTELLIGIBLE] 5-8-0-4-0-8-4—

9:44:34   [OFF-MIC CONVERSATION]

MALE VOICE:

Are you generating any airplanes?

MALE VOICE:

9:44:36   We got three up now.

NEADS MCC:

9:44:37   I got three up now [from Langley]. I got Otis in a turn. I got
two jets outta Otis in the turn. And I'm trying to contact Selfridge for another possible hijack in the Great Lakes area. . . .

9:44:52   . . . First Fighter Wing up—over to—I think—I think he's—
you might want to contact Bill. He said—he got stepped on.
It sounded like—

9:44:59   [OFF-MIC CONVERSATION]

MALE VOICE:

9:45:00   And tryin' to work on Selfridge.

9:45:01   [OFF-MIC CONVERSATION]

NEADS MCC:

9:45:03   Talk to me about Selfridge! Did anybody get contact with
him yet?

9:45:06   [OFF-MIC CONVERSATION]

MALE VOICE:

9:45:12   Good. They're mine.

NEADS WEAPONS [TO LANGLEY PILOTS]:

9:45:13   Quick 2-5, Huntress, confirm all birds squawking quad 7.

LANGLEY PILOT:

9:45:22   Affirmative. All birds are squawking quad 7.

9:45:24   [OFF-MIC CONVERSATION]

NEADS WEAPONS [TO LANGLEY PILOTS]:

9:45:25   Huntress copies all. Standby for the lat-long of the CAP point.

NEADS [TO MCC, REGARDING FIGHTERS FOR DELTA 1989]:

9:45:29   They got nobody there.

9:45:31   [OFF-MIC CONVERSATION]

MALE VOICE:

9:45:32   Just south of Toledo. We're talkin' to—with Toledo right now, and they may be able to get somebody airborne—

NEADS MCC:

9:45:35   Okay. Contact Selfridge. Selfridge is there, they've got F-16s . . .

             [OFF-MIC CONVERSATION]

NEADS WEAPONS [TO LANGLEY PILOTS]:

9:45:36   Quick 2-5, the CAP point: 3-8-2-5 north 0-7-7-0-2 west. How copy?

NEADS [TO MCC, RE FIGHTERS FOR DELTA 1989]:

9:45:47   What about Duluth?

NEADS MCC:

9:45:49   Duluth? They got no fighters.

9:45:51   [OFF-MIC CONVERSATION]

MALE VOICE:

9:45:52   We're callin' units to see if they have any assets in that area. We have a possible hijack.

9:45:57   [OFF-MIC CONVERSATION]

NEADS MCC:

9:46:00   Okay, talk to the Great Lakes area right now, we're looking

[to] Toledo to get somebody out there, and Selfridge and Duluth has night flying so there's nobody available—

MALE VOICE:

9:46:09   I'm sorry, sir. But here's the story. You're the closest guys. . . . That really is a hijacker up there. . . .

NEADS Weapons controllers continued to attempt to guide the Langley fighters, while MCC Nasypany struggled to find fighters available to scramble to intercept Delta 1989.

WEAPONS CONTROLLERS [TO LANGLEY PILOTS]:

9:46:18   Quick 2-5, traffic Bra 3-1-0-22, 25,000 tracking—

NEADS MCC:

9:46:23   What we're gonna have to do, we're gonna have to talk to the Commander there. He's gonna have to authority that—

9:46:29   [OFF-MIC CONVERSATION]

9:46:30   I'll work the deal. Yeah, Colonel Marr. He might need to call up—the Toledo guy. Okay? Press! . . .

9:47:44   We're tryin'—Toledo is gonna call me directly and ask the— whose authority—you know, we're gonna [UNINTELLIGIBLE]— have Colonel Marr come down. We'll do this whole homeland defense thing. I'll talk to him. I'll schmooze it. I'll get—I'll get some guys out there. . . .

These efforts were further complicated by the news, at 9:49, that the Pentagon had been hit.

9:49:02   [OFF-MIC CONVERSATION]

NEADS MALE VOICE:

9:49:06   Did you hear word the Pentagon got nailed?

NEADS MCC:

Pentagon just got hit.

9:49:08 [OFF-MIC CONVERSATION]

MALE VOICE:

9:49:10 We got anyone going after that Delta flight?

NEADS MCC:

9:49:12 We're trying.

MALE VOICE:

9:49:13 Okay. I just—

NEADS MCC:

Toledo.

Almost simultaneous with the news that the Pentagon had been hit was the news that the radio system was not sufficient to allow NEADS Weapons controllers to communicate with the Langley fighters over Washington.

9:49:16 [OFF-MIC CONVERSATION]

NEADS WEAPONS (MAJOR FOX):

9:49:21 They've run out of radios over Washington—

9:49:23 I'm trying to get the longitude but the friggin' computer hung on me as soon as I tried to do it.

NEADS MCC:

9:49:28 Okay.

NEADS WEAPONS (MAJOR FOX):

We've got somebody comin' to look at it. . . .

NEADS MCC:

9:49:33 Just do the best you can. Okay, what's the word on Toledo?

9:49:36   [OFF-MIC CONVERSATION]

MALE VOICE:

9:49:38   We all had the direction [UNINTELLIGIBLE].

9:49:40   [OFF-MIC CONVERSATION]

NEADS WEAPONS (MAJOR FOX):

9:49:41   And we're losin' radios out of those sites already and they're not even over Washington.

NEADS MCC:

9:49:44   God damn it! I can't even protect my NCA [National Capital Area].

The strain of coping with multiple reports and limited capabilities was starting to show on the NEADS floor. For all of the trillions of dollars that had been spent on America's post–Cold War defense posture, and for all of the attention that had been paid to the rising threat of domestic terrorist attacks, the infrastructure of alert sites and radar and radio communication that had been built during the Cold War had been allowed to deteriorate to the point that NEADS could not communicate directly with the fighters at low altitude over Washington; communications would have to be relayed either through the FAA or through a higher-flying fighter or tanker. Patience was wearing thin throughout the floor. The identification technicians were mystified that the FAA's Washington Center knew so little of what had happened.

NEADS ID:

9:44:11   Okay. The aircraft that he said was at White House is now near the Pentagon. I don't know where the hell they're getting their intel. I said Washington [Center, not FAA HQ] has no clue when I called Washington about it. They didn't know what the hell was going on. . . .

NEADS ID (OTHER):

9:44:53   They're showing it on TV now.

NEADS ID:

9:44:55 I don't know. [DIAL TONE] What the fuck is this about? [PHONE RINGS] Is that the one that Washington has no freaking—

The NEADS tracking and surveillance technicians struggled to find the coordinates for the White House to relay to the Langley fighters.

NEADS SURVEILLANCE 1:

0-3-2 is here . . .

NEADS SURVEILLANCE 2:

9:44:47 I know! If you just freakin' work with me for two seconds, we'll have it—

NEADS SURVEILLANCE 1:

9:44:50 Let's just calm down.

At the FAA's Command Center in Herndon, the news that the Pentagon had been hit came at 9:42 a.m. The Command Center was tracking United 93 and relaying the latest information regularly to FAA Headquarters in Washington. The FAA's national operations manager, Ben Sliney, reacted instantly by ordering all FAA facilities to instruct all aircraft to land at the nearest airport. There were some 4,500 commercial and general aviation planes airborne at the time. At 9:46, the Command Center advised FAA Headquarters that United 93 was "now twenty-nine minutes out of Washington, D.C." Three minutes later, the Command Center suggested pointedly to headquarters that someone should decide whether to seek military interception of United 93.

FAA HQ: They're pulling Jeff [Griffith, a senior manager] away to talk about United 93.

FAA COMMAND CENTER: Uh, do we want to think, uh, about scrambling aircraft?

FAA HQ: Oh, God, I don't know.

FAA COMMAND CENTER: Uh, that's a decision somebody's going to have to make probably in the next ten minutes.

FAA HQ: Uh, ya know, everybody just left the room.

At Andrews Air Force Base, near Washington, the Pentagon strike prompted the launch of the National Emergency Airborne Command Post, the so-called E-4B. The E-4B took off hurriedly at 9:43 from Andrews and was vectored initially toward Offutt Air Force Base, in Omaha.

AIR TRAFFIC CONTROL:
Okay, sir, I need a direction of flight. Do you have a flight plan in the system? . . . He wants to go to Offutt?

MALE VOICE:
He wants to go to Offutt.

AIR TRAFFIC CONTROL:
Yeah, okay. Just let him go. . . . Straight out.

The pilot of Venus 77, the airborne command post, then informed air traffic control that he wanted to fly to Wright-Patterson Air Force Base, near Dayton, Ohio, and was cleared to do so.

AIR TRAFFIC CONTROL:
Venus 77, please state your intentions.

VENUS 77:
Yes, sir, well, right now I just want to be cleared direct to Wright-Patterson.

Venus 77 turned to the west, just north of the no-fly area around Washington, D.C., then informed air traffic control that he wanted to turn back east and hold just south of Washington. The flight was cleared to do so at 9:47. It eventually settled into a holding pattern over Richmond, Virginia, perhaps awaiting the decision where to fly the president.

Vice President Cheney learned that the Pentagon had been hit while he was in the tunnel under the White House leading to the shelter. There was a secure phone, a bench, and a television in the tunnel. He saw television coverage of smoke coming from the Pentagon while he was in the tunnel, and asked to speak with the president. It took some time for the call to be connected.

President Bush's motorcade arrived at the airport in Sarasota between 9:42 and 9:45. During the ride the president learned of the attack on the Pentagon. The president called the vice president at about 9:45; according to notes of the call, the president told the vice president, "Sounds like we have a minor war going on here, I heard about the Pentagon. We're at war . . . somebody's going to pay."

Contemporaneous notes reflect that the vice president's wife, Lynne, arrived in the tunnel at 9:52, and that at 9:55 the vice president was still on the phone with the president. He advised the president, according to these contemporaneous notes, that three planes were missing and that, in addition to the two that had hit the World Trade Center, one had hit the Pentagon. When the call was over, Cheney and his wife moved to the shelter conference room.

Air Force One took off at 9:54 with no fixed destination. Vice President Cheney and the Secret Service had urged the president not to return to Washington, given the uncertainty of the situation. President Bush agreed reluctantly. *Air Force One* raced down the runway, took off, and flew as fast and high as possible.

Aboard United 93, the passengers and surviving crew were calling loved ones, advising them what had happened and learning about the other hijackings. At 9:37, passenger Mark Bingham called his mother. He told her that he was aboard United 93 and that the plane had been hijacked by three men who claimed to have a bomb. At the same time, passenger Thomas Burnett called his wife. He told her that the plane had been hijacked and that the hijackers claimed to have a bomb, and that one of the passengers had been knifed. He thought one of the hijackers had a gun, but he doubted they had a bomb, because he couldn't see it. He asked her if she had heard about any other planes; she told him that two planes had crashed into the World Trade Center. Burnett asked whether any of the planes that had crashed had been a commercial flight, like his own. Later, he called her again and told her that the passenger who had been knifed had died and that the hijackers were in the cockpit. He told her that "a group of passengers were getting ready to do something."

Passenger Jeremy Glick was on the phone with his wife and mother-in-law from 9:37 to 9:57. He told them that United 93 had been hijacked by three "Iranian-looking" men, with dark skin and bandannas. One of the hijackers said that he was carrying a bomb in a red box, and one was armed with a knife. The pilot, he said, had not made any announcements. The hijackers had herded the passengers to the back of the plane, and had entered the cockpit. Glick said he and the other passengers were thinking of "rushing" the hijackers; "the passengers were voting on whether to storm the cockpit and retake control of the airplane."

Passenger Todd Beamer contacted the GTE air phone operators at 9:44; the phone line remained open for the remainder of the flight. He told the GTE operators that the plane had been hijacked and that the pilot and first officer were lying dead or wounded on the floor of the first-class cabin. One of the hijackers had a red belt with a bomb strapped to his waist. Two of the hijackers, armed with knives, had entered the cockpit and closed the door behind them. The hijackers closed the curtain between first class and coach. Beamer said the plane was going up and down and had turned and changed direction. He said he and some other passengers were planning something and he was going to put the phone down.

At 9:50, flight attendant Sandy Bradshaw called her husband and talked to him for eight minutes. She was aware of the other hijackings that morning. Her husband told her that he had seen on television the results of the two planes' crashing into the World Trade Center. Sandy Bradshaw told him that the plane had been hijacked by three men, who were carrying knives and who put on red headbands as they were hijacking the plane. She said the passengers had been forced to the back of the plane and that the hijackers were up front. She thought they might be over the Mississippi River because they were passing over a wide river. She said the passengers were discussing how to overpower the hijackers, including boiling water to throw on the hijackers as they rushed them. At 9:57, she told her husband, "Everyone is running up to first class. I've got to go. Bye."

The passengers and crew of United 93 had come to the realization that they were the last line of defense; every element of the vast architecture of national defense, intelligence, and law enforcement, from the CIA and the NSA to DoD to State to the FBI to the FAA and NORAD, over years, then months, then weeks, then days, down to hours, to minutes, to seconds, had been stripped away. No one could save them now.

They gathered themselves in preparation to rush the hijackers. The GTE operator heard someone yell, "Are you guys ready? Okay! Let's roll!"

By 9:57, as the passengers and crew aboard United 93 began their rush up the aisle, NEADS personnel were tracking not United 93 but Delta 1989, although by that time they were almost certain that the Delta flight had not been hijacked. Any chance the NEADS air defenders had of learning about United 93 had been thwarted by the failure of FAA Headquarters to pass along the information it had been receiving regarding United 93 since 9:34, by the inability of the National Military Command Center to get anyone from the FAA on the Air Threat Conference Call despite repeated attempts, by the failure of the FAA executives on the White House videoconference to pass on the information, and by the direction of the FAA's Command Center in Herndon to the Cleveland Center not to call the military because that was FAA Headquarters' job. At 9:44, NORAD reported to the Air Threat Conference Call that Delta 1989 might be a hijacked plane based on the information NEADS had received from the FAA's Boston Center. Four minutes later, a caller from the White House shelter asked if there were any further reports of hijacked planes; the National Military Command Center's deputy director mentioned Delta 1989, reporting that "that would be the fourth possible hijack." There was no mention of United 93.

The essential "flaws by design" that separated the top policymaking officials within virtually every department of government from operational employees, and that left individual agencies largely isolated from one another and alienated from the national command structure, were now playing out in the frenzied and compressed final moments of United 93. Those desperate moments, then, were the trailing consequence of those years of frustrated attempts at reform and bureaucratic rivalry—of the CIA's failure to follow through on its director's declaration of war in 1998; of the FBI's unwillingness to follow through on Director Freeh's determination to make terrorism prevention the new priority of the Bureau; of both agencies' invocation of "the wall" to shield information from people in both agencies; of the Department of Defense's continued investment in Cold War strategies; of NORAD's inability to reorient its training even as it identified the emerging threat of a terrorist attack in the United States; and of the FAA's failure to translate its awareness of the emerging threat of a domestic terrorist attack, its awareness of the increased popularity of suicide attacks, and its awareness of the increasing threat of hijacking into any action designed to meet these threats. As a result, the passengers and crew of United 93, and of all the hijacked planes, and the people in the buildings of the World Trade Center and the Pentagon, were unprotected.

As 10:00 a.m. approached, the NEADS air defenders were following Delta 1989 as it circled over Ohio and ultimately landed in Cleveland. The flight had not been hijacked; the pilot had responded to an ACARS text message, and had communicated with air traffic control in Cleveland. The plane's transponder had never been turned off, so it could be followed easily on radar. In fact, minutes after reporting Delta 1989 to NEADS as a possible hijack, Boston Center's military liaison had called back.

FAA BOSTON CENTER:

9:45:25   Yes. That Delta 1989, they did reach 'em on ACARS.

NEADS ID:

9:45:30   It's 1989?

FAA BOSTON CENTER:

9:45:31   Yeah, Delta 1989.

NEADS ID:

9:45:33   Okay.

FAA BOSTON CENTER:

9:45:34   And they—got them on ACARS, told them to land Cleveland.
He acknowledged he would land Cleveland. So, he might not
be a hijack.

NEADS ID:

9:45:40   He may not be a hijack?

FAA BOSTON CENTER:

9:45:41   May not be a hijack.

NEADS ID:

9:45:42   All right. . . .

FAA BOSTON CENTER:

9:46:02   Yeah, he acknowledged on ACARS. He didn't acknowledge by
frequency. So, you know, he still could be. We're just not sure.
But—we—you might wanna keep tracking him. I'm gonna see
what he's—I mean, if he's going down, he might [UNINTELLI-
GIBLE] going down to land.

NEADS ID:

9:46:12   Okay.

FAA BOSTON CENTER:

9:46:13   Maybe not to crash the aircraft. So, we're not sure.

NEADS ID:

9:46:15   Copy that.

Five minutes later, they spoke again. NEADS sought clarification of
the status of American 11 as they followed Delta 1989:

NEADS ID:

9:50:23   Okay. Do you remember when we were talking about—the—
the aircraft by—you guys have any idea who that aircraft
was by—

FAA BOSTON CENTER:

9:50:29   By the White House?

NEADS ID:

9:50:30   Yeah.

FAA BOSTON CENTER:

We had thought for some reason to believe it was American
11. I don't know if we heard that from somebody else that
they had a visual on him that it was American Airlines or
what. We just don't know. So, we don't know—which aircraft
that was. So, and we have three calls—we don't know the
third call sign yet. So, we have two aircraft in the towers and
one in the Pentagon. And we don't know what that third call
sign was.

NEADS ID:

9:50:49   You don't know what the third call sign was?

FAA BOSTON CENTER:

9:50:51   No. We—we originally thought Delta 1989 was it. But now,
we have a third—that means it's, you know, possibly four air-

craft. However, are you still—are you still tracking Delta 1989?

NEADS ID:

9:50:59 Yes, sir, we still are. What—

FAA BOSTON CENTER:

9:51:00 Is—is he descending into Cleveland, or appear to be?

NEADS ID:

9:51:03 Right now, no. He's at—he's at 28,000 feet, 396 knots, just squawking his beacon code.

FAA BOSTON CENTER:

9:51:11 Still squawking—

[OVERTALK]

NEADS ID:

Yeah, it looks like he's by Toledo.

FAA BOSTON CENTER:

9:51:13 By Toledo. So, it doesn't look like he's landing?

NEADS ID:

9:51:15 No. . . .

NEADS ID:

9:52:02 They're—they're scrambling—

FAA BOSTON CENTER:

9:52:03 Okay.

NEADS ID:

9:52:04 They're on him.

FAA BOSTON CENTER:

9:52:05 There are fighters on him? Okay. . . .

NEADS MALE VOICE:

9:52:06   Nobody has scrambled. . . .

FAA BOSTON CENTER:

9:52:51   Yeah, you might wanna scramble on him.

NEADS ID:

9:52:52   Yeah—

FAA BOSTON CENTER:

Was he still heading westbound?

NEADS ID:

9:52:53   Yeah. We were trying to get Duluth. There was no one at Duluth. So now we're—yeah, he's heading westbound. Now, we're trying to get up Toledo and—scramble them. . . .

FAA BOSTON CENTER:

9:53:41   Oh, you'd have to talk to someone at Cleveland Center.

NEADS ID:

9:53:43   Okay. We're gonna try and get 'em on.

FAA BOSTON CENTER:

9:53:44   Okay.

NEADS ID:

Thanks a lot for your help.

FAA BOSTON CENTER:

9:53:45   Aright.

NEADS ID:

Bye.

The NEADS identification technician tried unsuccessfully to reach the FAA's Cleveland Center:

NEADS FEMALE VOICE:

9:54:21   In that book, in that—we used to have a book with numbers. [DIAL TONE] . . .

NEADS ID:

9:54:42   Wrong one. [BEEPS] My God. I can't get a hold of Cleveland. [SIGH] [DIAL TONE, DIALING, BUSY SIGNAL]

NEADS FEMALE VOICE:

9:55:03   Airport in Cleveland? [UNINTELLIGIBLE] airport, I don't know the name of the—what's that?

NEADS FEMALE VOICE:

9:55:07   Cleveland's right there.

NEADS FEMALE VOICE:

9:55:08   Right here?

NEADS FEMALE VOICE:

9:55:09   He's turning back. There's Cleveland right there. [UNINTELLIGIBLE].

9:55:12   [OFF-MIC CONVERSATION]

NEADS FEMALE VOICE:

9:55:15   A reference point. Just do a reference point. There you go. Go ahead. Huh?

9:55:21   [OFF-MIC CONVERSATION]

NEADS ID:

9:55:26   Okay. Cleveland's line is still busy. Boston's the only one that passed this information. Washington doesn't know shit.

The problems in communication were compounded moments later when the FAA's Boston Center called. One of the Otis F-15 fighters over New York had lost radio contact with NEADS and had called FAA's Boston Center to find out what to do.

NEADS ID:

9:55:52   Huntress I.D. Can I help you?

FAA BOSTON CENTER:

9:55:54   Scoggins, military. We have an F-15 holding. He wants to know if he should be—continue to hold or ready to go or—he's in the air.

NEADS ID:

9:56:00   You have an F-15 holding?

FAA BOSTON CENTER:

9:56:02   He's in the air. He wants to know whether he—he's waiting to get directions if he—if he needs to refuel or stay in the air, or I guess they're looking to decide whether—

NEADS ID:

9:56:09   Okay.

9:56:10   [OFF-MIC CONVERSATION]

NEADS ID:

9:56:11   Stand by—stand by one. Weapons? I need somebody up here that—

FAA BOSTON CENTER:

9:56:16   He's over at Kennedy.

NEADS ID:

9:56:17   He's over at Kennedy? Who's got the fighter over Kennedy?

FAA BOSTON CENTER:

9:56:20   Panta four-five. [UNINTELLIGIBLE] wants to know what he needs to do.

NEADS ID:

9:56:24   'Kay, what's his call sign? . . .

FAA BOSTON CENTER:

9:56:28   P-A-N-T-A, Panta 45.

NEADS ID:

9:56:30   All right. Stand by. I'm gonna let you talk to our Weapons officer.

FAA BOSTON CENTER:

9:56:32   Okay.

NEADS ID [TO WEAPONS OFFICER]:

9:56:34   [UNINTELLIGIBLE] there. They wanna know—Boston wants to know [UNINTELLIGIBLE] calling now, wanting to know if they're supposed to refuel or what.

9:56:41   [OFF-MIC CONVERSATION]

NEADS WEAPONS:

9:56:44   He's outta Otis?

NEADS ID:

9:56:45   Outta Otis?

FAA BOSTON CENTER:

9:56:46   Yeah. He's holding over at Kennedy, waiting for directions.

FEMALE VOICE:

9:56:49   Arighty. Stand by just a second. . . .

The NEADS personnel, who had attempted to scramble fighters from Air National Guard bases in Selfridge, Michigan, and Toledo, Ohio, then followed Delta 1989 as it turned toward Cleveland, descended, and landed.

FAA BOSTON CENTER:

9:57:46   Okay. So, is he—you still—where is he tracking now?

NEADS ID:

9:57:49   The one that he's tracking, he's at 30—hold on, I gotta fix my scope. Yeah, same guy. Go ahead and plug in. Okay, I got information for that F-15 [from Otis, holding over Kennedy Airport], hold on.

9:58:00   Okay. So, the F-15, we'd like to leave him under FAA control at a lower altitude. We want to keep him airborne. You can choose the altitude.

FAA BOSTON CENTER:

9:58:08   'Kay. . . .

NEADS ID:

Yeah, right. Now it looks like he's heading back towards Cleveland. His flight level is at 12,000 and descending.

FAA BOSTON CENTER:

9:59:10   One-two-thousand and he's heading into Cleveland, it appears?

NEADS ID:

9:59:12   Yeah. He's—

FAA BOSTON CENTER:

9:59:13   Okay.

NEADS ID:

—he's at 5,000 descending.

FAA BOSTON CENTER:

9:59:15   Okay.

NEADS ID:

Copy.

FAA BOSTON CENTER:

9:59:16   Alrighty. Thank you.

NEADS ID:

Thanks, sir.

Bye.

The fighters from Langley Air Force Base arrived over Washington and formed a combat air patrol (CAP) at approximately 10:00 a.m. The three fighters were handicapped in their mission, however, by degraded radio quality and a lack of information. Because there was no radio contact with NEADS at low altitude, one of the three fighters always flew high so that he could relay orders to the lower fighters, and the FAA air traffic controllers assumed control of the lower-flying fighters. The other problem was that the Langley fighters had no awareness of the hijackings; they knew and could see that the Pentagon had been hit, but they had no idea how. The lead pilot explained: "I reverted to the Russian threat. . . . I'm thinking cruise missile threat from the sea. You know, you look down and see the Pentagon burning, and I thought the bastards snuck one by us. . . . You couldn't see any airplanes, and no one told us anything."

The passengers and crew aboard United 93 had launched their desperate assault at 9:57. NEADS was following the Delta flight as it landed in Cleveland. The White House was requesting, on the Air Threat Conference Call, continuity of government measures, a fighter escort for *Air Force One*, and a CAP over Washington; the latter was already in place. The NMCC was still trying to get the FAA on the call. FAA Headquarters personnel were discussing what to do about United 93.

The sounds of the struggle were picked up by the cockpit voice recorder, which was recovered after the incident. On the tape, the sounds of struggle—shouting, crashing—grew louder, suggesting that the uprising was moving steadily toward the cockpit door. At 9:58:57, Ziad Jarrah, the hijacker pilot, told one of the other hijackers to block the cockpit door. He rocked the wings of United 93 sharply from side to side in an effort to throw the passengers and crew off balance. The assault continued unabated.

One minute later, Jarrah changed tactics, pitching the nose of the airplane up and down to disrupt the assault. There were "loud thumps, crashes, shouts, and the sound of breaking glasses and plates." At 10:00:03, Jarrah stabilized the flight path, then asked, "Is that it? Shall we finish it off?" One of his fellow hijackers responded, "No. Not yet. When they all come, we finish it off." Jarrah resumed pitching the nose of the plane up and down. At 10:00:26, a passenger yelled, "In the cockpit! If we don't, we'll die!" Sixteen seconds later, a passenger yelled, "Roll it!" A reasonable inference is that the passengers and crew had subdued the hijacker resistance outside the cockpit and were now at the threshold, ramming the door.

At 10:01, Jarrah stabilized the plane again, and said, "Allah is the greatest! Allah is the greatest!" He then asked, "Is that it? I mean, shall we put it down?" The other hijacker replied, "Yes, put it in and pull it down." The crashing noises continued. At 10:02:23, a hijacker yelled, "Pull it down! Pull it down!"

In its interpretation of the events, the 9/11 Commission concluded: "The hijackers remained at the controls, but must have judged that the passengers were only seconds from overcoming them." Jarrah banked the plane to the right and down; it rolled onto its back as one of the hijackers shouted, "Allah is the greatest! Allah is the greatest!" The sounds of shouting and crashing continued as the plane went down.

Heading almost straight down at 580 miles per hour, United 93 crashed into a field in Shanksville, Pennsylvania, about twenty minutes' flying time from Washington, D.C., at 10:03:11 a.m.

In the White House bunker, reports began coming in at 10:02 about an inbound aircraft, presumably hijacked. The reports were coming from the Secret Service, which was talking to someone at FAA Headquarters. Unbeknownst to the Secret Service and the White House, FAA Headquarters may have been following a computer projection of United 93's flight path, not the actual radar returns. Thus, over the succeeding minutes, updates would be offered reflecting United 93's coming closer and closer to Washington, when in fact it was already down.

NORAD had no knowledge whatsoever of this situation. At 10:07, its representative on the Air Threat Conference Call stated that NORAD had "no indication of a hijack heading to D.C. at this time."

The NEADS ID techs contacted Cleveland Center to confirm that Delta 1989 had landed, only to be told about United 93:

> **FAA CLEVELAND CENTER:**
> I believe I was the one talking about that Delta 1989.
>
> **NEADS ID:**
> Go ahead.
>
> **FAA CLEVELAND CENTER:**
> Okay, well—disregard that—did you—
>
> **NEADS ID:**
> [UNINTELLIGIBLE] planes are crashing through the—
> What we found out is that he was not a confirmed hijacked, however—
>
> **FAA CLEVELAND CENTER:**
> —okay, I—I don't want you to worry about that now. We got a United 93 out here. Are you aware of that?
>
> **NEADS ID:**
> United 93?
> We've got three more hijacked airborne.
>
> **FAA CLEVELAND CENTER:**
> That has a bomb on board.
>
> **NEADS ID:**
> A bomb on board? And this is confirmed? You have a mode three, sir?
>
> **FAA CLEVELAND CENTER:**
> No, we lost his transponder. What we wanna know is, did you scramble airplanes so that Delta 18—1989?
>
> **NEADS ID:**
> We did, out of Selfridge and Toledo, sir.

FAA CLEVELAND CENTER:

Did you? Did you? Are they in the air?

NEADS ID:

Yes, they are.

FAA CLEVELAND CENTER:

Is there any way we can get them to where this United is? . . .

NEADS MALE VOICE:

How do we—confirm that United's got the bomb on board?

FAA CLEVELAND CENTER:

He's—I heard on the frequency.

NEADS MALE VOICE:

Okay, we heard it on the frequency, yes.

NEADS ID:

It—it came across on the frequency. That's their confirmation
a bomb on board—

Even as Mission Crew Commander Major Nasypany was absorbing
the information that United 93 was hijacked with a bomb on board,
Weapons director Major James Fox shouted out an urgent message.

NEADS MCC:

10:07:16   Bomb on board. United 93. Out of Boston?

NEADS WEAPONS DIRECTOR FOX:

10:07:31   MCC, we've got an aircraft reported over the White House.
Intercept?

Mission Crew Commander Nasypany reacted instantly, then juggled the
crises of the aircraft over the White House and the news of a bomb on
board United 93:

NEADS MCC:

10:07:32   Intercept!

NEADS WEAPONS DIRECTOR FOX:

Intercept!

NEADS MCC:

10:07:35   Intercept and divert that aircraft away from there.

10:07:38   [OFF-MIC CONVERSATION]

NEADS MCC [TO COLONEL MARR]:

10:07:39   We—okay, we got that. Do you hear that? That aircraft over the White House. What's the word? . . .

10:07:45   Intercept and what else?

NEADS ID:

. . . bomb on board there, over Pittsburgh . . .

NEADS MCC:

10:07:48   Okay.

10:07:49   [OFF-MIC CONVERSATION]

10:07:50   Aircraft over the White House.

NEADS BACKGROUND MALE VOICE:

United 9-3. Bomb on board—

NEADS MCC:

10:07:55   Nope, not yet.

NEADS BACKGROUND MALE VOICE:

10:07:56   United 9-3? . . .

NEADS MCC:

10:07:58   How close are you to intercept [of the plane over the White House]? . . .

STAFF SERGEANT JEREMY POWELL:

10:08:10 They're right on him right now. They're going in now—

NEADS MCC [TO BATTLE CAB]:

10:08:12 They're going in right now.

10:08:13 [OFF-MIC CONVERSATION]

NEADS FEMALE VOICE:

10:08:15 Confirmed bomb on board. United 9-3—

NEADS MALE VOICE:

10:08:18 We don't have a position on it.

NEADS MCC

10:08:19 Got it. . . . Jamie, any words? Jamie?

10:08:44 [OFF-MIC CONVERSATION]

NEADS BACKGROUND MALE VOICE:

10:08:50 That might—be that fifth airplane.

10:08:52 [OFF-MIC CONVERSATION]

NEADS BACKGROUND MALE VOICE:

Had better days . . .

NEADS MCC:

10:09:11 Okay, we got a mode three on this—United 93.

10:09:15 [OFF-MIC CONVERSATION]

10:09:17 How close are ya? . . .

NEADS BACKGROUND MALE VOICE:

10:09:33 Going in for a Z-point . . .

FEMALE VOICE:

10:09:36 This is the guy with the bomb on board.

NEADS MCC:

10:09:37 Got it. . . . Look for him [United 93] . . .

NEADS BACKGROUND MALE VOICE:

I need a track number. . . .

NEADS MCC [TO BATTLE CAB]:

10:10:21 We're gettin' to it. We don't know where it is. We're—we're gettin'—track on it. . . .

10:10:27 Yeah.

[OFF-MIC CONVERSATION]

10:10:29 Okay.

10:10:30 [OFF-MIC CONVERSATION]

10:10:31 Got it.

NEADS BACKGROUND MALE VOICE:

United what?

NEADS BACKGROUND MALE VOICE:

United 9-3. Mode 3 15-27 . . .

NEADS MCC [TO WEAPONS DIRECTOR FOX]:

Negative. Negative clearance to shoot . . . Jamie . . . God-damnit! Foxy?

NEADS WEAPONS DIRECTOR FOX:

I'm not really worried about code words [authorizing a shoot-down] at this point.

NEADS MCC:

Fuck the code words. That's perishable information. Negative clearance to fire. ID. TYPE. TAIL.

Okay. Where's my bomb? Where's my bomber at?

High over Washington, one of the Langley fighters had spotted a target flying at low altitude near the White House. The fighter requested rules of engagement, and was told, "ID. TYPE. TAIL." In other words, even after the World Trade Center and the Pentagon had been struck, even after the intention of the hijackers to use planes as missiles was clear, the NORAD rules of engagement had not changed from the rules of a classic hijacking. There was no clearance to shoot the plane down. As Michael Bronner puts it, "At what feels on the tapes like the moment of truth, what comes back down the chain of command, instead of clearance to fire, is a resounding sense of caution." As it turned out, the plane that had been spotted over the White House was one of the other fighters from Langley; the fighter at high altitude had been sent to high altitude to relay radio transmissions to the other fighters and had not recognized the plane as one of his cohort. NEADS Weapons controllers struggled to pass the guidance to the Langley fighters:

> **NEADS WEAPONS:**
> Quit 2-6 status? SD, they're too low. I can't talk to them. They're too low. I can't talk to them.
>
> **MAJOR FOX:**
> Negative clearance to fire.
>
> **NEADS WEAPONS:**
> Okay. I told them mission is ID and that was it.
>
> **MAJOR FOX:**
> Do whatever you need to divert. They are not cleared to fire.

Word came back that the mysterious aircraft was one of the Langley fighters flying low. "That was cool," said a Weapons controller. "We intercepted our own guys."

For his part, MCC Nasypany was now directing the defense of America from the dim operations floor in Rome, New York, dealing simultaneously and adeptly with the interception of a plane over the White House and another flight with a bomb on board over Cleveland.

Down below the stray fighter, in the White House shelter, reports kept coming in from the Secret Service about the incoming aircraft. Sometime between 10:10 and 10:15, a White House military aide told the vice president that the aircraft was eighty miles out. The vice president was asked for authority to engage the aircraft. Scooter Libby described Cheney's reaction as quick and decisive: taking "about the time it takes a batter to decide to swing." He authorized the fighter pilots to engage. The aide returned a few minutes later, between 10:12 and 10:18, and informed that the flight was sixty miles out. The vice president reaffirmed his authorization of the shoot-down.

Josh Bolten, the White House deputy chief of staff, sat at the conference table with the vice president. He heard the vice president confirm the authorization to shoot down deviating aircraft and, after what he described as a "quiet moment," suggested that the vice president get in touch with the president to confirm the order. He told the 9/11 Commission that he had not heard any prior discussion with the president on the subject, and he wanted to make sure that the president was informed that the vice president had confirmed the order.

Vice President Cheney was logged calling the president at 10:18 for a two-minute conversation; the president confirmed the shoot-down order. White House press secretary Ari Fleischer's notes reflect that at 10:20 aboard *Air Force One*, "the president told him that he had authorized a shoot-down of aircraft if necessary." No prior notes reflect that authorization.

Much controversy has surrounded the issue of whether in fact it was the president or the vice president who had issued the authorization for fighter jets to shoot down deviating aircraft. In my view, the debate, on its merits, is trivial. Although by law only the president and the secretary of defense were empowered to issue such an order, and the vice president was not in the chain of command for such an order at all, given the chaos of the morning and the imminent peril in which everyone in the White House existed in those precious seconds, no one could have faulted the vice president, as the highest-ranking official remaining in the White House, for acting decisively to protect himself and the nation's capital.

The issue became controversial, in large part, because the president and vice president later insisted, adamantly, that the president had already authorized the shoot-down in an earlier conversation. Both men, however, were surrounded by people like Lynne Cheney and Ari Fleischer, who had a strong sense of the historic moment, and by officials whose job it was to record the significant events of the day. Although no single document captured every piece of critical information or every critical decision, all of the other important bits of information were captured somewhere. There is a record, for instance, of the call before 10:00, when the vice president informed the president that there were three hijacked planes, as there is a record of the conversation at 10:18, when the president confirmed the shoot-down order. There is no record anywhere of a prior conversation between the president and vice president regarding the shoot-down order. Given the historic nature of the order, it strains credulity to believe that such a conversation occurred and went both unrecorded and unremarked upon in its immediate aftermath.

Especially revealing, in this regard, is the manner in which the order was passed through the chain of command. The vice president's authorization was communicated to the NMCC at the Pentagon repeatedly between 10:14 and 10:18. It was apparently passed to NORAD and, through NORAD, to General Larry Arnold at CONR in Florida. At 10:31 a.m., General Arnold instructed his staff to broadcast the following message over a NORAD instant messaging system: "10:31 Vice president has cleared us to intercept tracks of interest and shoot them down if they don't respond, per [General Arnold]." If the vice president had truly been acting at presidential direction, he knew enough, and was experienced enough, to make clear in his authorization that he was acting at the direction of the president. He did not.

In the event, the shoot-down authorization, when it arrived on the floor at NEADS, at 10:32, caused considerable confusion.

NEADS MCC:
You need to read this. . . . The Region Commander has declared that we can shoot down aircraft that do not respond to our direction. Copy that?

NEADS WEAPONS CONTROLLERS:
Copy that, sir.

FLOOR LEADERSHIP:
So if you're trying to divert somebody and he won't divert—

NEADS WEAPONS CONTROLLERS:
[Colonel Marr] is saying no.

NEADS MCC:
No? It came over the chat. . . . You got a conflict on that direction?

NEADS CONTROLLERS:
Right now, no, but—

FLOOR LEADERSHIP:
Okay? Okay, you read that from the Vice President, right? Vice President has cleared us to intercept traffic and shoot them down if they do not respond, per [General Arnold].

The authorization was not passed to any of the pilots controlled by NEADS. Colonel Marr explained to the 9/11 Commission that he refused to pass it on because he was unsure of its ramifications. United 93 was confirmed crashed at 10:15, and there were no other targets by 10:32. Major Nasypany and Major Fox both told the Commission staff that they did not pass the order to the pilots over New York or Washington because they were unsure how the pilots would, or should, act as a result.

The authorization was also puzzling to Secretary of Defense Rumsfeld, who joined the Air Threat Conference Call at 10:39, and was briefed by the vice president.

> CHENEY: There's been at least three instances here where we've had reports of aircraft approaching Washington. A couple were confirmed hijack. And, pursuant to the President's instructions I gave authorization for them to be taken out.

There was a long pause. Finally, Vice President Cheney said, "Hello?" Secretary Rumsfeld responded:

> RUMSFELD: Yes, I understand. Who did you give that direction to?
>
> CHENEY: It was passed from here through the center at the White House, from the [shelter].
>
> RUMSFELD: OK, let me ask the question here. Has that directive been transmitted to the aircraft?
>
> CHENEY: Yes, it has.
>
> RUMSFELD: So we've got a couple of aircraft up there that have those instructions at this present time?
>
> CHENEY: That is correct. And it is my understanding they've already taken a couple of aircraft out.
>
> RUMSFELD: We can't confirm that. We're told that one aircraft is down but we don't have a pilot report that did it.

Thus, while the vice president and other leaders believed that the fighters circling above them had been passed the authorization to shoot down unresponsive flights, the orders actually conveyed remained the instruction that MCC Nasypany had shouted to Weapons director James Fox at 10:10: "Negative clearance to fire. ID. TYPE. TAIL."

Even as the vice president was briefing the secretary of defense on the applicable rules of engagement, another group of fighters was taking off from nearby Andrews Air Force Base with wholly separate instructions. These fighters, from the 113th Wing of the D.C. Air National Guard, launched as a result of information passed to General David Wherley by the Secret Service. General Wherley was talking to a Secret Service agent who claimed to be speaking on behalf of Vice President Cheney. The guidance he passed to Wherley was to send up fighters with orders to take out any aircraft that threatened the White House or Capitol. Wherley translated this in military terms as "weapons free," meaning that the decision to shoot rested in the cockpit of the lead pilot. General Wherley passed this instruction to the pilots that launched at 10:42. Neither the president, the vice president, the secretary of defense, the NORAD commander, nor anyone at NEADS was aware that morning that the Andrews Air Force Base fighters were airborne outside the military chain of command, operating under different rules of engagement from the Langley fighters in the same airspace.

The exploits of the Andrews pilots, and of Billy Hutchison in particular, have become the stuff of myth. Retold in numerous media accounts after 9/11, and most recently in Lynn Spencer's 2008 *Touching History*, the story is that Hutchison was returning from a training mission and nearly out of fuel when he was alerted that an aircraft—United 93—was hijacked and heading for Washington.

[He landed, then took off again, without refueling, and flew north at FAA direction, searching for United 93. Hutchison coordinated with the FAA, telling them to] give him a vector from his current location along with a distance to the target. This method works, and Hutchison quickly spots the aircraft [United 93] on his radar. But just after locating the target, United 93 disappears from his screen. It had descended too low, blending with the ground clutter—false radar returns resulting from the radar beam scattering off objects near the earth's surface. He struggles to spot the return again while he aims his F-16 up the Potomac. A minute later it reappears, as United 93 climbs back through 10,000 feet. . . . He begins to think about any options he has for taking out the airliner, other than crashing into it. He has 105 training rounds on board and he quickly comes up with a plan: he will try first to take the plane down with practice rounds fired into one of the engines, and then across the cockpit. He'll have to get close to attempt either. If that does not sufficiently disable the aircraft, then he will use his own plane as a missile. He thinks again of his son and prays to God that his mission won't end that way.

This is a thrilling, inspiring tale of fighter jock heroism. There is only one problem with it: It never happened. It is flat-out not true. Hutchison and his colleagues were unquestionably brave—even heroic—in taking off to defend Washington, but the radar and other records of the day indicate that the first Andrews fighter—Hutchison's—did not take off until 10:38, more than half an hour after United 93 had crashed and a good twenty minutes after the wreckage had been located. He landed a short eight minutes after takeoff. His instructions were not to hunt for United 93 but simply to fly past the Pentagon and upriver and radio back if he saw anything suspicious. He was not given the "weapons free" instructions; the fighters that left at 10:42 were. He never saw United 93 on his scope, and could never have intercepted it. When the 9/11 Commission staff questioned him about the disparities between the media accounts and what the radar returns and radio transmissions from the morning indicated, and asked in particular whether there might be tapes to which the Commission had not been given access—tapes that might support his public account—he stormed out of the room. "You know what happened," he said. "Why are you asking me?"

As early as 9/11 itself, the question of what happened was producing some bizarre accounts. It wasn't long before the Day of Days turned into the Tale of Tales. How that occurred, and the ramifications, are the subject of the next section.

PART FOUR

WHISKEY TANGO FOXTROT: THE TALE OF TALES

The government's response to the terrorist attacks on 9/11 did not cease with the response to the news that United 93 had crashed. The FAA was in the process of guiding 4,500 aircraft to land at their nearest airports; it did so without incident, in one of the more remarkable feats in aviation history. The military responded throughout the morning, raising the alert status of American armed services to DEFCON 3 just after 11:00, despite the fact that DEFCON 3 was a Cold War–era designation, devised to respond to a nuclear threat. By noon, Secretary Rumsfeld, Vice President Cheney, and General Eberhart put together a set of improvised rules of engagement that would have effectuated the shoot-down authorization. NEADS and the FAA established later that morning a twenty-four-hour, seven-day-a-week open line that operates to this day. The military made the transition nearly seamlessly into Operation Noble Eagle, a twenty-four-hour, seven-day-a-week guardianship of America's airspace that continued for months. The military's alert status has been heightened ever since.

Not surprisingly, however, even as operational responders were focused on the possibility of more attacks, the same question most Americans were asking the night of 9/11 was also ringing in the corridors of government at the highest levels: What the hell happened? President

Bush and Vice President Cheney, both of whom had come into office touting their business-management backgrounds, raised the question with staff and with the Cabinet. Just after noon that day, Vice President Cheney had told Richard Clarke, the veteran counterterrorism coordinator for the National Security Council who had chaired a crisis management conference call from the White House Situation Room that morning, to "prepare a briefing for President Bush when he lands in Omaha. And I need a timeline of everything you have done."

Andrew Card, the president's chief of staff who had been the secretary of transportation under the first President Bush, wondered what the role of air traffic controllers and the FAA had been. The vice president tasked the military almost immediately with finding out exactly what had occurred, and specifically with finding out whether the Air Force had shot down United Flight 93, the fourth hijacked plane that had crashed in Shanksville, Pennsylvania.

Fortunately for the historical record, the two agencies principally involved in the response on 9/11—the FAA and the military—were intimately acquainted with the "fog of war" that can occur in the moments surrounding a crisis, when human recollection becomes unreliable. Both had developed comprehensive information-retrieval systems designed to enable them to reconstruct events as they had actually occurred. Neither would be forced to rely on fallible human recollection.

The FAA taped every transmission between its controllers and the pilots of the flights under their control, and possessed the technology, through the flight data recorder, to reconstruct the flight path of every airplane, and to link that path with the cockpit voice recorder aboard the aircraft. The latter evidence would become particularly significant in reconstructing the last moments of United 93. When the National Transportation Safety Board synchronized the voices on the cockpit voice recorder with the simulated flight path from the flight data recorder, it became clear that the plane was not shot down; the flight of the plane matched perfectly the context provided by the voices on the tape. It was not crashed by the passengers and crew, nor was it crashed because of a cockpit struggle. As the final, clearly heard cries of *"Allah Akhbar"* made clear, it was the last desperate act of a failed mission, taken because the hijackers feared that the passengers and crew would retake the plane and land it safely.

The military had an equally sophisticated system of information retrieval in place. On the operations floor at NEADS, significant positions were taped, including that of the identification technicians, the Weapons team, and the mission crew commander. The taping system was an antiquated reel-to-reel design, but the conversations were ultimately converted to digital files without degrading the data. In addition, officers were assigned to back up key positions like the mission crew commander by maintaining logs, which recorded the significant conversations, developments, and orders of the day. Some of those logs were two- and three-way "chat" logs that enabled NEADS to communicate in real time with the Continental U.S. Region command (CONR) in Florida, and, through CONR, with NORAD Headquarters in Colorado.

Similarly, the Pentagon's National Military Command Center (NMCC) recorded the Significant Event and, immediately after, the Air Threat Conference Call; a log was maintained of the significant events and decisions reported on these calls. A log was also maintained of the significant discussions on the White House videoconference.

The officers involved in the response remained acutely aware, moreover, of these systems, and in fact relied on them. The NEADS mission crew commander, Major Nasypany, gave clear evidence of this when, in speaking with Weapons director James Fox, he decided to scramble the Langley fighters in response to the reports that American 11 was still airborne:

NEADS MCC:

9:07:20   Okay, Foxy. Plug in. I want to make sure this is on tape.

9:07:33   Okay, Foxy. This is what—this is what I foresee that we probably need to do. We need to talk to FAA. We need to tell 'em if this stuff's gonna keep on going, we need to take those fighters on and then put 'em over Manhattan, okay? That's the best thing. That's the best play right now. So, coordinate with the FAA. Tell 'em if there's more out there, which we don't know, let's get 'em over Manhattan. At least we got some kinda play.

Likewise, at 9:34, when the NEADS officers learned that American 77 was lost and the Langley fighters had been ordered to Baltimore, two Weapons controllers had the following exchange:

NEADS WEAPONS MALE VOICE:

9:34:34   Okay. Once we go to Baltimore, what are we supposed to do?

NEADS MALE VOICE:

9:34:36   Just have 'em contact us on the auxiliary frequency, 2-3-4 decimal six. We just need—instead of takin' handoff to us and us handin' 'em back, just tell Center they've got to go to Baltimore.

NEADS MALE VOICE:

9:34:47   All right, man. Stand by. We'll get back to you.

MALE VOICE:

9:34:49   Thanks, Papa Tango.

9:34:51   [OFF-MIC CONVERSATION]

NEADS MALE VOICE:

Why we doin' that?

9:34:53   [OFF-MIC CONVERSATION]

NEADS MALE VOICE:

9:34:54   I'm gonna choke that guy!

NEADS MALE VOICE:

9:34:55   Relax. [LAUGHTER]

NEADS MALE VOICE:

9:34:57   Hey, just remember, everything you say is being recorded.

NEADS MALE VOICE:

9:34:59   I know.

NEADS MALE VOICE:

The tapes will be played back.

NEADS MALE VOICE:

9:35:00   It's all good.

In part because of this awareness, the NORAD officers were diligent about updating the current situation as new information came in. Repeatedly that morning, NEADS personnel would restate the current level of awareness of missing flights, reported hijackings, and crash sites. For example, at 9:27 a.m., a NEADS officer stated for the record: "Three planes unaccounted for. American Airlines 11 may still be airborne but the flight that— United 175 to the World Trade Center. We're not sure who the other one is." The unfolding reality was recorded in logs maintained at various positions at NEADS, at CONR, at NORAD, and at the National Military Command Center at the Pentagon; the report that American 11 was still airborne opened the Significant Event Conference hosted by the Pentagon. Thus, as 9/11 Commission staff advised the Department of Defense Inspector General, NORAD's Headquarters intel chat log records at 9:24:39 that "original aa flt hijack is now headed to Washington scrambled lfi [Langley]," and then, at 9:25:13, that "arcrft that hit wt bldg not repeat not hijack aa acrft." The air warning log at NORAD records, at 9:27, "The original hijack a/c [aircraft] is still a/b [airborne] and head for Washington, DC. Otis F15 are trying to intercept the flight." It records, at 9:36, the Langley scramble: "LFI A/B Quit 25/26/27 3 A/B at time 1333 [9:33]." NORAD Headquarters chat log states, at 9:28: "R[eal] W[orld] H[ijacking] (original notification) assessed by Intel as heading to Washington DC/2XF-15s in tail chase."

For all of the chaos of that morning, the records made by the Department of Defense and the FAA document a remarkably coherent story of the sequence of events on 9/11, a sequence that is corroborated completely by the tapes recorded at NEADS, the Pentagon, and various FAA centers. Anyone examining the evidence yielded by the FAA and military information-retrieval systems could not have failed to reach the following conclusion regarding the events of 9/11: the military officers charged with leading the air defense mission did not receive notice from the FAA of any of the four hijacked flights in time to enable them to respond to the threat before the planes crashed.

The greatest amount of notice the military received of any of the hijacked planes was the eight minutes' notice NEADS received of the first hijacked plane, American Airlines Flight 11. The resulting scramble of fighters from Otis Air Force Base (on Cape Cod) occurred at 8:46 a.m., almost simultaneously with the impact of American 11 into the North Tower of the World Trade Center in Lower Manhattan.

The fighters from Otis were airborne at 8:52 a.m.

NEADS received notice of the second hijacked flight, United Airlines Flight 175, as it exploded into the South Tower at 9:02:40.

At 9:21, NEADS received notice that American 11, the first hijacked plane, had not hit the World Trade Center but was still airborne, heading for Washington, D.C.

As a result, the alert fighters at Langley Air Force Base were scrambled. The Otis fighters were initially ordered to tail-chase American 11, but this order was quickly rescinded and they remained over New York City.

NEADS received notice that American Flight 77 was missing, with no mention of its having been hijacked, three to five minutes before that airliner crashed into the Pentagon at 9:37:45. One to two minutes before impact at the Pentagon, NEADS received notice that an unidentified large plane was six miles southwest of the White House. NEADS did not scramble fighters from Langley Air Force Base in response to the report that the FAA was unable to locate American Flight 77.

NEADS received notice that Delta 1989 might be a hijacked flight at

9:42. NEADS was advised at 9:45 that it might not be hijacked and had agreed to land in Cleveland. NEADS never lost the flight on radar, and followed the flight as it landed in Cleveland at 10:00. NEADS established a track on the aircraft and forwarded it to CMOC, the only track forwarded that morning. NEADS scrambled fighters from Selfridge, Michigan, and Toledo, Ohio, to respond to Delta 1989.

Finally, NEADS received notice at 10:07 that United Airlines Flight 93 was hijacked, nearly five minutes *after* the flight had already crashed in Pennsylvania at 10:03:11 and some thirty-five minutes after FAA headquarters in Washington had been notified. The notice that NEADS finally received had come from the FAA's Cleveland Center, not from FAA Headquarters.

NEADS did not scramble fighters from Langley Air Force Base in response to the report of the hijacking of United Airlines Flight 93. The NEADS controllers never located the flight on radar. The Langley fighters did not know of its existence. No order was passed to the fighters to shoot down the plane if it approached the nation's capital.

To put the matter in the simplest terms, the Northeast Air Defense Sector had eight minutes' notice on one flight, five minutes' notice on another, and was notified post-crash on the other two. The notice that was received on the two planes before crash, moreover, did not specify the planes' locations. The authorization to shoot down deviating and unresponsive aircraft was received from the vice president at 10:31 a.m., fifteen minutes after NEADS learned that the last hijacked plane, United 93, had crashed. This order was never passed to the scrambled pilots over New York and Washington.

As the 9/11 Commission Report makes clear, every fact noted above is apparent on the face of the logs maintained that day; the various tape recordings made by the military and the FAA corroborate completely what the logs record.

Not surprisingly, however, confusion reigned in the early hours and days after the attacks. Two days after the attacks, on September 13, 2001, General Richard Myers testified before Congress about the events of

9/11. This was the government's first public accounting of the events, and it was confused. Senator Carl Levin (D-Michigan) asked whether the Department of Defense was "asked to take action against any specific aircraft? . . . And did you take action against—for instance, there has been statements that the aircraft that crashed in Pennsylvania was shot down. Those stories continue to exist." General Myers responded: "Mr. Chairman, the armed forces did not shoot down any aircraft. When it became clear what the threat was, we did scramble fighter aircraft, AWACS, radar aircraft, and tanker aircraft to begin to establish orbits in case other aircraft showed up in the FAA system that were hijacked. But we never actually had to use force."

> LEVIN: Was that order that you just described given before or after the Pentagon was struck? Do you know?

> MYERS: That order, to the best of my knowledge, was after the Pentagon was struck.

This answer bothered Senator Bill Nelson (D-Florida), who asked:

> NELSON: The second World Trade Center tower was hit shortly after 9:00. And the Pentagon was hit approximately 40 minutes later. That's approximately. You would know specifically what the timeline was. The crash that occurred in Pennsylvania after the Newark westbound flight was turned around 180 degrees and started heading back to Washington was approximately an hour after the World Trade Center second explosion. You said earlier in your testimony that we had not scrambled any military aircraft until after the Pentagon was hit. And so, my question would be: why?

> MYERS: I think I had that right, that it was not until then. I'd have to go back and review the exact timelines.

NELSON: . . . My question is an obvious one for not only this committee, but for the executive branch and the military establishment. If we knew that there was a general threat of terrorist activity, which we did, and we suddenly have two trade towers in New York being obviously hit by terrorist activity . . . then what happened to the response of the defense establishment once we saw the diversion of the aircraft headed west from Dulles turning around 180 degrees and, likewise, in the aircraft taking off from Newark and, in flight, turning 180 degrees? That's my question. I leave it to you as to how you would like to answer it. But we would like an answer.

MYERS: You bet. I spoke, after the second tower was hit, I spoke to the commander of NORAD, General Eberhart. And at that point, I think the decision was at that point to start launching aircraft. One of the things you have to understand, senator, is that in our posture right now, that we have many fewer aircraft on alert than we did during the height of the Cold War. And so, we've got just a few bases around the perimeter of the United States. So it's not just a question of launching aircraft, it's launching to do what? . . . In this case . . . my memory says that we had launched on the one that eventually crashed in Pennsylvania, I mean, we had gotten somebody close to it, as I recall. I'll have to check it out. I do not recall if that was the case for the one that had taken off from Dulles.

General Myers's evident confusion about precisely what had occurred prompted criticism in the media and a quick, if contradictory, response from the administration. Bradley Graham, writing in *The Washington Post*, noted that "questions about the time it took U.S. military planes to respond to the threat of several hijacked aircraft speeding toward the nation's financial and military centers have dogged the Pentagon since the attacks. . . . The matter has stood as emblematic of the U.S. government's overall lack of preparedness for the terrorist assault. Top Pentagon officials have been slow to respond to press inquiries for a timeline that would establish the exact times that civil aviation authorities became aware of the hijackings, when U.S. military commanders were notified and when U.S. fighter jets took to the air."

Major General Paul Weaver, the commanding general of the Air National Guard, which had responded on the morning of 9/11 under the command of the First Air Force, sought to answer some of these persistent questions. On September 14, 2001, speaking with reporters at the Pentagon, General Weaver, "pulling a chronology from his pocket," offered a detailed sequence of what had occurred on 9/11. He stated that at 8:53 a.m., seven minutes after American Airlines Flight 11 had hit the North Tower of the World Trade Center, "two F-15 fighters from Otis Air Force Base on Cape Cod, Mass., scrambled to chase the second plane that hit the trade center, United Airlines Flight 175, which had taken off from Boston at 8:14 a.m. and had deviated from its course."

General Weaver stated that the third flight, American Airlines Flight 77, took off from Dulles International Airport at 8:10 a.m., flew west for forty-five minutes, then turned east. "Whoever was flying it," General Weaver said, "had turned off the transponder," and the plane disappeared from radar. "They came back on the [radar]scope at 9:10 in West Virginia." The Northeast Air Defense Sector, Weaver stated, "scrambled F-16s that were on alert at Langley Air Force Base at 9:35. The crash happened at 9:37." General Weaver did not claim that the military had received notice that American 77 had been hijacked.

General Weaver added that "no National Guard or other military planes were scrambled to chase the fourth hijacked airliner," United Airlines Flight 93, which took off at 8:40 a.m. from Newark International Airport. General Weaver said that United 93 flew to the Ohio border, then "turned around real quick," ultimately crashing in a field in Pennsylvania at "10:10 a.m." Although the Langley fighters were patrolling Washington, General Weaver said, "There was no notification for us to launch airplanes" to respond to United 93. "We weren't even close." Besides, General Weaver noted, "What does he [the fighter pilot] do when he gets there? You're not going to get an American pilot shooting down an American airliner. We don't have permission to do that." Only the president, he stated, could issue such an order.

This account, offered days after 9/11, would be the last public statement uttered by General Weaver on the subject, and proved to be the most accurate account of events issued until the 9/11 Commission's investigation. It was, however, contradicted that very day by Deputy Defense Secretary Paul Wolfowitz. Appearing on public television's *NewsHour with Jim Lehrer*, Wolfowitz, when asked whether rules of engagement would have allowed the Air Force to shoot down United 93, said: "I think it was pretty clear at that point that that airliner was not under the pilot's control and that it was heading to do major damage. . . . We were already tracking in on that plane that crashed in Pennsylvania," Wolfowitz stated, adding that "it was the heroism of the passengers on board that brought it down but the Air Force was in a position to do so if we had to."

This view—that timely notice had been passed regarding United 93, that the fighters had been scrambled in response, that the president had issued the authorization to shoot the plane down, and that that order had been passed to the pilots, who were tracking United 93—quickly became official orthodoxy. His assertion that by the time United 93 was heading for Washington the fighters were tracking it and the shoot-down authorization had been given, was repeated on September 17 by Vice President Cheney during an appearance on *Meet the Press*.

As administration officials struggled in public to explain what had happened and when, personnel from both the Department of Defense and the FAA worked to piece the story together, preparing for a briefing at the White House on September 17. An e-mail sent from NORAD's Continental Region Headquarters in Panama City, Florida, just before midnight on September 16 commends the NEADS personnel "who dug up the requested information from your logs and tapes," and indicates that the information has been passed "to the proper FAA office," which will be "using this information to brief the White House tomorrow." The e-mail then asks for follow-up information about "United 93, 1408Z [Zulu time, i.e., 10:08]" and "Which center calls with information that UA93 . . . is heading for Cleveland? . . . 1415Z [i.e, 10:15]" and "Who reported to NEADS that aircraft had crashed?"

On the basis of information contained in the NEADS logs, which had been forwarded, and on transcripts obtained from the FAA's Cleveland Center, among others, the FAA compiled on September 17 a Summary of Air Traffic Hijack Events; this document was used to brief the White House. The FAA Summary, completed at 6:30 a.m. on the 17th, references explicitly the NEADS logs, noting, for instance, that at 8:40 "Northeast Air Defense Sector (NEADS) logs indicate they were notified by the Federal Aviation Administration of the events concerning AA 11," and that at 9:05 "Northeast Air Defense Sector (NEADS) logs indicate they were notified by the Federal Aviation Administration of the events concerning UA 175."

With respect to the other two flights, however, the Summary provides no notification times to NEADS or NORAD whatsoever. With respect to American 77, the Summary records that at 9:33, "an Operations Supervisor . . . advised the White House Office of the United States Secret Service of an unknown aircraft heading in the direction of the White House, fast moving. Meanwhile, a controller was providing the same information to controllers working at the [Reagan National Airport] Traffic Control Tower." The Summary makes no mention, however, of the notification to NEADS at 9:33 that American 77 was "lost," or of the notification to NEADS at 9:34 of an unidentified large plane six miles southwest of the White House, both of which are in the NEADS logs that the FAA reviewed.

The Summary's discussion of United 93 reflects a review of the transcripts from Cleveland Center but makes no mention of the 10:07 call in which Cleveland Center notified NEADS that United 93 was hijacked with a "bomb on board," which was duly noted in the NEADS logs and referenced specifically in the e-mail from CONR to NEADS late in the evening on September 16. The only entry recorded at 10:07 was that "a Falcon Jet reported observing puffs of smoke in the vicinity of UAL93's last known position." The FAA Summary was clear, however, that the hijacking occurred at 9:28, quoting from United 93's transmission of the attack as it occurred.

Thus, the FAA and NORAD went into the White House briefing on September 17 with notification times for American 11 and United 175, but with no notification times recorded for American 77 and United 93, despite the evidence contained in the transcripts and the logs. The Summary also reflected a time at which the FAA was notified that the Otis fighters were scrambled, but gave no account of the scramble of the fighters from Langley Air Force Base. Nor was any mention made of the mistaken report that American 11 was still airborne and heading for Washington.

The agencies' chronologies had changed by September 18, the day after the White House briefing. On September 18, the FAA generated another timeline; this document was for internal use. The September 18 chronology identified a time for the FAA's notification of the military regarding American 77: 9:24. With regard to the FAA's notification of the hijacking of United 93, the FAA's September 18 chronology indicates "N/A." That same day, NORAD issued a press release concerning its actions on 9/11. NORAD's press release also identified 9:24 as the notification time for American 77, and cited that notification as the trigger for the scramble of the Langley fighters. The press release reads:

FAA notification to NEADS 9:24
Fighter scramble order 9:24 *(Langley AFB, Hampton, VA, 2 F-16s)*

Like the FAA's September 18 document, NORAD's press release of the same date lists "N/A" as the notification time for the United 93 hijacking. The NORAD release explains that United 93 was discussed on an "open line" between FAA and DoD, then states:

Fighter scramble order *(Langley F-16s already airborne for AA Flt 77)*

Fighters airborne *(Langley F-16 CAP remains in place to protect DC)*.

Thus, the government emerged a day after the White House briefing with a unified account of the actions of the FAA and the military regarding the final two flights, American 77 and United 93. It was, moreover, an account that fit together nicely with the account provided publicly by Deputy Defense Secretary Wolfowitz and Vice President Cheney.

On October 25, 2001, NORAD Commanding General Ralph Eberhart appeared before the Senate Armed Services Committee to give the military's account of what had happened on 9/11. General Eberhart did not mention the mistaken report that American Flight 11 was still airborne and heading for Washington as a cause for the Langley scramble. Instead, consistent with the NORAD press release of September 18, he provided a timeline chart and verbal testimony that cited 9:24 as the notification time for American 77, implying that this notification prompted the scramble of the Langley fighters; he offered no notification time for United 93:

> SENATOR LEVIN: General Eberhart, there's been some confusion about the sequence of events on September 11 that maybe you can clear up for us. The time line that we've been given is that at 8:55 on September 11, American Airlines Flight 77 began turning east, away from its intended course. And at 9:10, flight 77 was detected by the FAA radar over West Virginia heading east. That was after the two planes had struck the World Trade Center towers.
>
> Then 15 minutes later, at 9:25, the FAA notified NORAD that flight 77 was headed toward Washington. Was that the first notification—the 9:25 notification—that NORAD or the DoD had that flight 77 was probably being hijacked? And if

it was, do you know why it took 15 minutes for the FAA to notify NORAD?

GENERAL EBERHART: Sir, there is one minor difference. I show it as 9:24 that we were notified, and that's the first notification that we received. I do not know, sir, why it took that amount of time for FAA. I hate to say it, but you'll have to ask FAA.

LEVIN: And do you know if that was the first notification to the DoD?

EBERHART: Yes, sir. That's the first documented notification that we have.

LEVIN: Either NORAD or any other component of the DoD?

EBERHART: Yes, sir.

LEVIN: If you could—for the record, I have a number of other questions relative to that issue which should be clarified, and I'm going to ask you those questions for the record to clear that up. We should get—it seems to me we all should have a very precise not only timetable, but a precise indication as to why other agencies, entities were not notified by FAA, if they weren't.

Perhaps you could make that inquiry for us, or we'll ask the FAA directly if you prefer; and also as to what notification was considered to the buildings in Washington once the concept was clear that this plane was headed toward Washington. But we'll save those for the record.

The next member of the committee in line to question Eberhart was Senator John Warner (R-Virginia), whose own extensive military background and familiarity with the military's procedures in conducting after-action reviews and identifying lessons learned led him to depart from his planned questioning of the general.

SENATOR WARNER: Mr. Chairman, you asked of our distinguished witness a very important question. I'm going to deviate from my planned opening here to say I guess I'm a little bit stunned that you don't know why that delay occurred. I would have thought by now all of you in this chain would have gone back, rehearsed these things, figured out what happened, what went wrong so that we ensure it won't happen again. If it was that significant delay and you can't tell us why, how do we leave with an assurance that you and your subordinates have taken steps so that it won't happen again?

General Eberhart responded to Senator Warner with reassurances, but he did not address the question of why the delay had occurred.

EBERHART: Sir, I assure you that we have, and we practice this daily now, and now it takes about one minute from the time that FAA sees some sort of discrepancy on their radarscope or detects a discrepancy in terms of their communication before they notify NORAD. So that certainly has been fixed.

I think at that time, the FAA was still thinking that if they saw a problem it was a problem that was a result of a mechanical failure or some sort of crew deviation. They weren't thinking hijacking. Today, the first thing they think is hijacking, and we respond accordingly.

Of course, if the kind of review Senator Warner referred to had been conducted, it would have disclosed that 9:24 was not the notification time at all, but that the first notification regarding American 77 occurred at 9:34, when it was reported "lost." Such a review would also, however, have raised the question of why the Langley fighters had been scrambled and vectored toward the Baltimore–Washington area, and would have compelled the disclosure that the Langley fighters were scrambled to intercept a plane mistakenly reported to be heading south toward Washington.

After the hearing, in responses submitted "for the record," NORAD stated: "The FAA notified the NEADS that American Airlines Flight 77 was headed toward Washington, DC. NEADS then passed this information to NORAD's Air Warning Center. . . . At 0925, the NMCC convened a Significant Event Conference and during that conference, at 0933, NORAD reported one more aircraft en route to Washington, D.C." As we have seen, this response was not accurate. The FAA never notified NEADS that American 77 was heading for Washington, D.C. There is no such notification recorded on any tape or in any log maintained at NEADS or at NORAD. Omitted from this account, moreover, was the critical fact that the "one more aircraft en route to Washington, DC" reported by NORAD was not American 77, as the answer implied, but American 11, a report that is reflected in logs up and down the NORAD chain of command, extending all the way to the National Military Command Center at the Pentagon.

With respect to United 93, General Eberhart repeated the claim that the military had been following the plane on radar and was in position to shoot it down if it approached Washington.

The next committee member to question the general was Senator Wayne Allard (R-Colorado).

SENATOR ALLARD: Thank you, Mr. Chairman.

As you know, General Eberhart, I am very interested in NORAD and so I'm particularly interested in how NORAD might interact with our various agencies, particularly the FAA. And I appreciate the question that was asked by Senator Carnahan, but I'm going to ask a little more detail. On September 11, my understanding is we had aircraft at least up in the air with the second plane to hit the twin towers; is that correct?

EBERHART: Yes, sir.

ALLARD: And so what I'm interested in knowing is, what was the process there and then how was that follow-up with the other aircraft that you identified that were coming or heading toward Washington, and how you responded? And how was the FAA interacting with NORAD in that whole situation, starting with that first plane that you deployed heading toward New York City?

EBERHART: Yes, sir. The first flight I think was American flight 11. The FAA, once they notified us and we issued a scramble order almost simultaneously to the first crash, tragically. That flight of two out of Otis Air Force Base, out of Cape Cod . . .

ALLARD: Let me understand—so right at the time the first aircraft was hitting the twin towers, you were being notified by FAA that you had another plane headed toward the towers, you just routinely brought another aircraft . . .

EBERHART: No, they notified us of the first hijacking just about the time that that airplane was hitting the tower.

ALLARD: OK.

EBERHART: And at that time, we issued a scramble order for the two F-15s out of Otis Air Force Base. We continued to send those airplanes toward New York City because initially, as we worked with the FAA, we weren't sure if that was the hijacked airplane. I mean, I hate to admit this, but I'm sitting there hoping that someone has made a mistake; there has been an accident; that this isn't the hijacked airplane, because there is confusion. We were told it was a light commuter airplane. It didn't look like that was caused by a light commuter airplane.

So we were still trying to sort this out, so we're moving the two F-15s and we continue to move them. They're flying toward New York City. In fact, they are eight minutes away from New York City when the second crash occurs. We didn't turn around. We didn't send them back.

ALLARD: They hadn't made a sighting of that . . .

EBERHART: Again, it's time and distance. It took them only six minutes to get airborne. Once we told them to get airborne, it took them six minutes to get airborne. I think this talks about the professionalism and training of these individuals. Tragically, there was just too much distance between Otis and New York City to get there in time to . . .

ALLARD: Did FAA then notify you that you had a second hijacked plane somewhere in there, and the planes up there were . . .

EBERHART: During that time, yes, we were notified, and again we'll provide the exact time line for the record.

ALLARD: I'm not interested in exact time lines as much as I am just how the FAA reacted with NORAD during this time period. And then you had the other two planes heading out. Then FAA continued to notify NORAD that you had two other potential hijackings, these headed for Washington; is that correct?

EBERHART: Yes, sir. The initial hijacking of the one, I think it's 77 that crashed into the Pentagon, we were working that with the FAA and we launched the airplanes out of Langley Air Force Base as soon as they notified us about hijacking. At that time it took those airplanes, two F-16s, again, six minutes to get airborne. They were approximately 13 minutes away from Washington, D.C., when that tragic crash occurred. Six minutes to get airborne, but still 13 minutes to it.

Now the last flight was a little bit different. I think it's Flight 93—United Airlines Flight 93 in Pennsylvania. At that time we were trying to decide, initially, if that flight was going to continue west and if there was some other target for that flight. Was it Chicago? Was it St. Louis? And what might we do to launch an aircraft to intercept it?

ALLARD: So FAA knew before it deviated its flight pattern that it was hijacked.

EBERHART: Yes. What we really knew is it was headed west, sir. It dropped off their radarscope. So it was headed west. And then they reacquired it. And at that time it became obvious to us that—we thought it was headed probably for Washington, D.C., but maybe New York City.

We elected at that time to keep the airplanes that were doing the combat air patrol over Washington, D.C., and New York City right where they were in case there was another airplane coming. And then our intent was to go out and meet that aircraft and destroy it if we needed to if it entered either Washington, D.C., or New York City airspace.

Again, General Eberhart's statement, with respect to American 77, that "we were working that with the FAA and we launched the airplanes out of Langley Air Force Base as soon as they notified us about hijacking" is a misleading conflation of events that never happened but were reported—the FAA's notification that American 77 was hijacked—with events that did happen but were never reported—that American 11 was still airborne and heading for Washington. Thus, NEADS was not "working that [i.e., the American 77 hijacking] with the FAA," because NEADS never received the notification that American 77 had been hijacked; the scramble of the Langley fighters did occur as an immediate reaction to a notification about hijacking, but that notification was not, as the testimony implies, a report that American 77 was hijacked, but the report that American 11 was still airborne and heading for Washington. Similarly, as we have seen, General Eberhart's testimony, regarding United 93, that "we were trying to decide, initially, if that flight was going to continue west and if there was some other target for that flight" is misleading, because it suggests that the military was following the flight on radar; in fact, NEADS never located United 93 on radar, because the plane had already crashed by the time NEADS was notified.

By the first anniversary of the attacks, the official version first put forward by Paul Wolfowitz had attained the status of national myth. This version acknowledged that there had been insufficient notice for the military to have responded to the World Trade Center attacks, but insisted that the fighters had narrowly missed arriving in time to intercept American 77 as it crashed into the Pentagon, and that the fighters were positioned and prepared to intercept and shoot down United 93 if it approached Washington.

This official version departed from the facts of the day in four critical respects. First, the official version indicated that the Langley fighters were scrambled in response to American 77, and thus omitted completely the pivotal report of the morning and the source of the Langley scramble: the report that American 11, the first hijack, was still airborne and heading for Washington. Second, the administration version insisted that the military was tracking United 93 and, as a consequence, was positioned to intercept the flight if it approached Washington. This was untrue; the military could not locate the flight to track it because it had crashed by the time of notification. Third, the official version insisted that President Bush had issued an authorization to shoot down hijacked commercial flights, and that that order had been processed through the chain of command and passed to the fighters. This was untrue.

Fourth, the administration version implied, where it did not state explicitly, that the chain of command had been functioning on 9/11, and that the critical decisions had been made by the appropriate top officials. Thus, the president issued the shoot-down order; top FAA Headquarters officials coordinated closely with the military; Transportation Secretary Norman Mineta issued the order to land all airplanes; NORAD Commanding General Eberhart monitored closely the decisions taken at NEADS and CONR; and so on. None of this captures how things actually unfolded on the day.

By the first anniversary of the attacks, this version had already been promoted aggressively by the government; it reached its apotheosis when it was recounted at length on September 11, 2002, for a national audience of tens of millions on an ABC News anniversary special.

CHARLES GIBSON, ABC NEWS: High overhead [after the Pentagon had been struck by American Airlines Flight 77], jet fighters arrive. Just moments too late. . . . In the Pentagon Command Center, General Winfield is juggling a secret conference call.

BRIGADIER GENERAL W. MONTAGUE WINFIELD, U.S. ARMY: We added the White House and we added *Air Force One* to the conference. All of the governmental agencies there that, that were involved in any activity that was going on in the United States at that point, were in that conference.

CHARLES GIBSON: Rumsfeld orders U.S. forces to DEFCON 3. The highest alert for the nuclear arsenal in thirty years. . . . While in Florida, the President hurries aboard *Air Force One*. . . .

[Note: The order to move to DEFCON 3 did not occur until after 11:00 that morning.]

KARL ROVE, WHITE HOUSE COUNSELOR: The President sat down in his chair, motioned to the chair across from . . . his desk for me to sit down, and before both we could, both of us could sit down and put on our seat belts, they were rolling the plane. And they stood that 747 on its tail and got it to about 45,000 feet as quick as I think you can get a big thing like that up in the air.

CHARLES GIBSON: It is 9:55 a.m. . . . Deep beneath the White House, Transportation Secretary Norman Mineta issues an unprecedented order.

NORMAN MINETA, SECRETARY OF TRANSPORTATION: The planes that are coming into the eastern seaboard, turn them around and get them going west. If they're going west, have them land at their destination, but in any event if they're not too far away, have them land.

CHARLES GIBSON: More than 4,000 planes are in the skies over the US. FAA policy allows pilots to use their own discretion to decide where and when they land in an emergency. But on this morning . . .

NORMAN MINETA: I said, "Screw pilot discretion, get the damn planes down." . . .

[Note: This order was not, it turns out, issued by Secretary Mineta at all, or even by FAA Administrator Jane Garvey; it was, instead, the initiative of FAA National Operations Manager Ben Sliney. By the time Mineta made those comments, the order had already been issued by Sliney and planes had already started to land.]

CHARLES GIBSON: Dozens of fighters are buzzing in the sky. F-16s scrambled at Andrews Air Force Base in nearby Maryland. . . . In the Pentagon Command Center, there's a report of another hijacked plane, United Airlines Flight 93.

[Note: By 10:00, there were only three fighters over Washington, the just-arrived F-16s from Langley Air Force Base. The first fighter from Andrews Air Force Base was not airborne until 10:38 a.m.]

GENERAL WINFIELD: We received the report from the FAA that Flight 93 had turned off its transponder, had turned, and was now heading for Washington, D.C.

[Note: The report concerning United 93 came from the FAA's Center in Cleveland to NEADS some five minutes after United 93 had crashed; FAA Headquarters, which received the report at 9:34, never passed it on and was not on the phone with the NMCC until 10:15 a.m.]

DONALD RUMSFELD, SECRETARY OF DEFENSE: We rapidly developed some rules of engagement for what our military aircraft might do in the event another aircraft appeared to be heading into some civilian, large civilian structure or population. . . .

[Note: The revised rules of engagement were not developed on 9/11 until nearly noon. At 10:10, when one of the Langley fighters mistook a plane flying over the White House for a potential target and requested rules of engagement, the NEADS MCC was absolutely clear about what those were: "Negative clearance to fire. ID. TYPE. TAIL."]

CHARLES GIBSON: It is just before 10:00 a.m., jet fighters swarm around the capital. . . . Only minutes before, the Pentagon was struck by a hijacked airplane. . . . But there is little the pilots can do, even though another hijacked aircraft, United Flight 93, is heading for Washington.

MAJOR DEAN ECKMANN, PILOT, AIR NATIONAL GUARD: At that point we had no authorization to shoot anyone down. . . .

CHARLES GIBSON: Cheney personally compiles a list of possible threats from the air. Of the flights that you didn't know where they were?

VICE PRESIDENT DICK CHENEY: That we couldn't account for.

DAVID BOHRER, WHITE HOUSE PHOTOGRAPHER: At first it was one of a few planes that they had questions about.

CHARLES GIBSON: White House photographer David Bohrer watches the moment and records it on film.

DAVID BOHRER: Eventually it narrowed to Flight 93. That was the biggest threat at that point.

KARL ROVE: If you take the trajectory of the plane, of Flight 93 after it passes Pittsburgh and draw a straight line, it's gonna go to Washington, D.C.

NORMAN MINETA: You just had to do something instantaneously.

DAVID BOHRER: There was a, a PEOC [Presidential Emergency Operations Center] staffer who would keep coming in with updates on Flight 93's progress towards DC.

CHARLES GIBSON: Did you have any thoughts at the time as to what the target of that airplane might be?

DICK CHENEY: I thought probably White House or Capitol. We found out later from interviewing people who were detained Al Qaeda members, that said the fourth plane was intended for the White House.

GENERAL WINFIELD: The decision was made to try to go intercept Flight 93.

DICK CHENEY: The significance of saying to a pilot that you are authorized to shoot down that plane full of Americans, is, a, you know, it's an order that had never been given before.

ANDREW CARD, WHITE HOUSE CHIEF OF STAFF: Very, very tough decision. And the President understood the magnitude of that decision.

CONDOLEEZZA RICE, NATIONAL SECURITY ADVISOR: The President did give the order to shoot down a civilian plane, if it was not responding properly. And it was authority requested through channels, by

Secretary Rumsfeld, Vice President passed the request, the President said, "Yes."

[Note: The authority was not requested through channels; when Secretary Rumsfeld joined the Air Threat Conference Call at 10:30 and was told about the shoot-down order by Vice President Cheney, he was clearly unaware of it. Whether the vice president had requested prior authorization from the president is disputed, but uncorroborated by the records of the day.]

DONALD RUMSFELD: It was a totally different circumstance for our country, the thought of having to shoot down one of our own civilian aircraft.

CHARLES GIBSON: Do you remember your own thoughts as to what you were thinking?

DICK CHENEY: Yeah, and that was a very difficult, difficult proposition, but it had to be done. If we had been able to intercept the planes before they hit the World Trade Center, would we? And the answer was, absolutely yes.

DAVID BOHRER: And the President gave the, the VP authority to make that call. It was a chilling moment, chilling moment.

GENERAL WINFIELD: The Vice President briefed into the conference that the President had given us permission to shoot down innocent civilian aircraft that threatened Washington, D.C. Again, in the National Military Command Center, everything stopped for a short second as the impact of those words sunk in.

[Note: When the vice president informed Secretary Rumsfeld that the president had passed the authority, there was a long moment of silence. But this occurred at 10:39, and everyone on the line by this time understood that United 93 had already crashed.]

COLONEL ROBERT MARR, U.S. AIR FORCE: The rules have changed. We could do something about it now.

CHARLES GIBSON: Colonel Bob Marr is in command at the Northeast Air Defense Sector base in Rome, New York.

COLONEL MARR: I got the call and . . . the words that I remember as clear as day [were], "We will take lives in the air to preserve lives on the ground."

CHARLES GIBSON: Marr orders his air controllers, tell the pilots to intercept Flight 93.

LIEUTENANT COLONEL DAWNE DESKINS, AIR NATIONAL GUARD: Nothing any controller would ever want to pass to a pilot, to shoot down an airliner filled with innocent people.

COLONEL MARR: And we of course passed that on to the pilots. United Airlines Flight 93 will not be allowed to reach Washington, D.C.

[Note: This never happened, as Colonel Marr later acknowledged to Commission staff, and he gave a very sound reason: The order was never passed to the pilots, because by the time it was received, NEADS was aware that United 93 had already crashed. (He offered no explanation as to why he said otherwise on ABC.) In addition, the order, which came from the vice president, was confusing to the NEADS commanders. The Langley pilots did not know about United 93, and were not told until much later that a plane, not a cruise missile, had hit the Pentagon.]

This version of events made for compelling television, and an equally compelling narrative, and was promoted extensively. Most prominently, it was featured in a BBC documentary, *Clear the Skies: 9/11 Air Defense,* and in a glossy official Air Force history titled *Air War over America:*

Sept. 11 Alters Face of Air Defense Mission, as well as in reports in major newspapers and in *Aviation Weekly.* The story seemed settled, consistent. It had been told repeatedly.

For that reason, when the work of the 9/11 Commission began, the air defense promised to be one of the easier parts of the story to put together. Charged with reconstructing the facts of the day of 9/11 at all levels of government, from the actions of President Bush to the actions of the first responders on the ground in New York City, I began to write a draft of Commission findings based on prior testimony and on open-source, public documents. This would, I believed, save time at the end of the Commission's work; we would merely have to corroborate the facts already set forth so extensively in the public record.

There were questions left unanswered by the government's version of events: When did the military learn that United 93 had been hijacked? When did the president issue the authorization to shoot down United 93? Where had the Langley fighters flown and when? But I expected that these questions would be resolved at one of the first Commission hearings, in May 2003.

At the May 23, 2003, hearing, Retired Colonel William Scott presented the Commission with a NORAD timeline of the operational facts of 9/11. This timeline reflected, among other things, FAA notice of the hijacking of United Airlines Flight 93 at 9:16 a.m. (forty-seven minutes before crash), and of the hijacking of American Airlines Flight 77 at 9:24 a.m. (thirteen minutes before crash), and indicated that the fighters at Langley Air Force Base were scrambled at 9:25 a.m. to meet the threat to Washington posed by American Airlines 77.

It quickly emerged that there was a problem with using 9:24—the time that had been settled on by both the FAA and DoD after the White House briefing on September 17, 2001—as the notification time for American 77, and as the event that triggered the Langley scramble. The representation that the Langley fighters were scrambled to meet the threat posed by American 77 puzzled Commissioners John Lehman and Richard Ben-Veniste in particular, who asked why, if that was the case, the radar reconstruction offered by the military showed the Langley fighters heading east, away from Washington, and then toward Baltimore, not Washington. If NORAD had received information that a third flight was heading east toward Washington, Commissioners Lehman and Ben-Veniste wondered, why didn't the Langley fighters fly directly to Washington? (In fact, as we have seen, once the NEADS MCC received that information, he did precisely that, declaring AFIO—Authorization for Interceptor Operations—and heading the fighters directly to Washington.) Retired Air Force General Larry Arnold explained:

9:24 was the first time that we had been advised of American 77 as a possible hijacked airplane. Our focus—you have got to remember that there's a lot of other things going on simultaneously here—was on United 93, which was being pointed out to us very aggressively I might say by the FAA. . . . We were advised [American 77] was possibly hijacked. And we had launched almost simultaneously with that, we launched the aircraft out of Langley to put them over top of Washington, D.C., not in response to American Airlines 77, but really to put them in position in case United 93 were to head that way. They were the closest fighters we had, and we started vectoring them to move towards the Washington, D.C., area.

With respect to United 93 and the shoot-down order, the testimony was confusing. On one hand, General Arnold conceded that the authorization did not come down until "about five minutes" after the plane had crashed, although this would have been timely notification had the flight continued on its way to Washington. On the other hand, General Arnold maintained that once the FAA had ordered all aircraft to land, the military was authorized to close the airspace around Washington and could have shot down any plane that did not respond to interception. This prompted Commissioner Ben-Veniste to ask: "If I understand the context of what you said about closing the perimeter around Washington, the president's directive or the vice president's directive would have been moot, because of the prior order, which would have enabled you to shoot down an unfriendly plane in that sector?" General Arnold answered: "We developed a certain—I guess the short answer, yes, that is correct. But it's very specifically in the Washington, D.C., area by presence that aircraft was hostile unless we could determine it was friendly."

As the Commission investigation continued, the confusion mounted. I abandoned my effort to complete a first draft based on public sources when it became clear that the information we began to receive in response to the Commission's document requests did not corroborate what the public had been told. There was no documented notification that American 77 had been hijacked; there was no documented notification that notice had been passed that United 93 had been hijacked at 9:16, as reported. We received a garbled and partial transcript from the NEADS floor, which was puzzling, given that Commissioner Ben-Veniste had asked General Arnold at the May hearing whether any of the conversations between NEADS and the FAA had been taped, and the general had testified, "Not to my knowledge." The transcript received by the Commission appeared garbled and partial; even this, however, failed to support the version of events set forth before Congress and the Commission, or in the media.

The situation was summed up aptly for the 9/11 Commission staff one afternoon by Kevin Shaeffer, one of my team's staff members. Kevin had been a rising star in the Navy before 9/11. An Annapolis graduate, on the morning of 9/11 he was working in Naval Intelligence at the Pentagon. By chance, Kevin had been standing behind a pillar when American 77 crashed into the Pentagon; everyone in his vicinity was killed. Kevin suffered severe burns over most of his body, and flatlined twice in the course of his recovery. His injuries had forced him to retire at age thirty from the military and abandon his dream of commanding a ship. He was still recovering when the 9/11 Commission's work began. He brought to our work a dedication and intense desire to know the truth of what had occurred that inspired all of us. I walked past Kevin's work space one afternoon late in the summer of 2003 and heard him muttering, under his breath, "Whiskey tango foxtrot, man. Whiskey tango foxtrot."

"What's that?" I asked. Kevin and Miles Kara (another team member, who was a Vietnam veteran and an Army colonel who left his position in the Department of Defense Inspector General's office of Intelligence Review to join the Professional Staff of the Joint Inquiry) laughed and explained that "Whiskey Tango Foxtrot" was a military euphemism for "What the fuck!"

I don't recall today the particular discrepancy between the official version of what happened on 9/11 and what we were discovering that prompted Kevin's utterance; there were so many that "Whiskey Tango Foxtrot" became a regular refrain for the members of my team. Among our Whiskey Tango Foxtrot moments, these stand out:

1. *The discovery that the FAA could not have notified NEADS at 9:16 that United 93 had been hijacked. In fact, the flight had not even been hijacked by 9:16; it was proceeding normally.* As described above, and as recorded on FAA tapes and the United 93 flight data recorder, the attack on United 93 occurred at 9:28 a.m. Thus, General Arnold's testimony, in explaining the Langley Air Force Base scramble, that "our focus—you have got to remember that there's a lot of other things going on simultaneously here—was on United 93, which was being pointed out to us very aggressively I might say by the FAA," might have served to explain why the Langley fighters took a circuitous route to Washington, but it could not have been true.

2. *The discovery that the FAA did not notify NEADS that American 77 was hijacked at 9:24, as represented to the public by the FAA and DoD since September 18, 2001, and as testified to before Congress and the Commission.* In fact, NEADS received no notification that American 77 had been hijacked at all. At 9:34, the FAA's Washington

Center reported that American 77 was missing; then, two minutes later, the FAA's Boston Center reported a plane six miles southwest of the White House.

3. *The discovery of the mistaken report that American 11 was still airborne and heading for Washington.* The effect of the testimony before Congress and the Commission that the Langley fighters had been scrambled in response to American 77, or United 93, or some combination of the two, had been to allow the witnesses not to mention the true reason for the Langley scramble: the mistaken report that American 11 was still airborne and heading south from New York toward Washington. That mistaken report appears in more logs, and on more tapes, than any other single event that morning, from the FAA's Boston Center, Command Center, and Headquarters to NEADS to CONR to NORAD to the Pentagon's National Military Command Center. It was the reason for the Langley scramble; it had triggered the Air Threat Conference Call. Yet it had never been disclosed; it was, instead, talked around, as in NORAD's testimony before Congress that "At 0925, the NMCC convened a Significant Event Conference and during that conference, at 0933, NORAD reported one more aircraft en route to Washington, DC." The clear implication of NORAD's testimony—submitted for the record, and not an extemporaneous utterance—was that the "one more flight" was American 77. But it was impossible to learn from the records of the Significant Event Conference that NORAD reported "one more aircraft" without also seeing that the "one more aircraft" was "American 11." The records, in other words, are flight-specific. Yet the mistaken report was never mentioned. Similarly, General Arnold testified before the Commission that the Langley fighters were scrambled in response to some combination of American 77 and United 93, but he never mentioned the mistaken report about American 11; later, however, he would demonstrate his

awareness of that report: "In fact, that airplane [American 11] was called possibly hijacked later on, which . . . caused further confusion, because we were not aware which aircraft actually crashed into the towers." The mistaken report was not, therefore, forgotten; its significance as the source of the Langley scramble was simply omitted, in favor of an explanation that continued to raise more questions than it answered.

4. *The discovery that the documents and other materials provided to the 9/11 Commission by the FAA in response to its document requests were significantly incomplete.* Early in the life of the Commission, the decision was made to proceed by document request rather than by subpoena. Although some staff members (including me) and commissioners disagreed with this decision, the reasons underlying it were valid. The Commission was concerned that issuing blanket subpoenas would result in litigation that, given the eighteen-month time frame allotted to the Commission to complete its work, might impair the Commission's ability to fulfill its mission. Detailed document requests were issued through the spring and summer of 2003; by early September, both the FAA and the DoD had certified to the Commission that they had fully satisfied the requests. By late September, having digested the information the agencies had provided, we began conducting field interviews at the FAA's regional centers. We found, to our astonishment, that the FAA had failed to provide significant tapes and transcripts from its investigation of the hijackings. The reason, we were told, was that the FAA thought we had asked for just the "accident package," the completed report, and not the "accident file," which consisted of all the raw material related to the incident. And when staff members John Azzarello, Miles Kara, and Geoffrey Brown visited the FAA's New York Center, they found that taped interviews of everyone involved in the response had been conducted on the evening of

9/11. When they asked why those tapes had not been turned over, they were informed that the tapes had been destroyed. Our team argued vigorously that, given these omissions, the FAA should be subpoenaed; thankfully, the Commissioners agreed.

5. *The discovery that the documents and other materials provided to the Commission by the Department of Defense were woefully incomplete.* When our team visited NEADS in October of 2003, we found, to our astonishment, that, contrary to General Arnold's testimony and to the materials that had been provided to the Commission, significant operational positions—that of the Mission Crew Commander, of the identification technicians, of the Weapons and Surveillance positions—were recorded as a matter of course. The significance of this news cannot be overstated. As we have seen, NEADS was the nerve center of the national response on 9/11. The tapes made on the NEADS floor offered the best opportunity to discover what the military refers to as "the ground truth" of that morning. These omissions, coupled with the fact we were unable to corroborate the official version of events on the basis of the materials we had seen, led us to recommend to the Commission that a subpoena also be issued to the Department of Defense. To their credit, a majority of the Commissioners supported the issuance of the subpoenas.

6. *The claim by senior officials at the FAA and the Department of Defense, once the subpoenaed documents had been turned over, that the senior agency officials had not made a serious effort to reconstruct the events of 9/11.* Once the subpoenaed tapes and other documents from the Department of Defense and the FAA arrived, and our team had correlated the conversations on the tapes with the information recorded on the various logs that were maintained that morning, few mysteries remained about the sequence

of events. Those mysteries—the source of the mistaken report concerning American 11, and the reported initial conversation between the president and the vice president concerning the shoot-down order—were joined by one of equal stature: Why was the official version of events at such variance with what the logs and tapes from the day revealed so clearly? The 9/11 Commission was not a criminal investigation; our job was to find the facts and write the history. We did not cross-examine the witnesses we interviewed but rather took them through the evidence in order to validate from refreshed recollections what the contemporaneous records showed. Still, it was impossible not to ask, particularly of those who had supported the official version in the public record, how it was that they had been so mistaken.

The uniform answer, from Colonel Marr at NEADS to General Arnold and Colonel Scott at CONR, to General Eberhart at NORAD, was that they really hadn't looked that closely. They had been too busy fighting the war on terror to take the time to do a careful reconstruction. For such senior officers, it was entirely plausible that they had been too occupied with the day-to-day business of conducting the war on terror to research the matter personally. That, in fact, would be their testimony before the Commission in June 2004. And yet, the official version had been presented in specific detail to Congress, to the Commission, to the BBC, to a national TV audience on ABC News, and in the official Air Force history, *Air War over America*. Before that, presumably, given the gravity and historical importance of the event, wouldn't the people in charge of the government— the president, the vice president, the secretary of defense—have demanded to know exactly what had happened? Wouldn't someone have been charged with reconstructing the events, given their importance? Was it believable that the Department of Defense would have allowed its officers to articulate and promote a version of what happened on one of the most important days in American history without taking care to make certain that it was accurate?

7. *The evidence that an effort was in fact made, in the days after 9/11, to reconstruct the events of the day, and that the correct timeline had been identified.* Commissioner Ben-Veniste noted as much at the Commission's June 17, 2004, hearing when questioning General Arnold: "I'm not going to go through it, but it is disturbing to see that there were efforts made at after-action reports which were available shortly after 9/11. There were communications which our staff has received with respect to e-mails that reflect some of the facts on a nearly contemporaneous basis with the 9/11 catastrophe that reflect a story that, unfortunately, is different from the one which was presented to this Commission earlier." Specifically, the Commission staff obtained the e-mail referenced earlier, sent late in the evening of September 16, 2001, from Brigadier General Doug Moore at CONR, under General Arnold's command, to NEADS. General Moore's e-mail commends the person at NEADS who retrieved the relevant information "from your logs and tapes," and indicates that it has been passed to the FAA, which would be using it "to brief the White House tomorrow" (i.e., on September 17). The e-mail then asks for follow-up information about, among other data points, United 93.

This e-mail is significant because it reveals that someone at NEADS had searched the relevant logs and tapes during the first week after 9/11 and identified the correct notification time for United Flight 93. That time, which was some five minutes after the plane had crashed, appeared in no timeline released officially or discussed, other than perhaps General Weaver's statement on September 14 that "There was no notification for us to launch airplanes [to respond to United 93]. We weren't even close." As we have seen, however, General Weaver's only public comment was quickly displaced in the official version of events by the version first espoused by Paul Wolfowitz, in which the military was portrayed as tracking United 93 and prepared to shoot the plane down if it approached Washington. Obviously, this version becomes impossible if the first notification the military received that United 93 was hijacked came after the plane had crashed; the military could never have tracked the plane. The day after the White House was briefed—on September 18—NORAD released its official timeline. Before then, NORAD's Office of Public Affairs prepared a draft release. As the Commission staff advised the Department of Defense Inspector General's office, the existence of the draft release, dated September 16, 2001, was revealed in interviews during the 9/11 Commission staff's visit to NORAD Headquarters. The draft release originally listed 9:16 a.m. for FAA notification of American Flight 77; this time did not appear in the final release of September 18. For United Flight 93, the time 9:16 is typewritten as the notification time. Between the September 16 draft and the September 18 final release, both times were changed. In the final release, the "No specific time available" for American 77 is changed to 9:24. The 0916 notification time for United 93 is deleted, and is replaced with the "N/A" entry mentioned above. The public affairs director told Commission staff that he deleted the 0916 notification time because he "lost confidence" in its accuracy, although he could not remember why he lost confidence at the time. He did not remember who told him that notification on American 77 occurred at 9:24. Thus, the Commission uncovered evidence both that the military was looking at the proper data to have discovered the truth during that first week, and that the notification times were being scrutinized closely, if not manipulated. Given that by September 16 the staff at NEADS had identified 10:08 as the notification time for

United 93, as reflected in General Moore's e-mail, it is a fair inference that NORAD "lost confidence" in 9:16 because it was informed of the correct time. Why, we wondered, if NORAD had "lost confidence" in 9:16 as the notification time for United 93 as early as five days after 9/11, had that time reemerged as the notification time in testimony before the Commission as late as May of 2003? Could it have been an effort to explain the direction the Langley fighters took without having to mention the mistaken report concerning American 11?

One answer to these questions, of course, is that, as General Eberhart testified before the Commission, "there's no scheme or plot to spin this story or to try to cover or take a bullet for anyone. . . . I can assure you that we didn't get together and decide that we were going to cover for anybody or take a bullet for anybody." In other words, the erroneous timelines resulted from human error, not calculation. Similarly, with respect to the failure to disclose the mistaken report concerning American 11 as the reason for the Langley scramble, General Arnold testified: "I guess my memory was not quite as good as it should be, and [the Commission] staff actually helped me out quite a bit in terms of this particular area, because I was never comfortable with the fact that some people have said that we had scrambled because of American . . . 77, and I knew that was not the case. So, I guess in the way that the human mind works, unfortunately, is we try to put things into some kind of category."

Anyone who has worked in government for a significant period will be sympathetic to the superior claim of incompetence over conspiracy. More often than not, government is too inept to be capable of successfully executing an elaborate scheme to conceal or deceive. That has certainly been my experience. In the case of the 9/11 timeline, both the erroneous 9:24 time given as the notification time for American 77 and the 9:16 time given for the notification regarding United 93 correspond to entries in the NEADS MCC log. At 9:16 the log records the tail number of a United flight. This tail number corresponds not with United 93, however, but with United Flight 175, which had crashed into the World Trade Center. A corresponding conversation on the subpoenaed tapes confirms that at 9:16 NEADS was receiving confirmation of the tail number of the United 175 flight. At 9:24, the log records the tail number of an American flight. This tail number refers not to American Airlines Flight 77 but to American Airlines 11, the first hijacked aircraft. The subpoenaed tapes confirm that this time corresponds to the receipt of the tail-number information on American 11 and to reports that American 11 was still airborne and headed toward Washington, D.C.

It is thus possible, if no one bothered to check the tail numbers in the log to see which flights they described, and if no one checked the MCC log against the information contained in other logs, and if no one checked with the FAA to verify the times at which the flights were hijacked, and if no one checked the information in the log against the tapes made of that morning, that the erroneous testimony proffered to Congress, the Commission, the media, and the public was simply the result of bureaucratic sloppiness. General Arnold, in particular, emphasized that he had not had access to the tapes concerning the mistaken American 11 report.

This conclusion was hard, if not impossible, to accept for several reasons. First, it conflicted with what the contemporaneous records of the day showed. As Commissioner Jamie Gorelick pointed out to General Arnold, "you said that the reason you were wrong was that you hadn't had an opportunity to listen to the tapes, or the tapes were inaccessible. But I mean, we have—and I'm just holding four of them—different [NORAD] headquarters and CONR logs that are—that clearly reflect that this scrambling was done in response to this phantom American 11, which didn't exist anymore. . . . Did you not look at the logs . . . ?" In other words, anyone who looked at the records would have discerned the ground truth of 9/11.

Second, it conflicted with what we had discovered about the extensive process that the government was undergoing that first week to piece together what happened. People were looking through the relevant records in the days after 9/11. The president and vice president had asked on 9/11 itself for an account of what had happened and of who had done what when. The press was already grumbling, by the time of General Myers's testimony on September 13, that the military had been slow to answer questions about what had occurred. The White House was scheduled to be briefed on September 17. We knew from General Moore's e-mail written late in the evening on September 16 that someone at NEADS was reviewing the "logs and tapes" and had identified the correct notification time for United 93 and for the report that the plane had crashed. We knew that this information was being shared with the FAA. We knew that NORAD had listed 9:16 as the notification time for United 93 in a draft press release but had changed it to "N/A" when it "lost confidence" in the time. We also knew that the time had reappeared in subsequent testimony. Why? In addition, we knew from the partial transcript that someone had been tasked with listening to and transcribing the tapes of 9/11, and had stopped. As Commission staff explained to the Department of Defense Inspector General, "During the week after 9/11, NORAD . . . detailed an officer with technical expertise from McGuire Air Force Base to begin the process of transcribing the operational tapes from NEADS on 9/11. This officer recalls having been visited personally by General Eberhart during the week or so that he worked on the transcription." Commission staff was told at NEADS that the reason the task had not been completed was that the officer, a senior noncommissioned officer, had caused the tape to malfunction and to "reformat"; he had been told to stop because DoD officials were concerned that the tapes would be lost. When the Commission staff interviewed the officer, however, he denied having caused the tape to malfunction and professed ignorance as to why he was asked to stop listening and transcribing. When asked what order of priority his task had been given previously, he indicated that he knew it was a high-priority assignment when he was visited by General Eberhart. When asked whether he was certain he had been visited by General Eberhart, he replied, "You tend to remember it when you're tapped on the shoulder, and turn around, and it's a four-star general." Finally, an e-mail provided to the Commission outside the Pentagon's process and recently released by the National Archives was, we felt, particularly revealing. In the e-mail, Colonel Robert Marr, the NEADS commander, explains why it was "easier" to explain to the public that the Langley fighters were scrambled in response to the report that American 77 was hijacked, even if that was not true:

> The answer on AA77 is not easy, nor is it pretty. At the time AA77 was occurring we were focused on UAL93 which was the only confirmed hijack that the FAA had identified to us. My records show UAL93 reported as hijacked at 0916L, once we found it and identified it's [sic] westerly heading, we scrambled Langley at 0924L just in case it turned around toward DC, which it did later. At 0924L we also received a call from the FAA about AA77 with a follow-up call at 0925L. It is easiest to explain the simultaneous scramble order with the AA77 notification as the scramble being against AA77—it takes a lot of time to explain to the public that you're scrambling fighters against a plane heading away from the possible target!

As we have seen, however, there are no records indicating that United 93 was reported hijacked at 9:16, or that the military found its "westerly heading," or that any call was received concerning American 77 at 9:24 or 9:25. And if Colonel Marr is willing to tell the public that the planes were scrambled in response to American 77 because it is difficult to "explain to the public that you're scrambling fighters against a plane heading away from the target," imagine his reaction to the even more difficult task of explaining that you're scrambling fighters against a plane that proved to be a phantom, that there was no awareness that American 77 was hijacked, and that there was no ability to track United 93's course because the plane had crashed by the time notice was passed. As the Commission staff advised the Department of Defense Inspector General, "Col. Marr attempted to explain the circuitous route of the Langley fighters in getting to Washington, D.C., by indicating that . . . they were scrambled in response to the 'earlier' report that United 93 was hijacked. Thus, the reintroduction of the discredited 9:16 notification time enabled NORAD to explain to the Commission the odd route of the Langley fighters in reaching Washington."

The third reason that it was difficult to accept that the testimony had been inadvertently in error had to do with motivation. It was impossible to ignore the effect of the version that emerged on September 18, 2001, with its omission of the report that American 11 was still airborne and heading for Washington, D.C., and its erroneous claim that the military had been aware of and tracking United 93: taken together, they made possible an official version of events that masked the level of confusion and the essential disconnect that existed between the top echelon of government and the people on the ground making decisions.

In the aftermath of 9/11, both DoD/NORAD and DoT/FAA, not to mention the White House, faced potentially embarrassing realities: the FAA, that its notification standard operating procedure for hijackings had been completely disregarded, and that the ad hoc notifications that were given left the military no realistic chance to intercept the aircraft; NORAD, that it had scrambled the Langley fighters in the wrong direction against a nonexistent target and that it was completely unaware of United 93—the fourth plane—when the flight was heading for Washington; the White House, that, regardless of who eventually issued the shoot-down authorization, national leadership had been irrelevant to the response to the attacks as they were occurring. By claiming that the fighters from Langley were scrambled directly in response to United 93 as well as simultaneously with the notification on American 77, officials were able to avoid admitting that the fighters were scrambled in response to the incorrect report that American 11 was airborne and heading toward Washington from the northeast—not from the west, the direction from which the Pentagon was ultimately attacked by American 77.

Perhaps more important, the erroneous testimony enabled federal officials to claim affirmatively that they were positioned and prepared to shoot down United 93 before it hit its target in Washington, D.C. Notably, Colonel Marr, the NEADS battle commander, states in the U.S. Air Force's official history of 9/11, *Air War over America*: "As United Airlines Flight 93 was going out [west, toward Chicago], we received the clearance to kill if need be." Thus the testimony was not simply wrong about facts; it was wrong in a way that misrepresented the competence and relevance of the chain of command to the response, and overstated, to put it mildly, the readiness of the national command structure to intercept and, if necessary, shoot down United 93 as it approached Washington, some ninety minutes after the attacks had begun.

It was difficult to decide which was the more disturbing possibility. To believe that the errors in fact were simply inadvertent would be to believe that senior military and civilian officials were willing to testify in great detail and with assurance before Congress and the Commission, to be interviewed by major media, to appear on national and international television and answer the same detailed questions, to cooperate in the preparation of an official Air Force history, and to brief the White House on what happened on 9/11 without bothering to make sure that what they were saying was accurate. Given the significance of 9/11 in our history, this would amount to an egregious breach of the public trust. If it were true, however, that the story was at some level coordinated and was knowingly false, that would be an egregious deception.

The 9/11 Commission lacked the time, the resources, and, in the view of most, the mandate to determine whether the untrue story resulted from deliberation or incompetence. The Commission found the facts of 9/11, and stated them clearly for the public record. In the course of our work, the Commission staff had pushed as far as it could its inquiry into how the story came to be. The staff persuaded the Commission, however, that the issue of whether the false accounts were knowingly false had to be pursued. The Commission referred the matter to the Inspectors General of the Departments of Transportation and Defense in late July 2004.

We submitted to the Inspectors General a detailed list of the relevant documents to review and people to interview. We were debriefed by the Inspectors General staffs as the Commission was disbanding in late August 2004.

Then we waited.

Those of us who had worked on the "Whiskey Tango Foxtrot" team placed bets on when the Inspectors General would issue their reports. Our betting centered on whether the reports would be issued before or after the 2004 elections, which were two months away; we felt that we had given them sufficient information about which documents and tapes to review and what issues to raise in their interviews that a few months would be sufficient to complete their review. Our eighteen-month investigation had done much of their work for them; a few more months should have been sufficient.

The 2004 elections came and went. So did calendar year 2005. So did the first half of 2006. Finally, on the evening of the Friday before Labor Day 2006, a release time calculated in government to avoid major press exposure, the Department of Transportation Inspector General released its report. The report centers on the two FAA documents put together during the week after 9/11. The first, dated September 17, 2001, was titled "Summary of Air Traffic Hijack Events." The Inspector General's Report notes that this document "was prepared for, and circulated to, FAA, DoT, and other government agencies." This document, the Commission learned, was also used to brief the White House on September 17.

The September 17 "Summary" was based on the NEADS MCC log and FAA transcripts, including transcripts from the FAA's Cleveland Center. The IG's Report points out that "both of these documents correctly recorded FAA's notification to DoD about the hijacking of United 93 as having occurred at 10:07 a.m. Despite the availability of this accurate information, FAA's September 17 'Summary . . .' is silent as to the time of FAA's notification to DoD for United flight 93."

When asked by the DoT Inspector General why they had omitted the notification time for United 93, the FAA executives involved in preparing the document stated that they did not believe they had an accurate notification time for United 93. The IG's Report concludes, "We do not find this explanation to be reasonable because the NEADS log—which the executive and manager cited was the source of the notification times for the three other hijacked aircraft—and the transcript from FAA's Cleveland Center (which was also available to them) show the correct notification time for United Flight 93."

Having concluded that the explanation for the omission was "not reasonable," the Inspector General's Report "considered whether the FAA executive and manager may have purposely omitted the notification time to avoid disclosing that FAA did not notify DoD until approximately four minutes after United 93 had crashed." The FAA executive and manager denied it, and the Inspector General's Report found the denials credible; after all, the IG's Report points out, the document did disclose that the FAA reported United 175 hijacked two minutes after that plane had crashed, and "We found no evidence to explain why the executive and manager would have purposely omitted one after-the-fact notification and not the other."

Ironically, this analysis turns on its head the answers given to the Commission by FAA executives. When asked by Counsel to the Commission John Azzarello why the agency had omitted the correct notification time for United 93, a senior FAA executive answered, "Because that time came after the crash, it hardly counts as notification." If that's the case, Azzarello pointed out, then why list the time for United 175, which was also after the crash? The FAA senior executive said that she didn't know.

Contrary to the Inspector General's conclusion, there is a distinction between United 93 and United 175 that could easily explain why the FAA would feel free to disclose one notification time but not the other: namely, the FAA's own differing levels of awareness. United 175 was difficult to identify as a hijacked plane. While the New York controller was following the progress of American 11 toward New York, United 175 deviated from its course and switched, but did not turn off, its transponder beacon code. Unlike American 11 and United 93, no one heard a transmission from United 175 indicating that the plane had been hijacked. That United 175 had been hijacked was an inference drawn by the New York air traffic controller, based on the plane's deviation from course, its failure to respond to attempts to contact it, and its eventual approach to New York City. By the time FAA was confident in its assessment that the plane had been hijacked, only seconds remained before it hit the World Trade Center.

By contrast, FAA controllers in Cleveland heard the attack on United 93 as it was occurring, and heard repeated transmissions from the hijackers. Within minutes of the attack, Cleveland Center had relayed word of the attack to the Command Center in Herndon and, through it, to FAA Headquarters in Washington. By 9:34 a.m., twenty-nine minutes before the plane crashed, Headquarters was aware that United 93 had been hijacked. By 9:36, Cleveland Center was requesting through the chain of command at FAA that the military be notified and that fighters be scrambled, and was offering to contact the military itself. As we have seen, however, Cleveland Center was instructed not to contact the military, and was assured that people higher in the FAA's chain of command were doing that. By 9:45, the Command Center in Herndon was warning Headquarters that time was running out for them to contact the military.

That contact was never made by Washington Headquarters. The notification that was made at 10:07 came from Cleveland Center, almost by accident. The point is this: The FAA had an institutional exposure in its handling of United 93 that it did not have with respect to its handling of United 175. Its failure for nearly thirty minutes, and after the attacks had been under way for nearly ninety minutes, to notify the military that United 93 had been hijacked was, quite simply, the greatest institutional failure on 9/11. Far from there being, as the Inspector General's Report concludes, "no evidence" to account for why one after-the-fact notification was included and not the other, there is perhaps the strongest evidence bearing upon credibility: evidence of a strong motive to conceal.

The Inspector General's Report is correct, in other words, that the

FAA's explanation for its omission of the notification time for United 93 is "not reasonable" given that the correct time was apparent on the face of the documents it was using to construct the timeline. The "unreasonableness" of this explanation, coupled with the agency's clear interest in not disclosing its failure to notify the military concerning United 93, is compelling evidence that the notification time for United 93 may have been omitted purposely.

The Department of Transportation Inspector General's Report concerning the agency's account of its notification to the military concerning American 77 also raises more questions than it answers. The report ascribes the FAA's acceptance of the 9:24 notification time for American 77 to a failure of the FAA person compiling the timeline to cross-check the tail number of the NEADS log entry with the plane it represented. Again, the question is whether the claim of negligence is credible when the same log notes, at 9:34, that American 77 is reported "missing." Wouldn't that later entry, which is the first time that "American 77" is mentioned, lead anyone relying on the log for notification times to make sure that the earlier entry of a tail number for a United flight did in fact refer to American 77?

The Inspector General also considered whether the FAA had been influenced by or coordinated its timeline with the NORAD effort that resulted in the September 18 press release. The report concludes: "Neither DoD/IG's investigation nor our investigation established any direct coordination between the FAA and DoD officials regarding the chronologies." This conclusion conflicts with the Commission staff's interviews, which, as the Inspector General's office was informed, "confirmed that the adequacy of the notification of the military was a 'topic of hot debate' in the days after September 11 between the FAA and the military. Jeff Griffith, the senior air traffic manager on duty at FAA Headquarters on September 11, recalled having heated conversations with General Arnold and others on the subject. He specifically recalled being informed by the military that their position was that no notice had been passed regarding the hijacking of United 93 before it crashed."

Accepting for the sake of argument the Inspector General's conclusion that there was no coordination between the agencies, it would point to a remarkable, if not astounding, coincidence: that both FAA and DoD, at some point between September 16 and September 18, arrived at 9:24 as the time for the notification of American 77 by making the identical and independent mistake of failing to cross-check the tail number of the flight listed at 9:24, and of failing to note the later entry of the specific notification of American 77 at 9:34. Furthermore, and perhaps more astoundingly, if the DoT IG's conclusion is correct, the agencies arrived independently between 9/16 and 9/18 at "N/A" as the proper notification time for United 93, notwithstanding that, as the report notes, "the NEADS log—which the executive and manager cited was the source of the notification times for the three other hijacked aircraft—and the transcript from FAA's Cleveland Center (which was also available to them) show the correct notification time for United Flight 93."

The DoT IG's Report completely ignores the intervening event that, had it been investigated, might well have accounted for the transformation in approach that occurred between September 16 and September 18: the White House briefing. The September 17 "Summary" that was used to brief the White House offered no notification times for American 77 or United 93. The answer proffered the Inspector General for this by the FAA officials who prepared the "Summary"—that they were uncertain of the times—would no doubt have been unacceptable to anyone charged with running the country. We do not know what transpired at that meeting: whether the times were worked out in discussion with the White House or whether the agencies were dispatched from that meeting to figure it out. We do know, however, that by the next morning both were reporting that 9:24 was the notification time for American 77's hijacking, which caused the Langley scramble, and that "N/A" was the appropriate time for United 93's hijacking, thus enabling all parties to claim that the national command structure had reasserted itself. The DoT IG Report's conclusion that this agreement was pure coincidence is not credible. Whiskey Tango . . .

If the DoT Inspector General's conclusions left us once more muttering "Whiskey Tango Foxtrot," the conclusions of the Department of Defense Inspector General's Report left us speechless. As with the DoT Inspector General's Report, its release was timed to generate as little public attention as possible. It was issued the afternoon of September 12, 2006, after the public had been inundated with September 11 anniversary media coverage.

The Department of Defense Inspector General's Report begins by mischaracterizing the 9/11 Commission's referral. The 9/11 Commission, the report begins, "alleged that DoD and . . . FAA officials at a Commission hearing made certain statements knowing them to be false." The Commission, of course, made no such allegation. The Commission documented the facts concerning what occurred on 9/11, the disparity between those facts and what the government had been telling the public with total assurance since 9/11, and the relative ease with which anyone looking could have uncovered those facts. In view of these circumstances, the Commission concluded, it was reasonable to question whether the officials involved had made false statements knowingly.

The DoD Inspector General's Report concedes, as it must, that "both DoD and the FAA provided the Commission with inaccurate information about their responses to the events of September 11, 2001. However," the Report continues, "we found no indication that these statements were intentionally false. Rather, we attribute the inaccurate statements to a lack of capabilities and thoroughness within DoD to accurately reconstruct the response to the sequence of events of September 11, 2001."

The report finds, "DoD forensic capabilities were inadequate to ensure accurate and timely reporting. . . . The lack of adequate forensic capabilities for maintaining logs, video and audio recordings, and storing radar information was a contributing factor to the inaccurate testimony. Individuals responsible for reporting on the response to the attacks were impeded because there were no standardized logs." If this is true, what General Arnold said is remarkable, as Commissioner Gorelick pointed out to him: "You said that the reason you were wrong was that you hadn't had an opportunity to listen to the tapes, or the tapes were inaccessible. But . . . we have—and I'm just holding four of them—different [NORAD] headquarters and CONR logs that are—that clearly reflect that this scrambling was done in response to this phantom American 11, which didn't exist anymore. . . . Did you not look at the logs . . . ?" The logs may not have been standardized, but as the 9/11 Commission Staff pointed out to the Department of Defense Inspector General, "NORAD's own Headquarters Intel Chat Log . . . record[s] at 9:24:39 'original aa flt hijack is now headed to Washington scrambled lfi [i.e., Langley],' and then at 9:25:13 '2 arcrft that hit wt bldg not repeat not hijack aa acrft.' Furthermore, the Air Warning Center log at NORAD . . . records, at 9:27, that 'The original hijack a/c [aircraft] is still a/b [airborne] and head for Washington, DC. Otis F15 are trying to intercept the flight.' It then records, at 9:36, that CONR has advised of the scramble at Langley: 'LFI A/B Quit 25/26/27 3 A/B at time 1333 [i.e., 9:33].' The NORAD Headquarters chat log states, at 9:28: 'R[eal] W[orld] H[ijacking] (original notification) assessed by Intel as heading to Washington DC/2XF-15s in tail chase.' "

The logs that were maintained reflected a completely consistent chronology of what occurred on 9/11, a chronology that was further buttressed by the partial transcript that was prepared based on the NEADS tapes. With respect to that issue, the DoD Inspector General accepted the representation that "DoD officials did not use the transcripts, even when available, to prepare the press releases and subsequent testimony to the Commission."

Indeed, the report concludes, "commanders throughout DoD did not place a high priority on developing accurate information and, after September 11, 2001, they primarily focused their efforts on identifying and correcting operational weaknesses. Gathering information related to the events of September 11, 2001, was considered an additional duty." Consider for a moment the implications of this conclusion. It assumes, first, that there is no connection between "identifying and correcting operational weaknesses" exposed by the September 11 attacks and "gathering information related to the events." This was, as noted, the refrain the

Commission heard from top NORAD commanders as its interviews progressed; they were simply too busy fixing the system and fighting the war on terror to concern themselves with piecing together the facts of 9/11. But how, one wonders, could the Department of Defense identify and correct operational weaknesses without knowing precisely what had occurred that morning? Take, for instance, the official version that emerged after 9/11, in which by the time United 93 was headed for Washington, the military and the FAA were coordinated with each other and with the national command authority and prepared to shoot down the plane. If the military officers who related this version before the Congress, the media, and the public truly believed all of this, they might have been led to draw the wrong conclusions about the steps they still needed to take to secure the nation's airspace. Beyond this, moreover, wouldn't the commanding officer of NORAD, or the chairman of the Joint Chiefs, or the secretary of defense, or the vice president, or the president of the United States have demanded to know what had happened? It is certainly understandable that senior officials like General Eberhart, or General Arnold, or Colonel Marr, were preoccupied defending the nation, but is it believable that they would not have ordered a thorough review of what had occurred, both to inform their ongoing efforts and to answer the growing demand from the public, Congress, and the media to know what had happened? And what about their duty to the commander-in-chief, whose office wanted within the first week an accounting of what had occurred? NORAD had been on notice, moreover, since at least Senator Warner's comments at the October 2001 congressional hearing, that "We're too busy fighting the war on terror" was an unacceptable excuse: "I'm going to deviate from my planned opening here to say I guess I'm a little bit stunned that you don't know why that delay occurred. I would have thought by now all of you in this chain would have gone back, rehearsed these things, figured out what happened, what went wrong so that we ensure it won't happen again. If it was that significant delay and you can't tell us why, how do we leave with an assurance that you and your subordinates have taken steps so that it won't happen again?" If the DoD Inspector General's Report is correct, that review never occurred. If that is true, it reveals a level of sheer incompetence and neglect of duty that is frightening.

There are, in sum, significant reasons to doubt the reliability of both Inspectors General's reports. Neither finds any evidence that the FAA and DoD coordinated their efforts after 9/11 to reconstruct the story. This conclusion is refuted by the e-mail from CONR to NEADS discussed above, which references the sharing of information, by the fact that NEADS provided its logs to the FAA, and by the fact that the agencies emerged on September 18 with identically erroneous notification times for American 77 and United 93.

Both Inspectors General read the Commission's referral as narrowly as possible, and thus addressed only the question of whether testimony presented to the Commission had been knowingly false, as though their appearance before the Commission had been the only venue in which FAA and DoD officials had set forth their account of what had occurred. In fact, as we have seen, they had been interviewed and had testified at length repeatedly before Congress and the public, and had set forth with total assurance a minute-by-minute account of what happened on 9/11 that was both self-serving and completely untrue. The putative failure to prepare adequately for testimony before the 9/11 Commission becomes less credible when one considers the many other occasions for which a review of the relevant logs and tapes was indicated. Would you, reader, testify before Congress or sit down before the hot television lights to talk about something as important to our history as 9/11 without preparing? Is that a believable conclusion? Nonetheless, the DoD Inspector General's Report dismisses the significance of these prior accounts by concluding, disingenuously, that it had "found no indication that the DoD officials made erroneous statements once they became aware of the inaccuracies" as a result of the Commission's work. Of course, at that point they had no choice. That analysis so deliberately misses the point that one is at a loss. The point, of course, is that from the first days after 9/11 on, everyone was on notice of the significance of the events and the importance of getting the facts straight, and those facts had been presented repeatedly. The account of 9/11 had been prepared not just for the Commission; it had been prepared for Congress, for the media, for the general public. The question is why it proved to be so wrong.

That determination to avoid the larger context of the Commission's referral suggests the greatest flaw in the IGs' analyses. Neither report takes note of the central consideration in any evaluation of credibility: Did the "inaccurate" story serve anyone's interest? If so, it is more likely to have been deliberate. There is no question that the official version of events that emerged in the weeks and months after 9/11 served the interest of every institution involved: the FAA was able to avoid disclosing that it failed to provide notice on United 93 for nearly thirty minutes, and that the notice it did provide came after the plane crashed; the military was able to avoid acknowledging that it scrambled the Langley fighters based on mistaken information, that it had never followed United 93 on its radarscopes, that it never received the shoot-down authorization from the president until United 93 had crashed, and that it never passed that authorization to the pilots; the White House was able to avoid disclosing the fact that it was, for all intents and purposes, irrelevant to the national defense during that critical period on 9/11. Critical to the ability of each institution to make those claims was the 9:24 notification time for American 77, which enabled officials to avoid mentioning the mistaken report concerning American 11, and the "N/A" time for United 93, which enabled each to claim that the national command authority had asserted itself and was prepared to take action against the final hijacking.

Thus, the Inspectors General looked into how the FAA's September 17 report was put together, and criticized the fact that no times were recorded for American 77 and United 93 despite the ready availability of those times. They apparently never considered, however, that the document was used to brief the White House on September 17, or that by the day after the White House briefing the agencies both cited 9:24—a time that General Arnold would later testify he "always knew" was incorrect—as the notification time for American 77 and, thus, as the reason for the Langley scramble. They never questioned why the 9:16 notification time for United 93 was discarded before September 18 as unreliable but later reappeared in public testimony. They never asked whether the White House briefing played a role in shaping the story and, if it did not, what did account for the agencies' account of the notifications for American 77 and United 93.

We may never know now the true "story of the story." But it is impossible to conclude honestly, from the two Inspector General reports, that the official version of the events of 9/11 was the result of mere administrative incompetence; too many questions remain unanswered. In the meantime, Whiskey Tango Foxtrot moments continue. Emboldened, perhaps, by the reports of the Inspectors General, retired General Larry Arnold (who "always knew" that 9:24 was the wrong time and that the Langley fighters were not scrambled in response to American 77) has written the afterword to *Touching History* by Lynn Spencer. The book's conclusions, General Arnold notes, "differ markedly from the account in *The 9/11 Commission Report*. . . . The corrections to the record are important, and I'm glad our people in the military were able to tell her their stories of the events of that tragic day. Lynn does not have a political agenda, as the 9/11 Commission clearly did." General Arnold goes on, "We believe we could have shot down the last of the hijacked aircraft, United 93, had it continued toward Washington, D.C., [though] the 9/11 Commission said we could not have done so. After reading this book, you decide."

Of course, the 9/11 Commission never concluded that NORAD could not have shot down United 93. The Langley fighters were airborne over Washington; anything could have happened as the plane approached the city. What the Commission did point out, however, was that the military's public confidence that it was prepared was based on an account of events that was quite simply, and demonstrably, based on untrue testimony, including in no small measure that of General Arnold himself, who told the nation that NORAD had been following United 93 for over forty-five minutes before it crashed, when in fact it never followed the plane. (Arnold later acknowledged that he was "wrong.") When one factors into the equation all the ways in which the truth differed from what the public had been told, even General Arnold would have to admit that the government's readiness to shoot down the last hijacked plane is a much closer question.

The question of what might have happened had the passengers and crew of United 93 not attacked the hijackers is ultimately unanswerable, and misses the larger significance of this account of what happened, and of what people said about what happened. History should record that whether through unprecedented administrative incompetence or orchestrated mendacity, the American people were misled about the nation's response to the 9/11 attacks. The story they were told gave a false assurance that by the time the last hijacked plane was heading for Washington, some ninety minutes after the attacks began, the military, from the commander in chief on down, had reasserted control over American airspace and was prepared to respond to the final attack. However one answers General Arnold's question, that wasn't true.

That false assurance masked the fundamental disconnects that existed that day: between and among agencies; between the bureaucracy within agencies and the agencies' departmental leadership; and also between the different agencies and the national leadership. This book has shown that those fundamental disconnects had existed throughout the five-year struggle against al Qaeda, and had beset virtually every agency of government charged with adapting to the new threat: the FBI; the CIA; the State Department; the Department of Defense; the Department of Transportation. In each case, agencies were able to identify the threat but were thoroughly incapable of changing the way they were configured, in order to respond to it. Emblematic of these failures is the ultimate Whiskey Tango Foxtrot moment to emerge from the 9/11 Commission's investigation: the image of former National Security Advisor Sandy Berger hiding documents in his socks, so desperate to prevent the public from seeing certain papers that he sneaked out of the National Archives and hid the documents at a nearby construction site so that he could shred them later. The desire to inhibit the discovery of historical truth, it turns out, is truly bipartisan, and—as the revelation that the CIA destroyed the tapes of its interrogation of detainees reveals—is not limited by government agency; it is endemic to the modern way of government.

Taken as a whole, the government's response to the emerging threat of terrorist attack was a stunning collapse of competence; 9/11 was its trailing consequence. The response on 9/11 replicated in compressed time the miscommunications, the garbled signals, the years of bureaucratic frustration that had preceded it. It was the product of a government that doesn't work, and the false story put forward about the events of that morning allowed the government to avoid the kind of searching reexamination of government that was appropriate to the situation, given the bureaucratic collapse that culminated in 9/11. Thus, years later, Richard Clarke could still believe that his high-level videoconference had been the nerve center of the nation's response; no one had done the thoroughgoing analysis that would have exposed the reality that national leadership was irrelevant during those critical moments. As a consequence, no one had acted to ensure that similar disconnects would not recur in a future crisis.

Instead, the principal response to the failure of bureaucracy was not an attempt to redefine government itself, but the creation of more government, more bureaucracy. Thus, in 2002, Congress and the Bush administration collaborated in forming a new federal department whose principal aim was to provide "homeland security." A loose agglomeration of disparate agencies, such as Immigration, Transportation Security, Secret Service, FEMA, the U.S. Coast Guard, all of which had some relation to homeland security, the department would face its first stern test in September 2005, when a long-anticipated threat approached the homeland. This threat came not in human form but in the form of a natural disaster. Nonetheless, as we shall see, the bureaucratic failures that resulted in 9/11 would be replicated, in virtually every respect, in the government's response to Hurricane Katrina.

PART FIVE

AFTERMATH: KATRINA AND THE CONSEQUENCES OF DENIAL

Like millions of Americans, I watched with a growing sense of dread in late August 2005 as Hurricane Katrina swept across Florida, then gathered itself over the warm waters of the Gulf of Mexico, growing to fill an enormous expanse of the Gulf as it churned slowly but steadily toward New Orleans. As the storm drew closer in its inexorable movement, the warnings issued by the National Hurricane Center grew dire. At 10:11 a.m. on Sunday, August 28, with the storm bearing down upon the city, the NHC issued an unequivocal advisory:

> Devastating damage expected. . . . Most of the area will be uninhabitable for weeks. . . . Perhaps longer. At least one half of well-constructed homes will have roof and wall failure. All gabled roofs will fail. . . . High rise office and apartment buildings will sway dangerously. . . . All windows will blow out. . . . Airborne debris will be widespread. . . . Persons . . . pets . . . and livestock exposed to the winds will face certain death if struck. Power outages will last for weeks. . . . Water shortages will make human suffering incredible by modern standards.

My own experience with emergency management tempered my apprehension, at least initially. Because New Jersey law locates the Office of

Emergency Management within the state police department, which in turn comes under the direction of the attorney general, when I assumed the office of Attorney General for New Jersey in June 1999, the operations of that state's OEM became, ultimately, my responsibility. I soon came to appreciate how challenging the work is and how extraordinarily competent are the emergency-management professionals at the state and county level, as well as our federal partners at FEMA. I worked with them through the remnants of Hurricane Floyd in 1999, which caused severe flooding in central New Jersey, through the millennium/Y2K preparations, and through 9/11 and the anthrax attacks that followed closely behind. Their work was government at its best. I assumed, as I followed Katrina's progress, that similar relationships obtained in Louisiana and New Orleans.

I also knew, from attending FEMA workshops and studying FEMA assessments over the years, that, as Douglas Brinkley puts it, "Most experts ranked a hurricane in New Orleans with an earthquake in California and a terrorist attack on New York as the gravest threats to the nation." I had attended a FEMA certification workshop in Manhattan, in which the scenario of a Category 3 hurricane striking New Orleans was played out in detail. The projected results had been devastating, but the level of detail involved in the presentation indicated that an emergency like the one Katrina promised to deliver had been anticipated and worked through in a painstaking manner. However powerful the storm, this would not be, I assured myself, another 9/11. Katrina would surprise no one.

Indeed, following 9/11, to strengthen national security, the government had undergone its most comprehensive reorganization since the Department of Defense and CIA were created after World War II to prevent another surprise attack like the one on Pearl Harbor. The creation of the Department of Homeland Security (DHS)—an agglomeration of twenty-two disparate agencies whose missions all related in some manner to the umbrella concept of homeland security, from Customs to Secret Service to the Coast Guard—had been opposed initially by the Bush administration, and remained controversial in its particulars even after it was formed. How, many asked, could the FBI have been excluded from a department whose mission virtually coincided with its own? In addition, many opposed the inclusion of FEMA, which had enjoyed a unique direct reporting relationship to the president of the United States since President Carter created it by executive order in 1979. Interposing layers of reporting between FEMA and the president, it was argued, would complicate the chain of command and add needless delay to emergency response. FEMA director Joseph Allbaugh, a Bush appointee, argued strongly against FEMA's inclusion. "I told him it was a big mistake," Allbaugh recalled telling Andrew Card, the White House chief of staff. "The fact that FEMA could report directly to the president, any president—Democrat or Republican or independent—was what made the agency effective."

At least under the original proposal, FEMA's role would have been enhanced by stripping related offices from other departments—namely, the FBI's National Preparedness Office, the Department of Health's National Disaster Medical System, and the Department of Justice's Office of Domestic Preparedness—and adding them to FEMA's core responsibilities. The idea, as Christopher Cooper and Robert Block describe it in *Disaster: Hurricane Katrina and the Failure of Homeland Security*, was to transform FEMA into the "central hub of the nation's homeland security efforts." But Congress blocked the transfer of the Office of Domestic Preparedness; the FBI gutted the staff of the National Preparedness Office before transferring it, and incoming Homeland Security Secretary Tom Ridge lost a turf battle with Health and Human Services Secretary Tommy Thompson over control of the National Disaster Medical System. It was a rare feat of bureaucratic alchemy; rather than being strengthened as a consequence of the 9/11 attacks, FEMA, the overseer of the nation's response to disasters, had been weakened.

Nevertheless, there was reason to be hopeful about the response as Katrina approached, if only because New Orleans's vulnerability was so well documented, in a series of well-researched articles by John McPhee and others. The consensus was that, as Mark Fischetti wrote in *Scientific*

American, "New Orleans is a disaster waiting to happen. The city lies below sea level, in a bowl bordered by levees that fend off Lake Pontchartrain to the north and the Mississippi River to the south and west." The levee system was antiquated and weakening by the year, and was designed to withstand only a Category 3 hurricane—if that. Reports of leaks and water-soaked yards in the vicinity of the Seventeenth Street and London Avenue canals had gone uninvestigated, even though, as Robert Bea of the University of California at Berkeley observed, "These are all signs that something is wrong. . . . It means your system is stressed." (Nevertheless, the New Orleans operations manager of the Army Corps of Engineers would insist after Katrina, "If someone had told us there was lake water on the outside of that levee—or any levee—it would have been a red flag to us, and we would have been out there, without question.")

But in the days leading up to Katrina, the Army Corps maintained its assessment that the levee system could withstand a Category 3 storm, and federal, state, and local officials participated in perhaps the most extensive dress rehearsal for disaster in American history. For eight days in late July 2004, many of them had gathered in Louisiana's emergency-management headquarters in Baton Rouge and worked through an extensive computer simulation of a Category 3 storm, Hurricane Pam, striking New Orleans. The notional exercise peaked on the third day, when "the room filled to capacity as Pam made landfall while about 270 emergency workers looked on. Representatives from the Pentagon, the Coast Guard, and FEMA mixed with National Guard officers, state disaster chiefs, and emergency personnel from dozens of parishes and the adjoining states of Arkansas and Texas. Pam made its predicted low-tech landfall: The model played out on a projection screen as . . . employees handed out documents describing the havoc Pam had wrought." Those results were sobering. The exercise assumed a relatively low evacuation rate, projecting that 600,000 people would choose to ride out the storm. The projected consequence: nearly 20,000 fatalities in New Orleans, and 40,000 more in surrounding parishes. Because of this dire forecast, and because of historic difficulties in evacuating the New Orleans area, Louisiana governor Kathleen Blanco directed the development of a "contra-flow" evacuation plan—allowing the state police to direct traffic flow in a single direction. In the opinion of most experts, the execution of this plan saved many lives during Katrina.

But the exercise exposed many more gaps in emergency preparedness: in the availability of temporary housing; in the adequacy of FEMA's supply chain of essential commodities like water; in the availability of telecommunications facilities; in the ability to evacuate the poorest residents; in the timing and process for reentry into the city after the storm. The gaps were left unfilled, moreover, when planned follow-up sessions were canceled by FEMA in early 2005 because of DHS budget cuts. Still, as Katrina bore down on New Orleans and the Gulf Coast on Sunday, August 28, 2005, it was an emergency that had been anticipated, the response to which had been planned for, coordinated. The "lessons of 9/11" had been embodied in the Department of Homeland Security, which, as a result of its own analysis of the response on 9/11 and the Commission's, had formulated and instituted the National Response Plan, designed to clarify lines of authority and response during a national crisis. Intended to be applicable to "all hazards," the NRP distinguished between, on the one hand, relatively routine natural and man-made disasters (hurricanes, floods, train wrecks, fires), for which state and local governments should take the lead in responding, backed by FEMA and other federal resources, and, on the other hand, "catastrophic events," by which it meant such disasters as would be expected to overwhelm the capacity of state governments—even multiple state governments—to meet. In the event of a catastrophe, the plan contemplated that the Department of Homeland Security would assume the lead in directing the response, backed by its constituent elements in FEMA and the Coast Guard, and by other federal agencies such as the Department of Defense, supporting the efforts of state and local governments. Once triggered, the National Response Plan would enable the Secretary of Homeland Security to convene the Interagency Incident Management Group, a panel of experts from across the federal government, to assist in managing the crisis. According to a leading text written before Katrina, the National

Response Plan "emphasizes unity of effort among all levels of government," and provided "the structure and mechanisms for the coordination of federal support to state, local, and tribal incident managers and for exercising direct federal authorities and responsibilities. . . . The fundamental goal of the NRP is to maximize available federal resources in support of response and recovery actions taken by state and local emergency officials."

To put the NRP into effect, the Department of Homeland Security had devised—in response to perceived problems in the chain of command on 9/11—the National Incident Management System (NIMS). The NIMS adopted the concept, endorsed by the 9/11 Commission, of an Incident Command System, in which complex events are managed by a "unified command": "Within this [unified command] framework, agencies are able to work together . . . to establish a common set of objectives and strategies and a single plan of action. . . . NIMS establishes standardized incident management processes, protocols, and procedures that all responders . . . federal, state, tribal, or local . . . will be able to [use] to work together with very little mismatch." In other words, the disconnects that had characterized the failure of response on 9/11—a consequence, the nation had been assured, of the utterly unexpected nature of the attacks, and which were set right by the time the final hijacked airliner was heading for Washington—would not recur during the response to Katrina.

Or so we were led to believe.

THE DAYS OF KATRINA
SATURDAY, AUGUST 27

In the early morning hours of August 27, Hurricane Katrina is about 450 miles southeast of the Mississippi River Delta, moving slowly (under 10 miles per hour), with sustained winds of 115 miles per hour. It is a Category 3 storm. Its projected path leads straight to New Orleans.

At 9:00 a.m., Plaquemines and St. Charles parishes issue mandatory evacuation orders. FEMA Director Michael Brown appears on national television later that morning to urge all residents of southeastern Louisiana to evacuate the area. The National Hurricane Center issues a hurricane watch for metropolitan New Orleans and indicates that Katrina could become a Category 5 (catastrophic) storm before making landfall. These developments cause state and local officials to begin to take action. The state of Louisiana calls 4,000 National Guard troops into service, and Governor Blanco activates the contra-flow evacuation plan, allowing the Louisiana State Police to set aside nearly every lane of highway for outward-bound traffic. At 5:00 p.m., Blanco and Mayor Ray Nagin of New Orleans hold a joint press conference. Mayor Nagin declares a state of emergency in New Orleans, but does not issue a mandatory evacuation order. Distressed by the dilatory response, National Hurricane Center (NHC) Director Mac Mayfield begins calling state and local officials at 7:30 p.m., emphasizing the dire nature of what they will be facing. After several attempts to reach Mayor Nagin fail, Mayfield reaches him through Governor Blanco; Nagin is at a restaurant with his wife. Mayfield tells Nagin he has "never seen a storm like this. I've never seen conditions like this."

As Saturday comes to a close, the government response to the approaching hurricane can be summarized as follows:

LOCAL

New Orleans's "Comprehensive Emergency Management Plan," which was written in 2000, has not been modified to reflect the lessons of the Hurricane Pam exercise. The plan concludes, with respect to evacuation, that "it must be understood that this Comprehensive Emergency Plan is an all-hazard plan. Due to the sheer size and number of persons to be evacuated . . . specifically directed long-range planning and coordination of resources and responsibilities efforts must be undertaken." The plan does call, however, for action to be taken at least 72 hours before an impending potentially devastating storm, in part in order to afford those residents who do not have personal means of transportation the opportunity to leave. Mayor Nagin has not issued an evacuation order. The city of New Orleans, as *The Washington Times* put it, "followed virtually no aspect of its own emergency management plan" and also "failed to implement most federal guidelines."

STATE

Governor Kathleen Blanco has activated the National Guard. She has put the contra-flow evacuation plan into effect. She has written President Bush, requesting that he declare a state of emergency in southeastern Louisiana; her letter has failed, however, to request the specific assistance the region would require in the immediate aftermath of the storm, focusing instead on boilerplate requests for debris-removal assistance and housing assistance. She has appeared at several news conferences to urge residents to evacuate and has held a conference call with Louisiana officials from coastal parishes trying to coordinate preparations. She has put the NHC director in touch with Mayor Nagin.

FEDERAL

President Bush has complied with Governor Blanco's request for federal assistance, authorizing FEMA to "coordinate all disaster relief efforts which have the purpose of alleviating the hardship and suffering caused by the emergency on the local population." FEMA Director Brown has appeared on network television and received a briefing from the National Hurricane Center. FEMA has dispatched two public affairs officials to Louisiana. FEMA has not sent emergency-response teams to the Gulf South region and has not otherwise mobilized the provision of emergency supplies. FEMA's deputy director of response, in an e-mail to FEMA's logistics chief, has urged: "If this is the 'New Orleans scenario' we're already way behind. Let's don't hold back. This may be IT!" According to Senator Mark Pryor (D-Arkansas), "When FEMA finally did show up, everybody was angry because all they had was a website and a flyer. They didn't have any real resources that they could give."

By 10:00 p.m., the NHC has escalated the hurricane watch to a hurricane warning. By midnight, Katrina has become a Category 4 storm, approximately 320 miles southeast of the Mississippi River Delta, moving toward New Orleans at eight to ten miles per hour.

SUNDAY, AUGUST 28

By 1:00 a.m. on Sunday, August 28, Hurricane Katrina has become a Category 4 storm. It is located 310 miles southeast of the Mississippi River Delta, moving toward New Orleans at eight miles per hour. By 6:15 a.m., the National Oceanic and Atmospheric Administration is reporting that Katrina is now a Category 5 hurricane. Its sustained winds are now 160 miles per hour. It is 250 miles south-southeast of the Mississippi River Delta, and it has accelerated to twelve miles per hour.

In the early morning hours, the U.S. Coast Guard begins positioning rescue assets in staging areas near the projected path of the storm. At 8:00 a.m., the Superdome opens in New Orleans as a shelter of last resort. The westernmost and coastal counties in Mississippi are ordered evacuated. President Bush calls Governor Blanco at 9:25, urging that New Orleans be ordered evacuated.

At 9:30 a.m., Mayor Nagin orders a mandatory evacuation of New Orleans. There are fewer than twelve hours remaining before the storm will begin to reach the city.

President Bush speaks via teleconference with the governors of Louisiana, Mississippi, Alabama, and Florida at 10:00. FEMA Director Brown arrives in Baton Rouge at 11:00.

By 3:00 p.m., cars are leaving New Orleans at the rate of 18,000 per hour; approximately 112,000 New Orleans residents do not have access to a car. By 4:00, over 350,000 people have evacuated from New Orleans, leaving approximately 100,000 behind. Thousands of people line up at the Superdome to take refuge there.

At 4:15 p.m., President Bush, Secretary of Homeland Security Michael Chertoff, and FEMA Director Brown participate in a conference call. Brown briefs his superiors on the likely effects of the storm: "We're going to need everything that we can possibly muster, not only in this state and in the region, but the nation, to respond to this event." On the call, the director of Louisiana's Department of Emergency Preparedness indicates that Katrina would be "catastrophic," but adds that that is what Louisiana has prepared to confront. "So," he concludes, "we're way ahead of the game there."

The outer bands of rain from Katrina reach the coast of southern Louisiana and Mississippi at 5:00 p.m. Approximately ten thousand people are now waiting in the Superdome for the storm; many thousands of others wait in houses and other buildings throughout the city. Mayor Nagin orders a 6:00 p.m. curfew. The last train leaves New Orleans at 8:30 p.m. with many empty cars.

At 9:00 p.m., the outer bands of tropical rain reach New Orleans. By 10:30, the last of the arrivals at the Superdome are searched and admitted. More than 10,000 people are being served by approximately 300 medical workers and staff members; security is provided by 550 National Guard troops.

By midnight, Katrina's storm surge has reached Mississippi's western coast. Residents in Waveland report a foot of water in their homes.

The government response on Sunday, August 28, has been as follows:

LOCAL

Mayor Nagin has ordered the mandatory evacuation, stating, "We are facing a storm that most of us have long feared. The storm surge will most likely topple our levee system." He has ordered a 6:00 p.m. curfew. He has not mobilized any of the city's buses for evacuation purposes or arranged for transportation out of town for anyone who did not already have access to a car or other means of evacuation. No special arrangements have been made for the elderly or sick. The mayor has sent a letter to the clergy at New Orleans' six hundred churches, urging them to assist people in evacuating. The Superdome has been opened as a shelter, and the city has made buses available to transport people to the Superdome. There is virtually no food or other supplies at the Superdome. The mayor has emphasized at a press conference that people going to the Superdome should bring bedding and food with them for five days. "You're going on a camping trip," he has said.

STATE

The contra-flow plan has facilitated the evacuation of tens of thousands—about 85 percent—of New Orleans residents. The National Guard has arrived to provide security at the Superdome. The Guard has asked FEMA for additional food and other supplies for the Superdome.

FEDERAL

President Bush has urged, by phone call to Governor Blanco, the mandatory evacuation of New Orleans. President Bush has participated in conference calls with the relevant governors, and with FEMA Director Brown and Homeland Security Secretary Chertoff. He has pledged the full support of the federal government in rescue and recovery efforts: "We are fully prepared to not only help you during the storm, but we will move in whatever resources and assets we have at our disposal after the storm to help you deal with the loss of property. And we pray for no loss of life, of course." FEMA Director Brown has arrived in Baton Rouge to oversee the rescue and recovery effort. On the conference call with the president, he has stated: "We've got everything we need from the federal government. . . . I want to see the supply chain jammed up just as much as possible. I mean, I want [more] stuff than we need. Just keep jamming those lines full as much as you can with commodities." Brown has also worried aloud about the capacity of the Superdome and about the fact that New Orleans is "not taking patients out of hospitals, [not] taking prisoners out of prisons," and that "they're leaving hotels open in downtown New Orleans." The Department of Homeland Security's infrastructure-protection division has put out a report, at approximately 4:00 p.m., warning that if the levees breach during the storm surge, it might take six months or more to drain the city.

Late in the day, FEMA is unable to deliver the additional food and other supplies requested by the National Guard, because the storm has begun to hit, winds are high, and the prestaged supplies are three hours away in Camp Beauregard, in central Louisiana. In addition, FEMA's advance teams have prestaged only one day's worth of food and ice, and "just slightly more water." The deputy director of response's urging, days before, to augment the supply chain has not resulted in significant action. In addition, FEMA has brought in only fifty generators, or half of what the Hurricane Pam exercise indicated were needed to pump out the city. Steve Sansone, of the Army Corps of Engineers, "just knew right then and there we couldn't execute the mission." The Pam exercise indicated that Louisiana would need 69 truckloads of water, 69 truckloads of ice, 34 truckloads of food, 28 truckloads of tarps, and 100,000 sets of bedding. By Sunday night, FEMA has staged 30 truckloads of water, 17 truckloads of ice, 15 truckloads of food, 6 truckloads of tarps, and a truckload of blankets. FEMA has prepositioned no cots and no plastic sheeting. Pam had disclosed the need for 400 buses and 800 drivers to be prestaged jointly by FEMA and the state and local governments to assist in rescue transportation. FEMA has no buses prestaged in Louisiana; New Orleans city buses have been left sitting in parking lots. A "Fast-Action Report" issued by DHS's National Infrastructure Simulation and Analysis Center has predicted, based on computer modeling, that the storm will breach the levees, obliterate communications networks, and leave "at least 100,000 poverty-stricken people" to fend for themselves. "The potential for severe storm surge to overwhelm Lake Pontchartrain levees is the greatest concern for New Orleans," the "Fast-Action Report" concludes. The U.S. Coast Guard is pre-positioned and on standby as the storm hits in earnest after midnight.

MONDAY, AUGUST 29

By 2:00 a.m., Katrina is 130 miles south-southeast of New Orleans, sustaining winds of 155 miles per hour; it is now a Category 4 storm. It is moving at twelve miles per hour.

At 3:00 a.m., according to National Guard reports, the Seventeenth Street Canal levee in New Orleans begins to give way. At 5:00 a.m., a civilian calls the Army Corps of Engineers to report that the Seventeenth Street levee has been breached. Rain is falling at a rate of one inch per hour as the storm approaches.

Katrina makes landfall at 6:10 a.m. near Buras, Louisiana, as a Category 4 storm. Winds are sustained at 145 mph. Every building in Buras is annihilated. The eye of the storm is less than seventy miles from New Orleans.

At 7:50 a.m., Katrina's storm surge reaches New Orleans, overwhelming the Mississippi River–Gulf Outlet and flooding St. Bernard Parish and the eastern reaches of New Orleans. Within minutes, water levels are at ten to fifteen feet in many neighborhoods. Throughout the night, the Army Corps of Engineers receives "hundreds of reports of failures or breaches," according to Colonel Richard Wagenaar, New Orleans district commander. The Corps has evacuated its New Orleans headquarters, leaving the commander and eight aides behind, with one SUV.

Mayor Nagin appears on the *Today* show at 8:00. He indicates that water is coming through the levees in places, and states that flooding is a certainty. "The only question is how much," he says. Within minutes, at 8:14 a.m., the Industrial Canal is breached, flooding the Lower Ninth Ward in New Orleans.

The flooding in St. Bernard Parish overwhelms St. Rita's Nursing Home, which has not evacuated. Thirty-five residents die before 9:00 a.m.

By 9:30 a.m., flood water in the Lower Ninth Ward is six to eight feet deep, and two holes have blown open in the roof of the Superdome. Power has failed throughout the region.

At 10:30, President Bush declares states of emergency in Louisiana, Alabama, and Mississippi. FEMA Director Brown issues an order at 11:00 requiring 1,000 FEMA employees to report to the Gulf region within two days.

The Emergency Operations Center in New Orleans learns at 11:00 that the Seventeenth Street Canal has been breached. Katrina is now a Category 2 storm, with sustained winds of 105 miles per hour.

At noon, FEMA Director Brown and DHS Secretary Chertoff participate in a videoconference with Governor Blanco and the White House. Brown relates that he has spoken twice that morning with President Bush, and that the president "had some questions about the Dome. He's asking questions about reports of breaches. He's asking about hospitals. He's very engaged." Governor Blanco states that "the Superdome structure is still sound, as far as we know." With respect to the levees, she indicates that "we heard a report, unconfirmed [that there had been a breach]. I think we have not breached the levee. We have not breached the levee at this point in time." She adds, however, that some neighborhoods are sitting in eight to ten feet of water, "and we have people swimming in there."

Shortly after noon, the hurricane begins to veer away from the coastal areas. The winds shift as the storm passes, sending the storm surge south.

At 1:00 p.m., Mayor Nagin announces the breach of the Seventeenth Street Canal. The Louisiana Department of Wildlife and Fisheries begins rescue operations, arriving in New Orleans with seventy boats. Private citizens are already rescuing people using private boats. Looting begins in New Orleans.

By 3:00 p.m., four feet of water is reported in the Lakeview District of New Orleans. The storm surge, which has reversed, now hits the levees supporting Lake Pontchartrain, widening the breaches. The London Avenue Canal levees are breached in two locations.

By 5:00 p.m., approximately a thousand rescued people congregate outside the Morial Convention Center and are told that buses will pick them up. The buses do not arrive. The Convention Center is locked; there is no food, water, or other supplies available at the center.

By 5:00 p.m., the Department of Homeland Security's Operations Center has received nine reports that the New Orleans levee system has been breached, and "at least eight other reports that huge swaths of the city were under water and that hundreds, perhaps thousands, of people were awaiting rescue in the sultry summer heat." Because federal officials had been assured by top officials in Louisiana and by the Army Corps of

Engineers to the contrary, however, the Operations Center's final report of Monday, issued at 6:13 p.m., concludes that "Preliminary reports indicate the levees have not been breached."

FEMA's representative in New Orleans, Martin Bahamonde, commandeers a Coast Guard helicopter at 5:15 p.m. and flies over the city, focusing on the Seventeenth Street Canal. Bahamonde estimates that 75 percent of the city is under water. Survivors are clinging to rooftops and trees. He calls FEMA Director Brown at 7:00 and relates the situation to him. Brown says he is calling the White House immediately. At 8:00 Bahamonde sees Mayor Nagin and briefs him. Nagin appears stunned.

By 7:00 p.m., the Coast Guard has begun helicopter rescue operations in New Orleans.

At 8:00 p.m., a distraught Governor Blanco speaks to President Bush, telling him, "Mr. President, we need your help. We need everything you've got." She does not cite specific needs.

At 9:30 p.m., DHS Chief of Staff John Wood is informed by FEMA Deputy Martin Bahamonde of the levee breaches and the massive flooding occurring in New Orleans. Bahamonde's report circulates through DHS, reaching Deputy Michael Jackson via e-mail at 11:05 p.m.; the White House receives a firsthand account of the levee breaks and flooding at 11:00 p.m.

As Monday ends, thousands of people with nowhere to go head to the Superdome. By Tuesday, more than 20,000 people will have arrived.

The governmental response as of Monday, September 29, 2005, can be summarized as follows:

LOCAL

Mayor Nagin has spent much of the day trying to figure out what has happened. This effort has been compromised by his remaining at the Hyatt Regency Hotel, not at the Emergency Operations Center. The New Orleans Police Department begins to encounter looting, and the command structure of the NOPD begins to dissolve. Many officers fend for themselves; some join in the looting. Others desert their posts. Douglas

Brinkley writes, "A few of those who stayed in New Orleans were 'outlaw' cops, not accountable to anybody—desperadoes looking for a quick score like a Panasonic plasma TV or a Sony CD player. Thugs with a silver badge. Pure and simple. Only now, standing in floodwater, their gunpowder wet, their toughness evaporated. They turned yellow. Dozens sank to looting and freebooting." Civic order has dissolved. Private citizens have begun rescuing others in private boats. Morial Convention Center personnel have been attempting to manage a growing crowd seeking to take refuge there, despite the lack of any preparation to house them.

STATE

The Louisiana Department of Wildlife and Fisheries has begun widely praised rescue efforts throughout the region, with a particular focus on New Orleans. Governor Blanco has urged President Bush to send "everything you've got" to the region. The Louisiana National Guard has attempted to manage crowd control at the Superdome.

FEDERAL

President Bush has pledged support for the region. The Department of Homeland Security has not activated the National Response Plan, because it has not credited the reports that the levees have been breached. The governor had reported earlier that they had not been breached, and the Army Corps of Engineers had concurred; these reports outweighed, in the judgment of DHS officials, the reports from the field, including that of FEMA's on-site official, as well as DHS's own "fast-analysis report," which had been e-mailed to the White House at 1:47 a.m. that morning and had stated that "the potential for severe storm surge to overwhelm Lake Pontchartrain levees is the greatest concern for New Orleans." The assumption of DHS officials has been that in the absence of a levee breach, the disaster would not rise to the level of a catastrophe, and would not justify invocation of the NRP. In fact, while the plan states that "all presidentially declared disasters and emergencies under the

Stafford Act are considered incidents of national significance," it does not set forth the specific conditions under which it is to be invoked. President Bush issued a declaration of emergency two days later, on Saturday, at Governor Blanco's request, but DHS officials believe that the NRP is not triggered until the DHS secretary declares an Incident of National Significance.

TUESDAY, AUGUST 30

In the early morning hours, the crowd outside the Morial Convention Center becomes unruly. The crowd smashes a locked door and begins to occupy the Convention Center. Mayor Nagin announces that the center will be used for the rescue and recovery operation after all, and that people may go there.

Between 1:30 and 3:00 a.m., power fails at Tulane University Hospital and Methodist Hospital when flood waters overwhelm the emergency generators. Several thousand patients and staff are stranded at New Orleans hospitals without power. Staff at Methodist Hospital begin hand-pumping oxygen into the lungs of people who had been on ventilators.

At 10:00 a.m., Mayor Nagin states that the effort to use sandbags to block the breach in the Seventeenth Street Canal levee have not been successful. He orders a mandatory evacuation of the city and empowers the police department to remove people against their will, if necessary. Fires and looting are reported throughout New Orleans.

The Louisiana Department of Wildlife and Fisheries operates more than 200 boats in the New Orleans area, rescuing hundreds of stranded residents.

The U.S. Coast Guard conducts rescue operations with 37 aircraft, 15 cutters, and 63 small boats.

Homeland Security Secretary Chertoff designates Katrina an Incident of National Significance, pursuant to the National Response Plan, and designates FEMA Director Brown the principal federal official to manage the rescue and recovery effort. The Department of Defense orders Northern Command to deploy all necessary assets to the Gulf Coast.

Conditions at the Superdome grow dire as the plumbing fails and the building is without air conditioning. Few FEMA supplies have arrived. No buses have been deployed by FEMA, the city, or the state. Landstar Trucking, the company with which FEMA has contracted for $100 million to provide buses in emergencies, assigns a subcontractor, Carey Limousines, to find buses. FEMA has assured state officials that buses are on the way.

At 10:00 p.m., Governor Blanco orders the Department of Social Services to find shelter for 25,000 people. At a news conference, she describes conditions at the Superdome as "very difficult": "They're putting more and more survivors into the Superdome. . . . But we're worrying first about the medically needy. So we have to set up shelters and make sure that their medical needs can be taken care of. Then in the next phase, we'll be looking for places to evacuate the rest of the folks at the Superdome."

New Orleans's buses sit in a flooded lot.

FEMA buses have yet to be deployed.

Social order continues to deteriorate as much of New Orleans sits in at least ten feet of water. The New Orleans Fire Department has trouble reaching fires; many buildings burn to the ground. Looting remains widespread.

The governmental response on Tuesday can be summarized as follows:

LOCAL

The mayor has ordered a mandatory—forced, if necessary—evacuation, and has announced that the breach in the Seventeenth Street Canal levee has widened. The police department has curtailed rescue efforts to concentrate on restoring public order. The fire department has struggled to reach burning buildings through the flood waters.

STATE

The Department of Fisheries and Wildlife rescues hundreds. The governor has ordered that shelter be found for 25,000 people. The National Guard has continued to attempt to keep order at the Superdome, and has assisted at the Convention Center.

FEDERAL

DHS Secretary Chertoff has triggered the National Response Plan, and has designated FEMA Director Brown as the lead federal official in coordinating the response. No buses and few supplies have arrived from FEMA despite assurances to the contrary. The Coast Guard has continued to rescue hundreds. The U.S. military has begun to mobilize to provide assistance.

WEDNESDAY, AUGUST 31

At 1:45 a.m., FEMA formalizes a request to the Department of Transportation for 455 buses and 300 ambulances.

With the number of refugees approaching 26,000, officials at the Superdome lock the doors as the day dawns.

By 8:00 a.m., two more hospitals, Charity and University, lose power as their generators fail. Governor Blanco attempts to call President Bush to tell him that "expected and promised federal resources still have not arrived." She does not reach the president; she later speaks with his chief of staff and tells him she needs as many as 5,000 buses.

At 8:00 a.m., President Bush participates in a videoconference regarding Katrina, led by FEMA Director Brown. Brown briefs the president, Secretary Chertoff, Karl Rove, and others about the efforts under way to repair the levee breaches and about the options available to evacuate people from the Superdome. According to White House press secretary Scott McClellan, "the President wanted to make sure that Mike [Brown] was getting all the cooperation he needed from all the different agencies within the federal government on the ground. And Mike expressed that he was getting good cooperation within the federal government."

This sentiment is echoed at 1:00 p.m. when Bush cabinet officials hold a press conference. Secretary Chertoff states that he is "extremely pleased with the response that every element of the federal government, all of our federal partners, has made to this terrible tragedy."

At 11:20 a.m., FEMA Director Brown receives an e-mail from Marty Bahamonde, stating, "The situation is past critical. Here [are] some things you might not know. Hotels are kicking people out, thousands gathering in the streets with no food or water. Hundreds still being rescued from homes. The dying . . . are being [medevaced]. Estimates are many will die within hours. Evacuation in process. Plans developing for dome evacuation but hotel situation adding to problem." FEMA Director Brown responds: "Thanks for the update. Anything specific we need to do or tweak?"

FEMA makes a formal request under the NRP to the Pentagon for fifty helicopters.

At 2:20 p.m., after being copied on an e-mail from FEMA Director Brown's assistant, in which she stated that "it is very important that time is allowed for Mr. Brown to eat dinner," Bahamonde responds, "I just ate an MRE and crapped in the hallway of the Superdome along with 30,000 other close friends so I understand her concern about busy restaurants. Maybe tonight I will have time to move the pebbles on the parking garage floor so they don't stab me in the back while I try to sleep, but instead I will hope [Brown's] wait at Ruth's [Chris steak house] is short."

By midafternoon, flood waters have stopped rising in New Orleans. The Army Corps of Engineers and the National Guard use helicopters to drop 5,000-pound sandbags and concrete highway barriers into the levee breaches. Governor Blanco issues an executive order allowing the state to commandeer all Louisiana school buses.

At 1:45 p.m., President Bush flies over New Orleans and the region aboard *Air Force One*.

At 2:00, the evacuation of the Superdome begins.

At 2:20, Governor Blanco calls the president again and speaks to him. She tells him she needs 40,000 troops. She tells him that she wants "to continue to be his partner in a unity of effort as is called for under the National Response Plan." Governor Blanco makes clear, however, that "I do not want to federalize the troops. What I want is some soldiers with equipment that can help us." Tensions rise among federal, state, and local officials as the White House begins telling reporters on background that the Katrina response is the fault of state and local officials.

At 3:00 p.m., President Bush presides over a task-force meeting at the White House to discuss the problems with the response, then details the federal response in an address to the nation. He explains that Secretary of Homeland Security Michael Chertoff, in charge of the federal task force, and FEMA Director Michael Brown, in charge of federal response and recovery efforts in the field, have been instructed "to work closely with state and local officials, as well as with the private sector, to ensure that we're helping—not hindering—recovery efforts." President Bush indicates that the National Guard has nearly 11,000 troops on active duty to assist governors and local officials, that FEMA and the Army Corps are working to repair the levee breaches, and that FEMA is moving into the affected areas "1,000 truckloads containing 5.4 million meals ready to eat . . . 13.4 million liters of water, 10,400 tarps, 3.4 million pounds of ice, 144 generators, 20 containers of pre-positioned disaster supplies; 135,000 blankets, and 11,000 cots. And we're just starting." Almost none of the items he mentions, however, will be available for days, or even weeks.

At 7:00 p.m., Mayor Nagin declares martial law in New Orleans.

By the end of the day on Wednesday, it is clear that the National Response Plan and the National Incident Management System have been irrelevant to the actual response to Katrina. On the ground, individual responders from the Coast Guard, FEMA, the National Guard, the Department of Fisheries and Wildlife, and the police and fire departments coordinate to address specific situations, often heroically; coordination is nonexistent, however, where the NRP and NIMS schemes dictate that it should be strongest, among the top officials who are supposed to constitute a "unified command." Rather than coming together, these officials proceed to polarize over the coming days, as each level of government begins to blame the others. Secretary Chertoff and FEMA director Brown fault each other. Governor Blanco repeatedly refuses overtures from Karl Rove to "federalize" the military response, viewing it as a partisan political gambit to place the blame for the failed early response squarely upon her shoulders. Beginning with a *Good Morning America* interview on September 1, President Bush insists that the reason for the difficulties in coordinating the response was surprise: "I don't think anybody anticipated the breach of the levees."

9/11 RECONSIDERED

At first glance, a comparison of the government's military and intelligence response to 9/11 and its emergency response to Hurricane Katrina may seem contrived. After all, 9/11 was a human-caused, quasimilitary attack, the most serious assault on America since Pearl Harbor; Katrina was a natural disaster—in economic and human terms, one of the greatest in our history. There was, moreover, little overlap in the government agencies involved: 9/11, as we have seen, involved the FBI, the CIA, the State Department, various attributes (principally NORAD) of the Department of Defense and the Department of Transportation (principally the FAA), while Katrina involved FEMA, the Coast Guard, and other attributes of the Department of Homeland Security (which was not created until after 9/11), plus the State of Louisiana and the City of New Orleans. They didn't even draw on the same elements of the National Guard. Perhaps most significant, 9/11 is considered, in emergency response parlance, a "high consequence, low probability" event, while Katrina is considered a "high consequence, high probability" event. The 9/11 attacks, in other words, although they were certainly possible, were not considered likely to occur. By contrast, Katrina—a hurricane of Category 3 strength or higher devastating New Orleans and the Gulf Coast region—had been considered a virtual certainty for decades.

Notwithstanding these differences—indeed, precisely because of them—I believe that a comparison of the government's efforts in responding to the two crises is essential to understanding our essential lack of emergency preparedness, and the role that the deception about the response to 9/11 has played in the failure to address it. For despite the dramatic differences in the two situations, what is striking is that the very different agencies involved in each failed and succeeded in precisely the same ways, both in the long lead-up to the events and in the days, hours, minutes, and seconds of crises themselves.

The same estrangement of the rank-and-file bureaucracy from upper-level management within agencies that beset the FBI and CIA in the time leading up to 9/11 also plagued FEMA, DHS, the city of New Orleans, and the state of Louisiana in the time leading up to and responding to Katrina, frustrating attempts to reconfigure departmental missions and assets to counter a clearly recognized threat. During the Katrina crisis, the high-level conference calls that played virtually no role on 9/11 in directing the response were replicated; the top officials were talking largely to themselves, and passing inaccurate information. Thus, Governor Blanco's assurances to federal officials that the New Orleans levees had not breached conflicted with the ground-level reporting from both her own employees and federal officials; her inaccurate reports were treated, however, as authoritative.

The bureaucratic unwillingness or inability to cooperate across departments crippled efforts to anticipate and respond to Katrina no less than it had crippled efforts to interdict and then respond to 9/11, preempting the possibility of a unified chain of command. Different agencies responded independently and haphazardly, with varying degrees of effectiveness. The Coast Guard performed heroically; the New Orleans Police Department abominably.

As with 9/11, there was an awkward and belated effort during Katrina to reassert the relevance of top officials to the response, even though they were largely irrelevant—even detrimental—to the vital decision making that was taking place on the ground. Governor Blanco's assurance that the levees had not been breached, for example, allowed federal officials to believe, falsely, that they did not need to activate the National Response Plan.

Finally, as on 9/11, the felt necessity to reassert the relevance of the top officials led the government during and after Katrina to "spin" the truth about what was occurring, just as it had on 9/11. A year after Katrina, in an interview on MSNBC's *Hardball*, former FEMA director Brown stated that his chief regret was that he had acceded to the White House's insistence that he "lie" about what had happened.

Q: What was the lie?

A: The lie was that we were working as a team and that everything was working smoothly. And how we could go out, and I beat myself up daily for allowing this to have happened, to sit there and go on television and talk about how things are working well, when you know they are not behind the scenes, is just wrong.

Q: So let me get this clear. Someone in the White House was telling you to lie?

A: Well, yes. They give you the talking points. Whenever you go out to do any interviews they always have the talking points. . . . That's just the way Washington, D.C., works and it's just wrong. . . .

Q: Then why did you lie? If you say they told you to carry that out, why did you carry that out?

A: . . . That's exactly why I think that's the biggest mistake that I made, was not leveling with the American people, and saying, you know what, this is a catastrophic event, and it's not working at the state, local, or the federal level.

As this book has shown, the process of "spin" Brown described—"The lie was that we were working as a team and that everything was working smoothly"—did not originate with Katrina. It originated in the week after 9/11, when the clear evidence of what had occurred that morning was ignored in service to the story that by the time United 93 was headed for Washington, the national command structure was "working as a team and . . . everything was working smoothly."

The "spin" approach may have worked for a brief time after 9/11. Over the long term, however, it compromised our preparedness and damaged the Bush administration tremendously. The 9/11 explanation raised more questions than it answered, and led many to call for the creation of the 9/11 Commission. In the case of Katrina, the vast gulf, between what government officials were describing and what the public could see was really going on—often on split-screen during press conferences—undermined the credibility of the Bush administration, for many, beyond repair. It certainly did for a freshman senator from Illinois named Barack Obama, who couldn't reconcile the images of death and suffering he had seen while listening to Cabinet officials "bristle with confidence . . . as they recited the number of evacuations made, military rations distributed, National Guard troops deployed." It felt, he thought, "as though nothing had happened."

More important, in my view, the administration's unwillingness to acknowledge the truth prevented it from seeing the implications of that truth: that what failed in both the 9/11 and Katrina responses was not a discrete agency or two, or a cabinet head, or a given bureaucracy, but government itself. We never undertook the kind of searching reexamination of government that the true history of 9/11 would have indicated; it was all too easy, once the false but reassuring story was told, to ascribe the faltering response to the unexpected nature of the attack, and to respond by simply creating a new department, more layers of bureaucracy, solving yesterday's problem at the expense of preventing tomorrow's. Katrina, a long-anticipated event, revealed that what was at fault was government itself, including the new structure created after 9/11.

The comprehensive reassessment of government that these failures demand will be a monumental task, beyond the scope of this book.

Nonetheless, the "ground truth" of 9/11 and Katrina does suggest some important starting points for reforming how the business of government is conducted.

REINVENTING GOVERNMENT, REVISITED

"If the agencies repeatedly fall short, one ought to at least consider the possibility that there is a systematic mismatch between what they are instructed to do and their capacity to do it." That statement was not made in reference to the performance of the federal government surrounding the events of 9/11 or Katrina, although it could well have been. Rather, it was the observation of a Brookings Institution fellow studying the efforts of the Social Security Administration to adjust to its new health care responsibilities in the late 1980s.

The rise of the administrative state from the 1930s onward, and the resulting exponential growth of bureaucracy at all levels of government, had spawned, by the time the Cold War ended, a vast literature concerning the nature of large organizations in general, and of government bureaucracies in particular. It also spawned frustration that led many in both parties to call for a dramatic reexamination of the role and scope of government. Accordingly, the incoming Clinton administration made the problem of bureaucratic effectiveness and adaptation to the post–Cold War world its top priority. President Clinton made clear that the end of the Cold War presented the nation with challenges that its bureaucracy was not configured adequately to address: "We have moved through a rapid transition at the end of the Cold War, and at the end of the traditional industrial economy. We've moved into a global economy with new challenges, new conflicts characterized by a high rate of change. . . . In that environment, the model that we have used to deliver government services and fill public needs is simply no longer relevant to the present, let alone the future."

Vice President Al Gore was tasked with leading the National Performance Review (NPR), a presidential task force on "reinventing government." In announcing the review, President Clinton stated, "Programs . . . are being undermined by an inefficient and outdated bureaucracy, and by our large debt. For too long the basic functioning of government has gone unexamined. . . . Our goal is to . . . change the culture of our national bureaucracy away from complacency and entitlement toward initiative and empowerment. We intend to redesign, to reinvent, to reinvigorate the entire national government."

The National Performance Review analyzed every executive department; the departments were tasked with creating "Reinvention Teams to lead transformations at their departments, and Reinvention Laboratories, to begin experimenting with new ways of doing business. Thousands of federal employees joined these two efforts." Among other findings, the review recommended that FEMA "shift its resources to respond to all hazards" and "develop a more anticipatory and customer-driven response to catastrophic disasters." The intelligence community, the review concluded, needed "to act more effectively and more efficiently as a team," because "the analytical issues the Intelligence Community faces are far more diverse and complex today [than during the Cold War], requiring new focus and new techniques. . . . The Intelligence Community lacks the connectivity and interoperability in its information systems to do its job efficiently and effectively." No recommendation pertained specifically to the divide between the FBI's intelligence and criminal investigations operations, but the review stated that the attorney general should "coordinate federal law enforcement efforts."

By the mid-1990s, when the fourth report of the National Performance Review was issued, the Clinton administration was confident that it was, in fact, "reinventing the way Washington works." Vice President Gore wrote, "The battle against the old forces of big government, central control and mistrust isn't won yet, but everything is moving in the right direction." A 1995 report focusing on "reinventing intelligence," picking up on the 1993 review's emphasis on the need for the intelligence community to "enhanc[e] Intelligence Community integration," "enhanc[e] Community responsiveness to customers," and "reassess . . . information collection to meet new analytical challenges," such as terrorism, concluded that "all of the NPR actions are being addressed at this time. More than 50% are complete, more will be complete soon, and all are either on or ahead of schedule." The review praised the intelligence community for "the proactive steps it has taken to meet the challenges of a changed world" and for meeting the challenge "to reinvent the intelligence process."

By the end of the Clinton administration, its "reinvention" of government was hailed widely as a success and was a cornerstone of Vice President Gore's campaign for the presidency. An assessment by Brookings Institution fellow Donald Kettl, issued in congressional testimony given in May 2000, concluded that the Clinton administration's "reinventing government" initiative had been successful in downsizing the federal government, in improving "customer service" and procurement procedures, and, through the reinvention labs, in encouraging innovative management approaches.

It is, however, impossible to square such glowing assessments with the history set forth in *The 9/11 Commission Report*, in the Report of the Congressional Joint Inquiry, in *The Looming Tower*, *Legacy of Ashes*, or *Spying Blind*, or in the early sections of this book, which detail the frustrated efforts of various agency heads to adapt their departments to the emerging post–Cold War reality of transnational terrorism. If the intelligence community's integration had truly been enhanced, how was it that key NSA intercepts had not been shared with other components of the community? How was it that CIA Director Tenet's declaration of "war" on al Qaeda did not resonate throughout the intelligence community? How was it that Tenet's efforts to require intelligence officers from different agencies to learn the details of their colleagues' jobs came to naught? How could the intelligence community's "connectivity and interoperability" have been so poor in the years, months, weeks, and days leading up to 9/11 if those issues had been "addressed"? How could FBI Director Freeh's heroic efforts to reorganize the Bureau so that it would

be positioned to combat terrorism—including his tripling of the terrorism budget, his expansion of the Joint Terrorism Task Forces, and his
expansion of the Bureau's overseas contacts—have failed to alter the
Bureau's culture? How could NORAD leadership's forward-looking attempt to salvage its mission by identifying terrorism as an emerging
threat to America's air sovereignty have led to nothing but the grudging
concession not to eliminate NORAD completely? Why were NORAD's
warnings that it could protect America's air sovereignty "in name only"
virtually ignored? Why were the FAA and NORAD looking at differently configured radar pictures and speaking different languages on 9/11?
Why was our national defense improvised on 9/11?

If the ability of bureaucracies to adapt rapidly to the new post–Cold
War world was the heart of the "reinventing government" movement, as
President Clinton had announced, 9/11 stands as its signal failure, but
there were troubling signs even as the review was under way. In 1998,
Donald Kettl observed that the "reinventing government" efforts suffered
from the failure to recognize that "a fundamental mismatch has arisen
between government's formal structures and processes and the realities of
what government does and how it does it. . . . The Clinton administration's
reinventing government movement has achieved notable and impressive
results. But at its core the effort has failed to grapple with [the] performance deficit and its underlying cause: the attempt to use processes built
for hierarchical authority to run a government built heavily on partner-
ships and run through proxies." Furthermore, as early as 1995, the Department of Defense's Defense Performance Review office was "closed, the
staff dispersed, and its remaining functions transferred." One Pentagon
official was reported to claim that DoD "intentionally disbanded the DPR
and allowed the program to be consumed by the bureaucracy it was meant
to streamline." Attorney General Janet Reno also resisted the recommendations of the National Performance Review that she more fully integrate
federal law enforcement by merging the FBI and the Drug Enforcement
Administration, and the Bureau made no progress in updating its technological assets. In short, the demonstrated incapacity of every relevant de-

partment of the federal government to adapt to the emerging threat posed by transnational terrorism belies the claim that the National Performance Review process had "reinvented government" to adapt to "new conflicts characterized by a high rate of change." The successes of the reassessments of government during the 1990s were real; FEMA, for instance, was "reinvented" and became, by all accounts, a high-performing agency. But the "reinvented" national-security structure in place in 2001 failed, ultimately, to fulfill the existential mission of the federal government: to "provide for the common defense." President Clinton's goal to "change the culture of our national bureaucracy away from complacency and entitlement toward initiative and empowerment" went tragically unrealized in the years, months, weeks, and days leading to 9/11. Amy Zegart's observation with regard to the intelligence community applies equally to the relevant government agencies: "The conceptual flaw . . . is their assumption that change and adaptation are the same. They aren't. . . . Organizations are constantly changing. The key issue is whether those changes matter or, more precisely, whether the rate of change within an organization keeps pace (or lags behind) the rate of change in the external environment. . . . Presenting only the litany of intelligence reforms gives the impression that America's intelligence system was succeeding when it was not."

Perhaps as egregious, there was no effort, after the 9/11 attacks, to reexamine systematically the role and nature of government in light of the prior reinvention initiatives and the failures that had led to the 9/11 attacks. Indeed, the academic literature falls silent after 9/11 on the whole question of reinventing government. As a consequence, the legislative reaction to the 9/11 attacks was simply to create a new executive department, the Department of Homeland Security. At hearings held to consider this move, Paul C. Light of the Brookings Institution urged Congress not to act to create a new department until it had assessed more fully the state of government organization generally: "I believe the creation of a cabinet-level department of homeland security would be more likely to succeed if it follows, not precedes, a top-to-bottom analysis of the federal hierarchy. It has now been more than fifty years since we last assessed the condition of the hierarchy in anything more than an ad hoc fashion. The result is a federal organization chart that was invented at the dawn of the Cold War for a nation and a world that have long ago moved on." That searching reexamination did not occur. The Department of Homeland Security was created, with the Bush administration's grudging acceptance, and the apparently genuinely reinvented FEMA was enveloped within it, along with other agencies. The debate as to whether FEMA's inclusion in DHS was ill-considered should have been ended by the dismal performance of the agency during Hurricane Katrina. Interposing a secretary of homeland security between the FEMA director and the president had created command and control confusion, delaying important decisions beyond the critical decision points; had led to the passing of inaccurate information; and had contributed to a breakdown in the personal relationship between the agency's secretary and director. Furthermore, the organizational charts developed by DHS to facilitate command and control during a crisis—the National Response Plan and the National Incident Management System—reflected, rather than transformed, a convoluted and hierarchical bureaucracy. Both failed embarrassingly during the response to Hurricane Katrina, as the unified command under the Incident Management System failed to take shape, the invocation of the National Response Plan was delayed, and the politicians scrambled to assign blame.

The ground truth of both 9/11 and Katrina, in short, points to the need for a closer look at the intractable problems of bureaucracy, and for a reexamination of the nature of government in crisis. Both events, moreover, suggest vital starting points for that reexamination.

STARTING FROM THE GROUND TRUTH

I am not a political scientist, nor am I qualified to expound a grand theory of "reinventing government." But my own experiences in managing emergencies as attorney general of New Jersey—including the state's response to 9/11—and my subsequent investigation of the government's responses to the emergencies caused by the 9/11 attacks and Hurricane Katrina, suggest that there are common characteristics of a government in crisis that can be anticipated, and hence addressed. Overarching theories are much less useful, in my opinion, than an inductive approach that plans to respond to crises in the way that experience teaches crises will be lived by responders. We should start, in other words, from the ground truth. In my view, that truth suggests the following basic starting points:

1. *Crises are lived from the ground up, not from the top down.* Accordingly, critical early decisions will have to be made by responders who are not the top officials, and who may not be federal officials. Planning for a crisis should accept that reality and empower and train people "on the ground" to make critical decisions.

    This reality held true at every level of the response to 9/11 and Katrina. On September 11, 2001, the carefully choreographed hijacking protocol—stipulating that the FAA's request for assistance would travel up that agency's chain of command, over to the secretary of defense, then down the military chain of command to NORAD and NEADS—was abandoned instantly, with the first hijacked flight, even before it was clear to anyone that the hijackers intended to use the plane as a weapon. The problem was that the hijacking protocol, which assumed a "standard" hijacking, with plenty of time to react, had never been adjusted to meet the kind of rapidly developing and evolving terrorist threat that President Clinton had identified, and of which senior officials were well aware. Great as it was, their awareness and concern did not move the bureaucracy, and so the hijacking protocol was undisturbed, the cockpit doors remained unsecured, the terrorist watchlists were not updated, the intelligence agencies continued to hoard information, the "wall" between intelligence and criminal investigations was not re-examined. As George Tenet writes, "The country had no systematic mechanism to translate foreign threats into a meaningful program of protection of the homeland."

Throughout the attacks, moreover, the national command structure—from the president to the vice president to the White House videoconference to the National Military Command Center to FAA Headquarters in Washington—was irrelevant to the critical decisions that had to be made, because top officials were receiving the relevant information too late. Major Nasypany at NEADS asked repeatedly what authority his fighters would be given once they intercepted the hijacked planes; General Arnold has insisted that, if necessary, he would have given the order to shoot the planes down even without authorization from the president. Dean Eckmann, the lead pilot from the Langley wing over Washington, told the 9/11 Commission staff, however, that he would have authenticated the order at least three times before executing it, and protocol at the time required that the president issue the order. The point is that no one before 9/11 had thought through the implications of the evolving terrorist threat sufficiently to force operational changes in the bureaucracy. Thus, NORAD's commanders identified the threat of terrorism as a justification for NORAD's mission, but that justification never reached to the level of NORAD's *operations*, which were still oriented toward the Russian threat on the morning of 9/11.

The irrelevance of the national command structure on 9/11 is also demonstrated by the inability of the decision-makers to piece together critical information concerning American Airlines Flight 77. By 9:10, two intermediate levels of government, the FAA's Great Lakes Region and the DoD's Rescue Coordination Center (ironically, located just across Langley Air Force Base from the air defense detachment) held specific, time-sensitive information concerning American 77, by flight number. Both entities knew that Indianapolis Center considered the flight to be lost, possibly crashed. There was, however, no feedback loop to national-level decision-makers. It is reasonable to infer that information concerning the loss of American 77 reported to FAA Headquarters or even the Command Center at Herndon and to the National Military Command Center at 9:10 would have been correlated to subsequent reports of another hijacked aircraft airborne and headed toward the nation's capital. Where the national command structure could have been "value-added," it was valueless. The echo chamber remained impenetrable.

During Katrina, an absurd disconnect occurred between people from the various agencies, notably FEMA, who were witnessing and reporting the levee breaches almost in real time, and the officials to whom they reported, who were slow to receive the information and who relied more upon their communications with each other than upon communications from their own people on the ground. Even when the National Response Plan was finally activated, it, too, proved to be "top-heavy," assuming a top-down command structure that simply was not practicable in the circumstances of the response.

As on 9/11, agencies on the ground had to act, and those who were empowered to do so, or who exercised initiative without waiting for official go-ahead, did the most effective work. Thus, the Coast Guard, like NEADS, stayed within its chain of command and performed its defined mission heroically. Similarly, the Louisiana Department of Wildlife and Fisheries was extremely effective operating on its own in rescuing flood victims. Those agencies that continued to depend on leadership that was not forthcoming, or that fell prey to a command-and-control collapse, such as FEMA (or, on 9/11, the New York Fire Department) were less effective. In some cases, as with the New Orleans Police Department (or, on 9/11, FAA Headquarters), organizational chaos set in.

The need to empower ground-level decision-makers appears to have been addressed in the context of airline hijackings, where the authorization to intercept and take action against the plane may be given at lower levels of command, and DHS has replaced the National Response Plan in part in response to its meltdown during Katrina.

Emphasis continues to be placed, however, on the primacy of "top officials" in directing the response to emergencies, and those protocols have been practiced in a series of so-called TOPOFF exercises begun in the wake of 9/11. The exercises were constructed, by most accounts, with little or no input from state and local law enforcement or first-responder communities, and they have been criticized as too expensive, too protracted, and too remote from anything resembling a real-world scenario. Then governor of Arizona Janet Napolitano wrote to Secretary Chertoff in October 2007, complaining of the deficiencies in the exercises. At her confirmation hearing as secretary of the Department of Homeland Security, in January 2009, she related that the exercises were on too large a scale to allow the development of networking, which is perhaps the most important aspect of any preparedness exercise; that they were too expensive to allow for frequent repetition; that information-sharing during the exercises was poor; and that, as of the time she left her governorship, she had received no feedback from DHS on the performance of the exercise. Russell Decker, the president of the International Association of Emergency Managers, told *The New York Times*, "If we're going to do these exercises, DHS needs to collaborate to a greater extent with local governments so we're not wasting resources, we're not spinning our wheels, and we're making the country safer."

Implicit in these critiques of the TOPOFF exercises is the reality apparent from the ground truths of 9/11 and Katrina: any exercise in which the response role of so-called Top Officials is emphasized will not conform to the way crises are lived in the real world. Federal officials—particularly top federal officials—are certainly essential in setting policy before an event, and may eventually play important roles in responding to crises, once the allowable interval between an event and the need for a decision has expanded beyond seconds and minutes to hours. But the reality is that most of the important early decisions in responding will have to be made by local and state officials, or, to the extent the federal agencies are relevant, by people other than the "top" federal officials. This was true at NEADS on 9/11, on the streets on New York and Washington on 9/11, and on the streets of New Orleans during Katrina. Responding effectively to future crises requires that the federal government work more closely with and empower both lower-level federal officials and local and state governments to make critical early decisions. A potential prototype might be the command structure at NEADS, in which the Mission Crew Commander was empowered to make critical decisions, while the Battle Cab Commander, one step removed from immediate decision making and thus able to view the situation from a broader perspective, could intervene where appropriate. Thus, Colonel Marr stepped in to cancel the tail chase of the phantom American 11 flight because of a well-founded concern that New York City not be left unprotected, and also intervened to prevent the reading of the vice president's direction that nonresponsive deviating flights could be shot down, out of a justifiable concern that there were no targeted flights when the directive came down, and some 4,000 planes were "deviating," landing at the nearest airport. That decision may well have saved hundreds of lives. Such a model is also consistent with how my office actually functioned, during my service as attorney general of New Jersey, in addressing such crises as Tropical Storm Floyd and 9/11. It became clear during each crisis that crucial decisions could not await authorization up and down the chain of command, and, frankly, that those closest to the crisis were better equipped to make immediate decisions. My role naturally evolved to reviewing and ratifying or modifying such decisions, rather than initiating them. That reality should be recognized in planning for decision-making in a crisis.

A corollary of the need to empower lower-level officials to make critical decisions is the commitment to support those decisions even if the outcomes are less than optimal. The kind of backbiting and scapegoating that occurred among the different levels of government in the aftermath of Katrina is unseemly and unacceptable, even if understandable.

2. *Communications will fail.* Emergency planning should assume this reality, even as a commitment must be made to improve crisis communications. If there was a single most urgent recommendation of the 9/11 Commission, in my view it was the recommendation relating to emergency communications, which stated: "The inability to communicate was a critical element at the World Trade Center, Pentagon, and Somerset County, Pennsylvania, crash sites, where multiple agencies and multiple jurisdictions responded. The occurrence of this problem at three different sites is strong evidence that compatible and adequate communications among public safety organizations at the local, state, and federal levels remains an important problem." Accordingly, the Commission recommended passage of legislation providing for the "expedited and increased assignment of radio spectrum for public safety purposes."

This recommendation remained unaddressed as of August 2005, when Katrina struck the Gulf Coast. Predictably, communications chaos ensued. Outrageously, the problem remains unaddressed as of this writing. In January 2006, President Bush signed legislation "reallocating analog bandwidth spectrum, including the provision of additional bandwidth for public safety purposes." The reallocation of bandwidth for public safety purposes was not scheduled to take place, however, until February

2009. The 9/11 Public Discourse Project, the nonprofit corporation formed to promote the implementation of the Commission's recommendations, stated: "First responders should not
have to wait three more years. . . . Congress should mandate the
reallocation of broadcast spectrum for public safety purposes by
January 1, 2007, or the earliest possible date." Three years and
more have elapsed, and the interoperable network has yet to be
established. The Federal Communications Commission, seeking
to expedite the build-out process for a nationwide interoperable
network, put the spectrum up for public-private partnership
bidding. No satisfactory bids were received. As of June 2009,
there was still no plan in place to achieve interoperability. As
a consequence, individual municipalities from New York to
Washington to San Francisco are going their own ways, attempting to build interoperability locally and regionally, and some—
including New York and Washington, D.C.—have reported
achieving success in developing interconnectivity among their
police, fire, EMS, and other local agencies. National interoperable
communications will not be achieved, however, for the foresee-
able future.

For this reason alone, planning for crisis communications
should assume breakdowns in primary and secondary communications systems. It follows from this assumption of failure that
planning should provide for redundant information-routing systems and, perhaps more important, should empower local decision making in situations where communications have failed.
This empowerment will prevent the kind of paralysis experienced during Katrina, when responders on the ground too frequently awaited guidance from above that, when it came, was
based on faulty information.

3. *Planning should favor smaller organizational units with clearly defined missions and tight command structures.* Experience has shown

that such organizations perform optimally during a crisis. Organizations like NEADS, in improvising on 9/11; or the various FAA centers and controllers, in bringing over 4,000 flights to safe landings on 9/11; or the U.S. Coast Guard, in rescuing thousands during Katrina; or the NYPD, in facilitating the evacuation of thousands from the World Trade Center on 9/11, all succeeded because, in James Q. Wilson's terms, the "system of coordination was designed to enhance in lower-ranking [responders] the capacity for independent action toward a general goal and within an overall system of discipline."

Conversely, larger organizational units with diffuse command structures and unclear direction have failed during prior crises. Thus, the FBI never completely accepted the new mission assigned to it by Director Freeh; as Amy Zegart puts it, "The FBI missed all of [the] clues to 9/11 because most officials were viewing events during the summer of 2001 as they always had: through law enforcement lenses." As for the broader intelligence community, as the 9/11 Commission concluded, its "confederated structure left open the question of who really was in charge of the entire U.S. intelligence effort."

This raises the question of what role the national command structure, sitting atop the panoply of local, state, and federal agencies should play in responding to a crisis. The answer suggested by the experience of 9/11 and Katrina, in my view, is that the national command structure is most relevant in the planning period before a crisis, in assuring that potential responders are acquainted with their potential missions and with their potential need for interaction, and in the period immediately after the most intense phase of the emergency has passed, when decision horizons can reasonably extend for several hours, if not days. In the heart of a crisis, however, when decisions must be made by the second, the national command structure is too remote and diffuse to be relevant.

4. *Failures occur along the fault lines between and within agencies, where missions are shared, and across which vital information must be passed.* More than anything else, the story of 9/11 is the story of how the 9/11 conspirators, however unwittingly, were able to exploit the fault lines that existed within and among America's national security agencies to evade detection. Thus, the FBI and CIA struggled to coordinate their intelligence reporting because of "the wall," an obstacle that also plagued the FBI internally as criminal investigators hesitated to share information with intelligence agents; FBI Headquarters' estrangement from the field offices resulted in the failure to communicate alerts raised in Arizona about Islamic extremists receiving flight training, and in Minnesota about Zacarias Moussaoui; George Tenet's effort to force employees of different agencies to understand their counterparts' jobs was ignored; the NSA's intercepts were not passed on; the FAA's no-fly list was not updated; and the FAA and NORAD struggled to view the same radar picture and to communicate clearly about it on 9/11. Most recently, George Tenet has warned that "nuclear terrorism falls between the seams of the counterproliferation and counterterrorism communities, not claimed by either and lying dangerously on the boundaries of both." Recognition that these fault lines pose the greatest likelihood of mission failure suggests that positions be cross-designated, so that a cadre of personnel works for several agencies, and bears the responsibility for ensuring that coordination does occur.

5. *The most difficult problem facing government in attempting to adapt to changing circumstances is inertia.* Bureaucracy is the enemy of preparedness, because bureaucracy survives not by solving problems but by managing—and, hence, perpetuating—them. Bureaucracy thrives by defining its mission broadly enough to acquire turf but narrowly enough to diffuse blame, should any-

thing go wrong. It will outlast any temporary steward, and it knows that. It is any administration's greatest challenge.

In overcoming bureaucratic inertia, it is not enough to identify a priority, or to change an organizational box or two; it is necessary to "drill down," to change work rules and to train staff to the new priority. The change in priorities must be reflected in mandated and trained changes in the way people actually perform their jobs. NORAD preserved its existence by changing its mission to acknowledge the terrorist threat, but that did not result in any change in the way NORAD's officers did their jobs. They were still, notwithstanding the change in mission, "looking out, not in" on 9/11. Despite the FBI's effort to reorient itself to anticipating criminal acts like terrorism, its law enforcement culture persisted. CIA director Tenet's declaration of "war" against al Qaeda in 1998 went largely unheeded, especially in the other national security agencies.

When I became attorney general for New Jersey, I was confronted by a racial-profiling scandal that had enveloped the New Jersey State Police. A decade before, one of my predecessors, Robert Del Tufo, had with tremendous foresight envisioned the trouble that could result from turning the state police into frontline combatants in the war on drugs. Accordingly, he had changed the standard operating procedures regarding roadside stops to require that state police have reasonable suspicion that a vehicle contained contraband before they requested permission to search the vehicle.

The reform that we put into place as a consequence of racial profiling built on Del Tufo's standard. We simply "drilled down" into the way troopers were conducting stops and changed the procedures and training to conform to the "reasonable suspicion" standard. Merely having the standard in place had proved to be insufficient.

Similarly, the trouble with many of the initiatives undertaken at CIA, FBI, NORAD, and other agencies before 9/11 was that they registered a level of concern—even urgency—without translating it into an operational context. Thus, a Presidential Daily Brief for President Clinton, dated December 4, 1998, declared that Osama bin Laden was "preparing to hijack U.S. aircraft and other attacks." Former CIA director Tenet points to this and other warnings issued by the intelligence service as evidence that the threat to civil aviation was clearly understood before 9/11, but concedes, "Unfortunately, even when our warnings were heard, little was done domestically to protect the United States against the threat. To cite two obvious and tragic failures, only after 9/11 were cockpit doors hardened and passengers forbidden from carrying box cutters aboard U.S. airliners." Despite the rhetoric about "reinventing" and making government more responsive, no one drilled the heightened level of urgency down to the point where government operations reflected the evolving threat that had been identified. Reinventing government, it turns out, is less an act of genius or imagination than one of persistence. It is the hardest work. The new mission must be reinforced constantly; it must reach the level of training; and it must change the way employees do their jobs, or it will not be accepted. It is that simple, and that hard.

6. *National security and public safety issues are not graded on a curve; they are strictly pass/fail.* Government officials must recognize this harsh reality, but we in the public must avoid the "heads must roll" mentality that, if allowed to continue, will discourage the best and brightest from the challenge of public service.

The suggestion of the CIA's Inspector General that George Tenet should be disciplined after the fact for failing to instill his "war" footing throughout the CIA before 9/11 would be laughable if it were not so scurrilous. Similarly, the calls for Michael Chertoff to resign in the wake of Katrina were absurdly unfair, a product of the media's desperation to have something provocative to say every hour of every day. We should encourage people of the caliber of Tenet and Chertoff to pursue public service, not attempt to humiliate them when things do not go well despite their best efforts.

Once we have elected or recruited them, however, there is a need to train incoming executives, most of all the president of the United States, in the mechanics of the business of government. The formation of a presidential academy, associated with the University of Virginia's Miller Center of Public Affairs or with the various presidential libraries, to train incoming administration officials in the nuts and bolts of running executive departments would go a long way toward sensitizing executives to the need for persistent follow-through in guiding agencies.

7. *Finally, a government reshaped by the lessons of its prior experiences requires candor.* Mayor Rudolph Giuliani demonstrated during and after 9/11 that leadership does not require dissembling. The mayor was so effective precisely because he stated precisely what he knew and what he didn't. His candor inspired confidence, even when his message was dispiriting.

The Bush administration, by contrast, demonstrated that leadership is undermined by dissembling. The false and misleading account the administration peddled about its response to the 9/11 attacks may have worked for a time. It may have emboldened the administration to put forward its misleading account of Jessica Lynch's capture and rescue and its false account of Pat Tillman's death. It even may have led the administration to shade the quality of information it possessed concerning weapons of mass destruction in Iraq; the jury is out on that question.

At the end of the day, however, the administration's story raised more questions than it answered, and led directly to the formation of the 9/11 Commission. When we were able to subpoena the appropriate records, and were easily able to reconstruct what had occurred, we presented the reconstructed timeline to a NORAD general in Panama City, Florida. His face reddened as he took in the disparity between what had happened and the official version; then he thanked us. "Looks like you've got the ground truth," he said. When a similar strategy of dissembling was attempted during Hurricane Katrina, no one needed subpoena power to see the ground truth. As Frank Rich put it, "The true Katrina narrative was just too powerful to be papered over with White House fictions."

Perhaps the most harmful consequence of the administration's continued insistence, in the face of evidence to the contrary, that operations were running smoothly, was the administration's own blindness, illustrated by Richard Clarke's good-faith account of the White House videoconference, to the reality disclosed by the ground truth of 9/11 and Katrina: that the task of "reinventing government" identified by President Clinton still lies ahead. Creating a new Department of Homeland Security, and fixing the obvious deficiencies exposed by the last crisis, does not address the reality that government, as it is currently configured, does not adapt fast enough to changing missions to be effective in the post–Cold War—and, now, post-9/11—world. My fervent hope is that now that we have learned the ground truth, we can start the important conversation about how to reconceive government the right way, from the ground up.

"SYSTEMIC FAILURES"

For all but one of the passengers lined up for boarding, Northwest Airlines' Christmas Day 2009 flight from Amsterdam to Detroit represents a brief and unlikely intersection of 278 destinies. Charlie and Scotti Keepman are eager, like many other passengers, to be home for the holidays, but they have two additional reasons to be joyful. They, along with their adult daughter, Ricki, are returning home to Wisconsin with two Ethiopian children they have adopted. Although security at the Amsterdam airport seems lax to Ricki, since they do not have to remove their shoes and Mrs. Keepman inadvertently carries a bottle of water onto the plane, they settle quickly into their seats at the back of the plane and try to keep their new family members entertained.

Jasper Schuringa, a Dutch filmmaker, is traveling to the United States on business. He passes through security uneventfully and takes his seat in row 22. Roey Rosenblith, who is returning home for a visit from his place of business in Africa, is impressed by the team of ten security screeners at the gate who interview each passenger. He is "frisked so thoroughly by the young Dutch security guard that I began to wonder if he was enjoying himself."

Canadian citizen Chandra Chopra is returning home from a visit to her native India. While waiting in line to pass through security, she notices a tall black man "lagging behind, hands on his forehead, lost in thought." "He was thinking very hard," she will recall. "I was thinking, 'Why is he standing like this?' They checked him again. He's the last one they let on the plane."

Like the other passengers, that man, later identified as Umar Farouk Abdumutallab, has pursued a unique life path to reach the line to board Northwest Airlines Flight 253 that Christmas morning. But in one radical respect he differs from the others. He wants their destinies to remain joined forever. He wants their lives to end that day.

BORN INTO A LIFE of relative privilege in Nigeria—his father is the head of a large bank—twenty-three-year-old Abdumutallab has distinguished himself throughout his young life for his piety. According to one of his cousins, Abdulmutallab condemned his father's profession as "immoral" and "un-Islamic" because bankers charge interest, and urged him to quit. He attended high school at the British International School in Lomé, the capital of Togo, where he was known as a devout Muslim who preached about Islam to his schoolmates.

For the 2004–05 academic year, Abdulmutallab studied at the Sana'a Institute for the Arabic Language in Sana'a, Yemen, and attended lectures at Iman University. The *Sunday Times* of London has reported that Abdulmutallab first met Anwar al-Awlaki, a radical Muslim cleric, in 2005 in Yemen. He attended lectures by al-Awlaki, and apparently began posting that year on the website "Farouk1986."

In September 2005, Abdulmutallab began studies at University College London. He became president of the school's Islamic Society. He organized a conference in January 2007 under the banner "War on Terror Week," which featured speakers including political figures, human rights lawyers, and former Guantánamo Bay detainees. One lecture, "Jihad v. Terrorism," was billed as "a lecture on the Islamic position with respect to jihad." During those years, Abdulmutallab "crossed the radar screen" of the United Kingdom's MI5 for radical links and "multiple communications" with Islamic extremists.

Notwithstanding MI5's notice, on June 12, 2008, Abdulmutallab applied for and received from the United States consulate in London a United States multiple-entry visa, valid until June 12, 2010. He attended an Islamic seminar at the AlMaghrib Institute in Houston, Texas, August 1–17, 2008.

In May 2009, Abdulmutallab tried to return to Britain for a program at what the British authorities concluded was a fictitious school. As a result, his visa application was denied by the United Kingdom Border Agency. His name was placed on a UK Home Office security watch list, which means, according to BBC News, that he could not enter the United Kingdom, though passing through the country in transit was permissible and he was not permanently banned. The United Kingdom did not share the information with other countries, because the application was rejected to prevent immigration fraud rather than for reasons of national security.

Abdulmutallab returned to Yemen in August to study at the Sana'a Institute for the Arabic Language in Yemen from August to September 2009. He appeared to have undergone a personality change: he was obsessively observant during his time there, "a loner" who wore traditional Islamic clothing. By September he was routinely skipping classes at the Institute and instead attending lectures at Iman University, a school suspected for links to terrorism. His family became concerned in August 2009 when he called them to say he had dropped out of school, but was remaining in Yemen. One classmate said that Abdulmutallab's had "told me his greatest wish was for sharia and Islam to be the rule of law across the world."

In October, Abdulmutallab sent his father a text message saying that he was no longer interested in pursuing an MBA in Dubai, and wanted instead to study sharia and Arabic in a seven-year course in Yemen. He stated that he would be getting this education for free, but would not disclose who was sponsoring him. He also sent text messages to his father making clear that he had "found a new religion, the real Islam" and that he had no intention of ever returning to his family. This was the family's last contact with Abdulmutallab.

He overstayed his student visa (which was valid through September 21). He left Yemen on December 7, flying to Ethiopia, and then two days later to Ghana. Yemeni officials have said that Abdulmutallab traveled to the mountainous Shabwa province to meet with "Al Qaeda elements" before leaving Yemen. It seems clear that among the radical elements in Yemen was the cleric al-Awlaki.

Al-Awlaki, the Imam in the Northern Virginia mosque attended by Hazmi and Mihdhar prior to the 9/11 attacks and a correspondent of the Fort Hood assailant in late 2009, is a continuous and disturbing link between the 9/11 attacks and subsequent acts of terror. There is evidence that al-Awlaki was also Abdulmutallab's recruiter and one of his trainers, and that the two met prior to the attack. In February 2010, al-Awlaki himself, in an interview published in Arabic by al-Jazeera.net, admitted that he taught and corresponded with Umar Farouk Abdulmutallab, but he denied having ordered the attack. Al-Awlaki said: "Umar Farouk is one of my students; I had communications with him. And I support what he did." He also said: "I did not tell him to do this operation, but I support it." In April 2010, al-Awlaki became the first American citizen approved by the government for targeted killing.

Ghanaian officials say Abdulmutallab was there from December 9 until December 24, when he flew to Lagos.

CHRISTMAS DAY, 2009. ABDULMUTALLAB travels to Amsterdam, where he clears security and boards Northwest Airlines Flight 253 en route to Detroit, Michigan. He has purchased his ticket with cash in Ghana on December 16. He takes his seat, 19A, and waits for his moment to strike. A six-inch packet sewn into his underwear contains pentaerythritol tetranitrate (PETN), a powder that becomes a plastic explosive when mixed with triacetone triperoxide (TAPN); he carries a syringe containing a liquid acid to activate the concoction. The plane takes off, and the flight proceeds uneventfully across the Atlantic Ocean.

Roughly eight hours after the flight has begun and shortly before the plane is to begin its descent, Abdulmutallab uses the restroom for twenty minutes. When he emerges, he indicates that he isn't feeling well. He returns to seat 19A, pulls a blanket over his lap, removes the syringe from his pocket, and injects the acid solution. If the substance detonates, all on board, and perhaps hundreds more on the ground, will die, and Abdulmutallab will have accomplished his mission. For the first time since 9/11, a major terrorist attack will occur on U.S. soil.

In the back of the plane, the Keepmans, tired from the long flight from Addis Ababa to Amsterdam to Detroit, are preparing their new family for landing when they hear "a pop, like a firecracker," and see smoke begin to fill the cabin. All around them passengers begin screaming; some leave their seats. They hear a commotion from the front of the plane as a male steward rushes past them to the rear to retrieve a fire extinguisher. He shouts at the passengers to remain in their seats. The Keepmans join hands with their children and begin singing "Jesus Loves the Little Children."

Passengers in the rows surrounding Abdulmutallab's seat also hear a loud popping noise, and smell a foul odor; some see Abdulmutallab's trouser leg and the wall of the plane on fire. Jasper Schuringa, the Dutch filmmaker seated on the other side of the plane and three rows behind Abdulmutallab, hurtles several passengers and jumps Abdulmutallab, wrestling him to the floor as flight attendants use fire extinguishers to try to douse the flames. "When I saw the suspect," Schuringa would recall, "that he was getting on fire, I freaked, of course, and without any hesitation I just jumped over all the seats, and I jumped to the suspect. I was thinking, like, he's trying to blow up the plane. I was trying to search his body for any explosives. I took some kind of object that was already melting and smoking out of him."

The aisle clogs with passengers trying to escape the flames and the stewards trying to extinguish them. Stewards pull off Abdulmutallab's burning pants and succeed in putting out the flames. Schuringa, holding Abdulmutallab firmly from behind, and others lead him up the aisle to a vacant seat, where he is handcuffed and otherwise restrained. Abdulmutallab has burns on his legs but remains calm. When asked by a flight attendant what he has in his pants, he replies: "Explosive device."

Schuringa's hands are burned. When he returns to his seat, the passengers and crew applaud. He has saved them.

IN THE IMMEDIATE AFTERMATH of the attack, similarities between the Christmas Day attack and the 9/11 attacks were dismissed as hyperbole. The notion that Abdulmutallab could have been part of a larger network seemed implausible, given the billions of dollars expended since 9/11, and the policy emphasis placed on strengthening America's early-warning systems and ensuring that vital intelligence information was shared. The State Department's TIPOFF list was now shared with the FAA, and compared with the FAA's "no-fly" list. Some seventy intelligence "fusion centers" had been established to ensure that local, state, and federal law enforcement were connected. Both formal and informal intelligence sharing with other nations was encouraged. The newly created Directorate of National Intelligence and National Counter-Terrorism Center were expressly charged with assimilating the intelligence received from disparate agencies and coordinating their efforts.

Even the best system would be vulnerable to an isolated individual, acting on his own to cause harm. In the early hours after the Christmas Day attack, that is what Abdulmutallab appeared to be. Within days, however, as details of his background began to emerge, it became clear that, as with the 9/11 hijackers, the failure to stop Abdulmutallab was not a consequence of his acting outside the reach or knowledge of government; it was instead, as President Obama put it angrily, a "systemic failure," a systemic failure that, in fact, repeated the essential characteristics of the pre-9/11 failures.

1. THE FAILURE TO SHARE INFORMATION ACROSS GOVERNMENTS AND AGENCIES

On November 11, British intelligence officials sent the United States a cable indicating that a man named "Umar Farouk" had spoken to radical cleric al-Awlaki, pledging to support jihad, but the cable did not reflect Abdulmutallab's last name. Just over a week later, Abdulmutallab's father made a report to two CIA officers at the U.S. Embassy in Abuja, Nigeria, regarding his son's "extreme religious views" and told the embassy that Abdulmutallab might be in Yemen. The suspect's name was added in November 2009 to the Terrorist Identities Datamart Environment (TIDE), but he was not added to the Terrorist Screening Database, nor was his U.S. visa revoked.

According to one report, United States intelligence officials requested that his U.S. visa not be revoked. The intelligence officials' stated reason was that revoking Abdulmutallab's visa could have foiled a larger investigation into al-Qaeda in Yemen; notwithstanding this degree of attention to Abdulmutallab, apparently no one was monitoring his travel on Christmas Day. The NCTC did not check to see whether Abdulmutallab's American visa was valid, or whether he had a British visa that was valid; therefore, it did not learn that the British had rejected Abdulmutallab's visa application earlier in 2009. The British did not inform the Americans of this rejection because the visa application was denied to prevent immigration fraud, not because of national security concerns.

2. THE FAILURE TO "CONNECT THE DOTS"

As on 9/11, a consequence of the failure of various governments and federal agencies to share the intelligence relating to Abdulmutallab was that no one assimilated and synthesized the intelligence. No one put together (1) the father's report of an estranged and potentially radicalized son in Yemen with (2) the NSA intercepts relating to the preparation of a "Nigerian" in Yemen for an attack, or with (3) the British intelligence relating to his radical religious views or the conversations of "Umar Farouk" with al-Awlaki or with (4) the British rejection of his visa application. The U.S. intelligence agencies' request that his visa not be revoked, if it occurred, was not accompanied by any attempt to track Abdulmutallab's travel or efforts to use that visa. Curiously, the State Department had decided that it would "question him about his ties to extremists if he chose to *renew* his visa." As Senator Susan Collins of Maine put it, "How he could have been a threat . . . in the *future* based on these extremist ties, but not a sufficient *current* threat to prudentially revoke his visa, defies both logic and common sense." His addition in November 2009 to the Terrorist Identities Datamart Environment carried no implications for the State Department's TIPOFF list, the FAA's no-fly list, or his visa status.

Like the 9/11 hijackers, and despite all the well-advertised (if not so well implemented) reforms and augmentations to the United States' national security apparatus, Abdulmutallab ran the gauntlet. He was able to travel relatively freely from Nigeria to England to Yemen to Ghana to Amsterdam to a descending altitude over Detroit. He did not escape identification but he did escape interdiction by the State Department, the CIA, the multifarious intelligence agencies under the supervision of the Pentagon, the FAA, and the intelligence and air traffic security forces of the United Kingdom, Nigeria, Yemen, and Holland, among others.

As during the development of the 9/11 plot, intelligence giving a partial identification, a critical NSA intercept, and the human intelligence supplied by relatives was never subjected to the elementary link analysis that would have supplied the connections. As on 9/11, government officials' after-the-fact explanation that they believed the threat posed by Al Qaeda in Yemen was directed overseas ignored the ease of global travel.

The result was that, as on 9/11, the passengers and crew aboard Abdulmutallab's chosen plane were left undefended. For all the reforms adopted, and all of the changes in governmental structure and process implemented after 9/11, their last best hope was once again themselves.

3. APPLYING THE LESSONS OF THE GROUND TRUTH

It is tempting, in light of the parallels between the failures leading to 9/11 and the failures leading to the Christmas Day attempt, to conclude that little has changed since 9/11 in our national preparedness, and that the United States is little, if at all, safer. In my view, that conclusion is unjustified. As former 9/11 Commission Chairman Tom Kean and Co-Chairman Lee Hamilton pointed out in testimony before Congress, "Since September 11, 2001, the NCTC [National Counter-Terrorism Center] and other government agencies have repeatedly connected the dots and shared information necessary to defeat terrorist attacks. Improvements have clearly been made although that sharing is not as prompt and as seamless as it should be." What, then, is the appropriate context in which to evaluate what President Obama called the "systemic failure" that resulted in a near-massacre on Christmas Day? I believe that, building on the case-by-case, inductive approach suggested in my analysis of 9/11 and Katrina, we can identify lessons learned that may make a difference in responding to future attacks and other crises.

First, the Christmas Day attack demonstrates once more that crises are lived not according to a government organization chart, where critical decision-making emanates from the top, but from the ground up, where people will be forced to make decisions above their job classifications and—unless reform is effected—beyond their competence. The events of September 11, Hurricane Katrina, and the Christmas Day attempted bombing, disparate as they are, share this characteristic: each required ordinary citizens—airline passengers, office workers, residents—to make critical, life-and-death decisions. Similarly, the alleged attempted bombing of Times Square on May 1, 2010 by disaffected American citizen Faisal Shahzad was interdicted primarily because a member of the public alerted police.

Applying the self-evident principle that we should plan to respond to crises the way we now know they will be experienced, it is disappointing that so little has been done to educate adult Americans in the rudiments of crisis response. Anyone trained in emergency response knows that people can be trained to think more clearly and calmly and to react more quickly in emergencies. We also know with certainty now that regardless of how much we spend on law enforcement, intelligence, and national defense, circumstances will arise in which ordinary people are confronted with extraordinary threats—storms, fires, floods, criminal or terrorist acts—and will need to know what to do. Beyond a fairly obscure advisory website, Ready.gov, however, there has been no national emergency preparedness education effort. Viewing crisis management from the ground up, such training on a national scale is imperative; its absence is perhaps the biggest flaw in our preparedness effort. The National Incident Management System (NIMS), a flow chart for national response that would make Rube Goldberg look like a minimalist, should also be revised in light of the knowledge that officers and emergency responders will have to make command-level decisions, particularly early in a crisis.

Second, the background of the Christmas Day attempted bombing brings into sharp relief the persistent reality that "failures occur along the fault lines between and within agencies, where missions are shared, and across which vital information must flow." Because failures of this magnitude were precisely what the Director of National Intelligence and the NCTC were established after 9/11 to prevent, moreover, the Christmas Day failure raises the question of how effective those reforms have been.

By establishing the Director of National Intelligence without the budgetary authority necessary to command compliance with its directives (an authority the 9/11 Commission had urged), and with the existing intelligence chains of command left intact, Congress perpetuated—and perhaps exacerbated—a critical ambiguity in the structure of the intelligence community. As Kean and Hamilton explained to the Senate Homeland Security Committee, "Ambiguities can contribute to mission confusion and to lack of clarity about lanes in the road. This is perhaps the greatest challenge facing the DNI. Is the DNI a strong leader of the intelligence community empowered to lead the IC as an enterprise? Or is the DNI a mere coordinator, a convening authority charged with helping facilitate common inter-intelligence agency agreement? The lack of settled clarity on its mission invites a host of other criticisms." In this critical respect, the 9/11 Commission's characterization of the intelligence community—that its "confederated structure left open the question of who really was in charge of the entire U.S. intelligence effort"—remains disturbingly true.

Third, the failure, in the months leading to Christmas Day, of the DNI, the NCTC, and various federal agencies to integrate the strands of intelligence regarding Abdulmutallab into a coherent picture bespeaks inertia, if not worse. Just as, prior to 9/11, FBI Director Freeh's reorientation of the Bureau, CIA Director Tenet's declaration of war on al Qaeda, and NORAD's reconception of its mission to counter the emerging terrorist threat failed to alter in any fundamental way the manner in which government officials performed their duties, so the establishment of the NCTC and the DNI have not led to the kind of integrative analysis necessary to identify and interdict threats like the one posed by Abdulmutallab.

This is not for lack of the necessary technical capability. Computer scientists have developed sophisticated software capable of the necessary intelligence integration and link analysis, and it is already in use throughout much of the intelligence community. Such tools are only as effective, however, as the quality of the data input. It seems clear that, as before 9/11, there has been a failure to redefine how line personnel actually do their jobs. As pointed out earlier, this bureaucratic resistance to change has been and will be any administration's greatest challenge. How should the Obama administration meet it?

The starting point is admitting how hard a task this is. A good illustration is the attack perpetrated in November 2009 by a military psychiatrist at Fort Hood in Texas. The perpetrator, Nidal Malik Hasan, MD, born in America of Palestinian parents, had started espousing fundamentalist Islamic views as early as 2005. On November 5, 2009, shortly after 1:30 p.m., Dr. Hasan took an empty seat at the Soldier Readiness Center where he worked, bowed his head, then stood, jumped onto a desk, shouted "Allah Akhbar," drew a FN-5-7, and fired more than a hundred rounds, killing thirteen and wounding forty-seven before he himself was shot.

A year earlier, officials at Walter Reed Army Hospital had become sufficiently concerned about Dr. Hasan's attitudes that meetings were held to discuss how to handle him. In December 2008, his case was referred to the FBI's Joint Terrorism Task Force. The Bureau examined evidence of email communications between Hasan and al-Awlaki—the imam involved in the Abdulmutallab case—and the concerns expressed by Hasan's colleagues, but concluded that "because the content of the communications was explainable by [Hasan's] research and nothing else derogatory was found, the JTTF concluded that Major Hasan was not involved in terrorist activities or terrorist planning." An after-action review conducted by the Department of Defense concluded that the Department was not as prepared as it should be to respond to internal threats, but avoided characterizing the incident as a terrorist attack; the report never mentioned Dr. Hasan's strong ties to al-Awlaki, or the fact that he shouted "Allah Akhbar" before opening fire.

In contrast to the Christmas Day attempted bombing, the Fort Hood case did not involve an interagency breakdown in communications; officials at Walter Reed Hospital became concerned about Dr. Hasan and relayed those concerns to the FBI. Intelligence agencies intercepted communications between Dr. Hasan and the radical imam with ties back to the 9/11 conspirators; those intercepts were also shared. So the dots were there to be connected; they were simply connected incorrectly. The Fort Hood case, in other words, involved human error; investigators misread Dr. Hasan. I believe the case also bears the earmarks of bureaucratic inertia; how much more would it have taken, one wonders, for the Bureau to have decided that Dr. Hasan was worth a closer look? If nothing else, the case raises the question of whether the stated change in mission has been accompanied by the necessary "drilling down" into how officials are performing their jobs to ensure that they are not simply checking off boxes or otherwise languishing in bureaucratic lassitude. Infusing the bureaucracy with an urgency commensurate with the threat to our national security remains the greatest challenge. Faisal Shahzad, the alleged Times Square bomber, was allowed to board a plane at JFK Airport despite having been placed in the FAA's no-fly list; the plane was about to take off when officials realized their oversight and stopped him. At this writing, moreover, Shahzad appears not to have been a lone wolf, but to have been trained by and part of a larger Taliban/Al Qaeda network that went undisturbed until Shahzad acted.

We should start, in other words, by recognizing how difficult a job it is to connect the dots, but we can never end there. We can never, in effect, grade the government's antiterrorism efforts on the curve. This is strictly a pass-fail game, and with respect to both the Fort Hood massacre and the Christmas Day bombing attempt—and perhaps with respect to the Times Square bombing attempt—the government failed.

Success turns ultimately, in my view, on appreciating the extent of the problem. The various failures in successive crises point to a larger failure: the inability to reconceive how government should be structured and work in the post-9/11 era. After all, the problems besetting our government in the terrorism context—inertia, the failure to integrate information across agencies, the dislocation of responsibility from budgetary authority—are not limited to that context, but are endemic to modern government as a whole. As Paul Light, author of *A Government Ill Executed*, puts it, "We're at a point right now where the federal government cannot faithfully execute the laws. If we're not quite on the brink of complete collapse, we're getting closer and closer. We've had a cascade of failures such as the sluggish response to Hurricane Katrina that show us that the government is having increasing problems delivering goods and services."

Add to that "cascade of failures" a further "sluggish response": the government's reaction to the BP Gulf oil catastrophe. As in Katrina, government officials spent critical days debating whether the gushing oil was "an incident of national significance" that would trigger the National Response Plan. Instead of, say, convening the leading engineering experts from industry, government, and academia to try to develop a solution, officials dithered over whether the administration should "own" the crisis. Now it owns them. Administrations change, but the essential problem persists. As I write, Congress is holding hearings lambasting BP and the administration. A senior official in the Department of Interior has been replaced, just as John Brennan was eased out of the DNI slot after the 9/11 intelligence failures. The terrorists plot. The oil gushes. The first tropical storms gather strength in the south Atlantic. The show goes on. But the task of "fixing" the intelligence or emergency response systems is inseparable from the larger task of reinventing government, with one vital difference. Given the stakes involved in the failure to protect public safety, it must be tackled first, and immediately.

TIMELINE OF HIJACKERS' MOVEMENTS, 1991–2002

The following chart highlights the travel of the al Qaeda hijackers and the contacts they had with government entities; it is illustrative, not exhaustive. Those contacts have been analyzed in a comprehensive 9/11 Staff Monograph, "9/11 and Terrorist Travel," which effectively dispels "the myth that [the hijackers' entry into the United States] was 'clean and legal.' It was not. Three hijackers carried passports with indicators of Islamic extremism linked to al Qaeda; two others carried passports manipulated in a fraudulent manner. . . . Two hijackers lied on their visa applications. Once in the United States, two hijackers violated the terms of their visas. One overstayed his visa. And all but one obtained some form of state identification. . . . In all, they had twenty-five contacts with consular officers and forty-three contacts with immigration and customs authorities. . . . They successfully entered the United States thirty-three times in twenty-one months, through nine airports of entry."

DATE	KHALID SHEIKH MOHAMMED (KSM)	OTHERS	AMERICAN 11	AMERICAN 77	UNITED 175	UNITED 93	NOTES
		Zacarias Moussaoui (ZM)	Mohammed Atta (MA)	Khalid al Mihdhar (KAM)	Marwan al Shehhi (MAS1)	Saeed al Ghamdi (SAG)	**Boldface entries** indicate direct contact between hijackers and government security entities.
		Tawfiq bin Attash (**Khallad**) (**K**)	Abdul Aziz al Omari (AAO)	Majed Moqed (MM)	Fayez Banihammad (FB)	Ahmed al Nami (AAM)	
		Zakariya Essabar (ZE)	Satam al Suqami (SAS)	Hani Hanjour (HH)	Mohand al Shehri (MAS2)	Ahmad al Haznawi (AAH)	
		Ramzi bin al Shib (RBAS)	Wail al Shehri (WAS1)	Nawaf al Hazmi (NAH)	Ahmed al Ghamdi (AAG)	Ziad Jarrah (ZJ)	
		Mohamed al Khatani (MAK)	Waleed al Shehri (WAS2)	Salem al Hazmi (SAH)	Hamza al Ghamdi (HAG)		
Brackets [ ] indicate gaps or uncertainty in sources; conflicts between sources are also noted.							
1991 [2]				HH: Saudi Arabia to Tucson			
EARLY 1992 [2]				HH: AZ to Saudi Arabia			
1992 [1]			MA: Egypt to Hamburg				
1994 [1]		K: Yemen to Afghanistan					Age 15
1994 [2]				NAH: Saudi Arabia			Contact w/ key al Qaeda facilitator
1995 [2]				KAM and NAH: Bosnia			Fight Serbs
1995 [1,2]		RBAS: Yemen to Hamburg					Under name Ramzi Omar (seeking asylum as Sudanese; **US visa application denied**)

EARLY 1996 [2,3]					KAM: Afghan training camp	
APRIL 1996 [2]		HH: Saudi Arabia to FL				
APRIL 1996 [1]				ZI: Lebanon to Greifswald, Germany		
MAY 1996 [2]		HH: FL to Oakland				Flight training
JUNE 1996 [1]			MASI: Bonn to United Arab Emirates (UAE)			
JUNE 1996 [1]			MASI: UAE to Bonn			
SEPTEMBER OR OCTOBER 1996 [2,3]		HH: CA to AZ				Attends flight school in AZ on several occasions, 1996–1999
NOVEMBER 1996 [2]		HH: US to Saudi Arabia				
1996–1998 [2]	MA: Travels in Middle East, returns to Germany					
MID-1996–EARLY 1997 [1]	From Tora Bora, Afghanistan, to India, Indonesia, Malaysia, Iran, Pakistan, and back to Afghanistan					Meets with Osama bin Laden (OBL)

Source Key: 1. *9/11 Commission Report* (http://www.9-11commission.gov/) 2. *Congressional Joint Inquiry Report* (http://www.gpoaccess.gov/serialset/creports/911.html) 3. *9/11 Timeline by Cooperative Research* (http://www.historycommons.org/project.jsp?project=911_project) 4. 9/11 Staff Monograph, "9/11 and Terrorist Travel" (http://www.9-11commission.gov/staff_statements/911_TerrTrav_Monograph.pdf)

DATE	KHALID SHEIKH MOHAMMED (KSM)	OTHERS	AMERICAN 11	AMERICAN 77	UNITED 175	UNITED 93	NOTES
1997[1]	To Karachi, then Afghanistan						Tries going to Chechnya; unable to travel through Azerbaijan, goes to Karachi, then Afghanistan
1997[1]		K: Still in Afghanistan					Fights Northern Alliance; loses leg; pledges alliance to OBL
1997[1]		RBAS: Germany to Yemen					**Asylum application denied**
1997[1]		RBAS: Yemen to Hamburg					Under true name
FEBRUARY 1997[1]		ZM: Morocco to Germany					City unidentified; moves to Hamburg in 1998
SEPTEMBER 1997[1]						ZJ: Greifswald to Hamburg	
NOVEMBER 1997[2]				HH: [Saudi Arabia] to US			To FL and AZ
1997 AND FIRST HALF OF 1998	Frequent travel between Pakistan and Afghanistan						
1998[1]		ZM: Moves to Hamburg	MA: Hamburg to Egypt to Hamburg				
1998[3]				NAH: Chechnya			

1998 [1]					MA and RBAS move into same apartment in April (MA's name on lease)
FEBRUARY–MARCH 1998 [1,2]			MA: Whereabouts unknown	MAST: Bonn to Hamburg	May be in Afghanistan
APRIL 1998 [2]		ZM: Afghanistan			At Khalden camp
JUNE 1998 [2]			MA: Egypt		**Applies for new passport**
AUGUST 1998 [1]				MAST: Hamburg to Bonn	School requires transfer back
LATE 1998 [2]		RBAS: Afghanistan (?)			According to "indications"
LATE 1998 OR EARLY 1999 [1]	Moves to Kandahar				At OBL's invitation
BEFORE EARLY 1999 [1]			KAM AND NAH: Visit Afghanistan "on several occasions"		Before selection for planes operation
1999 [1]		IC: Afghanistan to Yemen			**US visa application denied (under another name)**
1999 [3]	Philippines				In Philippines for "much of" 1999, planning to assassinate the pope
1999 [3]	Hamburg				Visits MA's apt. several times in 1999

Source Key: 1. *9/11 Commission Report* (http://www.9-11commission.gov/). 2. *Congressional Joint Inquiry Report* (http://www.gpoaccess.gov/serialset/creports/911.html). 3. *9/11 Timeline by Cooperative Research* (http://www.historycommons.org/project.jsp?project=911_project). 4. 9/11 Staff Monograph, "9/11 and Terrorist Travel" (http://www.9-11commission.gov/staff_statements/911_TerrTrav_Monograph.pdf)

DATE	KHALID SHEIKH MOHAMMED (KSM)	OTHERS	AMERICAN 11	AMERICAN 77	UNITED 175	UNITED 93	NOTES
SPRING 1999 [1]	Kandahar						Summoned by OBL in March or April, to learn al Qaeda will support planes proposal; meetings in spring w/ OBL and Mohammed Atef
APRIL 1999 [2]				HH: US to Saudi Arabia			Stays home for "a while," then whereabouts unknown—possibly training camps in Afghanistan
APRIL 1999 [1,2,4]				NAH AND SAH: Jeddah			Obtain US visas; OBL later tells KSM that KAM and NAH obtained visas for operation against US
APRIL 1999 [1,2,4]				KAM: Jeddah			Obtains US visa, expiration April 2000
APRIL 3–7, 1999 [2,3,4]				KAM, NAH, AND SAH: Jeddah			Obtain US visas at US Consulate (and attend "special training")
SUMMER 1999 [1]		K: Yemen to Afghanistan					
SEPTEMBER 1999 [2]				HH: Jeddah to Czech Republic (via bus) to Newark			Obtains US visa on second try
FALL 1999 [1,3]		K: Mes Aynak camp, Afghanistan		KAM AND NAH: Yemen and Karachi to Mes Aynak camp, Afghanistan			OBL selects 4 operatives for planes operation to attend training camp: K, NAH, Abu Bara al Yemeni from Karachi; KAM from Yemen

Date						Notes
OCTOBER 1999 [1,3]	To Karachi					Visit Mohamedou Ould Slahi, who instructs on obtaining Pakistani visas
LAST WEEK OF NOVEMBER 1999 [1,3]	**RBAS:** Duisburg, Germany	**MA:** Hamburg to Karachi; to Quetta, Pakistan; to Kandahar		**MAS:** Duisburg, Germany	**ZI:** Duisburg, Germany	Per Slahi's advice (instead of Chechnya), **with Pakistani visas**
EARLY DECEMBER 1999 [1]	**K:** Mes Aynak camp, Afghanistan, to Karachi		**NAH:** Mes Aynak camp, Afghanistan, to Karachi	**MAS:** Hamburg to Karachi; to Quetta, Pakistan; to Kandahar	**ZI:** Hamburg to Karachi; to Quetta, Pakistan; to Kandahar	KSM instructs on Western travel and culture, 1-2 weeks; NAH travels w/ K and Abu Bara al Yemeni
[EARLY DECEMBER 1999] [1]				**MAS:** Kandahar to UAE		To prepare for mission; after meeting with KSM (in Pakistan)
[EARLY DECEMBER 1999] [1]	**RBAS:** Hamburg to Karachi; to Quetta, Pakistan; to Kandahar					(About 2 weeks after MA, MAS, and ZI)
DECEMBER 1999 [2]		**MA:** Kandahar		**MAS:** Kandahar		At OBL's facilities
MID-DECEMBER 1999 [1]	**K:** Kuala Lumpur					Receives accommodations and assistance from Hambali (Riduan Isamuddin), w/ Abu Bara al Yemeni
LATE DECEMBER 1999 [3]			**NAH:** Karachi			Calls communications hub
DECEMBER 31, 1999 [1]	**K:** Kuala Lumpur to Bangkok					

Source Key: 1. *9/11 Commission Report* (http://www.9-11commission.gov/) **2.** *Congressional Joint Inquiry Report* (http://www.gpoaccess.gov/serialset/creports/911.html) **3.** *9/11 Timeline by Cooperative Research* (http://www.historycommons.org/project.jsp?project=911_project) **4.** *9/11 Staff Monograph, "9/11 and Terrorist Travel"* (http://www.9-11commission.gov/staff_statements/911_TerrTrav_Monograph.pdf)

DATE	KHALID SHEIKH MOHAMMED (KSM)	OTHERS	AMERICAN 11	AMERICAN 77	UNITED 175	UNITED 93	NOTES
JANUARY 1, 2000[1]		K: Bangkok to Hong Kong					US airliner ("casing flights")
JANUARY 2, 2000[1]		K: Hong Kong to Bangkok					
JANUARY 3, 2000[1,2]		K: Bangkok to Kuala Lumpur					
JANUARY 4, 2000[1]				NAH: Karachi to Kuala Lumpur			Date estimated: about 10 days after K and Abu Bara al Yemeni and about 1 day before KAM
JANUARY 5, 2000[1,2,3]				KAM: Sana'a, Yemen, to Dubai to Kuala Lumpur			**CIA monitors KAM as he leaves communications hub; obtains photocopy of his passport**
[AFTER JANUARY 5, 2000[1]]		ZM: Kuala Lumpur					Later in year than K, KAM, and NAH: receives accommodations and assistance from Hambali
JANUARY 5–8, 2000[3]	Kuala Lumpur	K AND RBAS: Kuala Lumpur		**KAM, NAH, and SAH: Kuala Lumpur**			In attendance at meeting (SAH in source 2; per source 3; very few sources corroborate this)
EARLY JANUARY 2000[1,2,4]					MASI: Pakistan to Germany		**Obtains new passport before leaving**

Date	K	KAM and NAH	MASI	ZI	Notes
JANUARY 8, 2000 [1,2]	K: Kuala Lumpur to Bangkok	KAM AND NAH: Kuala Lumpur to Bangkok			Travel together ("seated side by side"); KAM and NAH use Yemeni documents; Abu Bara el Yemeni can't get visa to Pakistan, so returns to Yemen
[A FEW DAYS BEFORE JANUARY 15, 2000]	K: Bangkok to Karachi				
JANUARY 15, 2000 [1,2,3,4]		KAM AND NAH: Bangkok to Los Angeles			Using Saudi passports; KSM doctors NAH's to look like he traveled to Kuala Lumpur from Saudi Arabia via Dubai
JANUARY 18, 2000 [2]			MASI: Dubai		Obtains 10-year multiple-entry US visa
JANUARY 31, 2000 [1]				ZI: Afghanistan to Hamburg	
[JANUARY 2000 [1]]	K: Karachi, Pakistan to Kandahar, Afghanistan				Reports on casing mission to OBL
BY FEBRUARY 4, 2000 [2]		KAM and NAH: Los Angeles to San Diego			About 2 weeks after arriving in LA
JANUARY–LATE FEBRUARY 2000 [1]			MASI: UAE to Saudi Arabia and Bahrain		Obtains new passport and US visa in UAE

Source Key: 1. 9/11 Commission Report (http://www.9-11commission.gov/) 2. Congressional Joint Inquiry Report (http://www.gpoaccess.gov/serialset/creports/911.html) 3. 9/11 Timeline by Cooperative Research (http://www.historycommons.org/project/project.jsp?project=911_project) 4. 9/11 Staff Monograph, "9/11 and Terrorist Travel" (http://www.9-11commission.gov/staff_statements/9II_TerrTrav_Monograph.pdf)

DATE	KHALID SHEIKH MOHAMMED (KSM)	OTHERS	AMERICAN 11	AMERICAN 77	UNITED 175	UNITED 93	NOTES
[AFTER JANUARY 31, 2000 1,2]	[Still in Karachi]	RBAS: Kandahar to Karachi	MA: Kandahar to Karachi				Instructed by KSM
FEBRUARY 25, 2000 1,2		RBAS: Karachi to Hamburg	MA: Karachi to Hamburg				RBAS arrives shortly after MA
SPRING 2000 2				HH: Afghanistan			
SPRING 2000 2	Pakistan to Afghanistan						At OBL's request
POSSIBLY MARCH 2000 1,3				KAM: Afghanistan	MASI: Germany		Per source 2, MASI returns to Germany in January 2000
APRIL 5, 2000 4				KAM AND NAH: San Diego			Acquire CA driver's licenses
MAY 2000 2				KAM AND NAH: Still in San Diego			Flight training
MAY–OCTOBER 2000 1,2,4		RBAS: Germany and Yemen					US visa request denied three times in Germany, once in Yemen
MAY 18, 2000 1,2,4			MA: Hamburg				Obtains US visa after getting new Egyptian passport
MAY 25, 2000 1,4						ZI: [ ]	Obtains US visa after getting new passport
MAY 29, 2000 2,4					MASI: UAE to Brussels to Newark		Detained briefly by US customs officers

JUNE 2, 2000 [2,3]	MA: Germany to Prague (via bus)				
JUNE 3, 2000 [2,4]	MA: Czech Republic to Newark				
JUNE 9, 2000 [2]		KAM AND NAH: San Diego to Los Angeles			
JUNE 10, 2000 [2,4]		KAM: Los Angeles to Yemen			
JUNE 20, 2000 [2]		HH: Afghanistan to Saudi Arabia			
[ARRIVES] JUNE 27, 2000 [2,3,4]				ZI: To Munich to US	**Earlier in year, reported losing Lebanese passport and obtained 5-year multiple-entry visa**
JUNE 27, 2000 [2,4]				ZI: [ ] To Venice, FL	**Violates terms of US visa by becoming a student**
EARLY JULY 2000 [2,3,4]	MA: New York area to Oklahoma City to Venice, FL		MAS: New York area to Oklahoma City to Venice, FL	ZI: GA to Venice, FL	
JULY 12, 2000 [4]					**NAH applies to extend stay in US**

Source Key: 1. *9/11 Commission Report* (http://www.9-11commission.gov/) **2.** *Congressional Joint Inquiry Report* (http://www.gpoaccess.gov/serialset/creports/911.html) **3.** *9/11 Timeline by Cooperative Research* (http://www.historycommons.org/project.jsp?project=911_project) **4.** 9/11 Staff Monograph, "9/11 and Terrorist Travel" (http://www.9-11commission.gov/staff_statements/911_TerrTrav_Monograph.pdf)

DATE	KHALID SHEIKH MOHAMMED (KSM)	OTHERS	AMERICAN 11	AMERICAN 77	UNITED 175	UNITED 93	NOTES
FALL 2000[2]		ZM: [ ] to Malaysia to Pakistan					To Malaysia for flight training, then back to Pakistan per KSM's instructions
SEPTEMBER 2000[2]		RBAS: Germany to Yemen					To apply for visa because denied in Germany
SEPTEMBER 3, 2000[4]							AAG applies for tourist visa to US with Saudi passport
MID-SEPTEMBER 2000[2]							MAS1 and MA apply to change immigration status from tourist to student
SEPTEMBER 25, 2000[2]				HH: Jeddah			Obtains student visa after initial denial
AFTER SEPTEMBER 25, 2000[2]				HH: Saudi Arabia to UAE			
EARLY OCTOBER 2000[2]		ZM: To London					
OCTOBER 2000[2]						RBAS: Yemen	Applies for US visa; denied again
OCTOBER 2000[2]						ZJ: FL to Germany to Paris	Travels to France with girlfriend (through August 2001, ZJ will take at least 5 trips outside US to visit family in Lebanon and girlfriend in Germany)
OCTOBER 17, 2000[4]					HAG: Riyadh		Applies for and receives US tourist visa

OCTOBER 23, 2000 [4]				MASZ: Riyadh		Applies for and receives US tourist visa
OCTOBER 28, 2000 [4]					AAH: Riyadh	Applies for and receives US tourist visa
OCTOBER 29, 2000 [2,4]					ZI: Returns to FL	
NOVEMBER 2000 [2]			HH: FL to CA			
NOVEMBER 20–21, 2000 [4]		SAS: Riyadh	MM: Riyadh			Apply for and receive US tourist visas
DECEMBER 2000 [2,3]			HH AND NAH: San Diego to Mesa, AZ			HH has "just returned to the US"; NAH moves from CA
DECEMBER 2000 [2]				MASI: To Hamburg to UAE		
DECEMBER 2000 [2]	ZE: []					2 US visa requests denied to travel to FL in January 2001
DECEMBER 2–9, 2000 [2]	RBAS: London					Stays at same dormitory as ZM
ARRIVES DECEMBER 8, 2000 [2,4]			HH: Dubai to Paris to Cincinnati to San Diego			
DECEMBER 9, 2000 [2]	ZM: London to Pakistan					

Source Key: 1. *9/11 Commission Report* (http://www.9-11commission.gov/) 2. *Congressional Joint Inquiry Report* (http://www.gpoaccess.gov/serialset/creports/911.html) 3. *9/11 Timeline by Cooperative Research* (http://www.historycommons.org/project.jsp?project=911_project) 4. 9/11 Staff Monograph, "9/11 and Terrorist Travel" (http://www.9-11commission.gov/staff_statements/911_TerrTrav_Monograph.pdf)

DATE	KHALID SHEIKH MOHAMMED (KSM)	OTHERS	AMERICAN 11	AMERICAN 77	UNITED 175	UNITED 93	NOTES
BEFORE DECEMBER 29, 2000 [2]					MASI: Returns to FL		
"HOLIDAY PERIOD" 2000–2001 [2,4]						Z1: Fl to Germany to Beirut; returns to FL via Germany	Stays home in Lebanon for a few weeks
EARLY 2001 [2]		RBAS: Spain					[Conflict in source: elsewhere says MA and RBAS met for progress meeting in Germany in early January 2001]
JANUARY 4, 2001 [2,4]			MA: Tampa to Miami to Madrid				
JANUARY 10, 2001 [2,4]			MA: Returns to FL				**Difficulty reentering because has no student visa**
2001 [2]		RBAS: Afghanistan and Pakistan					After meeting in early January, for several months, between Afghanistan and Pakistan
MID-JANUARY 2001 [2]					MASI: Fl to Casablanca		After MA returns to FL
JANUARY 18, 2001 [2]					MASI: Morocco to GA		**For flight training; difficulty reentering because has no student visa**
MID-JANUARY 2001 [2]			MA: To GA				
END OF JANUARY 2001 [2]						Z1: Fl to Beirut	

FEBRUARY 2001 [2]	MA: To Virginia Beach, VA			MAS1: To Virginia Beach, VA	
FEBRUARY 2001 [2]				ZI: Beirut to Germany	After "a few weeks" in Beirut
FEBRUARY 25, 2001 [4]				ZI: Returns to US	With business visitor visa
MARCH 2001 [2,3]			HH AND NAH: Phoenix to Falls Church, VA		By car, arriving "as early as" April 4
APRIL–JULY 2001 [2,3]	13 "muscle" hijackers arrive in US; those arriving in NY and VA settle in Paterson, NJ, area with NAH and HH				All pass through Dubai
EARLY APRIL 2001 [2]	MA: [Travel outside US]				To meet Iraqi intelligence officer, maybe under alias (per Tenet testimony, uncorroborated)
APRIL 12, 2001 [2]	WAS2: FL				Obtains FL driver's license
APRIL 18, 2001 [2]			MAS2: Miami to Amsterdam to Egypt		Visits MA's father in Egypt and obtains MA's international driver's license
APRIL 23, 2001 [3]	SAS AND WAS2: [ ] to Dubai to Orlando				
APRIL 23, 2001 [4]				AAM: Jeddah	Receives US tourist visa
MAY 2001 [3]	AAO: Saudi Arabia	KAM AND SAH: Saudi Arabia	FB: Saudi Arabia	SAG: Saudi Arabia	Obtain visa through "Visa Express" program (through travel agent, not consulate)

Source Key: 1. *9/11 Commission Report* (http://www.9-11commission.gov/). 2. *Congressional Joint Inquiry Report* (http://www.gpoaccess.gov/serialset/creports/911.html). 3. *9/11 Timeline by Cooperative Research* (http://www.historycommons.org/project.jsp?project=911_project). 4. 9/11 Staff Monograph, "9/11 and Terrorist Travel" (http://www.9-11commission.gov/staff_statements/911_TerrTrav_Monograph.pdf)

DATE	KHALID SHEIKH MOHAMMED (KSM)	OTHERS	AMERICAN 11	AMERICAN 77	UNITED 175	UNITED 93	NOTES
MAY 2, 2001[4]			MA: Miami			[ZJ]: Miami	Miami district immigration office: MA's 8-month visa rolled back to 7; other man (believed to be ZJ) receives 6-month visa; MA and ZJ obtain driver's licenses later same day
MAY 2, 2001[3,4]				MH: [ ] to Dubai to Washington	AAG: [ ] to Dubai to Washington		
MAY 2, 2001[2]					MASI: Egypt to Amsterdam to Miami		To date, 3 trips outside US and back
MAY 24, 2001[2]					MASI: New York to San Francisco to Las Vegas		
MAY 27, 2001[2]					MASI: Las Vegas to San Francisco to New York		
MAY 28, 2001[3,4]					HAG and MASI: [ ] to Dubai to Miami	AAM: [ ] to Dubai to Miami	
JUNE 8, 2001[3,4]			WASI: [ ] to Dubai to Miami			AAH: [ ] to Dubai to Miami	
JUNE 10, 2001[2]						ZJ: Las Vegas to Baltimore	
JUNE 12, 2001[4]						SAG: Jeddah	Obtains US tourist visa

JUNE 13, 2001 [2,3,4]				KAM: Jeddah	Obtains US visa using different passport from that used to enter US in January 2000
JUNE 26, 2001 [4]				HAG: FL	Obtains FL ID card
JUNE 27, 2004 [4]				SAG: To Orlando	Admitted to US as tourist after secondary inspection
JUNE 28, 2001 [2]		MA: Boston to San Francisco to Las Vegas			
JUNE 29, 2001 [4]		AAO: [] to Dubai to New York	SAM: [] to Dubai to New York		
JULY 1, 2001 [2]		MA: Las Vegas to Denver to Boston			
JULY 4, 2001 [2,3,4]			KAM: Saudi Arabia to New York		Passport invalid (no expiration date) and illegal (lied on application, saying never traveled to US before)
JULY 9, 2001 [2]	RBAS: Hamburg to Tarragona, Spain				Rental car in Spain, July 9–19; 1,908 kilometers
[JULY 9, 2001 [3]]				MASI: To Spain	"At about the same time" as RBAS
JULY 16, 2001 [2]		MA: Tarragona, Spain			Application to change visa to student status approved by INS next day

Source Key: 1. *9/11 Commission Report* (http://www.9-11commission.gov). 2. *Congressional Joint Inquiry Report* (http://www.gpoaccess.gov/serialset/creports/911.html) 3. *9/11 Timeline by Cooperative Research* (http://www.historycommons.org/project.jsp?project=911_project) 4. 9/11 Staff Monograph, "9/11 and Terrorist Travel" (http://www.9-11commission.gov/staff_statements/911_TerrTrav_Monograph.pdf)

DATE	KHALID SHEIKH MOHAMMED (KSM)	OTHERS	AMERICAN 11	AMERICAN 77	UNITED 175	UNITED 93	NOTES
JULY 19, 2001[2]			MA: Spain to Atlanta				Rental car returned, Madrid; 1,908 km on odometer
JULY 23, 2001[4]	Riyadh						**Using alias, obtains US tourist visa through Visa Express**
JULY 25, 2001[2]						ZJ: Newark to Germany	
AUGUST 1, 2001[3]			AAO: Las Vegas to New York				
AUGUST 1–3, 2001[2]		ZM: Oklahoma; RBAS: Düsseldorf and Hamburg					Wire transfer from RBAS to ZM
EARLY AUGUST 2001[4]			AAO: VA	KAM AND MN: VA		AAG: VA	**Obtain VA ID cards**
AUGUST 4, 2001[4]		MAN: Orlando					**Denied entry to US as MA waits for him**
AUGUST 5, 2001[2]						ZJ: Germany to [Newark]	
AUGUST 13, 2001[2]			MA: Washington to Las Vegas				
AUGUST 13, 2001[2]				HH AND NAH: Washington Dulles to Los Angeles to Las Vegas			
AUGUST 14, 2001[2]			MA: Las Vegas to Fort Lauderdale				

AUGUST 14, 2001 [2]			HH AND NAH: Las Vegas to Minneapolis to Baltimore		Arrested by INS
AUGUST 16, 2001 [3]	ZM: Minnesota				
AUGUST 27, 2001 [3]			NAH: Laurel, MD		Buys tickets online at Kinko's
AUGUST 28, 2001 [3]		WAS2: Fort Lauderdale		MASI: Miami	Buy tickets at ticket counters
AUGUST 31, 2001 [3]			HH: Totowa, NJ		Buys ticket from travel agent
FIRST WEEK OF SEPTEMBER 2001 [4]			NAH, KAM, MM, HH, SAH: NJ to Laurel, MD		
SEPTEMBER 5, 2001 [3]			KAM: BWI Airport (Baltimore)		Picks up tickets
SEPTEMBER 7, 2001 [3]		MA: Hollywood, FL		MASI: Hollywood, FL	Drink at sports bar with third, unidentified man
SEPTEMBER 9, 2001 [3]				ZI: MD to Newark	By car
SEPTEMBER 10, 2001 [3]		MA AND AAO: Boston to Portland, ME; SAS, WASI, WAS2: Newton, MA	KAM, MM, HH, NAH, SAH: Laurel, MD, to Herndon, VA	MASI, FB, MAS2, AAG, HAG: Boston	SAG, AAN, AAH, ZI: Newark

Source Key: 1. *9/11 Commission Report* (http://www.9-11commission.gov/). 2. *Congressional Joint Inquiry Report* (http://www.gpoaccess.gov/serialset/creports/911.html). 3. *9/11 Timeline by Cooperative Research* (http://www.historycommons.org/project.jsp?project=911_project). 4. *9/11 Staff Monograph, "9/11 and Terrorist Travel"* (http://www.9-11commission.gov/staff_statements/911_TerrTrav_Monograph.pdf)

DATE	KHALID SHEIKH MOHAMMED (KSM)	OTHERS	AMERICAN 11	AMERICAN 77	UNITED 175	UNITED 93	NOTES
SEPTEMBER 10, 2001 [3]	Afghanistan						MA calls KSM for final approval (call monitored by US)
SEPTEMBER 11, 2001 [3]			MA AND AA0: Portland, ME, to Boston				By plane
LATE SEPTEMBER 2001 [2]		ZE: Afghanistan					Per uncorroborated sources
SEPTEMBER 11, 2002 [2]		RBAS: Pakistan					**Captured after gun battle with Pakistani ISI and CIA personnel**

Source Key: 1. *9/11 Commission Report* (http://www.9-11commission.gov/) 2. *Congressional Joint Inquiry Report* (http://www.gpoaccess.gov/serialset/creports/911.html) 3. *9/11 Timeline by Cooperative Research* (http://www.historycommons.org/project.jsp?project=911_project) 4. 9/11 Staff Monograph, "9/11 and Terrorist Travel" (http://www.9-11commission.gov/staff_statements/911_TerrTrav_Monograph.pdf)

ACKNOWLEDGMENTS

So many people have assisted in this effort that it is hard to know where to begin in thanking them. First and foremost, I was privileged to work, on the 9/11 Commission, with a uniquely diverse and talented group of people. From top to bottom, the Commissioners and staff were extraordinarily smart, dedicated, and tireless. Many remain my close friends, and offered comments on the manuscript of this book. In particular, I thank the members of Team 8, the "Whiskey Tango Foxtrot" team: John Azzarello, Dana Hyde, Miles Kara, Kevin Schaeffer, Mark Bittinger, Charles Pereira, Geoffrey Brown, Cate Taylor, Lisa Sullivan, Joe McBride, George DelGrosso, Sam Caspersen, Jim Miller, Madeleine Blot, Emily Walker, and Ellie Hartz. Honorary WTF team members include John Raidt, Bill Johnstone, Warren Bass, Mike Hurley, and Bill Raisch. Thanks to John Azzarello, Dana, Miles, and Kevin for stepping up for me at a critical time in the Commission's work and "storming the Bastille" when deaths in the family required my absence. Thanks also to John, Kevin, and Ellie for serving in so many ways as the conscience of the Commission.

I have benefited enormously from research assistance provided by Rutgers Law students—now graduates—Megha Jonnalagadda and Jeff Stephens, and by Laurel DuMont. Thanks to Rachit Choski for assisting with the material for the afterword.

Thanks to the folks who made the film *United 93*—Paul Greengrass, Lloyd Levin, Kate Solomon, and Michael Bronner—for getting me to refocus on these issues. I'm particularly grateful to Michael, for his diplomatic skill in persuading the government to release the tapes and for providing me with some of the fruits of his research.

This project began with a call out of the blue from Flip Brophy of Sterling Lord Literistic, who had read a piece I wrote for the Newark *Star-Ledger* about Hurricane Katrina. Thanks to the *Star-Ledger*'s editor, Jim Willse, and to former *Ledger* editorial staff members Fraun Dauth, John Hassell, Tom Moran, and Deborah Jerome for giving me the freedom to write about whatever I chose in "Perspective." It was among the happiest experiences of my career. Flip Brophy is a great agent and now a great friend. She deserves enormous credit for introducing me to Rebecca Saletan, my editor, who has guided me through this process with professionalism and saintly patience while working at three different houses. Thanks also to Elaine Trevorrow, Anna Jardine, Nicole LaRoche, Geoff Kloske, Marilyn Ducksworth, and the rest of the crew at Riverhead.

This book is going to press at a time of fundamental change in my personal circumstances. I have been transitioning out of the private practice of law, transitioning into my new position as Dean of Rutgers School of Law, Newark, and completing this book simultaneously. Thanks to my law partners, John Azzarello, John Whipple, Jack Arseneault, and Dave Fassett, for their tolerance of me during this project. Thanks especially to John Azzarello, for his friendship, and to Jack, for allowing me the use of his condo in Mexico and for running Tres Bol, the best Irish pub south of the border.

In the crush of ending a law practice, startinq a new career in academia, and finishing *The Ground Truth*, I failed to acknowledge the vital assistance of Andrea Manna, without whom I could not have functioned, let alone finished, and the Hunterdon County Library in New Jersey, where much of this book was written. I also want to acknowledge the unflagging support of my new colleagues at the Rutgers School of Law in Newark, who have bolstered me through my first year in academia and supported the book without reservation. You have my abiding gratitude.

I thank all of those who have assisted in fact-checking, and apologize in advance for any errors of fact or emphasis that I may have missed despite my best efforts in the swirl of events; the responsibility is mine alone.

As always, thanks to Beth, my family, and my best friend of thirty-six years, Jes Staley, for their unconditional love and support. I owe particular thanks to my father, John J. Farmer, Sr., for giving me a love of language and history. My father, a Korean War veteran, and my grandfather Peter Farmer, an Irish infantryman who was wounded at the battle of the Somme and taken prisoner during World War I, used to allow me to watch and listen as they played cards late into the night. I didn't learn much about poker or pinochle, but I did gain a sense of how war is fought from the ground perspective, and a lasting respect and admiration for those who, standing at the end of the decision chain, must implement policies over which they have little or no control. And I also learned that, just as no one is always brave or always craven, so, for some people, physical courage is easier than moral courage. For those lessons, and for so much else, thanks.

NOTES

INTRODUCTION: THE VIEW FROM THE GROUND

1 *group of staffers and commissioners*. *The Ground Truth* relies heavily upon and reaffirms the facts set forth and conclusions reached in *The 9/11 Commission Report: Final Report of the National Commission of Terrorist Attacks upon the United States* (New York: W. W. Norton, 2004) and the detailed chronology set forth in the Commission's Staff Monograph, "Four Flights and Civil Aviation Security," September 12, 2005, http://www.archives.gov/legislative/research/9-11/staff-report-sept2005.pdf (hereafter: Third Monograph). Although *The Ground Truth* builds upon and is indebted to the work of my colleagues at the 9/11 Commission, the conclusions it reaches are entirely my own and should not be ascribed to the Commission, the Commissioners, or the 9/11 Commission staff members.

3 *evidence for an alternative explanation.* FAA Memorandum, Results of OIG Investigation of 9/11 Commission Staff Referral, August 31, 2006, p. 7.

3 *inadequate record-keeping procedures on 9/11.* Department of Defense Inspector General Report, September 12, 2006, p. 1.

7 *"Office of the Director of National Intelligence."* John Lehman, "We're Not Winning This War," *The Washington Post*, August 31, 2006, p. A25.

PART ONE. YEARS

14 *"the sensitive interrogation process."* The 9/11 Commission Report, p. 146.

14 *ongoing criminal investigation.* 9/11 Commission Staff Executive Director Philip Zelikow elaborated for Jane Mayer in her book *The Dark Side*: "There were problems from our perspective [with the detainees' answers]. There were internal and unexplained inconsistencies. There were cases where people were talking about things that were ripe for further examination. And there were other puzzling things," such as the lack of FBI involvement in the interrogations. "We inferred," Zelikow concluded, "that the interrogations were being conducted under highly unusual circumstances." Quoted in Jane Mayer, *The Dark Side* (New York: Anchor, 2009), pp. 279–280.

15 *his ambition was global.* See generally *The 9/11 Commission Report*, pp. 55–59; Lawrence Wright, *The Looming Tower: Al-Qaeda and the Road to 9/11* (New York: Alfred A. Knopf, 2006), pp. 170–73.

15 *"can be tackled."* Bruce James, "Middle East: Arab Veterans of the Afghan War—Trained Forces in Waiting," *Jane's Intelligence Review* 7, no. 4 (April 1995), quoted in Anonymous, *Through Our Enemies' Eyes: Osama bin Laden, Radical Islam, and the Future of America* (Dulles, VA: Potomac, 2003), p. 48.

15 *"after the seizure of power."* Emmanuel Sivan, "The Holy War Tradition in Islam," *Orbis* 42, no. 2 (1998), quoted in Anonymous, *Through Our Enemies' Eyes*, pp. 48–49.

15 *"on anyone's list."* Wright, *The Looming Tower*, p. 150.

16 *"animals would descend to."* Abd al-Bari Atawn, "Interview with Saudi Oppositionist Osama bin Laden," *Al-Quds Al-Arabi*, November 27, 1996, quoted in Anonymous, *Through Our Enemies' Eyes*, p. 46.

16 *non-Muslim presence in Arabia.* When Saudi Prince Sultan observed that "There are no caves in Kuwait," and asked "What will you do when [Saddam] lobs missiles at you with chemical and

biological weapons?" bin Laden reportedly replied, "We will fight him with faith." Lawrence Wright, *The Looming Tower*, p. 179.

16 *occupation of Muslim lands.* *The 9/11 Commission Report*, p. 59.

16 *claimed by al Qaeda associates.* Ibid., pp. 59–60.

16 *"'will wither away.'"* Anonymous, *Through Our Enemies' Eyes*, pp. 48–49.

17 *"a mostly black school in Greensboro."* Wright, *The Looming Tower*, p. 267.

17 *"policy favoring Israel."* *The 9/11 Commission Report*, p. 147.

17 *bin Laden's mentor . . . Abdullah Azzam.* Ibid., p. 146. KSM dates the meeting to 1989.

17 *phone calls in succeeding months.* Ibid., p. 147.

18 *when it accidentally exploded.* Ibid., p. 147.

18 *to discuss their common interests.* Ibid., p. 148.

18 *a fugitive from American justice.* Ibid., p. 73.

18 *to carry out his schemes.* Ibid., p. 489, note 14.

18 *"future anti-U.S. operations."* Ibid., p. 149.

18 *attacking the U.S. homeland directly.* Ibid., p. 489, note 13.

18 *crash airplanes into buildings.* Wright, *The Looming Tower*, p. 268.

19 *the Americans in February 2002.* Ibid., pp. 127–28.

20 *"and other signals every hour."* Amy Zegart, *Spying Blind: The CIA, the FBI, and the Origins of 9/11* (Princeton, NJ: Princeton University Press, 2007), p. 116, citing James Bamford, "War of Secrets: Eyes in the Sky, Ears to the Wall, and Still Wanting," *The New York Times*, September 8, 2002, section 4, p. 5. Of course, such capacity can be difficult to manage unless the government knows what types of people and information it is targeting. In the course of its work, the 9/11 Commission staff considered the interrelationship of the NSA and the other intelligence agencies, particularly the CIA and FBI, in numerous contexts. The staff looked closely at the NSA's involvement in piecing together the threat reporting about the Kuala Lumpur meeting and the developments of the summer of 2001, among other pivotal moments. Although Bamford's work is vividly drawn and adds value to the 9/11 history, his claim that the 9/11 Commission staff neglected to examine the relevant NSA documents is mistaken.

20 *imagery satellites.* See www.nro.gov.

20 *fought the Soviets.* See generally Steve Coll, *Ghost Wars: The Secret History of the CIA, Afghanistan, and Bin Laden, from the Soviet Invasion to September 10, 2001* (New York: The Penguin Press, 2004); George Crile, *Charlie Wilson's War: The Extraordinary Story of the Largest Covert Operation in History* (New York: Atlantic Monthly Press, 2003).

20 *benefactors like bin Laden.* 9/11 Commission Staff Statement, March 24, 2004.

21 *intelligence on bin Laden by 1996.* Zegart, *Spying Blind*, p. 22, citing Eleanor Hill, "Joint Inquiry Staff Statement, Part I," 107th Cong., 2d Sess., September 18, 2002.

21 *a short distance from CIA headquarters.* Zegart, *Spying Blind*, p. 77; *The 9/11 Commission Report*, p. 109.

21 *"to obtain nuclear material."* *The 9/11 Commission Report*, p. 109.

21 *to purchase nuclear material.* Coll, *Ghost Wars*, p. 367.

21 *"money to help the Taliban."* *The 9/11 Commission Report*, p. 110.

21 *"travels in Afghanistan."* Quoted ibid.

22 *"as long as this agency exists."* Coll, *Ghost Wars*, pp. 370–75.

22 *a plan to capture him.* Ibid., pp. 391–94; see also Tim Weiner, *Legacy of Ashes: The History of the CIA* (New York: Doubleday, 2007), pp. 468–69.

22 *"sounding the alarm."* Coll, *Ghost Wars*, pp. 416–17.

23 *estimated at $118 billion.* Chalmers Johnson, *The Sorrows of Empire: Militarism, Secrecy, and the End of the Republic* (New York: Metropolitan Books, 2004), p. 154.

23 *including terrorism.* Ibid.

23 *anywhere in the world.* *The 9/11 Commission Report*, p. 96.

23 *assassinate President George H. W. Bush.* Ibid., pp. 97–98.

24 *"and watchlist information."* Ibid., p. 95.

24 *designated by the State Department.* Ibid.

24 *presence on the terrorist watchlist.* Ibid., p. 80.

24 *every American community.* Ibid., p. 74.

25 *to coordinate investigations.* Ibid., pp. 81–82.

25 *responsibility for the attack.* Ibid., pp. 75–76.

25 *by the Justice Department.* The 9/11 Commission Report, p. 72; see also generally Jim Dwyer et al., *Two Seconds Under the World.*

25 *"crash an airplane into CIA headquarters."* Zegart, Spying Blind, p. 130.

26 *support of terrorist operations.* Ibid.

26 *first time in its history.* Zegart, Spying Blind, p. 131; see also The 9/11 Commission Report, pp. 76–77.

26 *"threaten vital American interests."* Quoted in Zegart, Spying Blind, p. 132.

27 *"provide backup security."* The 9/11 Commission Report, p. 83.

27 *specific plots and general threats.* Ibid.

27 *might pose a risk to aircraft.* Ibid., p. 84.

27 *other prohibited items.* Ibid.

27 *airport security systems.* "A Nation Challenged: Airports: F.A.A. Is Accused of Ignoring Security Lapses," The New York Times, February 27, 2002, p. A10.

28 *never reach their targets.* Remarks of Commissioner Jamie Gorelick, 9/11 Commission Hearing, June 17, 2004, transcript (available at http://www.9-11commission.gov/; hereafter "transcript").

28 *career agents and employees.* See also Douglas Stuart, *Creating the National Security State: A History of the Law That Transformed America* (Princeton, NJ: Princeton University Press, 2008); Ernest R. May, "The U.S. Government: A Legacy of the Cold War," in Michael J. Hogan, ed., *The End of the Cold War: Its Meaning and Implications* (New York: Cambridge University Press, 1992); and Graham T. Allison and Philip Zelikow, *Essence of Decision: Explaining the Cuban Missile Crisis,* 2nd ed. (New York: Longman, 1999), chap. 3.

29 *"to do so in any country."* Quoted in Coll, Ghost Wars, pp. 380–81.

29 *"attacks on American civilians anywhere in the world."* Walter Pincus, The Washington Post, February 25, 1998, quoted in Coll, Ghost Wars, p. 383.

30 *Pentagon identified "no showstoppers."* The 9/11 Commission Report, pp. 111–14.

30 *"perhaps using WMD."* Quoted in The 9/11 Commission Report, p. 112.

30 *July 23, 1998, came and went.* The 9/11 Commission Report, pp. 114–15.

30 *were never acted upon.* Coll, Ghost Wars, p. 642, note 12.

30 *disrupted his East African cell.* Coll, Ghost Wars, p. 404.

30 *bin Laden would likely attend.* Ibid., pp. 409–10. Coll notes that "participants later differed about the quality of the CIA's intelligence in the . . . meeting," with General Anthony Zinni in particular recalling that "the intelligence wasn't that solid."

31 *"might as well have been weed killer."* Weiner, Legacy of Ashes, p. 470.

31 *relations with the Taliban government.* The 9/11 Commission Report, pp. 121–22.

31 *ordering the missiles to be fired.* Coll, Ghost Wars, pp. 421–22.

31 *chances of success had been greater.* Ibid., p. 422.

32 *bin Laden and other al Qaeda leaders.* The 9/11 Commission Report, pp. 126–27.

32 *"But Clinton did not choose this path."* Coll, Ghost Wars, pp. 425–26.

32 *"convoluted and 'Talmudic.'"* Ibid., p. 426. Adding to the confused signals being sent to the intelligence community was President Clinton's handwritten note on the directive, redirecting the approval to capture only. No one, including President Clinton, recalls why he made that notation.

32 *"to take bin Laden alive."* Ibid., p. 427.

32 *"force against bin Laden."* The 9/11 Commission Report, p. 118.

32 *to kill or capture bin Laden.* Ibid., pp. 134–37.

33 *one of his lieutenants, Mohammed Atef.* See www.fbi.gov/wanted/terrorists/terbinladen.htm.

33 *or the CIA director.* Congressional Joint Inquiry Hearings (hereafter: Joint Inquiry), September 18, 2002, and July 24, 2003.

33 *the training camps of Afghanistan. The 9/11 Commission Report*, pp. 149–50. As the 9/11 Commission pointed out, as noted on page 14, reliance on KSM's version of events must be considered carefully, in light of the conditions under which he was held when he made the statements in question.

33 *"no resources or people spared in this effort."* George Tenet, quoted in Coll, *Ghost Wars*, p. 436.

33 *"and Other Attacks."* George Tenet, *At the Center of the Storm: My Years at the CIA* (New York: Harper Perennial, 2008), p. 105.

34 *"get another chance"* and *doubts about the intelligence. The 9/11 Commission Report*, pp. 130–31.

34 *"act on it."* Tenet, *At the Center of the Storm*, p. 109. The efforts to kill Bin Laden were also constrained, according to Tenet, by Attorney General Reno's view, communicated directly to Tenet, that "she would view an attempt to kill Bin Laden as illegal. Legal guidance by the attorney general matters." Ibid.

34 *"you get up with fleas."* Quoted in Coll, *Ghost Wars*, pp. 445–47.

34 *to launch cruise missiles. The 9/11 Commission Report*, p. 137.

35 *"We could take him out."* Quoted in Coll, *Ghost Wars*, pp. 449–50.

35 *an attractive future target. The 9/11 Commission Report*, p. 138.

35 *focus on the planes operation.* Ibid., p. 150.

35 *"governments in the Arab world."* Ibid., p. 154.

36 *the World Trade Center and the Capitol.* Ibid., p. 155.

36 *martial arts, explosives, and countersurveillance tactics.* Ibid.

36 *" 'a dead man' that night."* Quoted ibid., p. 140.

37 *the competence of the CIA.* Weiner, *Legacy of Ashes*, pp. 473–74.

37 *Bin Laden designated them for pilot training. The 9/11 Commission Report*, p. 155.

37 *"martyrdom opportunities for Yemenis."* Ibid., p. 156.

38 *how to function in America.* Ibid., p. 157.

38 *of less than 15 percent.* Ibid., pp. 142–43.

38 *"these targets will be in the U.S."* Quoted in Coll, *Ghost Wars*, p. 485.

39 *bomb Los Angeles International Airport. The 9/11 Commission Report*, pp. 176–78; Wright, *The Looming Tower*, pp. 335–39; Coll, *Ghost Wars*, pp. 482–83.

39 *"could not be more real." The 9/11 Commission Report*, pp. 178–80.

40 *"put into the trash."* Quoted in R. Jeffrey Smith, "More Details About Archives Case," *The Washington Post*, December 22, 2006, p. A31.

41 *access to original documents.* R. Jeffrey Smith, "Berger Case Still Roils Justice, Archives," *The Washington Post*, February 21, 2007. As 9/11 Commission Executive Director Philip Zelikow pointed out, the knowledge that Berger did have access to original documents, that he admitted to shredding three of them, and that he may have removed other documents "would have triggered some additional questions, including questions we could have posed to Berger under oath." Although the Commission had access to the *Millennium After-Action Review*, it is not known what notes, if any, and by whom, appeared on the documents shredded by Berger, or whether documents in addition to the *Review* were similarly removed and destroyed.

41 *"additional terrorist attacks here."* Art Moore, "Ashcroft: Berger Doc Exposes Security Lapse," July 20, 2004, WorldNet Daily.

41 *"and to be willing to die."* Wright, *The Looming Tower*, pp. 349–50.

42 *They returned in early January 2000. The 9/11 Commission Report*, pp. 165–67; Wright, *The Looming Tower*, pp. 349–50.

42 *also assisted Ziad Jarrah. The 9/11 Commission Report*, p. 167.

42 *"something nefarious might be afoot."* Ibid., p. 181; see also Wright, *The Looming Tower*, pp. 350–51; Coll, *Ghost Wars*, pp. 483–85.

43 *"any true threat posed."* Quoted in Wright, *The Looming Tower*, p. 351.

43 *"if a domestic angle arose." The 9/11 Commission Report*, p. 181. Lawrence Wright's version differs. He claims that the cable to foreign intelligence agencies "said that the FBI had been alerted to the Malaysia meeting and that the bureau had been given copies of Mihdhar's travel documents. That turned out not to be true." *The Looming Tower*, p. 352.

43 *golf course designed by Jack Nicklaus.* Wright, *The Looping Tower*, p. 311.

43 *"'Who are these dudes?'"* Coll, *Ghost Wars*, p. 484.

43 *the issue was forgotten.* Wright, *The Looming Tower*, p. 352.

44 *CIA's Counterterrorist Center was informed* and *"reignited interest in Khallad."* *The 9/11 Commission Report*, pp. 181–82.

44 *photographed with Mihdhar.* *The 9/11 Commission Report*, p. 182.

44 *"the 9/11 attack was lost."* Wright, *The Looming Tower*, pp. 351–52.

44 *acting like their old selves again.* *The 9/11 Commission Report*, pp. 167–68.

44 *to remain behind in Germany.* Ibid.

45 *"aliens seeking work in the United States."* Ibid.

45 *wired to them by KSM's nephew.* Ibid., p. 224.

45 *but bin Laden intervened on his behalf.* Ibid., pp. 221–22.

46 *to assist in investigating the attack.* Ibid., pp. 190–92.

46 *still an "unproven assumption."* Ibid., p. 194.

46 *both signals and human intelligence.* Ibid., pp. 194–95.

47 *"based on a 'preliminary judgment.'"* Ibid., p. 195.

47 *"dead certain of bin Laden's involvement."* Coll, *Ghost Wars*, p. 533.

47 *Nothing was done.* Ibid., pp. 535–36.

PART TWO. 2001

51 *under way by the Hamburg police.* *The 9/11 Commission Report*, p. 227.

52 *and meet with al Qaeda leadership.* Ibid.

52 *their flight-school training.* Ibid., p. 229.

52 *to get Florida driver's licenses.* Ibid., pp. 230–31.

52 *Mihdhar would join them in early July.* Ibid.

52 *the Cole had been linked to al Qaeda.* Ibid., pp. 236–37.

53 *"before reaching the United States."* Ibid., p. 236.

53 *"possibly the Africa bombings."* Quoted in Wright, *The Looming Tower*, p. 384.

53 *any of the participants.* *The 9/11 Commission Report*, p. 268; Wright, *The Looming Tower*, pp. 384–85.

54 *on January 5, 2000.* *The 9/11 Commission Report*, pp. 181, 267–68.

54 *with the FBI's criminal investigators.* Ibid., p. 269.

54 *He flew to Newark on July 4.* Ibid.; see also Wright, *The Looming Tower*, p. 385; James Bamford, *The Shadow Factory: The Ultra-Secret NSA from 9/11 to the Eavesdropping on America* (New York: Doubleday, 2008), pp. 58–59.

55 *"highest level since the millennium alert."* *The 9/11 Commission Report*, p. 255.

55 *in morning meetings with Tenet.* Ibid., pp. 255–56.

55 *"incarcerated in the United States."* Quoted ibid., p. 256.

55 *during the millennium crisis.* Ibid.

55 *"simultaneous—attacks."* Ibid., p. 257.

56 *"terrorist attack in the United States."* Quoted ibid., p. 258.

56 *"advisories to the field."* Ibid.

56 *"an alert about suicide pilots."* Quoted ibid., p. 272.

57 *"looking for vulnerability."* Tenet, *At the Center of the Storm*, pp. 151–52.

57 *"within the United States."* Quoted in *The 9/11 Commission Report*, p. 259.

57 *"plan and train for hijackings."* Quoted ibid.

58 *fearing detection.* Ibid., p. 243.

58 *close to Washington, D.C.* Ibid., p. 242.

58 *inform bin Laden.* Ibid., p. 244.

58 *easier to fly than Airbus.* Ibid., pp. 244–45.

59 *pass for wealthy Saudis.* Ibid., p. 245.

59 *live up to his commitment.* Ibid., p. 246.

59 *his final trip to Germany.* Ibid., p. 247.

60 *delayed, not canceled.* Ibid., p. 260.

61 *"Bin Laden Determined to Strike in US."* Quoted ibid., pp. 261–62.

61 *"Bin-Laden-related."* Ibid., p. 262.

61 *was sent back to Dubai.* Ibid., p. 248.

62 *in Las Vegas on August 13–14.* Ibid., pp. 248–49.

62 *airline tickets for September 11.* Ibid.

62 *She did not notify the FAA.* Wright, *The Looming Tower*, p. 398.

63 *"UBL . . . getting the most 'protection.'"* Quoted in Wright, *The Looming Tower*, p. 399; see also *The 9/11 Commission Report*, p. 271.

63 *"an ego-boosting thing."* *The 9/11 Commission Report*, p. 273.

63 *cockpit doors . . . unlocked during flight.* Wright, *The Looming Tower*, p. 396.

63 *Its investigation began on August 15.* *The 9/11 Commission Report*, p. 273.

64 *submit the FISA application.* Ibid., p. 274.

64 *a potential "suicide hijacker."* Ibid., pp. 274–75.

64 *should the White House prove too difficult.* Ibid., p. 248.

64 *in late August.* Coll, *Ghost Wars*, p. 564.

64 *planned his return for early September.* *The 9/11 Commission Report*, p. 249.

64 *in the days leading up to 9/11.* Ibid.

65 *search for Mihdhar.* Ibid., p. 271.

65 *"going as soon as possible."* Quoted in Zegart, *Spying Blind*, p. 158.

65 *"she put down 'routine.'"* Ibid.

65 *"crashing into the World Trade Center."* Wright, *The Looming Tower*, p. 396; *The 9/11 Commission Report*, p. 275.

66 *not within his portfolio.* *The 9/11 Commission Report*, p. 275.

67 *the Predator . . . an untested robot.* Coll, *Ghost Wars*, pp. 573–74.

68 *to his German girlfriend.* *The 9/11 Commission Report*, pp. 249, 252–53; see also Bamford, *The Shadow Factory*, pp. 78–79.

68 *decapitating the Northern Alliance.* Coll, *Ghost Wars*, pp. 574–75.

68 *a hotel in Herndon, Virginia.* *The 9/11 Commission Report*, pp. 252–53.

68 *"UBL-related covert actions contemplated."* Quoted ibid., p. 214.

69 *"flawed by design."* See Amy Zegart, *Flawed by Design: The Evolution of the CIA, JCS, and NSC* (Palo Alto, CA: Stanford University Press, 1999).

69 *"to rationalize society."* James Q. Wilson, *Bureaucracy: What Governments Do and Why They Do It* (New York: Basic Books, 1989), p. 376.

70 *"insulated . . . from outside interference."* Zegart, *Flawed by Design*, p. 184.

71 *"suited the task at hand."* Wilson, *Bureaucracy*, p. 365.

72 *surprise attack on the United States.* Zegart, *Spying Blind*, pp. 62–63.

72 *having defeated communism.* See Jeffrey R. Gerlach, *Pentagon Myths and Global Realities: The 1993 Defense Budget.* Cato Institute Policy Analysis 171 (1992).

72 *"forty-plus years."* Quoted in Weiner, *Legacy of Ashes*, p. 433.

72 *CIA budgets declined from 1991 to 1997.* Ibid., p. 434.

72 *"other parts of the U.S. government."* Zegart, *Spying Blind*, p. 27. Professor Zegart presents a trenchant analysis of these reports and their findings: "All of these reports offered not only extensive discussion of key problems, but specific recommendations to fix them. The studies issued a total of 514 recommendations; two-thirds of them, or 340, focused specifically on improving U.S. intelligence capabilities" (pp. 27–29).

73 *"an age of peace and security."* Council on Foreign Relations, "Making Intelligence Smarter" (Task Force Report, January 1996), p. 1.

73 *greatest danger to national security.* Zegart, *Spying Blind*, pp. 21–22.

73 *"no resources or people spared in this effort."* See discussion above, pp. 33, 38–39.

74 *none of these initiatives succeeded.* CIA Inspector General's Executive Summary, p. viii. See also Zegart, *Spying Blind*, pp. 80–82.

74 *"at any time prior to 9/11."* OIG Report on CIA Accountability with Respect to the 9/11 Attacks, Executive Summary, p. viii.

74 *"combating bin Laden."* CIA Inspector General's Executive Summary, p. viii.

75 *workers in the intelligence community.* Zegart, *Spying Blind*, pp. 82–83.

75 *"short shrift . . . from day one."* Ibid., p. 91.

75 *"'They were in governments.'"* Quoted ibid., pp. 93–94.

76 *remained constant from 1990 to 2001.* Ibid., p. 94.

76 *"designed . . . for a different enemy."* Ibid., p. 96.

77 *"over the past several decades."* Federal Bureau of Investigation, "Keeping Tomorrow Safe" (Draft FBI Strategic Plan, 1998–2003, unclassified version, May 8, 1998), p. 7, quoted in Zegart, *Spying Blind*, pp. 131–33.

77 *"to cover major criminal cases."* Ibid.

78 *with incompetent evidence.* For a thorough analysis of obstacles to interagency information-sharing, see Staff Monograph by Barbara A. Grewe, Senior Counsel for Special Projects, Commission on Terrorist Attacks Upon the United States, "Legal Barriers to Information Sharing: The Erection of a Wall Between Intelligence and Law Enforcement Investigations," August 20, 2004, http://fas.org/irp/eprint/wall.pdf. As Grewe aptly summarizes, "What had happened was a growing battle within the Department of Justice in the 1990s, and between parts of Justice and the FISA court, over the scope of the [Office of Intelligence Policy and Review's] screening function and the propriety of using FISA-derived information in criminal cases. . . . By late 2000, these factors had culminated in a set of complex rules and a widening set of beliefs—a bureaucratic culture—that discouraged FBI agents from even seeking to share intelligence information" (p. 35).

78 *"might target the United States itself."* Ibid., pp. 134–35, citing Joint Inquiry, p. 249.

79 *after the attacks on September 11, 2001.* Tom Pickard, Testimony Before the 9/11 Commission, April 13, 2004.

79 *"absolutely no comprehension."* Quoted in Zegart, *Spying Blind*, p. 141.

80 *in light of the Soviet collapse.* See James Carroll, *House of War: The Pentagon and the Disastrous Rise of American Power* (Boston: Houghton Mifflin, 2006), p. 468.

80 *approximately 3,500 warheads.* Walter LaFeber, *America, Russia, and the Cold War, 1945–1971* (New York: John Wiley & Sons, 1972), pp. 360–64.

80 *halted B-52 strategic alerts.* Carroll, *House of War*, p. 469.

80 *reduced by 25 percent.* Ibid., p. 434.

80 *"waiting them out."* Ibid., p. 469.

80 *vehicles from Italy and Pakistan.* Ibid., p. 467.

81 *"the nation's new situation."* Ibid., p. 451.

81 *"full-spectrum dominance."* LeFeber, *America, Russia, and the Cold War*, p. 371.

81 *from $260 billion to more than $300 billion.* Ibid., p. 385.

81 *"How the hell did that happen?"* Quoted in Carroll, *House of War*, p. 473.

82 *the first to fire nuclear weapons.* Ibid., p. 470.

82 *"and the Persian Gulf."* *The 9/11 Commission Report*, p. 203.

82 *"a new rival."* Paul Wolfowitz, Defense Planning Guidance, 1992, quoted in Carroll, *House of War*, p. 484.

82 *"Pax Americana."* Carroll, *House of War*, pp. 484–85.

82 *"weakened alliances and increased tensions."* The Project on Defense Alternatives, "The Paradoxes of post–Cold War US Defense Policy: An Agenda for the 2001 Quadrennial Defense Review," Briefing Memo 18, February 5, 2001, pp. 2–5.

83 *responsibility for the attack.* *The 9/11 Commission Report*, p. 202.

83 *in Wolfowitz's terms, "stale."* Quoted ibid., p. 202.

84 *at the behest of the Pentagon.* Zegart, *Spying Blind*, pp. 74–77. The five reports were issued by the U.S. Commission on the Roles and Capabilities of the U.S. Intelligence Community, the House Permanent Select Committee on Intelligence, the Council on Foreign Relations, the 20th Century Fund, and the National Institute for Public Policy.

84 *a threat to the continent.* The *9/11 Commission Report*, pp. 16–17.

84 *fourteen fighter jets on alert.* Leslie Filson, *Air War over America: Sept. 11 Alters Face of Air Defense Mission* (Panama City, FL: Tyndall Air Force Base Public Affairs Office, 2003), pp. 2–3.

84 *to 14 in 2001.* Ibid., p. 11.

84 *be phased out entirely.* "NORAD Strategy Review: Final Report," Department of Defense, 1992, p. 55, cited in *The 9/11 Commission Report*, p. 17.

85 *preservation of their command.* Filson, *Air War over America*, pp. 6–7.

85 *"almost went to the end game."* 9/11 Commission Hearing, June 17, 2004, transcript.

85 *"the air sovereignty mission."* Larry Arnold, Foreword to Filson, *Air War over America*, pp. iv–v.

85 *"large distances between the alert sites."* Larry Arnold, quoted in Filson, *Air War over America*, p. 36.

86 *"'we'll shut down now.'"* Arnold, quoted ibid., p. 37.

86 *"came down on 9/11."* Testimony of Larry Arnold, 9/11 Commission Hearing, June 17, 2004, transcript.

86 *"as many as you can."* Colonel William Scott (ret.), quoted in Filson, *Air War over America*, p. 39.

87 *"we had a viable threat."* Scott, quoted ibid., p. 40.

87 *"predicted they would strike."* Major General Haugen, quoted ibid., p. 38.

87 *"He didn't get any more forces."* Larry Arnold, Foreword, ibid., p. v.

87 *to defend the homeland.* See generally Filson, *Air War over America*; Eberhart interview, "Noble Eagle Without End," in *Air Force Journal*, February 2005, pp. 42–47.

88 *"externally were the CIA."* Testimony of General Richard Myers, 9/11 Commission Hearing, June 17, 2004, transcript.

88 *"the major role."* Ibid.

89 *"training for over-water events."* 9/11 Commission Memorandum for the Record, March 4, 2004, National Archives, 9/11 Commission Records, Dana Hyde files, Box 5, "DoD/NORAD."

89 *"those seven sites."* Testimony of General Richard Myers, 9/11 Commission Hearing, June 17, 2004, transcript. Commission staff member Miles Kara prepared a detailed briefing on the scope of NORAD training for hijack scenarios, which has recently been declassified; it is available at http://www.scribd.com/doc/10411947/NORAD-Exercises-Hijack-Summary. In addition, Kara has written and posted an article, "9-11: Training, Exercises, and War Games," available on his website at www.oredigger61.org. Training scenarios included hijacking a plane from London that terrorists intend to blow up over New York City, and use of a hijacked plane as a weapon. Again, the problem was not that such scenarios were not imagined, but that NORAD lacked the resources to reorient its mission even if it had viewed the exercise scenarios as real-world threats. As a consequence, the agency provided air sovereignty "in name only."

89 *"to balance that risk."* Ibid.

89 *"needs to be rectified."* Ivan Eland, "Tilting at Windmills: Post–Cold War Threats to U.S. Security," *Policy Analysis*, no. 332, February 8, 1999, p. 33.

90 *"viewed as a criminal act."* 9/11 Commission Hearing, June 17, 2004, transcript.

90 *along with NORAD's mission.* David F. Winkler, "Searching the Skies: The Legacy of the United States Cold War Defense Radar Program," U.S. Air Force Air Combat Command, June 1997, p. 47.

90 *"over the central part of the United States."* Arnold, quoted in Filson, *Air War over America*, p. 41.

90 *"more ready than we were."* Scott, quoted ibid., p. 41.

91 *by Defense Secretary Robert McNamara.* Testifying in 1966 before the House Subcommittee on Defense Appropriations, McNamara stated: "The elaborate defenses which we erected against the Soviets' bomber threat . . . no longer retain their original importance. Today, with no defense against the major threat, the Soviet ICBMs, our anti-bomber defenses alone would contribute very little to our damage limiting objective." Quoted in Winkler, "Searching the Skies," p. 37.

92 *"control of the airplane."* Testimony of General Ralph Eberhart, 9/11 Commission Hearing, June 17, 2004, transcript.

PART THREE. DAY OF DAYS

95 *over the North Pole.* See Michael Bronner, "9/11 Live: The NORAD Tapes," *Vanity Fair*, June 2006. Mr. Bronner, a former producer for CBS's *60 Minutes*, was instrumental in gathering the facts supporting Universal Pictures' *United 93*. In the process, he persuaded NORAD to make public the contemporaneous tapes from the morning of 9/11. The transcripts quoted in Part 3 are adapted from transcripts provided by Mr. Bronner; they have been revised by the author by comparing them closely to the tapes.

96 *Omari checked none.* Third Monograph, p. 2.

96 *He proceeded to the security checkpoint.* Ibid.

96 *Air Threat Conference Calls.* See *The 9/11 Commission Report*, p. 37.

96 *security of civil aviation.* See Andrea Canavan, *The Federal Aviation Administration* (New York: Chelsea House, 2003), pp. 35–38.

97 *screening for . . . onboard security.* Third Monograph, pp. 60–61.

97 *to further some political agenda.* Testimony of Jane Garvey before the 9/11 Commission, May 22, 2003.

97 *constituted a "last resort."* Third Monograph, p. 53.

97 *"thinking in that direction."* FAA, "2001 Terrorism Threat Prevention to Aviation Security Personnel at Airports and Air Carriers" (CD-ROM), slide 24, quoted in 9/11 Commission Staff Report, August 26, 2004, p. 53.

98 *to be prevented and countered.* Department of Transportation proposed rulemaking, 14 CFR Parts 107 and 139 Airport Security, "Final Rule," *Federal Register* 66, no. 137 (July 17, 2001).

98 *security should be ordered.* Third Monograph, p. 61.

98 *aircraft as a weapon.* Ibid., p. 55.

98 *renewed interest in hijacking.* Ibid., pp. 54–55.

99 *"would probably be preferable."* FAA, "2001 Terrorism Threat Prevention to Aviation Security Personnel at Airports and Air Carriers" (CD-ROM), slide 24, quoted in Third Monograph, p. 59.

99 *heightened threat environment.* Ibid., p. 57.

99 *"high degree of alertness."* FAA Report, Information Circular 2001-4A, July 31, 2001, quoted in Third Monograph, pp. 56–57.

99 *"the battle against hijacking."* Third Monograph, p. 58.

99 *targeting the transportation infrastructure.* Ibid.

100 *"lead the fight against it."* White House Commission on Aviation Safety and Security, Final Report to President Clinton, February 12, 1997, p. 4.

100 *"in carrying out their designs."* Ibid., p. 5.

100 *"countering emerging threats."* Ibid.

101 *"dissemination of intelligence."* Third Monograph, p. 64.

101 *"what's going on in Atlanta."* Quoted ibid.

101 *to assist in an investigation.* Ibid. Of course, as discussed earlier, much of the FBI itself was unaware of the Phoenix memo.

101 *the subject in January 2004.* Testimony of Cathal Flynn, 9/11 Commission Hearing, transcript, January 27, 2004: "I regret to say that I was unaware of the TIPOFF list and was unaware of it until yesterday."

102 *"specific to aviation at the time."* Testimony of Claudio Manno, 9/11 Commission Hearing, January 27, 2004, transcript.

102 *remained unimpaired.* Third Monograph, p. 69.

103 *"'we'll tell you.'"* Testimony of Cathal Flynn, 9/11 Commission Hearing, January 27, 2004, transcript.

103 *was ever interviewed.* CBC News, March 26, 2006, at www.cbc.ca/story/world/national/2006/03/22/moussaoui-trial.

103 *"more vigilant and cautious."* Testimony of John Raidt, 9/11 Commission Hearing, January 27, 2004, transcript.

104 *passengers on each flight for screening.* Third Monograph, p. 70.

104 *followed for some time.* Ibid., p. 71.

104 *planned to be a passenger.* Ibid., p. 2.

105 *in twelve seconds.* Ibid., p. 3. The 9/11 Commission staff's examination of the videotape revealed that they entered the walk-through metal detector at 5:45:03, and passed out of view of the video camera at 5:45:15.

105 *a camera or camcorder case.* Ibid., p. 3.

105 *Logan Airport at 6:45 a.m.* Ibid.

105 *Logan Airport without incident.* Third Monograph, pp. 5–6.

105 *and the departure gate.* Third Monograph. p. 18.

105 *by the CAPPS system.* Ibid., pp. 17–18.

106 *any of the men.* Ibid., p. 18.

106 *in seat 10B.* Ibid., p. 6.

106 *(seats 6C, 9C, and 9D).* Ibid., p. 18.

106 *followed shortly thereafter.* Ibid., pp. 27–28.

106 *for enhanced screening.* Ibid.

107 *their CAPPS selection.* Ibid.

107 *allowed to proceed.* Ibid.

107 *5E and 5F in first class.* Ibid., p. 28.

107 *also in first class.* Ibid., pp. 34–35.

108 *more than 25,000 flights.* Ibid., p. 60.

108 *"to try delaying tactics."* Ibid., p. 81.

108 *"negotiation, not confrontation."* Testimony of Jane Garvey, 9/11 Commission Hearing, May 22, 2003, transcript.

108 *"unseat the flight crew from the cockpit."* Third Monograph, p. 81.

109 *other FAA initiatives.* Ibid., p. 80.

109 *"I'm going to open the door."* Fort Worth Star-Telegram, January 10, 2001, p. 1.

110 *more than 73 million per year.* Canavan, *The Federal Aviation Administration*, p. 52.

112 *There was no response.* NTSB Report, Air Traffic Control Recording—American Airlines Flight 11, December 21, 2001.

112 *"something wrong with the frequency."* Peter Zalewski, interview with Tom Brokaw, NBC News, *Dateline*, September 11, 2002.

112 *"I think we're getting hijacked."* AAL Transcript, phone call from Betty Ong to Nydia Gonzalez, September 11, 2001.

113 *"I'm not sure."* Peter Zalewski, interview with Tom Brokaw, NBC News, *Dateline*, September 11, 2002.

113 *"We can't even get inside."* Betty Ong phone call, quoted in Third Monograph, p. 9.

113 *"on [radio frequency] 135.32."* Quoted in Third Monograph, p. 9.

113 *"American 11 trying to call?"* Quoted in Third Monograph, p. 10.

113 *"We are returning to the airport."* Quoted in *The 9/11 Commission Report*, p. 19.

114 *"Just stay quiet."* Quoted ibid. Also NBC News, *Dateline*, September 11, 2002.

114 *"'What's wrong with you?'"* Peter Zalewski interview, NBC News, *Dateline*, September 11, 2002.

114 *"worse than a normal hijack."* Ibid.

114 *and remaining flight crew.* Third Monograph, p. 10.

114 *was flying erratically.* Ibid.

114 *of the hijacking.* See *The 9/11 Commission Report*, p. 19; Third Monograph, pp. 10–11.

115 *including accidents and hijackings.* See *The 9/11 Commission Report*, pp. 14–16.

115 *coordination in handling the hijacking.* Third Monograph, p. 11.

115 *with New England Region.* Ibid.

115 *"might have been fatally stabbed."* Ibid.

115 *"any stupid moves."* Quoted in *The 9/11 Commission Report*, p. 19.

116 *contact the military.* Third Monograph, p. 12.

116 *"request . . . an escort aircraft."* See *The 9/11 Commission Report*, pp. 17–18.

116 *"in the event of an emergency."* Ibid., p. 18.

117 *"what was about to happen."* Ibid.

118 *"not an exercise, not a test."* Ibid., pp. 6–7.

122 *"mothballed in the [mid-1990s]."* Michael Bronner, "9/11 Live: The NORAD Tapes," in Paul Greengrass, *United 93: The Shooting Script* (New York: Newmarket, 2007), p. 106.

122 *"the Jetsons' garage."* Ibid.

123 *The time was 8:41. The 9/11 Commission Report*, p. 20.

124 *"way too low" . . . lost the connection.* Third Monograph, p. 14.

124 *"'broadcast by the American.'"* Dave Bottiglia interview, NBC News, *Dateline*, September 11, 2002.

124 *"stay in your seats."* NTSB Report, DCA01SA063, p. 8.

124 *pass the information on.* Ibid.

124 *"'thinks it's a hijack.'"* NBC News, *Dateline*, September 11, 2002.

124 *"we had no altitude . . . on him."* Ibid.

129 *"hitting up tracks."* Identification Technician Transcript, at 12:41:50. Note: The time-stamped hour is incorrect, but the minutes and seconds correspond to real time after 8:00 a.m.

129 *"we're doing the thing."* MCC Transcript, at 12:44.

132 *"oh three west . . ."* Identification Technician Transcript, at 12:44:50.

132 *"We didn't wait for that."* Testimony of Major General Arnold, 9/11 Commission, Washington, D.C., May 23, 2003.

133 *"'scramble the aircraft.'"* Major Larry General Arnold, quoted in Filson, *Air War over America*, p. 56.

133 *to Weapons director Major James Fox.* Ch. 2, MCC Op-Side, at 12:44:48.

133 *"I need a direction, a destination."* Ibid., at 12:44:58.

134 *"Yeah."* Identification Technician Transcript, at 12:47:57.

142 *"Sure."* Ibid., at 12:52:03.

142 *World Trade Center at 8:46:40 a.m.* I have used here, as the Commission did in its *Report*, a time of impact that corresponds to the time established by the National Transportation Safety Board. Seismic records, radar files, and other records support a time about fifteen seconds earlier.

142 *switched again to 3321.* FAA Timeline; *The 9/11 Commission Report*; Third Monograph, p. 15.

144 *"fighters in that location."* Identification Technician Transcript, Ch. 5, at 13:18:11.

144 *"Washington has no clue."* Ibid., at 13:44:15.

144 *NEADS that morning.* 9/11 Commission interview with Colin Scoggins, Nashua, New Hampshire, January 8, 2003. 9/11 Commission Memorandum for the Record (MFR), p. 2.

144 *the attacks were virtually over. The 9/11 Commission Report*, pp. 35–38.

145 *received no response.* Third Monograph, p. 21.

145 *"incidents going over here."* Quoted in Third Monograph, p. 21, note 163.

145 *continued off course.* Ibid.

145 *"Boston to L.A."* Quoted ibid., p. 21.

145 *hijackers were flying the plane.* Ibid., p. 21.

148 *"Yup."* MCC Transcript at 12:53.

148 *"What do you think? [LAUGHTER]."* Ibid., at 12:57:11.

148 *toward New York City.* Third Monograph, p. 22.

148 *"two of them."* Ibid.

148 *"any evasive action necessary."* David Bottiglia, on NBC *Dateline*, September 11, 2002.

149 *"into a building."* Quoted in Third Monograph, pp. 22–23.

149 *"situation going on here."* Third Monograph, p. 23.

149 *"another one coming in."* Quoted in *The 9/11 Commission Report*, p. 22.

150 *"quick on this."* Ibid., p. 23.

153 *"Thank you."* ID Tech Transcript, at 13:03:07.

153 *The time was 9:03:11.* Third Monograph, p. 24.

154 *trapped above the crash site.* *The 9/11 Commission Report*, p. 285.

154 *damage to the North Tower.* Ibid., pp. 286–87.

154 *if conditions warranted.* Ibid., p. 289.

154 *the ninety-first floor down.* Ibid., p. 293.

155 *"instantly doubled in magnitude."* Ibid.

155 *"caused by pilot error."* Ibid., p. 35.

155 *entered the classroom at 9:00.* Ibid.

155 *"America is under attack."* Ibid., p. 38.

155 *continued reading to him.* Ibid.

155 *hit the South Tower.* Ibid., p. 35.

156 *awaiting further information.* *The 9/11 Commission Report*, p. 37.

156 *"bin Laden's fingerprints all over it."* George Tenet, *At the Center of the Storm*, p. 161; Senator David Boren, on ABC News, September 14, 2002.

156 *any airport within Boston Center.* Command Center Tape Recording, Position 14, Line 5114, at 9:03 a.m.

156 *"we have planes."* Command Center Tape Recording, Position 15, Line 5115, at 9:05 a.m.

156 *"ATC Zero."* Daily Record of Facility Operations, FAA New York Center, p. 1.

156 *until further notice.* *The 9/11 Commission Report*, p. 23.

156 *in light of those events.* Ibid.; Command Center Tape, Position 15, Line 5115, at 9:05 a.m. to 9:07 a.m.

157 *"Thank you very much."* Command Center Tape Recording, Position 15, Line 5115 (p. 37 of Miller Transcript).

157 *of its carriers.* 9/11 Commission MFR, from Ellen King interview on April 5, 2004.

160 *Dulles at 8:20 a.m.* FAA Summary of Air Traffic Hijack Events: September 11, 2001, AAT-20, 9/17/01, Timeline for AAL 77; ZDC-ARTCC-212, Dulles ATCT LCW, at 12:19:20: "American 77 your departure frequency will be one two five point zero five runway three zero. Cleared for takeoff."

161 *Radio contact was routine.* ZDC-ARTCC-212, HNNR, at 12:40:13.

161 *turn right ten degrees.* FAA Summary of Air Traffic Hijack Events: September 11, 2001, AAT-20, 9/17/01; ZDC-ARTCC-212, HNNR, at 12:43:51 and 12:47:16.

161 *clearance instruction.* ZDC-ARTCC-212, HNNR, at 12:50:51 (transcript dated December 3, 2001).

161 *control of the cockpit.* Third Monograph, p. 608.

161 *the aircraft was observed descending.* FAA Summary of Air Traffic Hijack Events: September 11, 2001, AAT-20, 9/17/01, indicates time at 12:54:43; Commission interview with Richard Byard, Indianapolis, September 24, 2003, MFR, p. 1.

161 *as a primary target.* FAA Summary of Air Traffic Hijack Events: September 11, 2001, AAT-20, 9/17/01 indicates time at 12:56:19; Commission interview with Richard Byard, Indianapolis, September 24, 2003 MFR, p. 1; Commission interview with Linda Povinelli, Indianapolis, September 24, 2003 MFR, p. 1.

161 *to advise them of the situation.* ZDC-ARTCC-212, HNNR, at 12:57:39 (transcript dated December 3, 2001): "This is Henderson [sector]. American 77, I don't know what happened to him. I'm trying to reach somebody look[s] like he took a turn to the south and now I'm, uh, I don't know what altitude he's at or what he's doing last [UNINTELLIGIBLE] ah, heading towards Falmouth at 35[,000 feet]."

161 *"until we find out."* Transcript from Indianapolis ARTCC to NTSB #01-096, HNNR (dated October 4, 2001), at 13:06:39.

161 *projected flight path to the west.* FAA Summary of Air Traffic Hijack Events: September 11, 2001, AAT-20, 9/17/01: "[12:59:00] ZID [Indianapolis Center] controllers began coordinating with other controllers to protect the airspace and altitude of AAL 77's filed route of flight."

162 *radar identification.* FAA Summary of Air Traffic Hijack Events: September 11, 2001, AAT-20, 9/17/01: "[13:09:00] ZID notified Great Lakes Regional Operations Center a possible aircraft accident of AAL 77 due to the simultaneous loss of radio communications and radar identification."

162 *"to the rear of the plane."* Third Monograph, p. 31.

162 *flight services manager.* Ibid.

162 *possible crash of American 77.* Commission interview with John Thomas, Indianapolis, September 24, 2003, MFR, p. 2.

162 *reports of a downed aircraft.* Ibid.

163 *for that incident.* Third Monograph, p. 31.

163 *she was placing the phone call.* Ibid., p. 32.

163 *American 77, had been hijacked.* Ibid.

163 *American 77 might be a hijack.* Ibid.

165 *"all righty. Thank you—"* Identification Technician Transcript, at 13:17.

166 *"coffee? [LAUGHTER]"* MCC Transcript, at 13:19.

166 *they were heading northeast.* Third Monograph, p. 32.

166 *passed on this call.* The 9/11 Commission Report, p. 36.

166 *was a suspected hijack.* Command Center Tape, NTMO Position 26, Line 4530 (FAA Transcript, p. 15).

168 *"could be a third aircraft."* Identification Technician Transcript, at 9:21:10.

169 *"Bye. Okay."* MCC Transcript, at 13:21:37.

169 *"No problem."* SD2 Transcript (Surveillance Desk).

170 *identification for American 77.* FAA Summary of Air Traffic Hijack Events: September 11, 2001, AAT-20, 9/17/01.

170 *passed on this call.* The 9/11 Commission Report, p. 36.

170 *a combat air patrol at 9:25.* Third Monograph, p. 26.

170 *"taking off in the United States."* Third Monograph, p. 33.

171 *"That's great."* MCC Transcript, at 13:24:10.

171 *"who the other one is."* MCC Transcript, at 13:27.

171 *"will not stand."* Quoted in Sandra Silberstein, *War of Words: Language, Politics and 9/11* (London: Routledge, 2004), p. 18.

171 *unknown to the military.* Third Monograph, pp. 32–33. It has been established that two Dulles TRACON controllers had the following exchange shortly after 9:25: "See that no-tag?" "I do." (Or possibly "Thank you.") But neither of the controllers seems to have raised the issue to the area supervisor, and their exchange was never reported to the military, and thus did not play a role in the response.

172 *not join until 10:17.* The 9/11 Commission Report, p. 37.

172 *He lost her call at 9:31.* Third Monograph, p. 32.

172 *the approaching aircraft.* Ibid., pp. 32–33.

172 *"approaching Reagan National Airport."* The 9/11 Commission Report, p. 39.

175 *"headed towards Washington."* Identification Technician Transcript, at 13:32:36.

178 *"Thanks."* Ibid., at 13:32:36.

179 *the Pentagon or White House.* Third Monograph, p. 33.

179 *to the shelter at 9:36.* The 9/11 Commission Report, p. 40.

179 *"deviating away."* Third Monograph, p. 33.

180 *"going direct Washington. . . ."* MCC Transcript, at 13:36:23.

182 *"Get a Z point on that."* Ibid., at 13:37:23.

183 *"Push 'em back!"* Ibid., at 13:38:10.

183 *"especially FAA."* Richard Clarke, *Against All Enemies: Inside America's War on Terror* (New York: Free Press, 2004), p. 1.

184 *"It was now 9:28."* Ibid., pp. 4–5.

184 *Pentagon had been hit.* The 9/11 Commission Report, p. 36.

184 *"2 possibly 3 aloft."* Ibid., pp. 36–37.

185 *"over Washington" at 10:03.* Ibid., pp. 36–37.

185 *"to the National Military Command Center."* Ibid.

185 *"guidance to the operations team."* Ibid., pp. 462–63, note 189.

188 *and then to Cleveland Center.* See NTSB Report, December 21, 2001, DCA01SA065, pp. 1–6.

188 *traveling to see her.* See discussion above, pp. 51, 59–60.

189 *"Wind 290/50 ain't helping."* Quoted in Third Monograph, p. 37.

189 *"any ride reports?"* NTSB Report, DCA01SA065, p. 5.

189 *"point zero seven [radio frequency]."* Ibid., p. 6.

189 *"HIT TRADE CENTER BLDS."* Ibid.

189 *"intermittent light chop."* Ibid., p. 7.

189 *all flights in New York and Boston.* Third Monograph, p. 37.

189 *"United 93, Cleveland, roger."* NTSB Report, DCA01SA065, p. 7.

189 *landing flights in Philadelphia.* Third Monograph, p. 38.

189 *"confirm latest mssg plz—Jason."* Quoted in Third Monograph, p. 38.

189 *"Negative contact . . . United 93."* NTSB Report, DCA01SA065, p. 7.

189 *"Get out of here!"* Ibid.

190 *in a matter of seconds.* Third Monograph, p. 38.

190 *"ident, please."* NTSB Report, DCA01SA065, p. 7.

190 *several said that they had.* Third Monograph, p. 39.

190 *"stay in your seats."* NTSB Report, DCA01SA063, p. 8.

191 *"We have a bomb on board."* NTSB Report, DCA01SA065, p. 7.

191 *"Say again slowly."* Ibid.

191 *"So, sit."* Quoted in Third Monograph, p. 39.

191 *the sounds of her murder.* Ibid.

191 *as it turned south and east.* Ibid., p. 39.

191 *from 9:34 to 10:08.* Ibid.

191 *as the flight deviated.* Ibid.; see also NTSB Report, DCA01SA065, p. 8.

192 *killed a flight attendant.* Third Monograph, p. 40.

192 *working on it.* The 9/11 Commission Report, pp. 28–29.

192 *"Please remain quiet."* Quoted ibid., p. 29.

192 *There was no response.* Ibid.

193 *"Okay, bye."* Identification Technician Transcript (Rountree), at 13:38:35.

195 *"Boston? Okay."* Ibid., at 13:39:33.

196 *led to the call to NEADS.* The 9/11 Commission Report, pp. 27–28.

204 *"protect my NCA."* MCC Transcript, at 13:39:40–13:49:44.

205 *"Washington has no freaking—"* Identification Technician Transcript (Rountree), at 13:44:11.

205 *"Let's just calm down."* MCC Transcript, at 13:44:47.

205 *airborne at the time.* The 9/11 Commission Report, p. 29.

206 *"everybody just left the room."* Quoted ibid.

206 *"Straight out."* http://www.youtube.com/watch?v=dyanVli85gQ.

206 *"direct to Wright-Patterson."* Ibid.

207 *where to fly the president.* Ibid. Venus 77 was the so-called "mystery plane" of 9/11, photographed in the skies over Washington, unacknowledged by the Pentagon for years and unmentioned in *The 9/11 Commission Report.* The reason for the omission was that the administration deemed any information regarding the plane or its flight path highly confidential. Like other omissions, however, it has led some to believe that the plane played a significant

role in the events of that morning. It did not. In that respect, the omission of it was regrettable.

207 *"somebody's going to pay."* Quoted in *The 9/11 Commission Report*, p. 39.

207 *to the shelter conference room.* Ibid., p. 40.

207 *President Bush agreed reluctantly.* Ibid., p. 39.

207 *who claimed to have a bomb.* Third Monograph, p. 41.

208 *commercial flight, like his own.* Ibid., p. 42.

208 *"ready to do something."* Quoted ibid.

208 *"retake control of the airplane."* Quoted ibid., pp. 41–42.

208 *put the phone down.* Ibid., p. 43.

209 *"I've got to go. Bye."* Quoted ibid., pp. 44–45.

209 *"Let's roll!"* Quoted ibid., p. 45.

210 *"the fourth possible hijack."* Quoted in *The 9/11 Commission Report*, p. 38.

212 *"Copy that."* Identification Technician Transcript (Rountree), at 13:45:25–13:46:15.

215 *"Washington doesn't know shit."* Identification Technician Transcript (Rountree), at 13:50:23–13:55:26.

217 *"Stand by just a second. . . .* Ibid., at 13:55:52–13:56:49.

219 *"Bye."* Ibid., at 13:57:49–13:59:16.

219 *"no one told us anything."* Dean Eckmann, quoted in *The 9/11 Commission Report*, p. 45.

219 *what to do about United 93.* *The 9/11 Commission Report*, p. 38.

220 *"we finish it off?"* Third Monograph, p. 45.

220 *"only seconds from overcoming them."* Ibid., p. 46.

220 *"Allah is the greatest!"* Ibid.

220 *from Washington, D.C., at 10:03:11 a.m.* Ibid.

220 *it was already down.* *The 9/11 Commission Report*, p. 41.

220 *"a hijack heading to D.C. at this time."* Ibid., p. 42.

222 *"bomb on board—"* Identification Technician Transcript, at 10:07.

225 *"Where's my bomber at?"* MCC Transcript, at 14:07:07–14:10:25.

226 *"resounding sense of caution."* Bronner, "9/11 Live: The NORAD Tapes," in Greengrass, *United 93*, p. 131.

226 *"not cleared to fire."* Quoted ibid., p. 132.

226 *"We intercepted our own guys."* Quoted ibid., p. 133.

227 *authorization of the shoot-down.* *The 9/11 Commission Report*, p. 41.

227 *the vice president had confirmed the order.* Ibid.

227 *reflect that authorization.* Ibid.

228 *"don't respond, per [General Arnold]."* Quoted ibid., p. 42.

229 *"do not respond, per [General Arnold]."* Quoted ibid., pp. 42–43.

230 *"a pilot report that did it."* Quoted ibid., p. 43.

230 *"ID. TYPE. TAIL."* Ibid.,

231 *in the same airspace.* Ibid., p. 44.

232 *"his mission won't end that way."* Lynn Spencer, *Touching History*, p. 220.

PART FOUR. WHISKEY TANGO FOXTROT: THE TALE OF TALES

236 *and with the Cabinet.* See, generally, Frank Rich, *The Greatest Story Ever Sold: The Decline and Fall of Truth in Bush's America* (New York: Penguin, 2007); Bob Woodward, *Bush at War* (New York: Simon & Schuster, 2002).

236 *"everything you have done."* Clarke, *Against All Enemies*, p. 19.

238 *"we got some kinda play."* MCC Transcript, at 13:07:20.

239 *"It's all good."* Ibid., at 13:34.

239 *"who the other one is."* Third Monograph, p. 16.

239 *Conference hosted by the Pentagon.* The 9/11 Commission Report, pp. 34, 37.

239 *"headed to Washington DC . . . in tail chase."* Quoted in Memorandum from the 9/11 Commission Staff, July 29, 2004, p. 5. This document has been released from the National Archives, 9/11 Commission files, Daniel Marcus, Box 6, "Referral."

242 *"after the Pentagon was struck."* Myers Hearing Transcript, September 13, 2001, p. 11.

243 *"had taken off from Dulles."* Myers Hearing Transcript, September 13, 2001, pp. 35–36.

244 *"jets took to the air."* Bradley Graham, "Military Alerted Before Attacks," The Washington Post, September 15, 2001, p. A18.

244 *"We weren't even close."* Richard Whittle, "National Guard Raced After 2 Airliners," The Dallas Morning News, September 15, 2001; also Graham, "Military Alerted Before Attacks."

245 *"do so if we had to."* The NewsHour with Jim Lehrer, September 14, 2001.

246 *"aircraft had crashed?"* Quoted in 9/11 Commission Staff Memorandum, July 29, 2004, National Archives, 9/11 Commission files, Daniel Marcus, Box 6, "Referral."

246 *"events concerning UA 175."* See DoT Inspector General Report, August 29, 2006, Appendix 3.

246 *"[Reagan National Airport] Traffic Control Tower."* Ibid.

247 *"UAL93's last known location."* Ibid.

247 *"2 F-16s)."* Ibid., Appendix 2.

248 *"(Langley F-16 . . . protect DC)."* Ibid.

250 *"we respond accordingly."* October 25, 2001, Hearing, Senate Armed Services Committee, Transcript, pp. 7–9.

254 *"New York City airspace."* Ibid., pp. 16–18.

261 *"not be allowed to reach Washington, D.C."* ABC News, September 11, 2002. See http://s3.amazonaws.com/911timeline/2002/abcnews091102.html.

263 *"towards the Washington, D.C., area."* 9/11 Commission Hearing, May 23, 2003, transcript.

264 *"it was friendly."* Ibid.

267 *"crashed into the towers."* 9/11 Commission Hearing, May 23, 2003, transcript.

270 *"to this Commission earlier."* 9/11 Commission Hearing, June 17, 2004, transcript.

270 *"We weren't even close."* Richard Whittle, "National Guard Raced After 2 Airliners," The Dallas Morning News, September 15, 2001; also Bradley Graham, "Military Alerted Before Attacks," The Washington Post, September 15, 2001.

271 *"lost confidence" . . . at the time.* See 9/11 Commission Staff Memorandum, July 29, 2004, National Archives, 9/11 Commission files, Daniel Marcus, Box 6, "Referral."

272 *"take a bullet for anybody."* 9/11 Commission Hearing, June 17, 2004, transcript.

272 *"some kind of category."* Ibid.

273 *"look at the logs . . . ?"* Ibid.

274 *the tapes would be lost.* 9/11 Commission Staff Memo, July 29, 2004, from National Archives, 9/11 Commission Records, Daniel Marcus files, Box 6, "Referral."

275 *"away from the possible target!"* E-mail from Robert Marr to William Scott, June 2, 2003, from National Archives, 9/11 Commission records, Daniel Marcus, Box 6, "Referral." Colonel Marr's e-mail continues: "All I have is comments from the crew, but it appears that what really happened with AA77 is that the first call at 0924L was from another FAA center, I think it was Boston Center who called to say that something was happening in Washington Center that we needed to be concerned with (this would make sense because Boston now had our number whereas the other centers were just starting to get in the game). We called Washington Center and they said they didn't have time for us—there was a shift change going on. Their interest level obviously peaked quickly and we improved the comm. flow, although Washington never saw the track as far as I can tell. The approach controllers were the first to get a contact. I can't confirm these conversations and I'd have to do a lot of research to find out exactly which controller was taking those calls—we were a little busy. However, that's the closest I have come to reconstructing that particular event." Of course, more was available than comments from the crew, namely, the NORAD NEADS logs, which clearly reflect the mistaken report involving American

11, and the report, at 9:34, that AA77 is "missing"—an odd entry, if the flight had been reported hijacked ten minutes earlier. As noted, however, the 9:24 entry records the flight number of another flight, and does not relate in any way to American 77.

276 *"in reaching Washington."* Commission Staff Memorandum to the Inspector General, July 29, 2004, p. 3, from National Archives, 9/11 Commission Records, Daniel Marcus, Box 6, "Referral."

277 *"clearance to kill if need be."* Filson, *Air War over America*, p. 68.

278 *"and other government agencies."* Department of Transportation IG Report, August 31, 2006, p. 5.

278 *"notification to DoD for United flight 93."* Ibid.

279 *"time for United Flight 93."* Ibid., p. 6.

279 *"after United 93 had crashed."* Ibid., p. 7.

279 *"and not the other."* Ibid.

281 *"regarding the chronologies."* Ibid., pp. 6–7.

282 *"time for United Flight 93."* Department of Transportation IG Report, August 31, 2006, p. 6.

283 *"knowing them to be false."* Department of Defense IG Report, September 12, 2006, p. 1.

283 *"sequence of events of September 11, 2001."* Ibid.

283 *"no standardized logs."* Ibid., p. 2.

284 *"Did you not look at the logs . . . ?"* 9/11 Commission Hearing, June 17, 2004, transcript.

284 *"in tail chase."* 9/11 Commission Staff Memorandum, July 29, 2004, p. 5, from National Archives, 9/11 Commission Records, Daniel Marcus files, Box 6, "Referral."

284 *"testimony to the Commission."* Ibid.

284 *"considered an additional duty."* Ibid.

288 *"you decide."* Lynn Spencer, *Touching History: The Untold Drama That Unfolded in the Skies over America on 9/11* (New York: Free Press, 2008), pp. 285–86.

289 *closer question.* It's certainly not, moreover, a question that can be answered on the basis of the account in *Touching History*, which resurrects, as its best evidence that the military was ready for United 93, the adventures of Andrews Air Force Base pilot Billy Hutchison, who recounts taking off low on fuel and without weapons, and claims that he had United 93 in his sights when the plane went down. "*Thank God*, he thinks as he touches down at 10:35," the book concludes. When the Commission staff interviewed Hutchison at Andrews, we were truly puzzled. His dramatic story had been the subject of widespread media attention, and was vividly told, as it is in *Touching History*. The problem with the story was that the radar data showed that he didn't even take off until 10:38; the air traffic control records, further, never mentioned United 93. His mission was purely one of reconnaissance. When this was pointed out to Hutchison, he stormed out of the interview. "Why are you asking me?" he fumed. "You know the facts." *Touching History* adds value to the 9/11 story in recounting in vivid detail the FAA's success in landing more than 4,000 planes without incident; its unquestioning reliance on military anecdotes from the "fog of war" renders that part of the work inaccurate.

290 *is truly bipartisan.* A further WTF moment may yet emerge from the search to discover the source of the mistaken report concerning American 11. Independent researcher John Farmer (no relation, hard as that is to believe) has identified what may be critical omissions from the tape of two Dulles controllers at 9:25, referred to earlier, in which a primary radar track is noted. If the track was American 77, it is of obvious interest what was said after the track was spotted. That conversation, according to Farmer, is missing from the tape.

PART FIVE. AFTERMATH: KATRINA AND THE CONSEQUENCES OF DENIAL

293 *"human suffering incredible by modern standards."* National Hurricane Center, Advisory 23, issued August 28, 2005, quoted in Douglas Brinkley, *The Great Deluge: Hurricane Katrina, New Orleans, and the Mississippi Gulf Coast* (New York: William Morrow, 2006), pp. 79–80.

294 *"gravest threats to the nation."* Brinkley, *The Great Deluge*, p. 13.

295 *"made the agency effective."* Quoted in Christopher Cooper and Robert Block, *Disaster: Hurricane Katrina and the Failure of Homeland Security* (New York: Times Books/Henry Holt, 2006), pp. 76–77.

295 *"homeland security efforts."* Ibid., p. 80.

295 *FEMA . . . had been weakened.* Ibid.

295 *McPhee and others.* McPhee's *The Control of Nature* (1989; originally in *The New Yorker*); Mark Fischetti, "Drowning New Orleans," *Scientific American*, October 2001; John McQuaid and Mark Schleifstein, "Washing Away," New Orleans *Times-Picayune*, June 2002; an October 2004 *National Geographic* article, "Gone With the Water." Cited in Brinkley, *The Great Deluge*, pp. 14–15.

296 *"Mississippi River to the south and west."* Mark Fischetti, "Drowning New Orleans," *Scientific American*, October 2001.

296 *"your system is stressed."* Quoted in Marshall, "Levee Leaks Reported to S&WB a Year Ago," New Orleans *Times-Picayune*, November 18, 2005.

296 *"we would have been out there, without question."* Quoted ibid.

296 *"the havoc Pam had wrought."* Cooper and Block, *Disaster*, p. 17.

297 *"contra-flow" . . . saved many lives during Katrina.* Brinkley, *The Great Deluge*, p. 54.

297 *into the city after the storm* and *because of DHS budget cuts.* Cooper and Block, *Disaster*, p. 21.

298 *"state and local emergency officials."* See Jane Bullock et al., *Introduction to Homeland Security*, 2nd ed. (Burlington, MA, and Oxford: Butterworth-Heinemann, 2006), p. 357.

298 *"very little mismatch."* Ibid., pp. 350–51.

298 *Saturday, August 27.* The times are drawn from three principal sources: "A Nation Unprepared," Report of the Senate Homeland Security and Government Affairs Committee," Chapter 5, pp. 67–77; Brinkley, *The Great Deluge*, pp. 627–37; Cooper and Block, *Disaster*.

299 *before making landfall.* Brinkley, *The Great Deluge*, p. 625.

299 *"never seen conditions like this."* Ibid., pp. 57–58.

300 *the opportunity to leave.* Ibid., pp. 19–20.

300 *"most federal guidelines."* "New Orleans Ignored Its Own Plans," *The Washington Times*, September 9, 2005, quoted in Brinkley, *The Great Deluge*, p. 19.

300 *in touch with Mayor Nagin.* Brinkley, *The Great Deluge*, p. 38.

300 *"on the local population."* Ibid., p. 39.

300 *"This may be IT!"* Quoted in Cooper and Block, *Disaster*, p. 120.

300 *"resources that they could give."* Quoted in Brinkley, *The Great Deluge*, p. 37.

301 *toward New Orleans at eight miles per hour.* Ibid., p. 626.

302 *"way ahead of the game there."* Quoted in Cooper and Block, *Disaster*, p. 114.

302 *"likely topple our levee system."* Quoted ibid., p. 115.

303 *"on a camping trip," he has said.* Quoted ibid., p. 118.

303 *"no loss of life, of course."* Quoted ibid., p. 113.

303 *"as much as you can with commodities."* Quoted ibid., p. 114.

303 *"hotels open in downtown New Orleans."* Ibid.

303 *six months or more to drain the city.* Ibid., p. 115

304 *"just slightly more water."* Ibid., p. 119.

304 *"couldn't execute the mission."* Quoted ibid., p. 120.

304 *left sitting in parking lots.* Ibid., pp. 120–21.

304 *the "Fast-Action Report" concludes.* Quoted ibid., p. 123.

305 *with one SUV.* Quoted ibid., p. 140.

306 *"people swimming in there."* Quoted ibid., p. 138.

307 *"the levees have not been breached."* Quoted ibid., p. 149.

308 *"looting and freebooting."* Brinkley, *The Great Deluge*, p. 203.

308 *"greatest concern for New Orleans."* Quoted ibid., p. 279.

309 *under which it is to be invoked.* National Response Plan (2005), p. 7.

309 *declares an Incident of National Significance.* See Cooper and Block, *Disaster*, pp. 130–33.

310 *to find buses.* Brinkley, *The Great Deluge*, p. 396.

310 *"folks at the Superdome."* Quoted ibid., p. 338.

311 *as many as 5,000 buses.* Ibid., p. 392.

312 *"within the federal government."* Quoted ibid., p. 393.

312 *"to do or tweak?"* Quoted ibid., p. 395.

312 *"I will hope [Brown's] wait at Ruth's . . . is short."* Quoted ibid.

313 *the fault of state and local officials.* Ibid., p. 414.

313 *"And we're just starting."* Ibid., pp. 444–45.

316 *"or the federal level."* Hardball, MSNBC, August 28, 2006.

317 *"as though nothing had happened."* Barack Obama, *The Audacity of Hope: Thoughts on Reclaiming the American Dream* (New York: Crown, 2006), p. 230.

318 *health care responsibilities in the late 1980s.* Martha Derthick, *Agency Under Stress: The Social Security Administration in American Government*, quoted in Wilson, *Bureaucracy*, p. 368.

318 *and of government bureaucracies in particular.* See, for example, Wilson, *Bureaucracy*; Anthony Downs, *Inside Bureaucracy* (RAND Corporation, 1967); Gordon Tullock and James M. Buchanan, *The Politics of Bureaucracy* (Public Affairs Press, 1965); Raaj K. Sah, "Fallibility in Human Organizations and Political Systems," *Journal of Economic Perspectives* (1991), p. 67. See also Craig W. Thomas, "Reorganizing Public Organizations: Alternatives, Objectives, and Evidence," *Journal of Public Administration Research and Theory* 457 (1993); James Q. Wilson, "Thinking About Reorganization," in Roy Godson, Ernest R. May, and Gary James Schmitt, eds., *U.S. Intelligence at the Crossroads: Agendas for Reform* (Brassey's, 1995), p. 28.

318 *"let alone the future."* Bill Clinton, Foreword to Al Gore, *Common Sense Government: Works Better and Costs Less* (Honolulu: University Press of the Pacific, 2005), p. v.

319 *"entire national government."* Bill Clinton, Remarks Announcing National Performance Review, March 3, 1993, quoted in Al Gore, *The Gore Report on Reinventing Government: Creating a Government That Works Better and Costs Less* (New York: Three Rivers Press, 1993), pp. iv, 1.

319 *"Thousands . . . joined these two efforts."* Ibid., p. i.

319 *"federal law enforcement efforts."* Ibid., pp. 140, 143–44.

319 *"moving in the right direction."* Al Gore, *The Best Kept Secrets in Government: How the Clinton Administration Is Reinventing the Way Washington Works* (New York: Random House, 1996), p. 118.

320 *"to reinvent the intelligence process."* National Performance Review, Phase II Initiatives, Intelligence Community Report (1995), Appendix I.

320 *innovative management approaches.* Donald Kettl, "Has Government Been Reinvented," Testimony Before the Senate Government Affairs Committee, May 4, 2000.

321 *"and run through proxies."* Donald Kettl, "After the Reforms," Brookings Institution, April 1998.

321 *"the bureaucracy it was meant to streamline."* "Reinvention Efforts Stuck in Rhetorical Overdrive," *Washington Technology*, February 22, 1996.

321 *updating its technological assets.* Jerry Seper, "Reno Shoots Down Combining Agencies," *The Washington Times*, February 4, 2000, p. A7.

322 *"succeeding when it was not."* Zegart, *Spying Blind*, p. 20.

323 *"have long ago moved on."* Testimony of Paul Light before the Senate Committee on Government Affairs, April 11, 2002.

325 *"protection of the homeland."* Tenet, *At the Center of the Storm*, p. 516.

327 *no feedback . . . on the performance of the exercise.* Senate Homeland Security Committee, Confirmation Hearing of Janet Napolitano, Congressional Quarterly Transcripts Wire, January 15, 2009.

327 *"we're making the country safer."* Quoted in "Re-evaluation of National Security Ordered," *The New York Times*, February 16, 2009, p. A22.

329 *"remains an important problem."* The 9/11 Commission Report, p. 397.

330 *"or the earliest possible date."* FCC Public Hearing, July 30, 2008, Statement of John J. Farmer, Jr.

331 *"an overall system of discipline."* Wilson, *Bureaucracy*, p. 24.

331 *"through law enforcement lenses."* Zegart, *Spying Blind*, p. 167.

331 *"the entire U.S. intelligence effort."* The *9/11 Commission Report*, p. 93.

332 *"on the boundaries of both."* Tenet, *At the Center of the Storm*, p. 511.

334 *"carrying box cutters aboard U.S. airliners."* Ibid., p. 105.

336 *"papered over with White House fictions."* Rich, *The Greatest Story Ever Sold*, p. 201.

AFTERWORD

339 *"family members entertained."* NBC *Dateline*, January 10, 2010. Profile: The Passenger in Seat 19A; investigation into Christmas Day attempted bombing of Northwest Flight 253.

340 *"enjoying himself."* Jessica Leeder, *Globe and Mail*, December 28, 2009. "After 9 hours in the air, groggy passengers prepared for a routine landing. Then they saw the flames."

340 *"lost in thought."* Shama Chopra, quoted in Jessica Murphy, "A Loud Noise, Then Scream of Fire, Fire," *Toronto Star*, December 27, 2009.

340 *"on the plane."* Jessica Leeder, *Globe and Mail*, December 28, 2009.

340 *"for his piety."* Adam Nossiter, "Lonely Trek to Radicalism for Nigerian Terror Suspect." *The New York Times*, Januay 17, 2010, http://www.nytimes.com/2010/01/17/world/africa/17abdulmutallab.html?hp

340 *"urged him to quit."* Ibid.

340 *"the capital of Togo."* Samuel Goldsmith, "Father of Umar Farouk Abdul Mutallab, Nigerian terror suspect in Flight 253 attack, warned U.S," *New York Daily News*, December 26, 2009, http://www.nydailynews.com/news/national/2009/12/26/2009-12-26_father_of_umar_farouk_abdul_mutallab_nigerian_terror_suspect_in_flight_253_attac.html.

340 *"to his schoolmates."* Rich Schapiro, "Flight 253 terrorist Umar Farouk Abdulmutallab led life of luxury in London before attempted attack," *New York Daily News*, December 27, 2009, http://www.nydailynews.com/news/national/2009/12/27/2009-12-27_untitled__2london27m.html.

340 *"lectures at Iman University."* Ibid.; Mohammed al Qadhi, "Detroit bomb suspect 'smart but introverted' says Yemen classmate," *The National*, December 29, 2009, http://www.thenational.ae/apps/pbcs.dll/article?AID=/20091230/FOREIGN/712299856/1002/NEWS; Jon Gambrell, "Web posts suggest lonely, depressed terror suspect," Associated Press, December 29, 2009, http://www.thestar.com/news/world/article/743657--yemen-reveals-details-of-terror-suspect-s-time-in-country; Andrew England, "Quiet charm of student linked to airliner plot," *The Financial Times*, January 10, 2010, http://www.ft.com/cms/s/0/70f97fec-f73d-11de-9fb5-00144feab49a.html.

340 *"in 2005 in Yemen."* David Leppard, "MI5 knew of Umar Farouk Abdulmutallab's UK extremist links," *The Sunday Times*, January 3, 2010, http://www.timesonline.co.uk/tol/news/uk/article6973954.ece.

340 *"lectures by al-Awlaki."* Claire Newell, et al., "Umar Farouk Abdulmutallab: One boy's journey to jihad," *The Sunday Times*, January 3, 2010, http://www.timesonline.co.uk/tol/news/world/middle_east/article6974073.ece.

340 *"on the website Farouk1986."* "Online poster appears to be Christmas Day bomb suspect," CNN, December 29, 2009, http://www.cnn.com/2009/CRIME/12/29/terror.suspect.online/index.html. In a posting on February 20, 2005, he wrote:

Alright, i wont go into too much details about me fantasy, but basically they are jihad fantisies [sic]. I imagine how the great jihad will take place, how the muslims will win insha Allah and rule the whole world, and establish the greatest empire once again!!!

In a May 2005 posting, he referred to radical Jamaican-born Muslim cleric Abdullah el-Faisal, who had been imprisoned in the UK for urging his followers to murder Jews, Hindus, and Americans: i thought once they are arrested, no one hears about them for life and the keys to their prison wards are thrown away. That's what I heard sheikh faisal of UK say (he has also been arrested i heard).

340 *"began studies at University College London."* Rich Schapiro, "Flight 253 terrorist Umar Farouk Abdulmutallab led life of luxury in London before attempted attack," *New York Daily News*, December 27, 2009, http://www.nydailynews.com/news/national/2009/12/27/2009-12-27_untitled__2london27m.html.

340 *"president of the school's Islamic Society."* John F. Burns, "Terror Inquiry Looks at Suspect's Time in Britain," *The New York Times*, December 30, 2009, http://www.nytimes.com/2009/12/30/world/europe/30nigerian.html?_r=1&hp; Paisley Dodds, "UK knew US airline suspect had extremist ties," *The Washington Post*, January 3, 2010, http://www.washingtonpost.com/wp-dyn/content/article/2010/01/03/AR2010010300723_2.html.

341 *"former Guantánamo Bay detainees."* "Al-Qaeda 'groomed Abdulmutallab in London,'" *The Times*, December 30, 2009, http://www.timesonline.co.uk/tol/news/uk/article6971098.ece.

341 *"Islamic position with respect to jihad."* Ibid.

341 *"crossed the radar."* "America, al-Qaeda and home-made bombs: From shoes to soft drinks to underpants," *The Economist*, December 30, 2009, http://www.economist.com/world/unitedstates/displayStory.cfm?story_id=15179544&source=hptextfeature.

341 *"multiple communications."* David Leppard and Hala Jaber, *Sunday Times* UK, "Human rights gagged MI5 over jet bomber," January 10, 2010.

341 *"valid until June 12, 2010."* David Williams, Arthur Martin and Emily Andrews, "Did London turn him to terror?" *Daily Mail*, December 28, 2009; Larry Margasak and Corey Williams. "Nigerian man charged in Christmas airliner attack," ABC News, December 26, 2009, http://abcnews.go.com/Politics/wireStory?id=9426658; Scott Shane, Eric Schmitt, and Eric Lipton, "U.S. Charges Suspect, Eyeing Link to Qaeda in Yemen," *The New York Times*, December 26, 2009, http://www.nytimes.com/2009/12/27/us/27terror.html;

341 *"Houston, Texas, August 1–17, 2008."* Larry Margasak and Corey Williams, "Nigerian man charged in Christmas airliner attack," ABC News, December 26, 2009, http://abcnews.go.com/Politics/wireStory?id=9426658; Scott Shane, Eric Schmitt and Eric Lipton, "U.S. Charges Suspect, Eyeing Link to Qaeda in Yemen," *The New York Times*, December 26, 2009, http://www.nytimes.com/2009/12/27/us/27terror.html; Michael Graczyk, "Accused airline attacker attended Houston class," Associated Press, December 30, 2009, http://abcnews.go.com/US/wireStory?id=9451291.

341 *"a fictitious school."* Rich Schapiro, "Flight 253 terrorist Umar Farouk Abdulmutallab led life of luxury in London before attempted attack," *New York Daily News*, December 27, 2009, http://www.nydailynews.com/news/national/2009/12/27/2009-12-27_untitled__2london27m.html;

341 *"United Kingdom Border Agency."* Ibid.

341 *"he was not permanently banned."* "Bomb suspect Umar Farouk Abdulmutallab on UK watch-list," BBC News, December 28, 2009, http://news.bbc.co.uk/2/hi/uk_news/8432180.stm; Gordon Rayner, "Detroit terror attack: timeline," The *Telegraph*, December 30, 2009, http://www.telegraph.co.uk/news/worldnews/middleeast/yemen/6911200/Detroit-terror-attack-timeline.html.

341 *"for reasons of national security."* Mark Hosenball, Michael Isikoff and Evan Thomas, "The Radicalization of Umar Farouk Abdulmutallab," *Newsweek*, January 11, 2010, pp. 37-41, http://www.newsweek.com/id/229047.

341 *"in Yemen from August to September 2009."* Adam Nossiter, "Lonely Trek to Radicalism for Nigerian Terror Suspect," *New York Times*, January 16, 2010.

341 *"who wore traditional Islamic clothing."* "Nigeria: Abdulmutallab—More Trouble for Nigerian," *Daily Independent* (Lagos), December 30, 2009, http://allafrica.com/stories/200912310650.html. Sudarsan Raghavan, "Abdulmutallab's teachers, classmates at Yemen school say he became more religious," *The Washington Post*, December 31, 2009, http://www.washingtonpost.com/wp-dyn/content/article/2009/12/30/AR2009123002723.html?hpid=topnews.

341 *"a school suspected for links to terrorism."* Dan McDougall, Claire Newell, Christina Lamb, Jon Ungoed-Thomas, Chris Gourlay, Kevin Dowling and Dominic Tobin, "Umar Farouk Abdulmutallab: one boy's journey to jihad" *The Sunday Times*, January 3, 2010, http://www.timesonline.co.uk/tol/news/world/middle_east/article6974073.ece.

341 *"but was remaining in Yemen."* Karen DeYoung and Michael Leahy, "Uninvestigated terrorism warning about Detroit suspect called not unusual," *The Washington Post*, December 28, 2009, http://www.washingtonpost.com/wp-dyn/content/article/2009/12/27/AR2009122700279.html; Philip Elliott and Lolita Baldor, "Obama: US Intel Had Info Ahead of Airliner Attack," ABC News, December 29, 2009, http://abcnews.go.com/US/wirestory?id=9439201&page=3.

341 *"Islam to be the rule of law across the world."* Dan McDougall, Claire Newell, Christina Lamb, Jon Ungoed-Thomas, Chris Gourlay, Kevin Dowling and Dominic Tobin, "Umar Farouk Abdulmutallab: one boy's journey to jihad" *The Sunday Times*, January 3, 2010, http://www.timesonline.co.uk/tol/news/world/middle_east/article6974073.ece.

342 *"a seven year course in Yemen."* Ibid.

342 *" would be getting this education for free."* Ibid.

342 *"would not disclose who was sponsoring him."* Xan Rice, *The Guardian*, "Bombing suspect was pious pupil who shunned high life of the rich," http://www.guardian.co.uk/world/2009/dec/31/bombing-suspect-abdulmutallab-nigeria-home.

342 *"no intention of ever returning to his family."* Anthony Gregory, "Syringe bomber Umar Abdulmutallab chilling text messages to dad," *The Mirror*, January 1, 2010, http://www.mirror.co.uk/news/top-stories/2010/01/01/forget-me-i-m-never-coming-back-115875-21934727.

342 *"last contact with Abdulmutallab."* Dominic Kennedy, "Abdulmutallab's bomb plans began with classroom defence of 9/11," *The Times*, December 28, 2009, http://www.timesonline.co.uk/tol/news/world/us_and_americas/article6969075.ece

342 *"overstayed his student visa."* "Abdulmutallab Visited Yemen This Year; Airline Terror Suspect Spent More Than Four Months There, Yemeni Government Confirms," CBS News, December 28, 2009, http://www.cbsnews.com/stories/2009/12/28/national/main6031296.shtml?tag=contentMain;contentBody; "Yemen: Abdulmutallab Had Expired Visa; Suspected Terrorist Should Have Left Country in September, but Remained Illegally until December, Officials Say," CBS News, December 31, 2009, http://www.cbsnews.com/stories/2009/12/31/world/main6042470.shtml.

342 *"two days later to Ghana."* Ibid.

342 *"before leaving Yemen."* Adam Nossiter, "Lonely Trek to Radicalism For Nigerian Terror Suspect," *The New York Times*, January 17, 2010, http://www.nytimes.com/2010/01/17/world/africa/17abdulmutallab.html?hp. Retrieved January 17, 2010; NBC *Dateline*, January 10, 2010

342 *"denied having ordered the attack."* "US cleric: Accused plane bomber was my student," ABC News, Ahmed Al-Haj and Sarah El Deeb, http://abcnews.go.com/International/wireStory?id=9744188; Karen DeYoung, "Yemeni American cleric Aulaqi confirms contact with Nigerian suspect," *Washington Post*, February 6, 2010, http://www.washingtonpost.com/wp-dyn/content/article/2010/02/05/AR2010020504028.html;,MATT APUZZO and EILEEN SULLIVAN "Law official: Airline bomb suspect flips on cleric," ABC News, http://abcnews.go.com/Politics/wireStory?id=9753833

342 *"but I support it."* Robert F. Worth, "Cleric in Yemen Admits Meeting Airliner Plot Suspect, Journalist Says," *The New York Times*, January 31, 2010, http://www.nytimes.com/2010/02/01/world/middleeast/01yemen.html.

342 *"approved by the government for targeted killing."* "U.S. Citizen Anwar Awlaki Added To CIA's Target List," *Los Angeles Times*, April 6, 2010, http://articles.latimes.com/2010/apr/06/world/la-fg-yemen-cleric7-2010apr07.

342 *"when he flew to Lagos."* Sarah Childress, "Ghana Probes Visit by Bomb Suspect," *The Wall Street Journal*, January 5, 2010, http://online.wsj.com/article/SB126261251907114813.html?mod=googlenews_wsj.

342 *"cash in Ghana on December 16."* "U.S. officials investigating how Abdulmutallab boarded

Flight 253 as more missed red flags surface," *New York Daily News*, January 3, 2009, http://www
.nydailynews.com/news/national/2010/01/03/2010-01-03_plane_questions_dont_fly_right_
warning_signs_were_evident_yet_bomb_suspect_still.html?page=1.

343 *"sewn into his underwear."* Ibid.

343 *"a plastic explosive when mixed."* Malcolm W. Browne, "Readily Available, PETN Is Easily
Molded and Hidden," *The New York Times*, August 23, 1996, http://www.nytimes.com/1996/08/
23/nyregion/readily-available-petn-is-easily-molded-and-hidden.html?pagewanted=1.

343 *"to activate the concoction."* Kevin Krolicki and Jeremy Pelofsky, "Nigerian charged for trying
to blow up U.S. airliner," Reuters, December 26, 2009, http://af.reuters.com/article/worldNews/
idAFLDE5BP03M20091226.

343 *"'Jesus Loves the Little Children.'"* Meg Kissinger, *The Milwaukee Journal Sentinel*, December
27, 2009.

343 *"to try to douse the flames."* Hagar Mizrahi, "Dutch passenger thwarted terror attack on plane,"
Israel News, December 27, 2009, http://www.ynetnews.com/articles/0,7340,L-382544700.html.

343 *"smoking out of him."* Peter Slevin and Michael Sheer, "He's trying to blow up the plane," *The
Washington Post*, December 26, 2009.

344 *"but remains calm."* "How Nigerian attempted to blow up plane in US," *Vanguard*, December 27, 2009, http://www.vanguardngr.com/2009/12/27/how-nigerian-attempted-to-blow-up-
plane-in-us/comment-page-1.

345 *"did not reflect Abdulmutallab''s last name."* "Alleged Christmas Bomber Said To Flip On
Cleric; Official: Umar Farouk Abdullmutallab Says U.S.-Born Yemeni Cleric Anwar al-Awlaki
Instructed Him In Explosives Plot," CBS News, February 5, 2010, http://kdka.com/national/
Umar.Farouk.Abdulmutallab.2.1471361.html.

345 *"'extreme religious views.'"* Karen DeYoung and Michael Leahy, "Uninvestigated terrorism
warning about Detroit suspect called not unusual," *The Washington Post*, December 28, 2009,
http://www.washingtonpost.com/wp-dyn/content/article/2009/12/27/AR2009122700279.
html; Josh Meyer, "Suspect may have ties to Yemen militants," *Los Angeles Times*, December 27,
2009.

345 *"might be in Yemen."* Shama Chopra, quoted in Jessica Murphy, "A Loud Noise, Then
Screams of 'Fire, Fire!'" *Toronto Star*, December 27, 2009; Rich Schapiro, "Flight 253 terrorist Umar Farouk Abdulmutallab led life of luxury in London before attempted attack," *New
York Daily News*, December 27, 2009, http://www.nydailynews.com/news/national/2009/
12/27/2009-12-27_untitled__2london27m.html; Eric Lipton and Scott Shane, "More Questions on Why Terror Suspect Was Not Stopped," *The New York Times*, December 27, 2009,
http://www.nytimes.com/2009/12/28/us/28terror.html; "Obama orders review of U.S. no-fly
lists." AFP, http://www.google.com/hostednews/afp/article/ALeqM5g576mMIiaVSpiw-wwX9r-
Z7uECILA.

345 *"Terrorist Screening Database."* "Father of Terror Suspect Reportedly Warned U.S. About
Son," Fox News, http://www.foxnews.com/story/0,2933,581193,00.html.

345 *"nor was his U.S. visa revoked."* Dan McDougall, Claire Newell, Christina Lamb, Jon Ungoed-Thomas, Chris Gourlay, Kevin Dowling and Dominic Tobin, "Umar Farouk Abdulmutallab:
one boy's journey to jihad," *The Sunday Times*, January 3, 2010, http://www.timesonline.co.uk/
tol/news/world/middle_east/article6974073.ece.

345 *"his travel on Christmas Day."* "Terror Suspect Kept Visa To Avoid Tipping Off Larger Investigation," *The Detroit News*, January 27, 2010, http://detnews.com/article/20100127/NA-
TION/1270405/Terror-suspect-kept-visa-to-avoid-tipping-off-larger-investigation.

345 *"visa application earlier in 2009."* Mark Hosenball, Michael Isikoff and Evan Thomas, "The
Radicalization of Umar Farouk Abdulmutallab," *Newsweek*, January 2, 2010, pp. 37-41, http://
www.newsweek.com/id/229047.

345 *"national security concerns."* Ibid.

346 *"defies logic and common sense."* Opening Statement, Senator Susan Collins, Committee on
Homeland Security and Government Affairs, January 26, 2010.

347 *"as it should be."* Testimony of Thomas H. Kean and Lee Hamilton on behalf of the Bipartisan Policy Center before the Senate Homeland Security Committee, January 26, 2010.

348 *"a member of the public alerted police"* Michael M. Grynbaum et al., "Police Seek Man Taped Near Times Square Bomb Scene." The *New York Times.* May 2, 2010.

349 *"a host of other criticism."* Ibid.

349 *"entire U.S. intelligence effort."* The *9/11 Commission Report*, p. 93.

350 *"discuss how to handle him."* "Walter Reed Officials Asked: Was Hasan Psychotic?" NPR, November 11, 2009.

350 *"or terrorist planning."* David Johnston, "U.S. Knew of Suspect's Tie To Radical Cleric," *New York Times*, November 9, 2009, http://www.nytimes.com/2009/11/10/us/10inquire.html.

350 *"before opening fire."* Mark Thompson, "Fort Hood Report: No Mention of Islam, Hasan Not Named," *Time*, January 20, 2010.

351 *"realized their oversight and stopped him."* Mark Mazzetti et al., "Suspect, Charged, Said to Admit to Role in Plot," *The New York Times*, May 4, 2010.

351 *"undisturbed until Shahzad acted."* Mark Mazzetti et al., "Evidence Mounts for Taliban Role in Bomb Plot," *The New York Times*, May 5, 2010.

INDEX

John Farmer served as senior counsel to the 9/11 Commission, where his areas of responsibility included assessing the national response to the terrorist attacks and evaluating the current state of preparedness for terrorist attacks and natural disasters. In 2009 he became dean of the Rutgers University Law School. Farmer has also served as attorney general of New Jersey, as chief counsel to Governor Christine Todd Whitman, as a federal prosecutor, and as an advisor to the special envoy for Middle East regional security. His editorials and articles have appeared in the *New York Times, Washington Post,* and elsewhere. He lives in New Jersey.